PHILIP ROTH
AND THE JEWS

PHILIP ROTH
AND THE JEWS

ALAN COOPER

STATE UNIVERSITY OF NEW YORK PRESS

SUNY Series in Modern Jewish Literature and Culture
Sarah Blacher Cohen, Editor

Published by
State University of New York Press, Albany

© 1996 State University of New York

For information, address State University of New York
Press, State University Plaza, Albany, N.Y., 12246

Production by E. Moore
Marketing by Fran Keneston

Library of Congress Cataloging-in-Publication Data

Cooper, Alan, 1932-
        Philip Roth and the Jews / Alan Cooper.
        p.   cm. — (SUNY series in modern Jewish literature and
    culture)
        Includes bibliographical references and index.
        ISBN 0-7914-2909-1 (HC : acid free). — ISBN 0-7914-2910-5 (PB :
    acid free)
        1. Roth, Philip—Criticism and interpretation. 2. Jewish fiction-
    -History and criticism. 3. Roth, Philip—Characters—Jews.
    4. Roth, Philip—Religion. 5. Judaism in literature. 6. Jews in
    literature. I. Title. II. Series.
    PS3568.0855Z62 1996
    813'.54—dc20
                                                                    95-19591
                                                                       CIP

10 9 8 7 6 5 4 3 2

FOR ROBERT

Is it me? Is it me Me Me Me Me! It has to be me—but is it?
                    —*Ozzie Freedman, "Conversion of the Jews"*

*. . . to be raised as a post-immigrant Jew in America was to be given a ticket
out of the ghetto into a wholly unconstrained world of thought. Without an
old-country link and a strangling church like the Italians, or the Irish, or the
Poles, without generations of American forebears to bind you to American
life, or blind you by your loyalty to its deformities, you could read whatever you
wanted and write however and whatever you pleased. Alienated? Just another
way to say "Set free!" A Jew set free even from Jews—yet only by steadily
maintaining self-consciousness as a Jew. That was the thrilling paradoxical
kicker.*
                    —*Nathan Zuckerman,* The Anatomy Lesson

You think in the Diaspora *it's normal? Come live here. [Israel] is the* homeland
of Jewish abnormality. Worse: now we *are the dependent Jews, on your money,
your lobby, on our big allowance from Uncle Sam, while* you *are the Jews
living interesting lives, comfortable lives, without apology, without shame, and
perfectly* independent*. . . . We are the excitable, ghettoized, jittery little Jews of
the Diaspora, and you are the Jews with all the confidence and cultivation
that comes of feeling at home where you are.*
                    —*Shuki Elchanan,* The Counterlife

CONTENTS

PREFACE

This book was conceived partly out of puzzlement at the wide difference between my reading of Philip Roth and that of several of my friends. They seemed to take a position fixed around 1970 and incognizant of any development in the writer since that time. Informal surveys of academic colleagues and others confirmed the impression that many had a view of Roth as a kind of aging Peck's bad boy, but few were reading him, even as latter-day critics were giving him awards. Most still knew *Goodbye, Columbus* and *Portnoy's Complaint*, as much from the movies as from the printed word. What seemed to me to be lost in the general responses to Roth were his genuine artistic and Jewish developments since those early successes. Roth is much more complex, as both a writer and a Jew, than readers of his early works know; he has grappled with the most difficult issues that bind latter twentieth century Jewry and art. His manner of addressing these issues is partly playful, and to some readers, offputting. But it is a manner developed probing foibles widely shared. One of Roth's achievements is in revealing how flawed people experience themselves. I hope readers who have neglected Roth's works will be moved to pick them up and find that dimension. The rewards in store may be wonderfully surprising.

ACKNOWLEDGMENTS

An inescapable routine of full-time, year-round teaching would have made my task impossible were it not for a summer start-up grant from PSC/CUNY Research Foundation and the help of numerous friends and colleagues. First, I am most grateful to the librarians at York College, CUNY, for endless patience in retrieving and reproducing materials sometimes from great distances. Similarly, the good humor and patience of the staff at the Jewish Room of the New York Public Library, especially during a period of renovation at that facility, was most gratifying. The Anti-Defamation League of B'nai B'rith made available to me its extensive files of news clippings covering Roth's whole career, and I profited immeasurably by the vigilance of Hortense Nash, secretary in the Department of English at York College, who continued to spot items in the popular press that I would surely have missed. I thank the Central Conference of American Rabbis and the Rabbinic Assembly for circulating inquiries into sermons on Roth's early works, some of which bore welcome fruit. During dental sessions at which the conversation could flow only one way, I absorbed impressions and descriptions from Dr. William Kapner of his days growing up in the Weequahic section of Newark, of Weequahic High School and the Chancellor Avenue Elementary School, which Roth had attended and which formed so important a part of Roth's narrative landscape. From Stanley and Laura Kauffmann I heard first-hand accounts of Roth's New York years, the late sixties and early seventies, and from Ted Solotaroff accounts of Roth's earlier Chicago years. I profited from observations on Roth and the American literary scene by York professors Elaine Baruch, Sam Hux, Daniel Kelly, and Charles Shapiro, and on teaching Roth by Professor Krin Gabbard of SUNY at Stony Brook. Professor Michael Payne of Bucknell University was instrumental in securing for me Roth's undergraduate publications. Although working without an editor, I nonetheless was blessed with the generous kindness of my good friend and long-time associate, Joan Baum, who read about two-thirds of the manuscript and made invaluable editorial suggestions. The virtues of the manuscript owe largely to these people; the shortcomings are entirely mine. I appreciate the good humor of my family, who learned to forego my company and accept the competition of my computer on many a weekend and holiday. I thank SUNY Press for accepting a hybrid work: intended not only for scholarly readers but also for lay readers interested in American and Jewish cultural history, once a middle ground unreachable by either academic or trade presses. I am especially grateful to them for holding typesetting until July 1995 so I could include a brief discussion of *Sabbath's Theater* (September 1955) and to the *Forward* for securing that prepublication copy and permitting me to use material that would appear in its commissioned review. And finally, I thank Philip Roth for hundreds of hours of pleasure, some of it agonizing pleasure, spent reading and rereading his works.

Chapter 1

THE IRONIC AND THE IRATE

Since 1959 Philip Roth has been publishing steadily, an average of a book every twenty-three months—all but three having something to say directly about Jews. The cheers and the groans continue. While Roth has insisted he does not speak for American Jews or expound Judaism, he has given America a gallery of semitic stereotypes. Sophie and Alexander Portnoy,[1] Brenda Patimkin, Eli the Fanatic, and Nathan Zuckerman are household names. Zuckerman, himself a novelist taken by critics to be Roth's alter ego of the late seventies and eighties—to be the successor to Gabe Wallach, Alexander Portnoy, David Kepesh, and Peter Tarnopol—spent several novels protesting that he stood for nothing more than the power of art to illuminate life. From *The Ghost Writer* (1979)[2] to *The Counterlife* (1987)[3] Zuckerman kept declaring that *his* Jews were not *the* Jews and that his protagonists were not himself. He accused misreaders of willful self-impoverishment, of reducing fiction to some petty biographic detective game. Only fiction, this fictitious character insisted, has the power to convey the many-sidedness of fact.

Misunderstood Zuckerman, making those pronouncements to get the world off his back but with few illusions about getting himself off his back, was succeeded in the early nineties by a character bearing his author's name. Layered within Roth's fiction are authors and authors of authors, blurring the line between fiction and fact, all of them looking vainly for some boundary between their individual selves and their Jewish past—as if a statue could free itself from its stone and still have being. Some of Roth's latest fictions have invited readers playfully into the trap, that of identifying the "Philip" of *Deception* (1990)[4] and of *Operation Shylock* (1993)[5] with what they think they know of Philip Roth, the Jewish writer and biographer of his Jewish father. The confusions Roth once decried became his medium for sleight-of-hand demonstrations that the fiction writer is the teller of highest truth and that Jewishness is the perfect condition for exploring the American promise of freedom.

Roth's works have always irritated some readers; lately, the irritation has been intentional. Like Nietzsche, who wrote to be misunderstood, Roth has chosen to goad readers into thought, accepting some hostile reaction as part of the contract. Indeed, since the 1959 publication of his first book, *Goodbye, Columbus and Five Short Stories*,[6] Roth has been made increasingly aware that in trusting fiction to carry one's deepest thoughts and feelings, a writer, especially an ironic writer, takes risks. He mainly risks being identified with ideas or modes of expression he may only be using to dramatize more elusive concerns. For Roth the result has been more than the usual share of accusers and accusations. He has been accused of self-hatred yet of egotism, of anti-Semitism yet of Jewish parochialism, of a thinness of invention yet of flights of outlandish fancy, of being autobiographical and vengeful yet of borrowing personae from James or Kafka in lieu of a personal subject. Even some who have enjoyed Roth's novels have become accusers, feeling somehow they have been misled into profane laughter. And lurking behind all these has been the accusation of his trying to duck accusation by perverse strategies of anticipation or by intentional thwartings of public perception. When Roth labeled *Operation Shylock* a "Confession" from his real life, critics who charged him with having made the whole story up included some who had long declared him unable to invent anything he had not lived. So in *Sabbath's Theater* (1995),[7] he has tossed back at them a puppeteer instead of a novelist, as if he had not been ventriloquizing his characters all along.

Philip Roth has not generally taken to the air waves, used television interviews, or written prefaces to other people's books to explain to the public that perhaps they were not reading him right.[8] In the range of public exposure between what he has called "Mailerism," the direct taking on of the public as a figure whose life vies with his work, and "Salingerism," the hermitic retreat that ultimately refuses even to publish, he has taken a position midway, not courting the public outside the fiction—though becoming a public persona from within the fiction—yet sometimes answering criticism he has taken to be wrong-spirited. But early on he ruled out mass media exchanges or interviews about his work except in the literature sections of newspapers, usually at time of publication.[9] In seminars and forums of a purely literary nature he did attempt to clarify his art, but without reference to his personal life. The irony of this is that critics increasingly flushed him out. Having participated in the strictly literary exchanges, they brought to their popular reviewing aspects of Roth's personal life that he might once have preferred to keep private, and they made his efforts to remain above the fray increasingly part of the fray. Over the length of his career, Roth's most common response to this irony has been to make fiction out of it. As one critic has noted, however, "the ironical thing about irony is that those closest to you usually take it literally."[10] Writing about his having been misperceived didn't go far, in the late seventies and early eighties, toward pacifying a hostile public, but it may have paved the way for Roth's finest writing shortly thereafter. All he had to do was listen to one of his own novelist-characters, Peter Tarnopol: "Literature got me into this and literature is gonna have to get me out."

In the late eighties literature, it seems, got Roth out. Having weathered a stormy relationship with many of his readers—especially his Jewish readers—by hewing to his own line and holding out for judgment on his own terms, Roth with *The Counterlife* (1987) won the hearts and minds of some of his stoniest judges. In *The Counterlife* a mature Zuckerman, past rebelling at parents or protesting tribal censure, is suspended in a state of fictive uncertainty about his own identity: about how much he is the American, how much the Jew, how much the fiction writer, how much the Newark child trying to hold on to or repair to the myths of his own earliest security. And in continually refocusing Zuckerman's identity, Roth makes the reader refocus his own. *The Counterlife* thins the membrane through which experience and imagination nourish one another, letting certitude wait upon possibility. Repeatedly, just when the reader has identified himself with the travails of one character, Roth dissolves that character as the mere imaginings of another and forces the reader into yet another perspective on himself. By continually reopening the reader to new possibilities, *The Counterlife* had a liberating effect. To Roth, the praise and the acclaim in awards and prizes must have been gratifying.

But, as if to prove that what literature could get him out of, quasi-literature could get him back into, Roth, essaying forth with *The Facts* (1988),[11] plunged again into the thicket. He chose to lead his readers over so dubious a landscape of his own life and career, as almost to invite the old hostility. The works that have followed, especially *Patrimony* (1991),[12] which attracted Jewish audiences for what Roth might once have considered the wrong reasons, have somewhat compounded the conflict. And in *Operation Shylock*, pure invention and biographic and historic fact mingle like brush strokes of a single painting. The surreal result is an emerging Roth perspective that defies readers to separate out personal, tribal, national, global, and fictitious shadings of an irritating character very much their surrogate.

Why have readers so long and intently followed Roth's maps of misreading, pitching and lunging over broken terrain of critical and Freudian
clichés? What in Roth fascinates even skeptical readers, even as some of them
denounce him for reiterating mewling complaints or perpetrating tribal treachery? What do they find in his eternal revolving without resolving his characters'
troubles? Perhaps the late Anatole Broyard had part of the answer. Suffering
from terminal cancer and needing to unload his library to move into smaller
quarters, Broyard considered what to do with each author's works. About Roth
he mused,

> I felt that I had nursed him—or he had nursed me—through the long ill-
> ness of our literature. He was my cynical big brother and my crazy little
> brother, too. When he made a mistake—and he made a few—it was I
> who blushed. Like so many American readers, I felt that I had got glori-
> ously drunk with Philip Roth, we had gone skinny-dipping together, and
> had suffered with the same kind of women. I knew too much about
> him—and he knew too much about me—for me to give up his books.[13]

"Like so many *American* readers." Broyard, who was not Jewish, found in
Roth not just some initiator into mystic rites, but a brother, fully and equally
involved and at risk in the age. Not a sage outsider or a chorus, but a fellow
player in the American tragicomedy. Without having to offer answers "during
the long illness of our literature," Roth, it seems, could be trusted to air the
questions of sensitive young men who might once have counted upon literature
for answers. And that dual sensibility of cynical older brother and crazy
younger brother could be trusted not to mislead. Declaim as his characters
might against the unfairness of the world, in fiction Roth had mostly navi-
gated by irony to skirt extremes of sentimentality, cynicism and despair. His
material had provided a perspective on the changing American landscape. And
if Roth's combatants had Jewish accents, their conflicts had been recognizable enough in Peoria.

Broyard's words echo a statement made some three years earlier by
Primo Levi. Parting from Roth in 1986 after some four days together for a
New York Times interview that Roth was to publish, Levi had said, "I don't
know which of us is the younger brother and which is the older brother" (*Pat.*
211). Levi was apparently commenting on the mature Roth's understanding of
fiction, particularly Holocaust fiction, and on their novelists' bond of intense
introspection. Perhaps he saw pale reflections of his own survivor's guilt in
Roth's young heroes' wailing at sacrificing parents, or perhaps Levi saw a
mark of the "older brother" in these young heroes' ability to accept such ancient
sacrifices and go on. In the years since Levi's death, Roth has increasingly

assumed the voice of an aging generation, successors to the postimmigrants who dominated Jewish-American life in the middle of the twentieth century, forced to respond to the Holocaust.

Many of Roth's Jewish contemporaries had sensed in his early works a kinship closer than Broyard's American brotherhood. Ruth Wisse called Roth's

> the first literary voice that seemed to speak for our bunch, our group, our set, the particular gang of adolescents with whom I shared a mutual affection and an idea of what we stood against . . . a sensibility so familiar that it seemed to have come from our own midst, and in a sparkle of language . . . attractive to us. . . . Our affection for Philip Roth was part of the tenderness we felt for ourselves.[14]

Part of what they "stood against" was parental overprotection, being reined in by a now-comfortable generation seeking to keep them from dangers it had opened to them. Ironically, these young third-generation Jews sometimes seemed humiliated not by their own acts, but by their inbred ideals. Roth's characters are often caught redfaced between the generations. In book after book, young men struggle to enter American society on their own terms, trying to shake off, yet deeply appreciating, the limiting advantages of their ancient culture.

From the very start of Roth's career, questions about his literature have been intermingled with questions about himself: about his devotion to the Jews, about his feelings for family, about his attitude toward women, even about his personal life as a son, a brother, a husband or lover, and a nonparent—questions probed anew by Roth, himself, in the nonfictional *The Facts* and *Patrimony*. One hears about the "*Goodbye, Columbus* wars,"[15] about the uproar in the Jewish community over *Portnoy's Complaint*[16] and the continued attacks on Roth's subsequent publications by organized Jewry in its periodicals, its rabbinic sermons, its endless newsletters and discussion groups. But how extensive and how unalloyed was that hostility? In *The Facts* Roth tells of a traumatic encounter, of a near mob scene at (of all places) Yeshiva University, from which he had to be extricated by—irony of ironies!—Ralph Ellison; Roth offers that experience as just one example of the hostility of organized Jewry to his two great early successes. Were there other examples? Of what nature and to what extent? And, then, why Roth? Malamud married a Gentile, wrote Christological redemption pieces in Yiddish accents, and was loved by Jewish readers. Bellow married frequently—mostly younger and younger women, including Gentiles—presented assimilated Jews in ponderous intellectual style, and was and still is beloved as a true Jewish encyclopedist. As one critic put it in the mid-seventies, "Roth envies Bellow the old grace or magic or urbanity that turns away the anger of rabbis; while he, the author of *Portnoy's Complaint*, is denounced in every state of the union."[17] Indeed, Roth's writing about Jews has seldom been perceived as an act of love. And the guardians of Jewish perception were harsh in the postwar decades with any but clichéd loving of their people. Why Roth's immersion in the lives of Jews was seen as less loving than Bellow's is at least subject for speculation, but very respectable critics could take the questionings of his characters for a gauntlet to his people. Was it just some irritant in Roth, or did forces in the age itself contribute to this sensitivity? One might also ask why Roth's purposes were perceived so differently from those of these more accepted Jewish writers, how much more or less alienated or acculturated his characters were taken to be, or even how well and at what stages Roth knew his own purposes. Much of his journey out into the mediating world of fiction would be a quest to find the fountain light of his own seeing, a quest that would bring him back home.

To speak of a writer's purposes is necessarily to consider his view of man and of the role fiction can play in transforming his reader. Malamud's losers, *schlemiels* and *schlimazls*, are redeemed through their very loss. They sacrifice worldly recognition but find something new in themselves, often compassion for fellow suffering humans. The Jewish reader could easily join the gentile reader in feeling cleansed through that redemption. To read Malamud is to give up the world and to feel better for having given it up. But Roth's characters seldom accept their fate. Nor are his strivers like Bellow's strivers, who may succeed, even as they think they have failed, by finding "the consummation of [their] heart's ultimate need."[18] Roth's characters do not rest in loss of the world or feel redeemed at having wrested from that loss some single personal fulfillment. More than any other response to their own experience is the loss itself: seeing some illusion shattered without having it replaced by anything comforting. They do not even gain the emotional comfort of an overwhelming sadness, which might teach them that they can feel, and, in feeling, perhaps plumb the depth of their own humanity.

This seeming hardness in Roth has often been taken for personal failure, or selfishness. Where the reader, certainly the traditional Jewish reader, might expect a tender patting of the protagonist, Roth provides irony. And to many— in the early years especially among Roth's elders—that irony has seemed over-subtle or misapplied, allowing first-person narrators, in defending against the outrageous, to gloss the vicious. As a result, many readers, both Jewish and gentile, have felt left out of Broyard's asserted brotherhood. They wonder whether Roth has really been ahead of, or just insensitive to, his times. Has he shocked a sometimes grudging readership into recognizing their limitations and real possibilities or has he merely irritated people seeking solace in the human condition? In their questionings, of course, they have raised the ironic ante. As Wisse has suggested, if Roth has gotten his greatest mileage out of being a "critic of bourgeois complacency, what sweeter response than his constituency's cry of 'foul,' exposing that very obsession with propriety that he has been ridiculing?"[19] Part of Roth's "hardness" comes from leaving the questions festering in the fiction.

To try to answer any of these questions about Roth is to raise others, almost in serial logic, about modern life: questions about allegiance, maturity, freedom, family, the future of democracy, of Judaism, of Israel, the changing history of American Jewry in the postwar decades, indeed, the very questions about pluralism and multiculturalism that have recently challenged America. For whatever Roth's relationship to Jewish life might have been or might continue to be, he is an author very much bound by his times: cut off initially from European Jewish culture (though later rescuing lost works from that culture into English and assimilating the Holocaust), knowing far less about principles and practices—not to mention the scholarly tradition—of Judaism than about family-transmitted Jewishness, yet touched by values and assumptions of that tradition, and in childhood sufficiently content as both an American and a Jew not to seem disturbed by possible conflicts in these loyalties. Of this kind of Jewishness one may say of Roth what headmaster Rabbi Tzuref says to Eli (the fanatic) Peck about the Rabbi's ubiquitous gabardined assistant: "The suit the gentleman wears is all he's got." And as for Roth's qualifications to write about American Jews, he could answer with Eli: "I am them, they are me."

For Roth's generation of American-born Jews, it was normal to identify with the wider American culture, even as they sensed some incongruity between its popular images and the sounds and tastes of their own lives. Roth had come of age when normalcy was the last blooming of radio drama, was Gene Kelly and Frank Sinatra in sailor suits, was the postwar playing days of DiMaggio, Williams, and Musial (though for Roth, the stronger identification would have been with Duke Snider of the more proletarian Dodgers). Like the base line in a cardiogram, that view of normalcy became for a whole generation a measure for judging change. What would follow would be impure wars, greed, unheroic politicians, enterprises of no pitch or moment—the rewards of decency denied. Not that such failing was new in the world: it was just new to someone born to a lower middle-class family in 1933, for whose very people above all others the war had been fought, who could venture through American opportunity where his forebears had not—into old-line colleges and the American mainstream. Most of Roth's fiction has dealt with life in that imperfect postwar world, the life made for themselves by individuals with expectations and by institutions with power.[20] To be born into such innocence, into such expectations, was to be saddled with myths, with misconceptions that at once bolstered the egos of the youths of the age and threatened to unfit them for living in the real world. For young Jews the picture was further complicated by ties to family, parents who sacrificed for their advancement, and the sense of the forbidden—in foods, mates, pleasures. Such are the agitations of soul with which Roth has peopled his fiction.

Roth's late adolescence and early manhood were marked by rapid changes: from a secular Jewish childhood, secure in feelings for his family and friends, to beginnings in writing at a predominantly gentile college (producing formulaic stories without Jews or Jewish content), to a graduate school apostleship to literature that seemed to replace for a time the culture from which he had come (his rabbis now called Henry James, Gustave Flaubert, Anton Chekhov, and eventually Franz Kafka), to a brief stint in the army and back to doctoral studies punctuated and then terminated by publishing short fiction and some film reviews for *The New Republic*, to marriage and the dazzling success of the stories and novella—this time filled with Jews—which became the volume *Goodbye, Columbus*. He was, at twenty-six, a name.

In 1959 Roth was also a relative innocent in an age fast losing its innocence. Aware of some of the traps of normalcy, he had not yet learned the price of disclosing to a readership wearied with strife that normalcy was itself a trap. In 1959 America was already a dozen years into the cold war, had come through the McCarthy era and the Eisenhower years, trying to live its postwar dream of family togetherness, Doris Day, and the status quo. That there was rot in the society that had won the war and saved Europe for democracy was just hinted at in the quiz-show and Sherman Adams scandals. The police action in Korea was an unavoidable disturbance that the country had seemed to handle well. Rock music, drugs, Vietnam, the mid-sixties were still far enough ahead not to trouble dreams. Good-guyism marked the American self-image and invited everyone to work hard, raise families, get on the economic escalator, and be nice. Certain minorities, if they could blend into the split-level technicolor picture, were invited to the party. Even World War II itself, for those who had not fought or who had survived unscathed, was settling into romantic myth. Roth was just beginning to explore the frustration that comes from trying to live by myths. He did not yet fully realize that much of his work would be an attempt to demythologize the world so he could fathom its real offerings.

What Philip Roth was not in 1959 was a child of the thirties. The fact might be important to distinguish him from many of the critics he would encounter for a couple of decades. He had not come of age during the depression. He was not a joiner of movements, an active Marxist, or a social reformer. He had spent the first Roosevelt administration in the crib, the second in kindergarten and the elementary grades. While Arthur Miller, Alfred Kazin, Irving Howe, Saul Bellow, Bernard Malamud were arguing over the purges, the Hitler-Stalin pact, Rapp-Coudert, or Britain's white paper, children of Roth's age were tying on towel capes to play Superman or having cookies and milk with Jack Armstrong or Uncle Don. The onset of World War II meant collecting paper, rolling balls of lead foil from cigarettes, saving bubble gum picture cards not only of baseball players but also of generals and admirals, learning the opening bars of Beethoven's Fifth Symphony as the Morse code for V for Victory; it meant the adventures of buying Aircraft Spotters Guides and, for Roth, spotting imaginary submarines off the New Jersey beaches. In the comic books Superman was joined by Captain Marvel, Captain America, Slam Bradley, and three servicemen named Red, White, and Blue, who went to war along with Lucky Strike green. Roth's world of family, school, and baseball left little room for moral earnestness—or alienation. Looking back at the period in 1959, Roth could say that he had

> lived in comfort and ease; [his] father might have been struggling to pay bills, [his] mother juggling so as to make ends meet, but it was all hidden from their two children, masked by the spotless house, the starchily fresh linens, and the full, well-cooked meals.[21]

And when Roth's older brother was drafted into the service after the end of the war, Philip was the little man of the house, available to comfort mother in father's working absence and to absorb some of the psychological static energy that could crackle across generational insulation. The war had been over for a year before the little man was ready for bar mitzvah.

Another difference from some of his Jewish critics-to-be marked children of Roth's time and upbringing. His family had a socialist but not an active Zionist leaning. He was not sent to youth groups or summer camps where modern Hebrew would have been taught or spoken. He learned prayer-book Hebrew, sufficient for bar mitzvah and congregational reading, but not the language itself. He was fifteen, the age of strain on family ties and of looking elsewhere for identification, when Israel's nationhood was proclaimed. Whatever pride or hope for the State Roth might have known, it was not self-identifying or intertwined with personal dreams. Israel and Europe would eventually loom as commentary on his generation's personal and family tensions, but it is those tensions that have mostly moved American Jewish life and that have set the foreground of Roth's books.

Even now, Roth probes myths of Jewish history by suggesting that not Israel but America may be the true Zion. American Jews may be more at ease in their land than Israelis in theirs. Again the irony is double edged. Because Jews look more like old-line WASPs than do America's newest ethnics, they are being accepted into that mainstream more quickly and are in a position to render it less exclusionary. The distance American society and culture have traveled since

Roth's childhood can be sensed in the changing assumptions of Roth's books.

From all indications Roth was thoroughly comfortable among Jews during his family years. And by Jews he would have meant Ashkenazic Jews. Of some exotic Syrians encountered at the beach in summer he could say at the end of the fifties, "They were supposed to be Jews, but I never believed it. I still don't."[22] Jews looked and thought like his family and close friends. In a 1962 article Roth speculated that "Most of those jokes beginning, 'Two Jews were walking down the street' lose a little of their punch if one of the Jews, or both, is disguised as an Englishman or a Republican."[23] The punchline equation should not be lost. Jews were liberal, proletarian, demonstrative. They would love F.D.R. for the New Deal and his unrestrained, broad-smiling devotion to the laboring classes. Republicans were simply not to be trusted. Teddy Roosevelt had described the Episcopal church as "the Republican Party assembled for prayer." To Roth, as to his father, Republicans would remain just as out of touch with the masses in the personae of Dwight David Eisenhower, Richard Nixon, Ronald Reagan, George Bush, or J. Danforth Quayle, all of whom Roth would characterize in the popular press as slightly unreal. And genteel Gentiles, though they had left marks of their heritage on the public buildings of Roth's native Newark, were as remote to Roth as the Jews of Roth's day would be to the present black inhabitants of his old neighborhood.

Roth's Newark was, according to another of its natives, Leslie Fiedler,[24] already well declined into second-rate status even for a small city in the shadow of New York, and would soon lose its Jews to the postwar exodus to the suburbs. But for Roth it was an enclave of peace and comfort (his Weequahic High School was over 90 percent Jewish), having by some urban standards the advantages of a suburb: trees in abundance, a sandlot ball field at the school close by, two-family houses separated by tree-lined driveways. For a kid given to baseball, hanging out at candy stores or in the backs of cars, and needing to go downtown primarily to use the library, the neighborhood had a parochial security of its own. Culturally, it was located halfway between the middle America of *American Graffiti* and the ghetto of Chaim Potok's *The Chosen*: Jewish, baseball playing, but completely unlearned in Talmud or any but those rudiments of prayer that might be taught after school at the local synagogue. At a sufficient distance from the rougher neighborhoods of Newark, Weequahic was a refuge from all discomforts except the summer heat.

The young Philip Roth spent his summers at Bradley Beach, sharing summer houses, refrigerators, and the sense of an extended family with other Jewish households, where the accents, including those of immigrant generation grandparents, were stereotypically Jewish. In his memoir of that period, published just as Roth himself was first becoming a subject for critical attention,[25] he idealized his father as the selfless breadwinner who provided wife and child with relief from the summer heat, and he defined the challenge of childhood as swimming beyond the last rope that separates beach from ocean, of going beyond the boundaries of parental control. By his teens that control included curfews, relations with girls, possibly some expectations at holiday time. There was also, apparently, Roth's growing sense of being as strong willed as his father and of their heading for an inevitable clash. By the end of high school, as he indicates in *The Facts*, he wanted very much to break away, partly at least so as not to exacerbate these normal tensions into outright conflict.

Conflict, of course, is the province of the fiction writer, and the conflict over defining and becoming a man may yield considerable fiction, even without being resolved. How being a man affects tribal allegiance is a question that will divide a readership like Roth's. In Roth's fiction, characters often struggle to understand freedom. Especially in his early works, the striver after manhood often asserts himself against cultural bindings seen as shackles. The "ethnic" facing the majority world by trying to shake off signs of his provincialism or by becoming the exotic—most easily on the sexual battlefield—is almost a cliché. It would seem, however, that Roth at eighteen, like many of his characters into their fifties, saw manhood as requiring a letting go, a testing in some outer world unknown to his own people.

In choosing Bucknell University, after commuting for a year to Newark's own Rutgers campus, Roth was doing more than taking advantage of an upturn in family fortunes that allowed him to attend college "away." Nor was he merely following the only known path out, blazed by another neighborhood kid, as suggested in *The Facts*. Any Jewish boy who chooses, even in his second year, a small Protestant school

> where the bylaws stipulated that more than half the Board of Trustees had to be members of the Baptist Church, where chapel attendance was required of lowerclassmen, and where the one extracurricular organization for which most Bucknellians seemed to have membership cards was the Christian Association (*Facts* 61)

is making a positive decision. And what Bucknell seemed to offer to a boy who as a high school senior had served on the prom committee was a forties movie of college life, with fraternities, freshman hazing, and the small town with its soda shops nearby, a picture that had filtered into Weequahic on the movie screens and over the radio. At Rutgers, he asserts in *The Facts*, he had moved beyond Weequahic in the mix of other Newark ethnics and

> hadn't any doubts that . . . Jews were already American or that the Weequahic section was anything other than a quintessentially American

urban neighborhood, but as a child of the war and of the brotherhood mythology embodied in songs like Frank Sinatra's "The House I Live In" and Tony Martin's "Tenement Symphony," . . . [he] . . . was exhilarated to feel in contact with the country's much-proclaimed, self-defining heterogeneity. (*Facts* 37)

If he "hadn't any doubts" in his conscious mind, still his critics would wonder from what recesses he dredged up all those doubts in the minds of characters from Ozzie Freedman to Alexander Portnoy to Nathan Zuckerman. His buying into America may have carried with it a sizable emotional debt. Beneath the tranquil surface there may have been palpitations that only the fictive voice could relieve. If that is so, and "so" is neither knowable nor finally relevant to enjoyment of Roth's works, then it is a testimony to the power of fiction that it can employ feelings the memoirist may dismiss. Or so, at least, says Zuckerman, Roth's alter ego and pen pal of *The Facts* (164–65), commenting on Roth's Bucknell experience almost forty years later.

Roth's family had considered itself liberal—theoretically socialist— and cosmopolitan, yet they were most comfortable with people like themselves. Philip's father had just moved up in a gentile company, Metropolitan Life—from Roth's point of view Jewish merit breaking through gentlemen's agreements and improbability. To Roth there was some adventure in the prospect of going completely beyond their boundaries, in trying himself out in the land of forbidden pleasures, of *shiksas* and *sheygitzes*. It may well be that he was testing a sensed hypocrisy in one-world political messages delivered by parents who, nonetheless, associated most comfortably with their own kind.

In Lewisberg, Pennsylvania, and the environment of Bucknell, he saw a testing ground. Viewing the place as the guest of a neighborhood kid who had gone up a year or so before, he concluded that he indeed shared his friend's good feelings.

Lewisberg emanated an unpretentious civility that we could trust, rather than an air of privilege by which we might have been intimidated. To be sure, everything about the rural landscape and the small-town setting (and Miss Blake) [who had conducted his application interview] suggested an unmistakably gentile version of unpretentious civility, but by 1951 none of us thought it pretentious or unseemly that the momentum of our family's Americanization should have carried us, in half a century, from my Yiddish-speaking grandparents' hard existence in Newark's poorest ghetto neighborhood to this pretty place whose harmonious nativeness was proclaimed in every view. (*Facts* 46)

The "us" indicates Roth's identification at the time—with *his* peers, *his* generation, rather than with Jewish tribalism. It also shows the extent to which the older generation of lower middle-class Jews took its cue for navigating the American academic landscape from its children.

When Roth began writing stories for a literary magazine he had helped found at Bucknell, his thoughts were not on things Jewish. His undergraduate fiction is as bleached, and about as tasty, as white bread. Indeed, as Roth put it himself, the stories,

> set absolutely nowhere, were mournful little things about sensitive children, sensitive adolescents, and sensitive young men crushed by coarse life. The stories were intended to be "touching"; without entirely knowing it, I wanted through my fiction to become "refined," to be elevated into realms unknown to the lower-middle-class Jews of Leslie Street. . . . To prove in my earliest undergraduate stories that I was a nice Jewish boy would have been bad enough; this was worse—proving that I was a nice boy, period. The Jew was nowhere to be seen; there were no Jews in the stories, no Newark, and not a sign of comedy—the last thing I wanted to do was hand anybody a laugh in literature. I wanted to show that life was sad and poignant, even while I was experiencing it as heady and exhilarating; I wanted to demonstrate that I was "compassionate," a totally harmless person. (*Facts* 60)

A harmless *non*person, he might have said, for without the Jewish sensibility that was introduced just a few years later into the *Goodbye, Columbus* stories, Roth's undergraduate fiction, for all its striving, was lifeless. Roth would be a writer about Jews, it seems, or no writer at all.

And five years after college, having just published his first volume, five of whose six stories involved the subject of Jewishness (and the sixth had a Jewish protagonist), feelings for his family and his people as he had remembered them in his childhood were, in general, very warm.[26] Indeed, fifteen years later still, in 1974, after numerous assaults on his allegiance to Jews and the accusations that he had betrayed his family in *Portnoy*, he could say,

> I am probably right now as devoted to my origins as I ever was in the days when I was indeed as powerless as little Freedman [the child protagonist of "The Conversion of the Jews"] and, more or less, had no other sane choice. But this has come about only after subjecting these ties and connections to considerable scrutiny. In fact, the affinities that I continue to feel toward the forces that first shaped me, having withstood to the degree that they have the assault of imagination and the test of sus-

tained psychoanalysis (with all the coldbloodedness *that* entails), would seem by now to be here to stay. Of course, I have greatly refashioned my attachments through the effort of testing them, and over the years have developed my strongest attachment to the test itself. (*RMAO* 9–10)

By that "assault of imagination" Roth meant having let his imagination play upon these materials over a period of time, having done, that is, the work of the fiction writer. Some part of that imagining involved his father, who represented in Roth's 1959 memoir of Bradley Beach summers, "my ideas of how difficult it was to be a man." Through a lifetime of fiction writing that difficulty remained close to consciousness in characters like Wallach, Portnoy, Tarnopol, Kepesh, Zuckerman, "Philip Roth," and Mickey Sabbath and even tempted Roth out of fiction into the chancier worlds of *The Facts* and *Patrimony*. But "the test itself," the writing of fiction rather than any particular subject matter, has been for most of these last several decades, Roth's "strongest attachment." Roth's 1974 reflection declared complementary articles of faith: he must live by being himself—a large part of which is Jewish—and by writing fiction, an activity not merely of telling but also of learning. By infinitely engaging himself on paper, even more than by a finite psychoanalysis, he would rework experience into art.

But "assault of imagination," the work of the fiction writer, Roth already knew in 1959, should begin in sympathy and neither flatter nor condemn its subject. So when the first reviews of *Goodbye, Columbus* praised Roth's artistic control and maturity, his having come into the literary world, as Saul Bellow would say, "with nails, hair, and teeth, speaking coherently,"[27] praise that was followed shortly by both the Jewish Book Council's Daroff Award (1959) and the National Book Award in fiction (1960), Roth should have had little reason to anticipate that characters and situations in his stories could be viewed as grotesques, as distortions used for condemning his own people. Indeed, some of the very stories that would receive the harshest treatment from his coreligionists received individual awards—the *Paris Review*'s Aga Khan Award for "Epstein" and inclusion of "The Conversion of the Jews" in the 1959 and "Defender of the Faith" in the 1960 editions of *The Best American Short Stories*.

Yet, even before the publication of the book, during the two or three years of magazine publication of some of the stories that would compose the book, Roth had begun to receive harsh reactions in letters to the editors; and before the reviewing season was out, from pulpits and in journals, Roth would be accused of portraying Jews as materialistic hedonists ("Goodbye, Columbus"), Rabbis as child abusers and hypocrites ("Conversion of the Jews"), Jewish soldiers as shirkers of duty ("Defender of the Faith"), Jewish fathers as philanderers ("Epstein"), and Jewish suburbanites as insensitive, ignorant assimilationists ("Eli, the Fanatic"). From Roth's standpoint, some of the characters he was "condemning" were actually characters of whom he was fond, all of them characters he felt he understood. None of them were meant to be whole categories of Jews—not *all* rabbis, or *all* fathers, or *all* soldiers, or *all* suburbanites. Some he had met "when [he] was indeed as powerless as little Freedman," before he had embarked on that distancing from powerlessness that was part of the artist's quest. Some of it, for example, the essential plot of and nonjudgmental attitude toward "Epstein" (*RMAO* 173), had been absorbed at family dinners presided over by Herman Roth, the "bard of Newark," a title conferred with the recollection: "That really rich Newark stuff isn't my story—it's his" (*Pat.* 181). Yet, while America was giving Roth the National Book Award, some spokesmen for organized Jewry were giving him the business. What was going on?

What was going on had as much to do with the state of American Jewry as with the literary venturings of Philip Roth. Postwar Jewry, still staggering from the revelations of the Holocaust, was reading Elie Wiesel's *Night*, and Andre Schwarz-Bart's *The Last of the Just* and producing Anne Frank's diary on Broadway. It was reading a literature of pride and propaganda such as Leon Uris's *Exodus*, whose stereotyping made all Jews saintly victims and by implication all critics persecutors. In America, Jews were moving from the cities to the suburbs and joining congregations and organizations to establish a new kind of Jewish life in the new communities. They were breaking down the barriers to medical and law school admissions, and in enormous numbers they were entering the graduate schools and establishing careers as academicians. In all this they were doubly sensitive of their image in the world and of the possibility of other holocausts. Whether what had happened in Hitler's Germany could happen in the United States was a constantly renewed topic of debate.

At the same time American Jewry was caught in a paradox as old as the history of its people, a conflict implicit in Judaism itself. For Judaism is at once a folk (or tribal) religion and a religion that proclaims universal principles. Since its rituals and references are grounded in the experience of the Jewish people, its teachings cannot simply be adopted by or grafted onto some other people having no continuity to Jewish history and life. Yet Judaism has always asserted that it has something to teach the world, and teaching requires contact. Within Judaism itself there have always been conflicts over the extent of that contact, extremists at one end preaching assimilationism and at the other end sanctifying xenophobia. And especially since the enlightenment there has been a sensed danger in the opening of the democracies, an anxiety that Western Jews have mostly suppressed. They have built great societies on the opportunity for integration and fulfillment. But the idea that personal fulfillment might include integration as one of its choices, or that integration might threaten group survival, is a paradox not easily acknowledged in the American Jewish consciousness. American Jews have not perceived themselves as having to declare for survival or for integration. As Charles S. Liebman has said,

> Most Jews are not interested in the articulation of either position. On the contrary, the typical Jew is more anxious to find an ideological position which denies the existence of any tension between survival and integration.[28]

What the "typical Jew" in the late fifties tended to do was to insist that Jews could be liberal, open to opportunity, loving of their people, and strong enough to resist finding any undue attraction in the values of the larger society. If tensions arose over intermarriage or loyalties within families, over perceptions of Israel, over liberalism and conservatism, over allegiances within the family of nations, the particular resolutions of these tensions were so articulated as to seem to be Jewish values, though they ". . . are not values per se . . . [but] only the means to strengthen what the Jewish community really considers most important: Jewish identity and communal survival."[29] So what was going on when Philip Roth published *Goodbye, Columbus* was far more complex than he might have been ready to understand.

In one sense, Roth might have already thought of himself as beyond any possible hubbub. For though he had found his true voice writing about New Jersey Jews, he had done so at a distance from Newark—while teaching in Chicago and Iowa and sliding toward his marriage with a gentile mother of two that would take place just as *Goodbye, Columbus* was being published. Roth's relationship with Margaret Martinson Williams would provide subject matter and perspective for his next several novels—and would eventually add "misogynist" to the epithets of his critics. That relationship would be his way of testing the gentile side of the American coin. But it was the Jewish side with which Roth would increasingly test the ring of the American dream, in fiction and criticism. And soon the response to his first volume would fix him in Jewish controversy for the next several decades. Robert Alter defined the fix two years before *Portnoy*:

> It is easy enough to imagine how exasperated a writer of serious ambition must feel to find himself trapped, as Roth has been, by his own initial success, securely tucked away by the public into a special pigeonhole of genre writing.[30]

"Perhaps," suggested John Gross, "it would have been as well for Philip Roth if he hadn't been cited again and again as a leading member of the new school of American-Jewish novelists."[31] Gross saw the citation as a ". . . portentous . . . label hung round his neck," under whose weight, one was to infer, Roth was not ancient enough a mariner to navigate easily. While he would eventually make that albatross a subject for fiction in the Zuckerman books, his first response was to take on the criticism in serious literary forums. Roth's efforts, though irritating to his antagonists at the time, have been illuminating to critics ever since.

Roth's immediate forays, published as "Writing American Fiction" in *Commentary* of March 1961, "Some New Jewish Stereotypes" in *American Judaism* for Winter 1961,[32] and "Writing About Jews" in *Commentary* of December 1963,[33] explore problems raised by the realities of the new America: that the world of the tabloid was so bizarre that it stymied the imagination of the fiction writer, that Jewish kitsch neutered Jewish subject matter, and that establishment Jews saw self-criticism as stimulating anti-Semitism. In retrospect, the three essays seem to map territory for and chart courses into Roth's career. As manifestos, they identify the corruptions in American society that would frustrate his heroes; they justify bland plots in modern novels on the grounds that any momentous plotting must pale beside the horrendous realities revealed daily in the press; they score facile chauvinism; they even note that some young Jewish men, suffocating under the attentions of their mothers, envy the child neglect or abuse practiced by some gentile parents. This last phenomenon Roth discovered, not in his own notebooks, but as a recurring theme in fiction submitted by his Jewish students— half a dozen years before the writing of *Portnoy*. As Roth would declare in retrospect, these essays were not so much a deliberate program for the future as they were a defense of his past writing and an opportunity to take stock of the present.

> Because recognition—and with it, opposition—came to me almost immediately, I seem . . . to have felt called upon both to assert a literary position and to defend my moral flank the instant after I had managed to take my first steps. . . .[34]

Against the notion that he was a threat to the Jews, Wisse has said,

> he could argue, and did, that his mockery was only proof of their normalization, and that by doing what writers habitually do, singling out their own group for attention, he was showing confidence in their American security and strength.[35]

It is noteworthy that Roth at this time, whatever he may have begun to find out about the world beyond Weequahic, still saw that world as open to him. Within a decade he would be increasingly fascinated by Kafka, whose works operate from the premise that the world is closed to their protagonists, probably because Kafka, from very early, had come to see the world as closed to himself, his family as having been inadequate to prepare him to live in it. But the happy child—father of the man—that had been Philip Roth had little in common with the blighted child that had been Franz Kafka.

Roth's three essay-manifestos also set out his "preoccupation with the relationship between the written and the unwritten world" (*RMAO* xi), a distinction articulated by Paul Goodman for the two planes on which a writer simultaneously lives. And over the decades, as Roth mingled imaginatively his changing sense of America, the Jews, and himself, he would find himself increasingly preoccupied with the "simple distinction (embracing a complex phenomenon)" (*RMAO* xi) implied by Goodman's term. For Roth, a distinction between the "written and unwritten worlds" was

> . . . more useful . . . than the distinction between imagination and reality, or art and life, first, because everyone can think through readily enough to the clear-cut differences between the two, and second, because the worlds that I feel myself shuttling between every day couldn't be more succinctly described. Back and forth, back and forth, bearing fresh information, detailed instructions, garbled messages, desperate inquiries, naive expectations, baffling new challenges . . . in all, cast somewhat in the role of Barnabas, whom the Land Surveyor K. enlists to traverse the steep winding road between the village and the castle in Kafka's novel about the difficulties of getting through. (*RMAO* xi–xii)

But the relationship between these two worlds would become more complex and less clear-cut as Roth's pursuit of fiction-making continued. True, every writer lives a life who.se facts are different from and only imaginatively reconstructed or elaborated into the written world of his making. But Roth would come increasingly to view any life consciously experienced as a story with its own shadings and colorings. Fiction-making is not just imagining, it is also conceiving the goings on of real life: the unwritten world is never experienced uninterpreted. For Jews, the "people of the book," whose group experience is largely pinned, not to a place on the map but to lore and law—to an already existing written world—the separation is even more problematic. Increasingly Roth would see that the fixed fiction—the written world—is only arbitrarily fixed: to come closer to the unwritten reality it has to be ever more ambiguous, multidimensional, and contradictory. Writing fiction is not only carrying messages across from the unwritten to the written world, it is living intensely without the comfort of finality. And the uncertainty inherent to being Jewish raises the intensity a few powers more. To his characterization of *The Castle* as "Kafka's novel about the difficulties of getting through" he adds that it is "also about what comes of taking yourself too seriously—or is it what comes of believing you are not being taken seriously enough? Or is that the same thing?" Comic self-deflation, Kafka's saving grace, would serve Roth well long after 1959.

At the time Roth wrote the materials of *Goodbye, Columbus*, his particular quest was to be a fiction writer, not a spokesman for Jews. He had come to understand that the good story was usually to be found close to home, to one's own experience; and his experience had been of neighborhood, of school, of the army, of starting out into the adult world, some of it the experience of Jews in conflict with aspects of America. Their accents he knew, their feelings he could explore, but he had no program of particular Jewish ideology, no strategy for Jewish, as against human, survival. His conflicts would be about authority and relative position, about going beyond the last rope with parents, teachers, officers, about going into the American landscape and beyond parochial bounds. And his imaginative assault was many sided: conjuring what it means to be a child, to be an expectant father, to be a middle-aged man despairing of his lost youth, to be a noncommissioned officer poised between the army establishment and the recruits—as Roth's father had been between officers of the great insurance company and lowly policyholders in the ghettos. Roth imagined their souls in conflict, sometimes in conflict with such Jewish survival mechanisms as keeping kosher, filling the table and everyone at it, building the business ostensibly for the children, joining the congregation (or the country club), revering the rabbi, seeing the psychiatrist (or the plastic surgeon), avoiding needless contact with the *goyim*.

Doubting the efficacy of these survival mechanisms could seem like attacking the Jews. And portraying mostly doubters, the young, the rebellious, the irreverent—albeit constrained by good Jewish upbringing—was asking for trouble from the guardians of Jewry in 1959. After all, where in the *Goodbye, Columbus* stories was the victim of anti-Semitism, was the saintly grandmother, was the rabbi sacrificing for his people, was the union organizer, was the Zionist leaving his books for the plow in Jezreel, was the assimilated tycoon realizing too late his loss of soul in having become a Jewish Bounderby? American Jewry may have been an amalgam of waves of immigration, settling differently into the American landscape. Grandees, Marxists, Zionists, Freudians may hardly have spoken to one another. But every present ripple of every past Jewish wave had its journal—and its reviewer seeking in vain for his Jew in this Jewish writer. That Roth was contemplating, as he would phrase it later, "the problematical nature of moral authority and of social restraint and regulation . . . the question of who or what shall have influence and jurisdiction over one's life" (*RMAO* 84) was not so apparent in the description of the Potamkins' wedding or of Eli Peck's cold dinner during his wife's "Oedipal experience" with her unborn baby.

As would more often be the case following publication of *Portnoy's Complaint*, anger at the details could blind one to the serious thesis beneath. And for all the sophistication of the Jewish reading public, their strongest tradition had a good strain of sentimentality—with its emphasis on family, mothers, children. For almost two centuries, sentimentality had been a hem against the unravelings of modernism, warding off threats of separation and chaotic invidualism. Roth would quickly be identified with attacks on mothers and family. Yet, in the periodicals over the decades critics would achieve much more consensus in condemning Roth in general than in identifying or analyzing specific evils in his work.

Roth's fiction mostly starts within the experience of a "human character," what he has called "the country's private life" (*RMAO* 122), never with contemplations of society as such. Any translation of individuals into social categories Roth leaves to the reader—or critic. He places his character in some heady experience and gives the reader, not analysis of its moral dilemma, but its smells, sights, voices, temperatures. At his best, he correlates these physical aspects with the moral dilemma: all those young men of appetite but not taste, of blocked expression but ample effusion are presented, as Hermione Lee points out, in

> novels . . . full of tasting and eating, licking and chewing, vomiting, regurgitating, weeping and excreting, and, conversely, of forbidden foods, constipated fathers, teachers with migraines, and women who prefer not to suck cocks or drink sperm. Roth is, preeminently, the novelist of orifices and blockages, of frustrated gratification.[36]

The major orifice in Roth's work is the mouth, locus of ingestion but also of speech, of saying, of storytelling, of wisecracking, of complaining, of informing, of declaring, of responding. Mouths are symbolically fed by mothers or substitute aunts or wives, self-stuffed by compulsives usually while spewing or ranting—the labial traffic moving in two directions—invaded by forbidden foods or sexual objects or organs, protected by dentists, usually failed doctors impotent to do more for a body than polish its smile. Little in Roth's novels centers on muscles or hands or backs or legs, except when the subject is baseball, the silent other side, the graceful representation, of at once individualism and belonging, of having made it in America.

The relationship of America and its Jews has changed significantly during Roth's career. American Jewry has become more open and less defensive about its identity but at the same time more assimilated. Its chief opposition and antagonists are no longer traditional power establishments but underclasses touched by Jewry's recent middle-management authority, now threatening it in the streets and through power clashes in the academy. But early in Roth's career, following the reaction to *Goodbye, Columbus* and the cause *célèbre* of *Portnoy's Complaint*, as Roth's attention to the problem of Jewish conflict in America became intensified by his need to come to terms with his own unforeseen rejection, he created a gallery of testifiers, many of them writers, whose mouths or pens (the recorder of considered speech) addressed and readdressed the Jewish question.

The main Jewish question, raised in magazines, newspapers, and surveys, usually in response to an internal debate in Israel, was Who (and by implication, what) is a Jew. The American spin on the question, iterated by Roth's protagonists, was Why should my being Jewish keep me from sharing in the American dream? Or conversely, How, being Jewish, is it that I *do* seem to be sharing in that dream? Sometimes "being Jewish" meant a word on a medical or army record, but mostly it meant something in the gut that said no to participation or pleasure in unfamiliar pursuits. So in addition to all the orality suggested in characters' names and by words within titles such as "Complaint," "Lippman," "Professor," "Defender," "Writer," "Word Smith," "Fasting," "Breast," and "Zuckerman" (sweet), there is the vocabulary of independence: "Unbound," "Letting Go," "Goodbye," "Beyond," "Desire," "Orgy," "Lonoff," "American," and even, in Roth's uses of the terms, "a Man," "Life," and "Counterlife." Many of Roth's testifiers are men like himself, born in 1933, often in or near Newark, whose lives bear surface resemblances to Roth's, with names suggesting nice Jewish intellectuals—Klugman (smart), Kepesh (of the head, but ineffectual), or Zuckerman (sugar). Five of them, Wallach, Kepesh, Tarnopol, Zuckerman, and "Philip Roth"—spread throughout eleven works—are novelists or teachers of literature. And literature becomes the medium through which these protagonists—and their author—assimilate America into their Jewish selves and themselves into America and the wider world beyond. The younger protagonists fight off the control of Jewish parents threatening their personal independence; the older protagonists, largely writers, fight off the control of organized Jewry threatening their artistic independence and the guilt of having escaped the Holocaust; the protagonist of *Operation Shylock* strives for balance between the Diaspora that nurtured him and the Zionism that would pull all Jews into the modern vortex of their ancient culture. Bearing his author's name and the surface facts of his author's career, he is the "Philip Roth" most people conjure when contemplating the well-known Jewish self-hater, a fictitious "Roth" thrown back at a readership that has created it.

Roth sets his novels at different times during the postwar decades, some-times back a dozen or so years before the period in which he writes them; they most often reflect the predicaments of younger men than their author, or of ear-lier stages in his career. Some of the heroes develop nonsequentially, their middle age written about before their youth, or their backgrounds and parentage changed in later stories. David Kepesh suffers his metamorphosis in *The Breast* (1972)[37] after a life of sensation and diminishing erotic prowess that Roth would eventually spell out in its prequel, *The Professor of Desire* (1977).[38] Nathan Zuckerman is at first the invention of Peter Tarnopol, the novelist-pro-tagonist of *My Life as a Man* (1974),[39] who creates him differently in the two "Useful Fictions" that precede his "True Story," making him in one an army company clerk, in the other an accountant. Later Zuckerman becomes the writer-protagonist in five consecutive works of fiction published between 1979 and 1987. In these, his surface life and parentage differ from those of his earlier manifestations, though he shares something of their sensibility. Zuckerman's own notorious novel, *Carnovsky*, written between the first and second of these five works, draws its allusive value—without having actually to be quoted—from its identification with *Portnoy's Complaint.*[40] By mid-career Roth could play his fiction off against the public myth of his life, in the tradition of Byron—but unlike Byron, spending a fairly unremarkable existence largely behind a typewriter. Finally, Zuckerman is Roth's pen-pal alter ego in *The Facts* (1988), eventually to be replaced by "Philip" and "Philip Roth" of *Deception* and *Operation Shylock* and by Mickey Sabbath of *Sabbath's Theater* (1995).

Roth has been noted for his fine ear and his mastery of narrative voice, which has ranged from complex Jamesian refinement to manic obsession. But as part of the reaction against *Portnoy*, many readers impatient with Roth's manic mode cut themselves off from some of his most powerful writing. While the *Goodbye, Columbus* stories went through scores of printings as classroom fare, such hard gems as "On the Air,"[41] "'I Always Wanted You to Admire My Fasting'; or, Looking at Kafka,"[42] and "The Prague Orgy"[43] remained com-paratively unknown. These pieces, which subject culture to tests of tyranny, use Jews as touchstones, much as do some of the works Roth edited in the series "Writers from the Other Europe." "On the Air," with its racial slurs, despising of Gentiles, and Jewish chauvinism, is not only a devastating example of black humor at its best, it is an explication of Jewish insecurity in America, despite myths of identification, among the postimmigrant generation Jews of the thir-ties and forties. "The Prague Orgy" is perhaps the finest exposition by an American writer of Communist-generated cynicism behind the iron curtain. In the manic "On the Air" and the wistful, recently anthologized "Looking at

Kafka," Jews are swallowed by America. In "The Prague Orgy" a liberated American Jew feels the impotence of his freedom to affect the Communist world. Roth brings to these accounts the double vision of his Jewish humor, his victim-heroes decrying yet resigning themselves to cosmic absurdity.

While some of these short forms well accommodate the manic tone, some longer works do not. The prophetic, just pre-Watergate *Our Gang*[44] and the often hilarious but overburdened *The Great American Novel*[45] almost blow themselves out of the water. Yet these, too, reflect a value system that grew out of Roth's Jewish Newark background: opposition to power and privilege, the natural hating of red-baiters and bald-faced opportunists like Nixon, the ease with which an American establishment can brand its critics or nonconformists with labels like "red" or "un-American" and expect the masses mindlessly to demand their subjugation. The tones of Roth's novels over the period from 1959 to the mid-nineties have varied from the Jamesian omniscience of his longest novel, *Letting Go* (1962)[46] to the depressed stammer of *My Life as a Man* (1974), to the wistful reflectiveness of *The Professor of Desire* (1977), to the increasingly concise shocks of the Zuckerman novels, to the squeezed-dry Pinteresque shorthand of *Deception* (1990), to the challenging postrealism of *Operation Shylock* (1993). Threading these works is an American's attempt to filter out illusions from the world through the agency of a wry Jewish sensibility. What an opportunity for misunderstanding! And what a set of chances for Roth to return volleys right at the feet of his critics.

Chapter 2

STARTING OUT

Roth's undergraduate and graduate-school fiction, bland stories "set nowhere," barely hint at the career to come. While they do show Roth's concerns with self-definition, their voices squeak. By comparison the *Goodbye, Columbus* stories, written soon after, resonate with overtones of the Jewish condition: Jews trying to define themselves getting mixed messages, hearing at the same time the siren song of America and ancestral voices cautioning restraint. These Jewish overtones give authenticity to what in the student stories are mere gropings after sincerity, plucking at strings that have no sounding board.

The student work, formulaic and full of telegraphed punches, strains to present characters and situations more posited than known: a normal child envying institutionalized children; a child of one philosophy teacher snubbing the child of another because he's "not allowed to play with Pantheists"; a just-widowed mailman, about to retire during the final days of World War II, saving himself the agony of delivering a "regret to inform you . . ." letter from the War Department by letting the wind blow it away; a young would-be novelist in a bar abandoning his just-rejected manuscript when he realizes—all in one drunken afternoon—that he has not lived and therefore has no truths to tell, that his "glass is empty"; a stock boy in a department store discovering the phoniness of people of wealth and authority; a little boy who has been lied to about deaths in the family paying the price of his mother's ill-conceived deception. In this last story, written when Roth was already a graduate student at Chicago, the child, left alone at home while his "missing" stepfather is being buried, wanders out, meets a stranger who guides him to the family funeral, and is run over by a car before the eyes of his overprotective mother.

The stories are slight not just because the situations are contrived (the philosophy professor's child story is, after all, a shaggy-dog campus in-joke) and not just because most of them are narrated from the point of view of children or youths. Rather, they share an indictment the young rejected novelist in the barroom levels against himself: that he knows nothing about life. Unfortunately, his narrator had no idea how a young man making that discovery might behave—certainly not by abandoning a manuscript he had worked on for thirteen months, to be swept up or stolen in a bar, melodramatic as that might seem. Nor is there anything convincing in the manner of his getting drunk or of his expressing despair. One suspects that his author did not yet know much about drunks. The stock boy has a few rings of experience. But by and large, their author had not heard them speak, had not witnessed their agony. What the stories show is that Roth had done homework in Lit but not yet in living.

Take, for example, this paragraph from the story of the young rejected novelist:

> He shook his head vigorously, as a dog who emerges from a puddle of muddy water shakes himself. It had been, he consoled himself, a dirty, dizzy afternoon. The dirtiness? That, of course, referred to what had happened inside the publishing house; the dizziness referred to his two block walk from the publishing house to the bar in which he now sat—drunk. For two New York blocks the pedestrian traffic had swarmed over him; yet, incredible though it may appear, he could neither remember one incident that had occurred, nor recall the face of one of the hundreds that had passed him. Was this unusual though: could he now, he challenged himself, recall, this minute, the faces he had lived with for twenty-one years? His mother, for example. . . . Why, of course, she . . . has . . . STOP, his ego screamed, push that thought into the Pandora's box of truths you don't even realize is bursting within you![1]

The passage has the ring of a wooden nickel. The doggie shake of the young man's head is imposed observation: it has nothing to do with a drunk about to console himself. And a young man sloshed for the first time would not analyze and defend at length his choice of adjectives ("dizzy" and "dirty") or find "incredible" his failure to note the faces he had passed on a two-block walk, or consider that, nevertheless, "pedestrians" had "swarmed" over him en route. These misfortunes of narrative inexperience pale, of course, before the stridency at the end of the passage: the character's hearing his "ego scream" or the "Pandora's box of truths." (Not only does that unfortunate phrase "burst . . . within" the young man here, it recurs three times before the end of the narrative.) If the passage is noteworthy at all, it is as contrast to the Roth of "Goodbye, Columbus." Neil Klugman's self-discovery scenes are epiphanies: the reflection in the Lamont Library door, the hollow prayer in St. Patrick's Cathedral; they indicate growth not only in craft but also in understanding. Young men in fiction written just a couple of years later will still need to tell truth, but it will be *their* truth drawn from their lives and their cultures. And their author will observe them at arm's length with an undercutting irony.

The student stories show neither introspection nor *this* author's experience. And as a result their conflicts never rise to issues. Each protagonist is isolated, without a culture to give his strivings more than perfunctory interest. Where the later stories will see America through the eyes of outsiders trying to bend it to their needs, and will resonate with their idiom, the early student stories, even collectively, have no location, no authentic voice. They present problem situations, easily resolved. The one about the retiring mailman may use later Rothian motifs— inexplicable ailments, radioland as Middle America—but the story has little more than a premise to offer. The mailman's pain in bearing tragic news and his discovery of eternal peace in surrendering his will to the wind are equally unconvincing. The mailman, Mr. Thorn, is only a set of specifications: recently widowed, for sympathy with the G.I. loss; almost retired, for the finality of his one act and the totality of his transformation. But he has no life except that of the one conflict. When he speaks, only in reverie or prayer, it is in a toneless voice used solely to give information. To compare his musings with those of, say, Lou Epstein is to move from a premise to a person. Here is Thorn muttering to himself:

> I could put my bag down here and look and see if the letter is there, and if it's not I can start enjoying my last day right this moment. One way or the other I'll know, and if, if I do have to suffer, well. . . . But every day, every single day for months I have thought of doing the same thing, of looking, and every day I've decided against it. Why start now. he mumbled. [sic][2]

How different is the troubled mind of Lou Epstein, overheard as he lies beside his sagging wife, Goldie. Downstairs, his daughter—that ". . . twenty-three-year-old woman with 'a social conscience'! . . . [who] . . . hunts all day for a picket line to march in so that at night she can come home and eat like a horse. . . ." and her fiance, "that guitar plucker . . ."—are making love.

When Epstein tossed in bed and heard their panting and zipping it sounded in his ears like thunder.

Zip!

They were at it. He would ignore them, think of his other problems. The business . . . here he was a year away from retirement he had planned but with no heir to Epstein Paper Bag Company. He had built the business from the ground, suffered and bled during the Depression and Roosevelt, only, finally, with the war and Eisenhower to see it succeed. The thought of a stranger taking it over made him sick. But what could be done? Herbie, who would have been twenty-eight, had died of polio, age eleven. And Sheila, his last hope, had chosen as her intended a lazy man. What could he do? Does a man of fifty-nine all of a sudden start producing heirs? (*GC* 205)

Epstein is no mere idea. His pain and his idiom, both from sources older than he, give him life. Simple remarks carry overtones, like the irony in his line about not producing heirs. In its echo of the biblical Naomi, it not only gives him a Jewish context but also isolates him in a woman's world. Epstein's radical shrew daughter had once been a rosy-cheeked baby; and his Bab-O-smelling, cooking machine of a wife had once been young and sexually stimulating. After discovering his nephew making love to the girl across the street, his sense of loss leads him to an affair with the girl's widowed mother. But Epstein is too old and too long governed by traditional values to manage an infidelity. His rash act sets in motion a series of events he cannot control: produces an irritation that his wife concludes is syphilis, deposits his entire family in his bedroom to witness the naked evidence, plunges him defiantly into the widow's house, brings him down with a heart attack, and subjects him to the ambulance-delivered moralizings of his wife and the emergency medic. And beneath it all, he agrees with them. His whole heritage has trained him for responsibility, not pleasure. The issue for Epstein is not just whether a man can get a little relief from a trying situation, but whether a responsible, middle-aged Jewish husband and father dare entertain liberating thoughts that fly in the face of his defining heritage.

How much richer a narrative conception have these values created for "Epstein" than the thin linearity of "The Final Delivery of Mr. Thorn." Thorn is made lonely by being placed alone: his sorrow is posited as feeling for a stranger's loss. Epstein is lonely though not alone. (He wishes he were. He thinks he would know what to do with another chance if he were not choked with a disappointing family.) His sorrow is for his own loss of youth, opportunity, and fulfillment. Thorn is let off the hook. After surrendering the letter to the wind, he sleeps well and will no longer be troubled. Epstein ventures into adultery, ridicule, illness, and final entrapment in his stagnant situation. Thorn's oath as a mailman, which he can break guiltlessly through a technicality, is coterminus with his job; Epstein's marriage vow, branded in his childhood flesh by the seventh commandment, is not even coterminus with his breath: he could be held to it by a grieving widow. The one character has been thought up; the other, imaginatively realized from countless observations.

The child characters in the student fiction also lack the authenticity of those in *Goodbye, Columbus*. In "The Fence,"[3] the ten-year-old narrator who wishes he were an orphan has no child sound. His ". . . the winey carpet faintly brushed against my toes" is too sophisticated, more like a grownup narrator looking back. But even his grownup sound is false: "I had wished that when I was born again—for like all children, I believed in reincarnation—I would be an orphan." What children believe in reincarnation, or even think about it? Or what man recalling his childhood would conclude so? These thoughts are mouthed to advance the plot, which in this case involves a contrast between privileged "normal" children and orphans. In "Philosophy, Or Something Like That,"[4] Roth imitates the breezy voice of a young Salinger narrator. In "The Day It Snowed",[5] the story about the little boy who is lied to about death, there are echoes of Hemingway's *In Our Time,* without any of its truth, and some of the naïveté of Henry Roth's David Schearl, without any of his pain or fear. Sydney, the child talking, is supposed to be too young to know of death, so all his speculations about the disappearances of close family and the absences of his mother at the times of funerals are given as ignorant innocence. But he is ignorant of much more than death. He is ignorant of any ritual or family custom into which to place it and of the questions that a real child would ask. He has no referents and no particular background. His childish speculations on the mystery of death convey no culture's memory or teachings.

Sydney's dead Aunt Wilma and Uncle Carl could have been anybody's aunt and uncle. The family has no ethnicity. The cemetery, gratuitously described "like a brown and green ocean stuck with white buoys," makes the place too uniform to be a Jewish cemetery. No grays, no odd sizes, no anarchic variety that observation outside the movies might have disclosed. The description is a forced turn of phrase. And the message—too loud, too clear—that a child who is kept from knowing the truth, even by a well-intentioned family, will be the worse for the overprotection, gets translated into the melodramatic death of the young boy. If the idea of withholding pain from the young is a culturally based notion, Roth does not say so. Nor does the old man who finds the child wandering in the streets and takes him to the cemetery represent any particular ethnic value system. The plot requires someone to enlighten the child. So he is brought in to explain to Sydney that a disappeared stepfather could not have been the child's only father, that he must also once have had a biological father and that the term "disappeared" as used by his family really means "dead." His remarks are intended to calm the child by telling him that the dead are not really missing and therefore no longer to be vainly sought. But he is a mere contrivance for ending the story. When Sydney tries to comfort his mother with this startling new idea, her recoiling at such interference makes her send the old man away and creates the reaction in the boy demanded by the plot.

> For a moment Sydney did not see the old man leaving, and he clutched his mother's dress and yelled in his thin glass voice, "Momma, he is dead and that's good. Momma, you can stop looking, I can stop looking!" But then Sydney turned and saw the old man moving away under the oak trees, and he broke for the side walk, crying, "Mister, Mister Man, please come back—" but before he could reach the sidewalk, the big black hearse, like an angry whale, came charging down the left side of the road to be first in the funeral line, and it crushed the boy to the ground, like feet crush acorns, and it shattered forever his thin glass voice.

It would be hard to guess, from the sound of this narrative, that its author was Philip Roth. His later Gentiles had, even in their Gentileness, some flavor arising in their author's mind as contrast to some Jews. Not just Gentiles, but *goyim.*

Two years after writing "The Day It Snowed" Roth published "The Conversion of the Jews," set in the pulsating childworld of little Ozzie Freedman. It is a story about a Hebrew-school child who reacts against his rabbi's abuse by running to the roof of the synagogue, holding everyone hostage to his seeming threat to jump, and getting the rabbi and other children to make vows that stick in their craw. Ozzie's relation to other children, to his mother, to his teacher-tormentor, Rabbi Binder, to gentile society as represented by the firemen who come to rescue him from the synagogue roof is made believable by Roth's knowing touches of description and voice. Here is Ozzie describing to his friend Itzie his encounter with Rabbi Binder after Ozzie has suggested in class that Jesus could have been born of a virgin:

> "And he kept explaining about Jesus being historical, and so I kept asking him. No kidding, Itz, he was trying to make me look stupid."
> "So what he finally do?"
> "Finally he starts screaming that I was deliberately simple-minded and a wise guy, and that my mother had to come, and this was the last time. And that I'd never get bar-mitzvahed if he could help it. Then, Itz, then he starts talking in that voice like a statue, real slow and deep, and he says that I better think over what I said about the Lord. He told me to go

to his office and think it over." Ozzie leaned his body towards Itzie: "Itz,
I thought it over for a solid hour, and now I'm convinced God could do
it." (*GC* 142)

Earnest as this last statement seems, and even naive, it is something like a
punch line. The reader doesn't expect "God" to be the "it" Ozzie was thinking
over. Here is a quality virtually missing from the student fiction: a play of
irony that, however subdued and chastened to other fictive demands, balances
moral earnestness. Roth, according to Albert Goldman, had learned

> to be funny when he was a child, probably on those walks from
> Chancellor Avenue grade school in the Weequahic section of Newark to
> the little Hebrew school fifteen minutes away. In that precious quarter of
> an hour those highly regimented Jewish kids could blow off steam and
> subject the pyramided pieties of their world to a healthy dose of dese-
> cratory humor. For a few minutes they could afford to be bad. Being
> bad and being funny were much the same thing in Roth's mind.[6]

Roth's dropping the high moral tone between "The Day It Snowed" at
age twenty-one and "The Conversion of the Jews" at age twenty-three paralleled his unleashing into fiction those funny-bad Jews he had loved in his
Newark childhood. Even in college, although his writing was "serious," he
had occasionally relaxed in the trusted company of close faculty. They were

> . . . the first gentiles to whom I'd ever given an insider's view of my
> Jewish neighborhood, my family, and our friends. When I jumped up
> from the table to mimic my more colorful relations, I found that they
> were not merely entertained but interested, and they encouraged me to tell
> more about where I was from. Nonetheless, so long as I was earnestly
> reading my way from Cynewulf to *Mrs. Dalloway*—and so long as I
> was enrolled at a college where the five percent of Jewish students left no
> mark on the prevailing undergraduate style—it did not dawn on me that
> these anecdotes and observations might be made into literature. . . . How
> could Art be rooted in a parochial Jewish Newark neighborhood having
> nothing to do with the enigma of time and space or good and evil or
> appearance and reality? (*Facts* 59)

But those are the very concerns of Ozzie and Itzy expressed in the accents of
the Weequahic forties.
     Even when Roth forces the theme, as he still tends to do in "The
Conversion of the Jews," the sense of real goings-on absorbs the material and

gives it overtones of meaning. Ozzie, like Sydney, has only his mother as close family, and like Sydney, reasons about grownups from bits of evidence; but Ozzie's evidence has a context:

> When his mother lit the candles she would move her two arms slowly towards her, dragging them through the air, as though persuading people whose minds were half made up. And her eyes would get glassy with tears. Even when his father was alive Ozzie remembered that her eyes had gotten glassy, so it didn't have anything to do with his dying. It had something to do with lighting the candles. (GC 143)

Candle lighting is, of course, Mrs. Freedman's connection to tradition. In having Ozzie associate her arm movements with gestures of persuasion, Roth may be pushing the boy's suspicion of adult authority, but he gets the physical description right. Arm movements will figure later in Ozzie's birdlike flappings on the roof, as he initiates himself into the mysteries of total free will, but here they represent the mother's peace in unquestioning surrender, and her glassy eyes—no metaphoric contrivance like Sydney's glass voice—touch this child so that a moment later "he felt his own eyes get glassy." At Hebrew school Ozzie's rationalism may verge on agnosticism, but his home-rooted attachments are Jewish and nourishing.

Both "The Day It Snowed" and "The Conversion of the Jews" concern freedom from adult oppression, but in "The Conversion," as in the other Goodbye, Columbus stories, Roth takes the protagonist's resistance to the forces trying to define him, elaborates it into a contemporary issue, and gives it perspective through irony or humor. That children should not be lied to is a limited truth. That a child nurtured within a religious tradition feels betrayed by the dogmatism of his own mentors is a greater one. For Ozzie Freedman, as for Stephen Daedalus before him, the test of received tradition is how authority responds to the questioning child. Roth makes his Jewish child defeat his tormentors by magnifying their own absurdity. And for doing so, Roth, too, would have to dig in his heels and fight off critics. The actions of both character and author were as much a commentary on the condition of Jewry in mid-century America as Stephen's rejecting the Church and Joyce's fleeing the country were a commentary on the state of Catholicism in turn-of-the-century Ireland.

Ozzie's questioning of his rabbi's dogma may touch theology (the tactic of responding to the charge of blasphemy with a countercharge of greater blasphemy is right out of John Locke), but it is less theology than it is pique. Rabbi Binder seems arbitrary to Ozzie at first partly because he makes Judaism seem to grant only its own miracles while denying those of Christianity, but even more because Binder is a bully and a hypocrite. He invites open discussion of any issue but will not allow and cannot answer questions about the virgin birth. And when Ozzie flees to the roof—in pure mindless reaction to a slap—and forces the rabbi and the other Hebrew-school children to genuflect and admit that the Christian miracle is as possible as, say, the creation, he is testing freedom, not theology.

And yet, this child's tug-of-war with authority, humorously portrayed, draws into it the struggle of secular Jewry against orthodox teaching and, implicitly, the effect of public education. In postwar America the middle class still seemed like the model for the future, and its future lay in public education. But in the cities that education had not yet been overwhelmed by welfare or drug problems, nor had the psychedelic-rock-astrology nexus or creationism yet made inroads into science to weaken the hold of rationalism on impressionable minds. The distinction between knowledge and belief was important. National heroes included quiz-show contestants. An education separated from indoctrination was still the signal achievement of public school systems protected by the First Amendment. Most middle-class, urban, Jewish kids still went to public schools and got their Jewish education in after-school synagogue schools like Rabbi Binder's. In this setting liberal thought and Judaism seemed to walk hand in hand. Often quoted in Jewish congregations was Edmond Fleg's affirmation, "I am a Jew because the faith of Israel requires of me no abdication of the mind."[7]

That abdication, which Rabbi Binder denies in his lectures but demands in his punishments of Ozzie Freedman, sparks the tension and humor of the story. Ozzie is a child trying to escape the authority of grownups, as every child must eventually do—that is a common denominator of Roth's early fiction—but he is more. He is a Jewish child, already God's rival for family devotion in the age of the child-centered home. Even the orphaned Ozzie, whose bedraggled mother can lose her patience, has status in 1950s America. And the power that status gives him, dancing on the edge of the roof and waving his arms, is a product of the half-century of movement from the Pale of Settlement to the American suburbs. Unlike David Levinsky in Poland in the 1880s, Ozzie Freedman in Newark in the 1950s takes neither illogic nor a slap from his rabbi sitting down.

Of course, Ozzie knows nothing of the history surging through his veins. He gets slapped and he runs. And Roth keeps him in perspective. He's a frightened, plucky kid. Roth contrasts Ozzie's childish remarks with analogies that set him off and yet suggest the universality of his situation. Ozzie's most profound statements are inadvertent. His "You don't know anything about God!" the remark that finally draws the slap, is shouted impetuously at Binder's back. That Ozzie may be summing up the point of the Book of Job—that is, that God is too mysterious for man to know anything about Him for certain—does not soften Binder's response. And Ozzie's most profound question, asked and then reiterated on the roof, "Is it me? Is it me ME ME ME ME! It has to be me—but is it!"—the question that every Roth protagonist will ask himself through the next forty years of fiction writing—comes unexpectedly and is muted almost as quickly by Roth's narrative voice:

> It is the question a thief must ask himself the night he jimmies open his first window, and it is said to be the question with which bridegrooms quiz themselves before the altar.
> In the few wild seconds it took Ozzie's body to propel him to the edge of the roof, his self-examination began to grow fuzzy. Gazing down at the street, he became confused as to the problem beneath the question: was it, is-it-me-who-called-Binder-a-bastard? or, is-it-me-prancing-around-on-the-roof? However, the scene below settled all, for there is an instant in any action when whether it is you or somebody else is academic. The thief crams the money in his pockets and scoots out the window. The bridegroom signs the hotel register for two. And the boy on the roof finds a streetful of people gaping at him, necks stretched backwards, faces up, as though he were the ceiling of the Hayden Planetarium. Suddenly you know it's you. (*GC* 148)

Ozzie's situation on the roof is poignant and funny. When the actor Bob Dishy read "The Conversion of the Jews" to an audience at New York's Symphony Space theater as part of that institution's annual celebration of the short story form, it was met with ample laughter. But that was 1988. In 1956, and later as part of the 1959 book, Ozzie's making the whole group below aver that God could make a child without intercourse was a bit touchier to Jews. His vengeful follow up of having them all say they believed in Jesus Christ was too much. There was limited appreciation of the joke or, one might suspect, of Ozzie's last requirement: "Promise me, promise me you'll never hit anybody about God." Apparently, lots of Jews would have given his author what Rabbi Binder gave Ozzie, and more.

Shortly before the end of the story there is a moment of choosing for Ozzie—his rabbi kneeling, trembling, and begging him not to be a martyr, his friends shouting for him to jump and become a "Martin"—when Ozzie's question shifts from "Is it me?" to "Is it us? . . . Is it us?" His whole assertion of freedom is given a group context. It is not Ozzie versus his people, but Ozzie as one of his people seeking room to find himself within the tribe, but unbound from arbitrary authority. Ironically using a question about Jesus, in whom he has no personal stake, little Freedman frees himself (and his fellows) from the bindings of Binder, a Promethean act. All Roth's other protagonists in the *Goodbye,*

Columbus stories struggle the same way: to replace with their own values bindings they feel imposed by the group. As for Roth's Jewish readers, many
would accuse him of mere indulgence or, worse yet, betrayal for focusing on "Is
it me?" Very few would recognize that Roth's context for the question was that
other question, "Is it us?"

Reviewing *Goodbye, Columbus* in *The Reconstructionist* (March 4,
1960), Harold Ribalow says of Roth that ". . . he writes out of hatred more often
than not," that "his people are so unsympathetic that you find yourself not car-
ing for them, their troubles and the ways in which they try to solve their problems," and that his stories are "open to the charge of anti-Semitism." Four
years later Oscar Janowsky would say of Roth that

> . . . his rebellion against the Jewish world from which he springs is so
> extreme that the characters he describes are frequently unconvincing and
> revolting. . . . The umbilical cord which ties the author to his Jewish
> past is torn with such violence that the clinical details of the rupture
> obscure every other element."[8]

These condemnations, one by a partisan Jewish publicist and one by a respected
scholar, are somewhat restrained compared to the views of countless rabbis
expressed in pulpits and of letter writers to the review columns and magazines
in which the various *Goodbye, Columbus* stories originally appeared. But they
show how the insecurity of the times could color critical judgment. Of another
Goodbye, Columbus story, "Defender of the Faith," Ribalow writes

> . . . I do not think anyone will deny that it is a vivid and, in a way, bril-
> liant story about a Jew in the United States Army who spends all his
> time, energies and abilities in trying to fool everyone with whom he
> deals, to get away from every responsibility. It is a story about a perfect
> "goldbrick," a hateful, miserably phony type. Grossbart, the faker, is a
> Jew who exploits his Jewishness in every possible way to avoid work, to
> get off the Army base. Grossbart is constantly dealing with a fellow Jew,
> Sergeant Marx, and uses psychological pressure to get what he wants . . .
> you remember Grossbart as the meanest, most unsavory Jew you have
> come across in years, and you cannot help being revolted by him. (13)

Grossbart is almost everything Ribalow says he is, and yet Ribalow is wrong in
his most essential point: "Defender of the Faith" is not a "story about [this] perfect 'goldbrick'"; it is a story of conscience about the sergeant who has to deal
with him. It is Marx's story, told in Marx's narrative voice, much more than
Grossbart's. Over a generation of college students, most of them gentile, have

not failed to grasp that point. Appearing in several—including the most widely read[9]—freshman English anthologies, the story has been presented—and elucidated in ample study notes—as a model of moral dilemma played out in the psyche of its protagonist, Sergeant Marx.

And, indeed, Marx moves from dilemma to dilemma, as he considers Jewish issues for perhaps the first time: whether he has not helped save Jewry from Hitler only to deliver it into bland assimilation, whether the army that fights for democracy should not consider the pluralism of its own citizenry and attempt to provide special sabbath observances and kosher food for Jewish soldiers, whether the pressures of war and army conformity have too easily severed Marx's own ties with his Jewish tradition. These are not new issues. During World War I, one of the improvised choruses of "Inky Dinky Parlez Vous" advised that "many a son of Abraham is eating ham for Uncle Sam," and the case of an army doctor who chose to wear a yarmulke during surgery would hold the headlines a generation after this story was published. Roth presents an issue so universal that it anticipates the very criticism that would be leveled at the narrative. At the end of the story Grossbart shouts, ". . . There's no limit to your anti-Semitism, is there! . . ." as earlier he had averred, "I've run into this before, but never from my own!"

In slowly succumbing to Grossbart's suggestion that his G.I. heart has hardened by disassociation from his Jewish roots, Marx lets guilt—and a dose of sentimental memory—color judgment.

> Out of the many recollections that had tumbled over me these past few days, I heard from some childhood moment my grandmother's voice: "What are you making a *tsimas*?" It was what she would ask my mother when, say, I had cut myself with a knife and her daughter was busy bawling me out. I would need a hug and a kiss and my mother would moralize! But my grandmother knew—mercy overrides justice. I should have known it, too. Who was Nathan Marx to be such a pennypincher with kindness? Surely, I thought, the Messiah himself—if he should ever come—won't niggle over nickels and dimes. God willing, he'll hug and kiss. (*GC* 193)

This self-examination comes after Marx has just written a weekend pass, against the rules of basic training, to allow Grossbart and his two Jewish fellow trainees to go to an aunt's home for a (as it later turns out) fictitious, month-late special seder. That Marx can derive Portia's "quality of mercy" scruples from the homey teachings of his Jewish grandmother or that Roth neatly distinguishes for his reader the Jewish idea of the messiah as separate from God and still anticipated—these gifts to a general readership could not move critics like Ribalow to modulate their attack. To them, fear that Gentiles would take all Jews to be like Grossbart overrode every other consideration.

A subtext of the story is the war itself and its background assimilation of Jews and Gentiles in the army. Marx has fought in the already concluded European phase of the war, which began as Germany's war against the Jews. His commanding officer, Captain Barrett, uses him as an example to answer Grossbart, flattering Marx with the status of hero. Grossbart wants to avoid the dangers of the remaining action in the Pacific by being shipped back to New Jersey. Both Grossbart and Barrett are using Marx.

Marx's redemption comes in a hard but fair act. Grossbart finally makes the move he has been building toward throughout the story and, deserting the two other recruits he has claimed to champion, finds another Jewish patsy to reverse his combat orders and keep him from being sent to the Pacific. But Marx has the orders restored. He alleges to the commanding officer that he is doing so at Grossbart's bidding, ironically explaining that the "boy" is indeed the patriot he has painted himself as being, one who wishes fervently to remain with his friends assigned to the remaining war zone. Roth makes Marx the titled "Defender of the Faith" by having him refuse to allow other characters in the story to perceive the Jews as seeking—or getting—special treatment. The resolution is finally of Marx's conflict. Having been forced to reconsider his Jewish difference, he lets his duty as soldier properly prevail. He is equally the sergeant of all his recruits.

> With a kind of quiet nervousness, they polished shoes, shined belt buckles, squared away underwear, trying as best they could to accept their fate. Behind me, Grossbart swallowed hard, accepting his. And then, resisting with all my will an impulse to turn and seek pardon for my vindictiveness, I accepted my own. (*GC* 200)

There is real anti-Semitism in the story, but it is not Roth's. Sergeant Marx is torn not only between two impulses but between two representative characters. Grossbart is one. The other, Captain Barrett, is perhaps more sinister because totally unaware: like most of America, he sees no reason to know who Marx is. In one statement he both honors Marx's military record and erases his identity. Barrett's "native corn," as Roth would call it elsewhere, chills as much as Grossbart's weaseling enrages.

A few years later, in "Writing About Jews," Roth would say about this story, as indeed about "Epstein," that his characters had their seeds in fact, in people who impressed him with their human failings, and that it was their generalized human condition that interested him primarily. But he also saw that inextricably wound into and giving special character to their conflicts were their attitudes toward Jewishness.

Grossbart is depicted as a single blundering human being, one with force, self-righteousness, cunning, and, on occasion, even a little disarming charm; he is depicted as a man whose lapses of integrity seem to him so necessary to his survival as to convince him that such lapses are actually committed in the name of integrity. He has been able to work out a system whereby his own sense of responsibility can suspend operation, what with the collective guilt of the others having become so immense as to have seriously altered the conditions of trust in the world. He is represented not as the stereotype of The Jew, but as a Jew who acts like the stereotype, offering back to his enemies their vision of him, answering the punishment with the crime. Given the particular kinds of humiliations and persecutions that the nations have practiced on the Jews, it argues for far too much nobility to deny not only that Jews like Grossbart exist but that the temptations to Grossbartism exist in many who perhaps have more grace, or will, or are perhaps only more cowed, than the simple frightened soul that I imagined weeping with fear and disappointment at the end of the story. Grossbart is not The Jew; but he is a fact of Jewish experience and well within the range of its moral possibilities. (*RMAO* 158–59)

Roth was defending his own writing against the charges of anti-Semitism and self-hatred that had become by then a common indictment. Part of his theme was that a writer must achieve a certain sympathy even for the most failed human beings, Epstein, for example, so that the reader can derive, not as moral judge but as expanded consciousness, a sense of what that act of failing is like. What is of interest to Roth in Epstein's being Jewish is not that Jews do or do not commit adultery—of course they do—or whether in representative proportions. Rather, he said, ". . . I seem to be interested in how—and why and when—a man acts counter to what he considers to be his 'best self,' or what others assume it to be, or would like it to be" (*RMAO* 152). The range and degree of accusations contained in the letters Roth received either directly, or indirectly from his publishers, would seem a fiction writer's exaggeration today. Indeed, they would become the stuff of fiction when Roth dealt with them later in the Zuckerman novels. But in "Writing American Fiction" he would turn the charge of self-hatred on his accusers, many of them rabbis, who, he demonstrates, need a Jewry under siege, even if from their own, so unconfident are they of their congregants' ability to read competently on their own.

Jewish subject matter and tones, then, were Roth's legitimate material. Jewish voices bring the *Goodbye, Columbus* stories alive because they had resonated through Roth's formative years. Moreover, Jews were uniquely suited to test America as an idea. Roth saw how America's supposed equality and liberty, its infinite opportunity, inspired some Jews, intimidated others, produced in still others centuries-old reflexes and defenses. The eternal Jewish conflict, today the conflict of "ethnics" everywhere, of maintaining their identity while participating in a wider national life, vitalized their stories. But for Roth, even more interesting than conflicts between Jews and Gentiles may have been conflicts, which his rabbinic critics would confirm, among Jews living self-consciously in the presence of Gentiles. Ozzie Freedman's rebellion would be less troublesome if he didn't drag the Christian majority's religious doctrine into Hebrew school and then require their representative firemen to hold his safety net. Captain Barrett and the other G.I.'s are very much part of the conflict between Grossbart and Marx. And it is the whole society of Woodenton, the silent gentile community whom the Jews feel compelled to placate, that sets the conflict going in "Eli, the Fanatic."

"Is it me?" "Is it us?" Eli Peck, assimilated Jew of neutral surname in suburbia, is at a loss to define himself even before this narrative begins. His first words in the story are about *his* unease, his awkward fit in Woodenton. Rabbi Tzuref, the Hasidic thorn in the progressive Jews' side, has welcomed the "weary" Eli into his mansion-turned-yeshiva by remarking on the length of Eli's work day. Disarmed by kindness, Eli drops the prosecutorial tone he had prepared and sighs, "It's the commuting that's killing. . . . Three hours a day . . . I came right from the train." And before even knowing the facts of Eli's case against Tzuref, the reader is invited to wonder why this man has made himself a "commuter"—defined in a light verse of the day as "One who shaves and takes a train/ And then rides home to shave again." A busy city lawyer, Eli adds three more stressful hours to his workday to spend the night in this bedroom community. The reason, it is soon apparent, is to prove that he has made it in America. Eli has settled for a "me" that seems safe: progressively Jewish, he and his friends in Woodenton are indistinguishable from the Gentiles; all they need do is refrain from making waves; but Eli, whose wife fashionably worships Freud and "domestic happiness," is given to nervous breakdowns, and the Jews of Woodenton must pay for their tranquility by keeping out their more apparent, less suitable coreligionists. Eli's task, after commuting from the city where he works to the suburbs where he sleeps, is to represent the other overnighters in excising from their tenuous midst a ghetto of war-displaced yeshiva students who would live and work, night and day, in this, their other Eden. And Eli is performing this service *pro bono*, to pay his dues so that, as his wife puts it, "the community's temper would quiet, and the calm circumstances of their domestic happiness return." A bumbling knight errant he may be, but Eli's story is a quest in the archetypal sense: he must find himself and confirm that "it is me." And Roth intensifies the pressure because whatever Eli's real "me" is, Eli has only a couple of days to identify it before he must pass it on to an heir. His wife is about to give birth, and at the end of the story the Eli that comes to see the child must be an Eli confirmed by his quest.

Roth introduces an element of mysticism into this otherwise open, contemporary atmosphere. It is an element that weakens the thematic resolution but deepens by its overtones the feeling for the conflict. Tzuref's assistant is a Hasid in black coat, traditional broad-brimmed hat, and protruding *tzitzit* fringes. He is otherworldly, almost mute, something between a figure out of Chagall and Harpo Marx. His traversings of the glossy Woodenton landscape are what most upset the assimilationist Jews. Roth makes him Eli's doppelganger. As Eli finds himself less able to demand Tzuref's removal—Tzuref claims that the children are all one extended family and therefore not in violation of the zoning laws—Eli brings the assistant a green suit of his own to replace the black caftan, leaving the gift at his door. He finds in exchange the assistant's black garments now at his door, and in his nervous condition, dons them to show the man reciprocal acceptance. But Roth has the black clothes claim Eli in almost mystic fashion: Eli tries to inhabit them in acceptance of traditional faith, even as the "greeny" now goes up and down the village in Eli's suit. The question of identity is absurdly joined as the two men mirror one another. Roth needs Eli's emotional illness to make this work (illness will justify exceptional behavior in future Roth stories as well), but the device makes Eli's resolution of the question of Jewish-American identity merely eccentric.

Of course, real resolution is impossible. Eli cannot get from some here to some there because he is nowhere. What made him susceptible to pressure in the first place—not from Gentiles, but from Jews insecure about Gentiles—was a vacuum of personal Jewish identity. He cannot fill that vacuum by a sudden decision to embrace ultra-orthodoxy. That could come only from another lived experience, not from guilt about nonexperience. He dons the black gabardine which is not his and vows that he and his son will wear it ceremonially every year; but Eli has no standing in or understanding of that mode, or any alternative Jewish mode, of living. Eli's breakdown, requiring sedation and removal by the men in white, is the consequence of his being unable to travel any Jewish distance himself.

Jewish identity here is not just a matter of choosing temple affiliations or of taking adult education courses in Jewish history. Eli, educated professional, knows of the Holocaust, and must know something, however rudimentary, about the forms of his religion, but has joined these suburban Jews in escaping far from their roots. They may not even have a temple of their own: one of Eli's protesting Jewish neighbors says that on Sunday's ". . . I drive my oldest kid all the way to Scarsdale to learn Bible stories. . . ." Scarsdale is a half-hour commute from New York; Woodenton, an hour-and-a-half commute for Eli, is located an hour further from the city than Scarsdale. Even if Roth is allowed his fictitious sense of space and distance, he has clearly placed these Jews far from their roots.

Sometimes, to stack the deck, too far. The Jew who drives his child to Scarsdale continues, ". . . and you know what she comes up with? This Abraham in the Bible was going to kill his own *kid* for a sacrifice. She gets nightmares from it, for God's sake! You call that religion? Today a guy like that they'd lock him up." Irving Howe justifiably objects that even this Philistine cannot be so ignorant of "this Abraham" as to speak this way, that Roth is giving him not what the man would say, "but what Roth thinks his 'real' sentiments are."[10] But this assimilated Jew's real sentiments are for moderation, for replacing paradox with scientific truth, religious mystery with ethics—perhaps tinged by, but certainly not in the grip of, emotion. The neighbor's speech concludes, "This is an age of science, Eli. I size people's feet with an X-ray machine, for God's sake. They've disproved all that stuff, Eli, and I refuse to sit by and watch it happening on my own front lawn".[11] The "it" is his notion of religion as mystery—symbolized by the yeshiva and the "greenie" in his black gabardine—mystery whose ethical questions are not fathomed in platitudes about social moderation. Ironically, like the displaced Tzuref, these Woodenton Jews are also Abrahams, but of a perverse kind. They have left their urban Chaldea to sojourn in the promised suburbs, all too ready to sacrifice their children's heritage on an altar of conformity. Or like the Israelites at the foot of Sinai, ready to proclaim their ease their faith.

Eli is placed between an old and a new neither of which can suffice. How widespread that conflict might be, it is doubtful that even Roth could have known, for in 1959 the march of modernism seemed inexorable. The as-yet-unforeseen rise of fundamentalism—among Hasidim in America or Israel, among Iranians or Arabs, among peoples of the Indian subcontinent—would be inimical to the still prevailing idea of progress, with its ties to science. The corresponding impulse toward separatism and ethnic faction was also unforeseen. "Eli the Fanatic" seemed to the average reader to have but limited implications—a mere phase of Jewish acculturation. But it is a phase in a larger sweep of history, in a struggle for ascendancy within peoples between mind and heart. Judged today, after united Jewish protests over the racial murder of a Hasid in Brooklyn's Crown Heights, any Jewish stigmatizing of the ultra-orthodox might seem self-hatred in the extreme; but conflicts between modern and Hasidic Jews—over residential zoning, over school taxes, over participation in a range of civic enterprises—has, if anything, grown since 1959, and the Woodenton Jewish attitude has perhaps changed less toward Hasidim than toward the once-prevailing WASPs. More at home now in America, Jews can get annoyed with Hasidim or

Lubavitchers on their own, without being prodded by thoughts of the Gentiles. Yet the larger question for each Jew has not gone away: what mix of tradition, ritual, belief, and commitment to pluralism constitutes a "yes" to the question "Is it me?"

Eli's fanaticism, his donning the old-world wardrobe, raises a question of sanity: his and his neighbors'. For Eli, craziness is failure to recognize the vacuity of Woodenton Jewishness. For his neighbors, it is any attempt to go back to the past. Roth may mean Eli to be redeemed in his breakdown at the end, but it is a redemption suitable only for the styling of a short story. Eli's agony will have been short-lived, a gesture. He is not likely to convert his wife or control the upbringing of his son, or live the adored exotic in their midst. He undergoes no intensive penance and purgation like that of, say, *The Magician of Lublin*. Roth raises the question of how to be Jewish in the presence of a larger gentile society and clothes the asking in symbolism: the Hasidic garb and the "blackness within," the hilltop Yeshivah from which Eli comes down, Moses-like, to the worshipers of the golden calf. These symbols serve to dramatize the dilemma of "Is it us?" But resolving the question was not what Roth was about in this or the other *Goodbye, Columbus* stories. Raising it, in numerous contexts, was task enough.

Looking back some dozen years later, Roth wondered whether it had not been too much task. Jewish audiences, and sympathetic Gentiles, had found common ground in reading and viewing stories about unfair treatment of Jews by Gentiles. *Gentleman's Agreement* had been successful on both page and screen, and Gregory Peck (could his surname have suggested Eli's?) had spoken not only persuasively in the cause, but, from a certain admiring perspective, with grace under fire and gentility. Still, Roth mused,

> I did not realize at the time that I had turned the familiar subject of anti-Semitism somewhat on its head and that, in writing of the harassment of Jew by Jew rather than Jew by Gentile, I was pressing readers to alter a system of responses to "Jewish" fiction to which they had perhaps become more than a little accustomed. Had I been fully alert to the demand being made and the expectations being bucked, I might not have been so bewildered by the charges of "anti-Semitism" and "self-hatred" that were brought against me by any number of Jewish readers following the publication in *The New Yorker*, in 1959, of "Defender of the Faith." Only five thousand days after Buchenwald and Auschwitz it was asking a great deal of people still frozen in horror by the Nazi slaughter of European Jewry to consider, with ironic detachment, or comic amusement, the internal politics of Jewish life. In some instances, understandably, it was asking the impossible. (*RMAO* 174)

In the title novella Roth would view the question of "Is it us?" from the perspective of his own generation. Neil Klugman would be the first of that series of young men born in 1933 who would populate much of the later fiction. The dirty linen in "Goodbye, Columbus" would flap for decades.

One of the great artistic (though certainly not commercial) misfortunes of Roth's early career was the release of the movie of "Goodbye, Columbus" in the same year that *Portnoy's Complaint* was published. The double whammy of decrying Jewish guilt on paper and splashing Patimkin opulence on screen would seal the Jewish self-hatred indictment against Roth for decades. Worse, still, the movie, in shifting the geography from New Jersey to Westchester and in muting the internal monologue, took Neil out of Newark and, largely, the conflict out of Neil. But the conflict is in Neil in ways that his actions alone cannot disclose. At key times in the book Roth gives him dreams or meditations that color the actions, or nonactions, as the case may be. They reveal a character adrift but clever, capable of fooling himself by playing mind games with his identity, but sensing, even as he criticizes everyone else's values, that his nihilism is void of values too. In the movie script, employing pure action and dialogue, Neil wins the word games but loses his self-criticism. Brenda becomes the prime mover (a task for which Ali MacGraw was hardly adequate, making all the moves zombie moves); Neil remains little more than her love slave to be discarded when she is through with him.

In "Goodbye, Columbus" Roth was writing more than a summer romance, though that in its most basic outline is the plot. A young man romances a young woman during summer vacation, and when fall necessity banishes summer idleness and everyone must go back to doing something and being someone other than a consumer of time and dreams, Romeo is banished and Brenda, without the moxie of a Juliet or any desire to risk inconvenience, returns to being her mother's daughter. Beyond that plot stand all the differences in social system and expectations between medieval Verona and mid-twentieth-century America—differences, however, that were only a generation or so old. For in their sexual mores and social mobility, immigrant Jews were much closer to Verona than to Short Hills. The third generation loosed into an upwardly mobile world many bright young people educated on other people's sweat; they might test their intellectual merit but rarely their characters. Scorning business, assuming a new permissiveness, and silencing their parents with academic abracadabra, they got to assert not so much their wills as their willfulness. Trying to climb some magic staircase, many would wind up, like Neil, walking the plank.

Neil, who identifies himself by his oppositions, not by his affirmations, is, like Eli, without locomotion. From a lower middle-class family, dependent on his education for a career, he has temporarily stalled in a respectable enough job at the Newark Public Library, helping people a bit but himself not very much. He disdains business. He has cut his hawsers; he has no motor of his own; he can but drift. In a Jewish value system he does have his maleness, suited out not for battle but for prize. He is a catch, provided he behaves. But unassertive males find—or create—overassertive females. Neil, still with the power to resist being caught but no power to move himself or to move Brenda out of her sphere, ends where he began, except for the experience itself. And in that Roth remains ambiguous. Neil may have learned something useful, but maybe not.

The title "Goodbye, Columbus" is suggestive more than it is concrete. From its specific reference to a university's farewell ceremony at Columbus, Ohio, it ripples outward to embrace dreams of escape and waking realities of immigrant populations. Columbus is, after all, the patron saint of immigrants to America, and, sailing at the time of the Jewish expulsion from Spain, particularly associative for Jews. People who would have called goodbye to the real Columbus were not only Spaniards looking west but, a few months later, West Indians looking east, resembling the Gauguin figures that fascinate the black boy in the Newark library. In Neil's dream, he and that boy are anchored at such an island on a ship that begins mysteriously to drift them seaward, against their wills and away from their havened paradise, while the natives chant "Goodbye, Columbus . . . goodbye, Columbus . . . goodbye . . . ," echoes from Ron Patimkin's phonograph record preserving college dreams. "Columbus" suggests opportunity, dreams of escape to paradise, for Neil, climbing the "hundred and eighty feet that make summer nights so much cooler in Short Hills than they are in Newark," for the black boy, climbing to the library stacks where he can safely read his book without subjecting it to the dangers of the ghetto. Neil and the boy are intertwined in their Columbus-like venturings. Neil, as if to preserve the boy's dream, keeps the book illegally out of circulation for the boy's exclusive use. And when Neil leaves the boy to go to Brenda, he sees Short Hills in his "mind's eye, at dusk, rose-colored, like a Gauguin stream." The summer in Short Hills, the paradise of sex without responsibility, the Patimkin refrigerators and table bulging with fruit like a tropical island all play into Neil's illusion, in which drift is movement and lunch almost free. "Oh, Patimkin! Fruit grew in their refrigerator and sporting goods dropped from their trees." Neil's final awakening is another goodbye: after his attempt to discover America in Short Hills and Boston, he says his goodbye to the myth that began with Columbus and takes his first steps back into the Newark library, this time by choice or perceived necessity, rather than just by drift.

"Goodbye, Columbus" pits the urban values of immigrant settlers against the suburban leisure values of the postwar generation. The former, used to working hard and getting nothing free, are represented by Mr. Patimkin, Neil's Aunt Gladys and Uncle Max, Neil's asthmatic parents (now removed to

Arizona) and their son, recently returned from the army. Patimkin Sink is located in Newark's black ghetto, and Mr. Patimkin, for all the comfort of the house he has provided his family in Short Hills, is more at home at work. But his children and to a lesser extent his wife have shed the ghetto for the suburbs (but storing their old furniture in the attic as though the dream might end), and their life centers at the country club. Ghetto values are crowded and shared; suburban values, individualistic. Aunt Gladys's house offers Neil neither privacy nor expectation that privacy will be needed; to phone he must retreat to a closet. At Short Hills everyone has a separate bedroom and little chance of being interrupted once behind closed doors. The dining room in which the family gathers once a day to confirm their corporate existence hears no shared concerns, echoes no wisdom to help its inhabitants in their goings forth. It is a place to display the consumerism of eating and the opulence of being served. At Short Hills, where Patimkins give poor imitations of Gentiles, just fixing bumpy noses and learning American sports, all is overdone.

Brenda is the chief representative of the new generation. She may have weak eyesight without her glasses, but her main employment does not require good vision. It is not to see but to be seen. She is aware of her attractions, of other eyes on her, and is clever about getting what she wants, for both the short and the long run. She meets Neil at the country club to which he has inveigled an invitation from a cousin, and she allows him to admire her and invites him to spend his vacation time at her house. But she is always running away from conversation with Neil, and he limits his own remarks to quips, as she seems to require. Conversation implies commitment; her relation to Neil is merely athletic, even in bed. Her brother, returning from a jock college, but deprived of his father's ghetto education, is hapless at Patimkin Sink. He has nothing of the "goniff" in him needed to succeed in his father's kind of business. Mr. Patimkin glances toward Neil in hopes that not all of the Newark instincts are out of him and that he might fare better in the world of Patimkin Sink if Brenda decides to keep him.

Neil's problem is what to do with his life. It is the problem of freedom, a product of modern times. The question was not asked in fixed societies when children's occupations were predetermined—girls to be wives and boys to be whatever their fathers were—and when the purpose of life was to have a family, maintain close ties to relatives, celebrate one's people's holidays, and support the politics of one's class. For Roth's generation, freedom was the new given; and this first of Roth's major fictions to explore the question of what one does with one's life undertakes not the sociologist's but the writer's task: to show the alternative traps of powerlessness and arid opulence.

To the extent that Roth drew Neil from his own experience, Newark and the library may symbolize respectively his unwritten and his written life. But to the extent that Neil is not Roth, he has no sense of a life's work to give him purpose, nor much of a purpose to give him life. His courting of Brenda had employed terms and deeds of competition; he had swum, raced, and played, sometimes fiercely, against her. But he had competed *for* her only against her mood swings, her indifference or arbitrariness: it was always in her power to let him continue in, or to bar him from, the race. When Neil is in Harvard Yard at the very end of the story, Brenda having kissed him off and he trying to settle something about his identity before returning to Newark, he sees his reflection in the glass front of the Lamont Library, and, as always when he consciously confronts himself, he uses the language of competition, as if he believed his fate, like a sprinter's kick, could be summoned from within.

> What was it inside me that had turned pursuit and clutching into love, and then turned it inside out again? What was it that had turned winning into losing, and losing—who knows—into winning? I was sure I had loved Brenda, though standing there, I knew I couldn't any longer. (*GC* 135)

Winning and losing, of course, are Patimkin terms: Brenda on the tennis court, Julie at table tennis or getting extra foul shots, Ron the once and always star center, Mr. Patimkin forcing his supplier to meet his price, Uncle Leo at the wedding telling Neil to play his cards right and win a place at Patimkin Sink, Brenda eternally locked in rivalry with her mother, sundry Patimkins winning new noses. But for Neil, winning Brenda could only mean buying into all those values and becoming a commodity in the bargain. He could not win her sexually, for she had given herself casually, and therefore meaninglessly and controllingly, at the start. He could not win her mind, for—with all her being adept at word games and a Radcliffe girl—she showed no mind to win. What he could win, what had attracted him in the first place despite all his denials to himself and ironic put-downs to her, was her life—with no sweat except the intentional, athletically induced variety. Instinctively Neil had always known that he could win Brenda only by losing himself to what Bellow would call, "the vacuity and mindlessness of Pig Heaven."[12] But "pursuit . . . winning . . . and losing . . ." were not Neil's sources of pleasure or his strength. And so his meditation in front of the Lamont Library is an act of self-styling, a refusal to acknowledge his more natural tendency to drift. In the story it is also an echo of an earlier meditation, Neil's "prayer" in St. Patrick's Cathedral.

Saul Bellow's favorable review of "Goodbye, Columbus"[13] expresses one strong reservation about Roth, the evidence for which he finds in that St. Patrick's meditation. Neil has gone there to wait out Brenda's being fitted for a diaphragm in a doctor's office across from Bergdorf Goodman's—"a perfect place," Neil muses, "for Brenda to add to her wardrobe." Neil's meditation is in the form of a "little speech" to himself.

. . . Can I call the self-conscious words I spoke prayer? At any rate, I called my audience God. God, I said, I am twenty-three years old. I want to make the best of things. Now the doctor is about to wed Brenda to me, and I am not entirely certain this is all for the best. What is it I love, Lord? Why have I chosen? Who is Brenda? The race is to the swift. Should I have stopped to think?

I was getting no answers, but I went on. If we meet You at all, God, it's that we're carnal, and acquisitive, and thereby partake of You. I am carnal, and I know You approve, I just know it. But how carnal can I get? I am acquisitive. Where do I turn now in my acquisitiveness? Where do we meet? Which prize is You?

It was an ingenious meditation, and suddenly I felt ashamed. I got up and walked outside, and the noise of Fifth Avenue met me with an answer:

Which prize do you think, *schmuck*? Gold dinnerware, sporting-goods trees, nectarines, garbage disposals, bumpless noses, Patimkin Sink, Bonwit Teller—

But damn it, God, that *is* You!

And God only laughed, that clown. (*GC* 100)

When Bellow had finished reading the book, he reread this passage twice more, and on third reading found it "a little too cozy." Bellow asks, "Why should it please God that we are carnal or acquisitive? I don't see that at all." Nor should we. Nor should we think Roth did. Nor does the story indicate that Neil does "think" it, though it says he says it. Bellow "assume[s] Mr. Roth is saying that it would be a deadly offense to confuse God with Bonwit Teller and garbage disposals, with goods and money." But Bellow concludes that Roth ". . . doesn't say it well; he is confused, nervous, wry, and somewhat too aware that this is a shocking way to address God. And in St. Patrick's, too, perhaps displeasing the Catholics as well as the Jews." Bellow goes on to say he knows Roth's "meaning" in the novella: "the world is too much with us, and there has never been so much world." But Bellow does not consider that Roth may not be the one who is confused and trying to shock, that rather the wry tone may be Neil's attempt to find some role for himself.

"Meaning" is Bellow's word, used shorthand in a review, not intended to call down I. A. Richards upon his head. And so even allowing Bellow his license and setting aside layers and complexities of meaning, there is still the question of whether he has got Roth's broadest meaning through Neil's meditation. Neil begins by wondering whether he can call his "self-conscious" words a prayer. The answer is no. "Self-conscious," as Neil uses the term, is not meditation or genuine prayer. It is the wise-acre styling of someone conscious of being out of place, defiant rather than worshipful. All Neil's ironies are defenses in exposed circumstances, the opposite of his dream states. They are competitive chiding, as about Brenda's nose, when the moment threatens to evoke other sentiments, sentiment at all. Neil has no fear that a personal God is listening and judging. Neil says that at twenty-three he'd like to "make the best of *things*." "Things" isn't exactly God's domain, unless one has posited a material, acquisitive, totally antispiritual God for the purpose of testing one's independence in defiance. In such a purely material or physical world, "the doctor" can indeed "wed" Brenda to Neil, for no spiritual coupling is being anticipated, although the price of any coupling, permanence in Patimkinland, makes Neil "not entirely certain this is all for the best." The "God" Neil is self-consciously and defiantly praying to is Mammon, and Neil is teasing him slightly with biblical misquotation, and from the most pessimistic of books, Ecclesiastes, with its imagery of competition: "The race is to the swift. Should I have stopped to think?" In their competitive racing around Short Hills, Brenda has proved the swifter. "What is it I love, Lord? Why have I chosen? Who is Brenda?" These could be the desperate musings of Faust, but they are ironic because Neil has not done the choosing, and Brenda, who has, is not the self-evident answer to "What is it I love?" Neil is styling the possibilities of this "ingenious meditation" as he posits the Mammonite theology: "If we meet You at all, God, it's that we're carnal, and acquisitive, and thereby partake of You. I am carnal, and I know You approve, I just know it," the last clause undercutting the certainty of the rest. "But how carnal," he wants to know, "can I get?" and for "get" we are to read "get away with being." "I am acquisitive. Where do I turn now in my acquisitiveness? Where do we meet? Which prize is You?" This language of competition, as in the later meditation before the Lamont Library, is self-deceiving. Neil is not carnal or acquisitive. His natural spot is in the Newark library, not the office of Patimkin Sink. But this image of the Mammonite and the voluptuary is one he wants to think he can aspire to. It is the promise of America—that everyone can get to Short Hills and have athletic equipment growing on trees. To an immigrant-descended Jew it is also *tref*. Wanting it is being bad. And what Neil wants is the right to be bad. It is the ultimate promise of Columbus. But "Man proposes, God disposes." In the Yiddish proverb that Roth would have heard as a boy, "a man tracht, Gut lacht." And so when Neil, with Faustian bravado, says, "But damn it, God, that *is* You!" he answers himself, "And God only laughed, that clown."

But Roth knows this: he wrote it. Neil Klugman wants to be bad; Philip Roth wants to explore what it is like to want to be bad—that is, acquisitive and carnal—when one is essentially good—that is, restrained by moral upbringing and cultural values, what it is like to want to act "counter to what he considers to be his 'best self.'" Roth poses that as a Jewish problem reified in the postwar economic upsurge; yet he views this Jewish problem as but a concentrated form of a larger American problem.

Postwar America seemed to promise each man as much as he could take. A little cleverness, a little industry, perhaps a few connections could land almost anyone on easy street, in a home that was a veritable health club. But how healthful was a life whose only quest was for easy street, where the orgy of *getting* ended merely in the anticlimax of *having* or the itch of *comparing*? If all that was left of human aspiration was to have a little more than the next fellow, where was the humanity of the aspiration? Was this the end and the purpose of all that Jewish immigration in the holds of steamers—of Malkas, and Yettas, and Minnas cramped in the wake of Nina and Pinta and Santa Maria? Did "goodbye, Columbus" mean goodbye to the immigrant quest, destined to run aground in Short Hills and Woodenton? Or was that quest no more than material in the first place, the whole third wave a reaching after economic opportunity rather than religious freedom? Or even if for religious freedom, not for the freedom to practice Judaism but, as Arthur Hertzberg has suggested, the freedom to live as Jews without necessarily practicing Judaism? Roth would be criticized for criticizing the Jews, but what he was criticizing was their settling for a purely material definition of America, for the price they would pay in loss of spiritual values. Ben Patimkin had cut his clan off from ever finding kinship with the black boy in the library. Eli Peck, wishing to be true to his newborn son but able only to choose falsely—between two identities neither of which is himself—is doomed to walk the earth without a soul.

Yet none of this comes across in apocalyptic terms. Roth is without *sturm und drang*. The *Goodbye, Columbus* stories, except for "Defender of the Faith," are largely funny, even when, as in "Epstein" or "Eli the Fanatic," they are sobering or touching. What the decision to go to his Jewish material allowed Roth to do two years after writing the last of the lifeless student stories was to observe what he had known, rather than have to strain to simulate the white-bread America he had posited in college. And what he largely observed when he observed Jews was their unease in their new situation. America was like an ill-fitting suit. It would have them square their shoulders when they felt like slouching, keep in their shirttails when they felt like scratching. Roth's deft observation of the details of rooms, tables, country clubs, synagogues is counterpoised against another kind of observation—of behavior that does not quite suit the decorator's intent.

> We did not eat in the kitchen; rather, the six of us—Brenda, myself, Ron, Mr. and Mrs. Patimkin, and Brenda's little sister, Julie—sat around the dining room table, while the maid . . . served us the meal. . . . Mr. Patimkin . . . was tall, strong, ungrammatical, and a ferocious eater.

When he attacked his salad—after drenching it in bottled French dressing—the veins swelled under the heavy skin of his forearm. He ate three
helpings of salad, Ron had four, Brenda and Julie two, and only Mrs.
Patimkin and I had one each. . . . Mrs. Patimkin . . . disastrously polite to
me, . . . gave me the feeling of some captive beauty, some wild princess,
who has been tamed and made servant to the king's daughter—who was
Brenda. (*GC* 21)

Dear Mr. Tzuref:
        Our meeting this evening seems to me inconclusive. . . . It seems to
me that what most disturbs my neighbors are the visits to town by the
gentleman in the black suit, hat, etc. Woodenton is a progressive suburban community whose members, both Jewish and Gentile, are anxious
that their families live in comfort and beauty and serenity. This is, after
all, the twentieth century, and we do not think it too much to ask that the
members of our community dress in a manner appropriate to our time and
place. (*GC* 261–62)

The unease, whether from trying too hard to fit or from squirming at the absurdity of trying, is apparent wherever Roth's Jews have to take America head on.
That part of Neil—or Eli, or little Ozzie Freedman, or Epstein—that wants to be
bad is absurdly funny. Many a literary hero has fallen in the heroic quest to be
good—noble, grand, spiritually transcendent. It is a peculiarly Jewish burden,
as Roth sees it, to have to aspire to be bad. The very intensity with which his
poor, blocked creatures struggle to cut loose might dismay readers unsuscepti-
ble to the humor, might become grounds for those charges of Jewish self-
hatred that Roth would endure, even from readers themselves given to sighing
that goodness is no easy burden. But this desire of many American Jews to
prove they belonged by coolly being bad would infuse Roth's major works in
the decade and a half following *Goodbye, Columbus.*
        Roth worked his Jewish materials in the conviction that they contained
universal elements and that working close to the society he had known would
set his imagination free. As Roth would put it years later, speaking in the third
person of the youth he had been when he wrote these stories, "Altogether
unwittingly, he had activated the ambivalence that was to stimulate his imagination for years to come and establish the grounds for that necessary struggle
from which his—no, my—fiction would spring."[14]
        But Roth had good backing to go forward in the struggle, in spite of the
narrower critics. Even if some of Roth's riskiest tones could elude even
Bellow's discernment, Bellow spoke for those whose trust was in literature. His
1959 review of *Goodbye, Columbus* concludes:

Not all Jewish readers have shown themselves pleased with Mr. Roth's stories. Here and there one meets people who feel that the business of a Jewish writer in America is to write public relations releases, to publicize everything that is nice in the Jewish community and to suppress the rest, loyally. This is not at all the business of Jewish writers or of writers of any kind, and those touchy persons who reproach us with not writing the Jewish Elsie Dinsmore over and over again are very like the Russian authorities who created socialist realism. No quantity of Elsie Dinsmores from Mamaroneck will decrease anti-Semitic feeling. The loss to our sense of reality is not worth the gain (if there is one) in public relations. . . .

My advice to Mr. Roth is to ignore all objections and to continue on his present course.

Whether Saul Bellow would eventually concur in Roth's view of his true course is another question. Roth wrote most of *Goodbye, Columbus* from Bellow's home turf. But it wasn't so much Chicago that Bellow would bring to his Jewish readership as it was Russia, Poland, Germany, France—the grand literary tradition of Europe. One of their own could compete with Dostoevsky, Tolstoy, Mann, Gide in worldliness and sophistication. Roth would go another way—seemingly the way of the rebellious American *pisher*. A quarter of a century after giving Roth his blessing, Bellow could quip to Dick Cavett, "What has Roth got?" What Roth had got was what neither Malamud, setting his America in some mythic *shtetl*, nor Bellow, celebrating the intellect and culture of the immigrants, had yet reached for: a way to test the survival of their tradition in the real landscape of the new America.

Chapter 3

BIOGRAPHY VERSUS THE BIOGRAPHICAL

Roth's early career seems to have moved in decades. *Goodbye, Columbus*, his first big success, was published in 1959, *Portnoy's Complaint*, his second big success, in 1969, and the first of the Zuckerman novels, *The Ghost Writer*, in 1979. These and some of the novels in between were taken as disguised autobiographies, as Roth developed a reputation for airing his own personal problems before the public. But it would be another decade before Roth would oblige with his own personal disclosures.

Before the autobiographical *The Facts* (1988) and *Patrimony* (1991), all Roth's narrative books were fiction; their themes and characters were fair game for criticism. Not so yet their author's life: most critics' attempts to construct Roth's biography from the fiction were mere surmises, often way off base and irrelevant to appreciation of the novels.[1] But in disclosing the limited facts of *The Facts* and in making his father's life and death a public subject, Roth gave the nineties an opening for legitimate speculations on the uses of his own life in his fiction. He also gave himself an opening for distorting that life in his namesake characters of *Deception* (1990) and *Operation Shylock* (1993). One cannot appreciate those books without some knowledge of Roth's later career and second marriage, for they invite the identification and tease with intentional distortion. But before *The Facts* one could draw from the early novels no certain knowledge of Roth's life.

What *The Facts* would finally disclose or confirm is that whole episodes and some key plots of the sixties' and seventies' novels were indeed drawn from Roth's young adult life, that major characters were fictionalizations of friends, relatives, lovers, and his first wife. Indeed, that wife, Margaret Martinson Williams, the Josie Jensen of *The Facts* (in the closing section, Roth's alter ego, Zuckerman, advises him to disclose her real name), is traceable in characters and situations of *Letting Go*, *Portnoy's Complaint*, and *The Professor of Desire* and is the provenance and almost the very *raison d'être* for *When She Was Good*[2] and *My Life as a Man*.

In that respect, the common reference to *When She Was Good* as "the book without Jews" is but a half-truth. Writing it, Roth was conscious of the contrast between his wife's perception of her upbringing and his view of his own Jewish experience. Lucy Nelson, based loosely on his wife, would have to wrench herself from indifferent, sometimes even hostile, parents and a dominating grandfather; but Roth made her the antithesis of his own supportive family's gradual letting go. Any constraint by his family that Roth had felt, he acknowledged as loving concern, an extreme form of which he would pursue as a Jewish, though not necessarily a personal, malady in *Portnoy's Complaint*. But Lucy Nelson saw her family as incapable of nurturing—though it had been her grandfather's obsession to protect the whole family from a strain of rural brutality—and her response was to seek someone outside the family who would love her, someone built for responsibility. Of course, Lucy could not acknowledge the logical corollaries of her deprivation: that she was incapable of feeling loved or other than betrayed, perpetually abandoned; and, therefore, that she would have to be betrayed by whichever shining knight came along next. Roth confined Lucy to a gentile world, instead of having her find a Jew just begging for an unpassable test of manhood, but that was a literary decision: Roth would stay out of the autobiographical (a decision he reversed with *My Life as a Man*) and try imaginatively to understand the gentile, as distinguished from the Jewish, working-class mind. Perhaps that decision also allowed Roth to postpone—indefinitely, it would appear—facing in fiction the question of what made young men of his background take on responsibility for neurotically dependent women. In *When She Was Good*, the Protestant Roy Bassart, marrying Lucy Nelson after impregnating her in the back seat of a car, is doing what Middle America regarded as the decent thing. But Jewish Paul Herz, Gabe Wallach, Peter Tarnopol, David Kepesh, Nathan Zuckerman, and even Alex Portnoy pursue (not merely fail to avoid) relationships with neurotic gentile women. And the reason why is not just that these men define their manhood by the weight of the emotional and personal responsibility they can bear. The question that Roth did not answer in his mid-life fiction, that indeed he left on his agenda at the end of *The Facts* and but lightly touched on in *Operation*

Shylock, is *why* they define manhood so. But then, as Roth would acknowledge in another context, his "obsessional theme is the one [a novelist] least understands. . . ."[3]

The title *The Facts*, like most Roth titles, has at least two implications. The first, which he alluded to while writing the book, is the raw material on which mind and imagination work to create fiction.

> . . . imagination . . . clubs the fact over the head, . . . slits its throat, and then with its bare hands, . . . pulls forth the guts. Soon the guts of facts are everywhere, the imagination is simply *wading* through them. By the time the imagination is finished with a fact, believe me, it bears no resemblance to a fact.[4]

Facts, that is, are the stuff of the unwritten world being prepared for delivery to the written world, but hardly to be trusted, for in merely being apprehended they have already been assaulted by the imagination.

The other implication of the title *The Facts* is a clarification for the record in a legal proceeding. That proceeding is "the case" against Roth, primarily by establishment Jews, the by-then three-decade-old charges of anti-Semitism, betrayal of family, misogyny, shallowness of imagination, and self-pity. Roth testifies to present his side of the case but suffers his imaginative self—in the guise of his then most recent incarnation, Zuckerman—to offer objections that this truth is not the whole truth and certainly not nothing but the truth. Zuckerman stands for the view that no man can tell the truth about himself because his fiction-making faculty is always at work. This device allows Roth to add to the record but to invite critical challenge. In choosing to disclose limited portions of his biography, he seeks to dispel some of these age-old charges, but in choosing the parts to tell and the point of view from which to tell them, he maintains his fiction writer's duty to question his own motives and his own facile acquittal. As the Zuckerman voice points out at the end, "Your Jewish readers are finally going to glean from this what they've wanted to hear from you for three decades. That your parents had a good son who loved them" (*Facts* 166). In thus making his *Facts*, like his fiction, an exercise in double vision, Roth asserts the supremacy of the fictive imagination over the notion that there can be uninterpreted "fact."

Roth presented *The Facts* in 1988 as a vindication of—and a provocation to question further—his life up to 1968, especially his involvement with two gentile women, one whom he married and the other from whom he fled, after a five-year affair, when he finally became legally free to marry her. What the two women share, one in her active competition with him and the other in her passive sympathy, is a soul-sapping dependence on the man they attach themselves to. They both represent the drowning victim who calls for a life preserver only to pull her would-be rescuer into the maelstrom with her. *The Facts* makes it clear that one key to most of Roth's fiction of the sixties and seventies was the influence, one way or the other, of his first wife. But the fictive reworking of that biographical material was not unlike his practice in reworking other relationships in his life.

Characters and situations scattered through Roth's fiction are either identified in *The Facts* as autobiographical or have analogs described or mentioned in enough detail to suggest Roth's life as their source. As will be shown more fully, his Jewish high school environment at Weequahic was also Portnoy's; his censure and near expulsion for violation of a boarding house restriction with "Polly" is the source of a similar episode in *When She Was Good*; his college seminars with his teacher, Mildred Martin, become the reminiscence in "Salad Days" about similar seminars with Miss Caroline Benson; his refusal to continue ROTC training becomes Nate Zuckerman's of the same story and the rationale for both author and character to enter the army as enlisted men rather than as officers; his backache discharge from the army becomes the conflict for "Novatny's Pain"; the Jewish girl from New Jersey called in *The Facts* "Gayle Millman" (these name changes are supposed to protect anonymity) is the prototype for the oversexed Sharon Shatzky (who laments that her last name is nothing more than the past tense of "Shitzky"), and for Dina Dornbusch, both from *My Life as a Man*, and probably for a good part of Brenda Patimkin; the "May Aldridge" (her real name was Ann Mudge)[5] with whom he spent a good part of his life after the breakup with his first wife and immediately after her death becomes Susan McCall in *My Life as a Man*; his mother's bachelor artist brother may have suggested aspects of Paul Herz's uncle Asher; his Uncle Ed's having taken him for a drive to Princeton for a football game and to see Einstein's house when Roth was in grade school seems the circumstance from which the plot of "On the Air" grew; his friendship with Theodore Solotaroff in Iowa was the basis for many details of the Paul Herz story in *Letting Go*; and on and on into the parallels of the Zuckerman novels and *Operation Shylock* and numerous echoes in *Sabbath's Theater*.

Roth's fictive use of his life has thus been extensive. It has also been largely misunderstood. Some clarification might come from a close look at his use of his own family. A casual reader in 1990 might have associated Roth with an aging Alex Portnoy, a writer still brooding on mothers. But the book he produced about a parent was not about Mrs. Roth, it was about Mr. Roth. This was the Mr. Roth of Philip's childhood, the Mr. Roth who was Mr. Roth before critics began "Mr. Roth"ing the son, the Mr. Roth paralleling all those fathers in the novels of the seventies and eighties who—as shall be seen—somehow came, for their protagonists, to represent the Jews, the Mr. Roth who was now passing on the name and the heritage for good.

Patrimony is nonfiction. It certainly struck a chord in the year of *Final Exit* about respecting the person of the aged infirm, and it is in a way a piece of loyalty rewarded—Herman Roth had been "a fiercely loyal and devoted father who had never found a thing in [Philip's] books to criticize." Indeed, *Patrimony* won the Book Critics Circle award for biography for 1991. However, as will be seen, it is a book that strives earnestly to paint a remarkable portrait of a fairly unremarkable man. Except, perhaps, to his son. What comes across more than any actual heroism is the son's need to find, and success in finding, something heroic in the father—this despite the countervailing need to be truthful about the old man's sometimes bullying assertiveness— and Roth's need to be vindicated as the good son. Odd, perhaps, for Roth, but right for this book, is the lack of any ironic point of view. There is no alternative voice—no Zuckerman as in *The Facts*—to challenge the earnest, straightforward telling, and whether Roth took liberties with facts in private situations, only he can know. What makes the unremarkable remarkable is Roth's presentation of his father as at once unique and representative. Closing a life of duty and but small pleasures is a realist facing death without need of myth, supremely conscious of himself as a Jew, yet passing on a Jewishness not of religious ritual but of earned place. *Patrimony* also unlocks that easily overlooked vein in Roth's fiction, the use of fathers, which turns out to be far more remarkable than the ballyhooed use of mothers. The major use is the test of manhood, and a significant part of the test is the patrimonial link to the Jews.

Roth weaves the surface facts of his father's life into many of his fictions. In "Salad Days," the first of the "Useful Fictions" that introduce *My Life as a Man*, Mr. Z., as the protagonist Nathan (Nate) Zuckerman's father is called, owns a shoe store and drives himself and other people hard to make it succeed. Milton Lippman, the narrator-protagonist of "On the Air" also owns a shoe store. Herman Roth had failed at running "a family shoe store" (*Facts* 21) some years before becoming an agent for Metropolitan Life, and before Philip was born. In "Salad Days" Nate's parents drive him to Bass, the gentile Vermont college with weekly chapel that resembles Roth's description of Bucknell; and the whole section on Nate's adolescence and undergraduate days, replete with conflicts over Nate's desire to make independent decisions, dramatized in telephone arguments with Mr. Z., may hint at what lay behind Roth's "increasing friction between my father and me" (*Facts* 37) in Roth's own later adolescence. No small part of that was a similarity of wills and a tendency to dismiss opposing points of view and those that hold them, to take decisive actions regardless of others' opinions. Herman Roth's disposing, without his son's permission, of his stamp collection (*Patrimony* 29–30) may have indicated an inability to respect his son's sovereignty that no doubt found other daily expression as well. While these last details do not appear in the fiction, the feeling tone behind them often does.

Portnoy's Complaint, only one of many novels incorporating aspects of Herman Roth, perhaps best shows the transforming fictive imagination at work. The overall impression of Portnoy's father that survives a reading of the book is of a milquetoast, his social impotence symbolized by his constipation, the same motif Roth had used seven years earlier in *Letting Go* to show Mr. Herz's dying grief over his son Paul's intermarriage. But in *Portnoy's Complaint*, which, as shall be seen, Roth wrote in stages and from conflicting original intents,[6] there are counterbalancing aspects of Jack Portnoy as a loving, almost heroic father. He is "the Jackie Robinson of the insurance business" (8), integrating district management as the first Jew to head up a New Jersey office of a great company, clearly modeled on Metropolitan Life and on Herman Roth's achievement despite his having had only an eighth-grade education. And one passage in particular may show how the fiction writer transforms autobiographical material. In 1959, when Roth was first breaking upon the literary scene with *Goodbye, Columbus*, and reluctantly (he has declared) embarking upon marriage, he published that *Harper's* memoir of his childhood summers at Bradley Beach, "Recollections from Beyond the Last Rope." In it he idealizes his father with this passage:

> Usually he took off the last week of July and the first in August; otherwise he would stay in the city during the week and drive down on weekends. Sometimes, though, our old Pontiac would pull up at LaReine Avenue smack in the middle of the week: the city was too hot. "You can't even breathe," he tells my mother. "The humidity," she'd say.
>
> On these surprise visits he would usually arrive about seven thirty without having had dinner. But dinner would wait—despite the protest of my mother—while he tossed away his wrinkled city clothes and changed into a bathing suit. I carried his towel for him as he headed down the beach for a dip. I would be dressed, the salt and sun showered off me, and my hair parted and slicked down. There was a roughened iron rail that ran the length of the boardwalk, and I sat on the edge of it and watched him down below as he stepped into the water.
>
> He entered slowly, lingering a long while with the water licking up at his knees. Then he would make a cup with his hands and in the thin after-supper dimness he would pour the water on his face and down the back of his neck. All my ideas of how difficult it was to be a man, to work and support a family, seem to me to have come not so much from being told about the difficulties, as from observing the kinds of relaxation the difficulties led you into; as for work, it made you want to pour a handful of cool water on your face and neck, it made such a simple thing a pleasure. I could tell that by the way he rubbed the water on his arms

and massaged it into his shoulders. He would take so much time just
getting *ready* to enter the water that I knew a lot of policies must have
lapsed or almost lapsed that day. I had no clear idea, however, of how he
prevented them from lapsing, of what exactly he did. What did he do
during the day? and when we were away, what did he do at night? Who
did he listen to the radio with? He missed us—I was sure of that—and
though he would never indulge his loneliness, it must have pleased him
when the day's temperature and humidity became so unbearable that he
felt justified in fleeing the city for the night. He paid, most of the time,
however, in money and loneliness for our comfort. The heat in the summer was the enemy of women and children: *we* had to be saved from
it. . . . Finally I would watch him lower himself into the water to swim,
and then to turn over and float on his back. Behind us the sun was perfect
and red, and when its light broke out on the water I knew I was seeing
something beautiful. My father floated so still—he worked so hard and
then he came in and he was glowing, like the sea, from those last pure
spikes of light.[7]

Sentimental, perhaps, but undoubtedly heartfelt. Roth had no need yet to prove
he was a good son. Alexander Portnoy's constipated father was years away
even from contemplation, and Nathan Zuckerman's father, dying (in a 1981
novel set in 1969) with a curse of his son on his lips, did not yet need the disassociation Roth would provide by dedicating his 1987 novel, *The Counterlife*,
"To my father at eighty-five" or by writing his 1991 *Patrimony*.

Roth used this *Harper's* passage again when he came to write *Portnoy's
Complaint*. Note the change of tone to suit Alex the analysand:

In summer he remains in the city while the three of us go off to live in a
furnished room at the seashore for a month. He will join us for the last
two weeks, when he gets his vacation . . . there are times, however, when
Jersey City is so thick with humidity, so alive with the mosquitoes that
come dive-bombing in from the marshes, that at the end of his day's
work he drives sixty-five miles, taking the old Cheesequake Highway—
the Cheesequake! My God! the stuff you uncover here!—drives sixty-
five miles to spend the night with us in our breezy room at Bradley
Beach.
     He arrives after we have already eaten, but his own dinner waits
while he unpeels the soggy city clothes in which he has been making
the rounds of his debit all day, and changes into his swimsuit. I carry his
towel for him as he clops down the street to the beach in his unlaced
shoes. I am dressed in clean short pants and a spotless polo shirt, the

salt is showered off me, and my hair—still my little boy's pre-steel wool hair, soft and combable—is beautifully parted and slicked down. There is a weathered iron rail that runs the length of the boardwalk, and I seat myself upon it; below me, in his shoes, my father crosses the empty beach. I watch him neatly set down his towel near the shore. He places his watch in one shoe, his eyeglasses in the other, and then he is ready to make his entrance into the sea. To this day I go into the water as he advised: plunge the wrists in first, then splash the underarms, then a handful to the temples and the back of the neck . . . ah, but slowly, always slowly. This way you get to refresh yourself, while avoiding a shock to the system. Refreshed, unshocked, he turns to face me, comically waves farewell up to where he thinks I'm standing, and drops backward to float with his arms outstretched. Oh, he floats so still—he works, so hard, and for whom if not for me?—and then at last, after turning on his belly and making with a few choppy strokes that carry him nowhere, he comes wading back to shore, his streaming compact torso glowing from the last pure spikes of light driving in, over my shoulder, out of stifling inland New Jersey, from which I am being spared. (*PC* 29–30)

Clearly, Roth is borrowing from his decade-old *Harper's* passage here in *Portnoy*. But how little of it remains directly quoted. Roth changes the tense from past to historical present, as suits the Portnoy tone of voice. Then he systematically reduces the touches of admiration and devoted gratitude, placing Jack Portnoy at arm's length from, and in embarrassing contrast to, his would-be-easeful, Americanized son. In the family memoir, Roth's father "would pull up" in his Pontiac, declaring of the hot city, "You can't even breathe." He would proceed over the protests of his wife to "toss... away his wrinkled city clothes." He is decisive and assertive. But Jack Portnoy, driven from the city by dive-bombing mosquitoes, is immediately a victim, and he remains so as he "unpeels the soggy city clothes." In the memoir, after Roth's father "change[s] into a bathing suit," there is no narration of his doings between ". . . he headed down the beach for a dip" and ". . . he stepped into the water." Jack Portnoy "clops down the street to the beach in his unlaced shoes," in klutzy contrast to his son. The details of placing his watch in one shoe and his glasses in the other all support the image of an overly prudent, passive man. In the memoir, little Philip had merely "dressed, . . . showered . . . and [had his] hair parted and slicked down." But the boy who has to watch Jack Portnoy clop and fuss with his watch and glasses is "now dressed in clean short pants and a spotless polo shirt" (thanks, no doubt, to stricturing Sophie) with his shower-clean hair "*beautifully* parted and slicked down." These adjectives score the complaining Alex's perceived incongruity between father and son.

What is the feeling tone of each man's immersion in the sea? In the memoir, Roth's father "step[s] into the water . . . enter[ing] slowly, lingering a long while with the water licking up at his knees." This, in contrast to the drive down, gives a sense of relief from the heat. And after briefly mentioning the cupping of hands and pouring of water over the man, young Philip derives his filial lesson: his "ideas of how difficult it was to be a man . . . from observing the kinds of relaxation the difficulties led you into." The mystery of manhood, awe-inspiring but demonstrably within reach, is being passed from father to son.

What lesson does Alex Portnoy derive? "To this day I go into the water as he advised . . . ," a lesson in caution, in being repressed, in ". . . avoiding a shock to the system." Whereas Herman Roth would "lower himself into the water to swim, and then to turn over and float on his back" sportively like a man at ease, Jack Portnoy, Alex recalls, ". . . turns to face me, comically waves farewell up to where he thinks I'm standing, and drops backward to float with his arms outstretched." Herman Roth, whose work in the city is seen by his son as some religious mystery, came to the beach and conquered the heat. Jack Portnoy comes defeated "from making the rounds of his debit all day" and, as viewed in retrospect on the analyst's couch, humiliates his son with his myopia and his ineptitude.

Finally, there are the spikes of light. In the memoir the setting sun was "perfect and red," illuminating "something beautiful." So when Philip's hard-working father finished floating, "he came in and he was glowing, like the sea, from those last pure spikes of light." Alex Portnoy, on the other hand, can tell it only with a sigh: not the hushed "My father floated so still," but "Oh, he floats so still"; and with guilt: "—he works, so hard, and for whom if not for me?"; and with a description of total ineptitude: "...turning on his belly and making with a few choppy strokes that carry him nowhere, he comes wading back to shore"; and finally with a coda omitting the beauty but preserving the guilt: "his streaming compact torso glowing from the last pure spikes of light driving in, over my shoulder, out of stifling inland New Jersey, from which I am being spared." "Driving" changes the point of view. No longer do we have a rhapsodic movie fadeout. The eye that was carried from the illuminated body "glowing, like the sea," outward toward the sunset is now driven "in" by spikes that seem to impale the poor victim. Gone is the mystic bond to the mainstay of the family. In Portnoy's complaining the hero has been replaced by the martyr.

And yet Portnoy's is not an altogether negative description. Love filters through. Alex's feelings for his father are in great conflict, and he has brought himself to a state of heightened agitation unloading on his psychiatrist. Roth builds that conflict by tapping feelings for his own father, muting some and exaggerating others. He adds elements of experience of other sons' feelings for other fathers (*RMAO* 142, 33–41). But he does it imaginatively, which means that in the writing he becomes Alex Portnoy, and speaks like him. Navigating in the character's guise, Roth as novelist steers sometimes very close to and veers sometimes very far from his sense of himself. In these heightened states he may unlock sides of himself and reveal feelings that he would not acknowledge in a critical or autobiographical frame of mind. But the reader can't know that and doesn't have to. Neither can the critic. The question for both is whether this character, with his conflicts, in this state of mind, would say these things. Their believability is their test of truth. Their testing as ideas must be made in the context of the novel: why is this character saying these things here and now? not, what right has this author to say these things? In this case, how does Alex sound when he gets on the subject of Jack Portnoy? One part of that answer is a mixture of contempt, guilt, and love; but it is not how Roth at twenty-six had sounded when recording memories of his father.

Close as the *Portnoy* passage is to the memoir, then, it is not autobiography. It is fiction. Indeed, as Roth would come increasingly to see, they are both fictions, though of different orders. In the one, the memoir, he is recalling, sentimentally, rites of passage. It has a point of view and a story to tell, though the same facts might have been assembled to serve another theme in another mood. But as a memoir using real names it avoids fictive reorderings and seems to talk directly to the reader. The other, the novel, invites the reader into an imagined situation. Not to learn about what really happened once to make this author who he is, but to experience what it is like to see the world through the eyes of a wildly neurotic and consequently impotent man. It tells truths, and they are Roth's truths, but not in service of some message. Any message is the whole experience, its tones, its contradictions, its outbursts and insights—even its incorrect insights when a character is comforted by them, or motivated to act, or to refrain from acting. Multidimensional, ambiguous, more than its immediate seeming, the novel is not an essay, man speaking thoughtfully to man, but an imitation of that pulsating mystery we call life.

Roth's seeming abuse of his father in *Portnoy* is just that, a seeming. As is the whole character of Sophie Portnoy, as is the sister whose underwear Alex abuses and whom letter-writing readers excoriated Roth for abusing in the novel, though he never himself had a sister. But it was a mighty seeming, apparently a convincing seeming to have generated so much heat.

The heat would carry over for years. Roth's greatest controversies, both with organized Jewry and with the critics, came during the decade and a half following publication of *Portnoy's Complaint* (1969). Indeed, so intense was this new flack that many people must have forgotten about the older wars. Roth's defenders often wrote reviews in the form of a sprung surprise: they would begin by quoting abusive reviews by other critics and then identify the invective as not new, but old brickbats from 1959 to 1960, hurled against *Goodbye, Columbus*. These critics apparently needed to remind readers, in light of the new outrage, that they had been outraged before. The intervening decade had been comparatively quiet. The serious Jamesian and Flaubertian efforts of *Letting Go* and *When She Was Good* had drawn (as will be seen) milder responses from the critics, while Roth's defensive literary essays and forum appearances had attracted principally literati and academicians. During that interim the public had still awaited fulfillment of Roth's early vaunted promise, hoping for tomes that would address important social, including Jewish, concerns. But what a reactive public could not yet know was what would become clear to scholars only in hindsight: that the evolving subject matter in Roth's work was a weaving of many concerns. What he had to say about upbringing, breaking from the family, and struggling for self-definition would be interwoven with thoughts on the artist's right or ability to assert new values, with questions about the effects of his art on the artist, on the wider culture, and on the Jewish culture that produced him, and later in a calmer vein, with revaluation of that upbringing and of the stories all people tell one another to establish who they are. Increasingly, it would reflect a changing Jewish consciousness of being a Jew.

When the new hostility arose, it went beyond the claim that *Portnoy* was a dirty book. It was largely reaction to another feature of Roth's subject matter: the strivings after license by young men brought up to be good. That the young men suffered for their desires, and never fulfilled them anyway, would not placate many readers. Rather, readers often tended to view the sufferings as comeuppance to characters identified with the mewlings of their author. *Portnoy's Complaint* (1969) is about impotence caused by culture conflict, *My Life as a Man* (1974) about marital entrapment elaborated into writer's block, *The Professor of Desire* (1977) and *The Breast* (1972) about the waning and finally the loss through metamorphosis of male sexuality. Jewishness was an issue in all of them, specifically the conflict between the contradictory ways Jews are perceived, ways Roth would characterized as "the nice Jewish boy" and "the Jewboy." Many readers complained that the novels were just compendiums of sex, ranting and betrayal by young Jewish men, and labeled them all as mere ventings of egoism. Even when an entirely different kind of book appeared amidst all this in 1973, its ironic title, *The Great American Novel*, was deemed immediately suspect and discouraged many would-be readers. They assumed that the cover phrase was not so much a title as a self-promoting blurb for another egoistic, probably anti-Semitic, diatribe. This for a book about baseball, whose title spoofed a wacky novel within the novel, whose targets were the abuses of red-bating and the sellout to big money—both issues that most Jews at the time would have supported—a book containing few Jews in very minor positions.

In the four novels about waning or lost powers, the seeming excesses of the protagonists did push against the existing bounds of decorum. As such, these books risked offending some part of their readership. But, as shall be seen, one of Roth's issues in these books is decorum itself: the extent to which decorum embraced for itself might be an offense to one's personal freedom. If observing decorum meant suppressing one's own nature, containing one's vital forces, and complying with some imposed duty, how could one square observing standards of decorum with being true to one's own self (in the reiterated terms of Roth's fiction, with being "a man")? A man had either to betray himself or seem to betray his friends and relatives by refusing to live their fiction of him. But if their fiction has already been so successfully imposed that he has bought into it and is already his own worst betrayer, couldn't his struggle to leave the abyss of decorum be almost heroic? From the very start, Roth's subject matter, whatever else it might also have been, had been fiction—the fiction we are asked to live, the fiction we create to survive, the fiction we oppose to the fictions imposed, the writing or rewriting of ourselves. And since every fiction is a betrayal of an opposing fiction, another embedded subject in Roth's work has been betrayal.

The earliest betrayers in Roth's work were authorities or authority figures: parents, rabbis, officers, the army, America itself, perceived to have misused their power, turning on those who had trusted them. But all the way through from little Ozzie Freedman to Philip of *Deception* (1990), "Philip Roth" of *Operation Shylock* (1993), and Mickey Sabbath of *Sabbath's Theater* (1995), the betrayed have also been betrayers. Freedman, Epstein, Marx, Peck, Klugman, Portnoy, Kepesh, Tarnopol, Zuckerman, "Philip," and ultimately "Philip Roth" and Sabbath, in asserting themselves against some force, succeed or fail by betraying some assumed allegiance. In such charged circumstances it may have been inevitable that Roth, too, would be labeled a betrayer (in part, for using everyone and everything as material for his fiction) rather than a mere anatomist of betrayal. But these embedded conflicts—fiction/antifiction, betrayed/betrayer—(even when the betrayal is mere deception) vitalize the subject matter of the novels. Characters of two minds take life from their continued self-questionings. Double-mindedness, tragic to a Hamlet, can be, in a Jewish heritage, excruciatingly comic.

In *Portnoy's Complaint, The Breast, My Life as a Man*, and *The Professor of Desire* the protagonists all tell their own stories, in howls and whispers of unburdening. One of their burdens is a part of the Jewish heritage that all Jews share, the secular as well as the religious, and it is another embedded theme in all of these works. It is the notion, if not the outright idea, of chosenness. That notion, which can uphold the innocent idea of "the nice Jewish boy" by contrasting it to the less innocent idea of "the *goyish kopp*," which can read its own moral constraints—its answering, as the ads say, to a "higher authority"—as an unacknowledged sense of superiority, pervades the unconscious of Roth's protagonists even as they consciously seek to prove that they are the same as everyone else. It both helps them endure failure and guarantees that in some aspects of their quest they must fail. Roth's nice Jewish boys want to be "libidinous slobs" (*RMAO* 243), but they consider the libido the forbidden prerogative of Gentiles. In each of these first person narratives, the easiest kind to confuse with autobiography, particular aspects of the Jewish difference early become obsessive challenges to the protagonists. For Portnoy Jewish restraint is symbolized in the *kashruth* laws, which the culture extends to anything that comes in contact with the mouth, to unkosher sex, to social interaction with Gentiles. All is summed up in Alex's desecration of the family meal, a piece of liver, which, once put to double purpose, will never again qualify for him as food:

> my first piece I had in the privacy of my own home, rolled round my cock in the bathroom at three-thirty—and then had again on the end of a fork at five-thirty, along with the other members of that poor innocent family of mine. (*PC* 150)

Their "innocence," that is, ignorance of his defilement, intensifies Alex's guilt. Unconsciously, he has bought into the Jewish myth of purity through separation, an aspect of chosenness that has worked pretty well for his people since the biblical Daniel's time. But that same valued kosher purity has impeded his quest for America, which Alex wants fully to enter, even if he has to blaze a trail through every blond, pug-nosed cheerleader from sea to shining sea. He learns that what he would do is not what he can do: wrestling with guilt, the onanist is pinned by impotence.

Of course, as discussion of *Portnoy* will make clear, *kashruth* is only emblematic of Alex's larger problem. He is at war with his upbringing as a nice Jewish boy. In a secular Jewish family, a large part of that role consisted in being a model citizen, a practice that began in the public school system. A nice Jewish boy did his homework, obeyed the rules, and used the opportunity that had been denied his parents and his European counterparts to excel in scholarship. Alex Portnoy was the valedictorian of his high school and the law review editor at Columbia, and is an Assistant Commissioner for The City of New York Commission on Human Opportunity in the Lindsay administration. Like all Roth's Jewish protagonists from Neal Klugman on, he has parleyed the life of the mind into a respectable and responsible career. The other protagonists are mainly writers and professors. But what they profess is at war with their desire for sexual adventure, and not only have they not resolved that conflict, but they do not even know whether it is the sex or the adventure that most moves them. For to be a nice Jewish boy is not only to be good, it is also to be safe. But to conquer America, or to write about or profess the meaning of life, they feel, one has to risk dangers, to take on the conflicts oneself. How can the nice Jewish boy become the great public servant, teacher, or writer without getting deeply involved in the nonkosher act? To sing the songs of experience one must put by the songs of innocence. There cannot be accomplishment, they feel, in playing life safe.

It is difficult to determine just why and when these became themes that would preoccupy Roth. The Zuckerman voice at the end of *The Facts* hints that the anger was always there, right in his nice Jewish childhood, that it was partly "the angry Jew . . . [that] . . . hurled you, howling, into a struggle with repression and inhibition and humiliation and fear. Fanatical security, fanatical insecurity—this dramatic duality that you see embodied in the Jews, . . . is where the drama is rooted . . ." (180). Such anger might underlie his need to get away, even to choose a career that could take him away. At least from college on, the quest was to be a writer, and to a college-trained lit major starting out in the fifties the great tradition was Anglo-American in its values and Protestant-genteel in its transmission. Young Jews were being "refined" by the English Department even as they were inheriting its mantles. Indeed, something of that danger may have been perceived, however fuzzily, by one antagonist at the Yeshiva University mob scene who shouted at the fleeing Roth, "You were brought up on anti-Semitic literature! . . . English literature! . . . English literature is anti-Semitic literature! (*Facts* 229)" Although the tormenter may have had nothing more definite in mind than a facile association of "English literature" with Shylock and Fagin, and a dash of "The Nun's Priest's Tale," or the easy exclusion of Jews from society in novels of manners, it was also true that steeping oneself in the Oxbridge tradition and its American paleface counterpart tended to Anglicize one's values and point of view, however slightly or unwittingly. In Anglican high culture Jewishness had no place.

Roth wanted to become a writer and to support himself as a college English teacher. But going to the Midwest armed with little more than his discipline as a student was not just moving a bit further from the ghetto, it may have been stepping right into a gentile ambush. He could not perceive it as such because he was not the only Jew in town, and the others of his society were comfortable in their male Jewish bonding and kibitzing, even about literature: referring, for example, to Henry James's Elizabeth Archer as a "shiksa" (*Facts* 114–15). Indeed they stressed their ghetto style to resist becoming high Anglos. Nevertheless, he was vulnerable in his itch to test his Jewish metal against that of more "American" ethnics, especially in the arena of romance. In his academic and artistic life, he was well surrounded by like-minded Jews, and he had his routine of reading, writing, attending lectures, and grading freshman themes to keep him on course. Yet, romanticize these activities as he might, along with the suede-patched arm sleeves in which they were performed, outside the book world they may have made him ripe for plucking amidst the Aryan corn.

What he carried of Jewishness with him was his early Newark perspective—thoroughly American though totally Jewish—and his willingness to explore his view of that emerging Jewish life in fiction. Perhaps he knew intuitively that to master that material he had to loosen his ties to the community that had produced it. Just that disengagement, begun in the army, and the away-from-home perspective of colleagues, may have spurred him to continue writing the stories that would become *Goodbye, Columbus*.

Intellectually, Roth did not feel a bit alienated in Chicago. He has since described his graduate-school and brief teaching life there as more nurturing and psychologically easeful than New York ever became. The University of Chicago was a mecca of progressive—and Jewish—thinking and creativity. Roth and other young writer-teachers, among them Ted Solotaroff and George Starbuck, would read and criticize drafts of each other's stories. And after Starbuck moved on to become an editor at Houghton Mifflin, he eventually solicited remembered stories of Roth for the volume that would become *Goodbye, Columbus*. Indeed, it was Starbuck's selection of the strongest stories that gave Roth's first book its Jewish cast.

One of Roth's teacher-colleagues, who invited well-known writers to address his students, took an occasion to use Roth's still unpublished "The Conversion of the Jews" as a piece for criticism by his students and his day's visitor, Saul Bellow; and so Bellow had coffee with and first became aware of the young writer. Roth was too "in awe of him" (and eighteen years his junior) for a friendship to develop;[8] however, the episode was characteristic of the nurturing environment for writers that was Chicago.

But literature was not all of life in Chicago. As Roth put it, "I had nothing to do with any but literary or bookish people. I should say bookish men. With women I was more ecumenical."[9] Indeed, artistic needs would become entangled with personal inclination, which was for escape from the ghetto and exploration of America. He carried, he says in *The Facts*, a picture of "Gayle Millman," that Jewish girl from New Jersey who, in her parents and her independence of spirit seems remarkably to resemble Brenda Patimkin.

> Over a period of two years, while I was in graduate school and in the Army, Gayle and I were equally caught up by an obsessional passion yet, returning to Chicago in September 1956, I thought my voyage out—wherever it might be taking me—could no longer be impeded by this

affair, which as I saw it, had inevitably to resolve into a marriage linking me with the safe enclosure of Jewish New Jersey. I wanted a harder test, to work at life under more difficult conditions. (*Facts* 89)

His meeting with Margaret Martinson Williams would provide the test—and drive Roth's writing—for the next two decades. In *The Facts* he presents her as the serpent of his personal fall. As for his state of innocence preceding the fatal encounter, he would characterize it as

> that exhilarating, adventurous sense of personal freedom that had prompted the high-flying freshman-composition teacher, on a fall evening in 1956, to go blithely forward in his new Brooks Brothers suit and, without the slightest idea that he might be risking his life, handily pick up on a Chicago street the small-town blond divorcee with the two little fatherless children, the penniless ex-waitress whom he'd already spotted serving cheeseburgers back in graduate school, and who'd looked to him like nothing so much as the All-American girl, albeit one enticingly at odds with her origins. (*Facts* 160)

What, one wonders, was "enticing" about being "at odds with her origins"? Was she more likely now to romanticize the Jew? Was it just the bond of youthful rebellion, his facile equating of his growing pains—his still trying to go beyond the last rope—with her actual victimization? Was it guilt at having outstripped his father, coloring Newark and its Jews with a wash of parochialism? Ironically, it turns out that not Margaret, but "Gayle," was the independent one; Margaret, his "Maggie," would become to him the leach. "Gayle," he found out years later, after packaging her neatly as predictable Brenda and nymphomaniacal Sharon and Dina, took her own "voyage out" to Europe, where she became "the most desirable woman of *any* nationality between the Berlin Wall and the English Channel" (*Facts* 90).

Margaret Martinson Williams would give him a permanent wound and much material for literature, albeit some of it greatly obsessed, as his critics at the time, without the facts of the case, would intuit or merely charge. Maggie may well have contributed, through contrast, to the perspective that made Brenda a princess, for in on-again, off-again fashion Maggie was with Roth for the three years preceding their marriage and publication of *Goodbye, Columbus*. She may also have provided *Letting Go* with the neurotic clinginess of Marge Howells and some of the tough cheeriness mixed with inclinations of vindictiveness of Martha Reganhart. Like Martha, she was a widow with two young children, who had worked as a waitress near the University of Chicago, with a penchant for taking courses to give herself an identity beyond that of the wife and daughter of abusive gentile men. (Even Norman Podhoretz, who decried what he saw as the unremitting gloom of *Letting Go*, found Martha "the only character that Roth seems genuinely to like.")[10] If Maggie's situation gave rise to Martha's, so might aspects of her personality. Maggie may have had more of a sense of humor than Roth would later admit, may have provided the child-rearing scenes of *Letting Go*, may have offered more than the fascination with a victim that Roth claims was the case in *The Facts*. They lived together, discussed the movies he would review in *The New Republic*, allowed others to see them as a couple (*Facts* 91–93). As they played their respective personal fictions off, contrapuntally, against each other, she provided him with the outline and thesis of *When She Was Good*, he provided her with an attractive picture of responsibility and mental health, "motivated," he would later think, "by an egoistic young lover's predilection for intimacy and sincerity . . ." (*Facts* 93). After he had fled from her to New York's East Village to resume the writer's and teacher's stoic life in a tenement near Tompkins Square Park, Roth tells in *The Facts*, she followed and tricked him into marriage by the very switch of a urine specimen bought from a pregnant Negro woman he would later describe as Maureen's ploy in *My Life as a Man*. In all the neurotic ways of insinuating herself into his professional life, insisting that she was his real editor, turning violently on him when he tried to undo the match, it seems she *was* Maureen. His teaching her about life-in-literature and learning from her about life-in-life probably contributed to Kepesh's relationship with Helen Baird in *The Professor of Desire*. Roth's unsuccesful attempts to detach himself from her despite the stacked deck of New York's then stringent divorce laws, he living meanwhile his life with Ann Mudge, gave him the Susan McCall episodes of *My Life as a Man*. Maggie's violent death in a car accident in Central Park became Maureen's death in an auto accident in Boston. Release from her debilitating threat of perpetual alimony allowed him, he conjectured, to set about putting in place the disparate elements of *Portnoy's Complaint* and the sense of freedom to command its sometimes rollicking tone. He saw her as the gentile femme fatale and himself as the Jewish innocent, categories he elaborated into generalization. Closing his comparison of "Josie" (Maggie) with "Gayle Milman," Roth would conclude in *The Facts*,

> I had got everything backward. Josie, with her chaotic history, seemed to me a woman of courage and strength for having survived that awful background. Gayle, on the other hand, because of all that family security and all that father love, seemed to me a girl whose comfortable upbringing would keep her a girl forever. Gayle would be dependent because of her nurturing background and Josie would be independent because of her broken background! Could I have been any

more naive? Not neurotic, naive, because that's true about us too: very naive, even the brightest, and not just as youngsters either. (*Facts* 90)

"Us"! In book after book Roth has characters wonder at the seeming toughness of the knocked-about, worldly seeming gentile woman, and just as consistently he has some voice—parent's or brother's or even the hero's own unconscious—telling the young Jew he's riding into trouble, advice he won't appreciate until it's too late. When after years of fantasizing being fellated by some *shiksa*, Portnoy picks up "The Monkey" and has the experience with a virtuosa of the art, he muses "What a find. . . ! What a mouth I have fallen into! Talk about opportunities! And simultaneously: *Get out! Go! Who and what can this person be!*" (*PC* 158). In a phone conversation, Peter Tarnopol tells his parents, over their logical objections, that he is marrying Maureen. His mother finally gets down to the most basic question:

> "Peppy," asked my mother, "do you—love her?"
> "Of course I do." And what did I want to shout into the phone at that very moment? *I'm coming home. Take me home. This isn't what I want to do. You're right, there's something wrong with her: the woman is mad. Only I gave my word.* (*MLAM* 203)

When in "Courting Disaster" the narrator tries to explain why Nathan came to marry Lydia Ketterer, abused child and beaten wife and now single mother of a hapless little daughter, he muses that ". . . it was *precisely* 'the uniform dismal situation' that did more for Lydia's cause than all the companionable meals and walks and museum visits and the cozy fireside conversations in which he corrected her taste in books" (*MLAM* 81). Lydia's was the "cause," Nathan's the education obligated to serve the cause. After Lydia's death, Nathan runs off with her daughter to Italy in not-quite-Humbert Humbert fashion (he had not consciously coveted the girl while Lydia was alive) and lives in guilt-stricken exile, wanting nothing so much as acceptance back into the family bosom by his aging parents. But the very upbringing they had provided defeats him. Nathan tries to assess his situation in light of the times: "From what I read it would appear that in post-Oswald America a man with my sort of record can go about his business without attracting very much attention"; however, he is "too humiliated" to go home (*MLAM* 86–87). When David Kepesh marries the beautiful Helen Baird, former mistress of a wealthy adventurer who had whisked her out of college to the Far East to become a dragon lady among the super rich, Kepesh's marriage comes after a three-year courtship consisting mostly of his demystifying her image, of reorienting himself to see her as another occidental case of *shiksa*-gone-housewife.

I marry Helen when the weight of experience required to reach the monumental decision to give her up for good turns out to be so enormous and so moving that I cannot possibly imagine life without her. Only when I finally know *for sure* that *this must end now*, do I discover how deeply wed I already am by my thousand days of indecision, by all the scrutinizing appraisal of possibilities that has somehow made an affair of three years' duration seem as dense with human event as a marriage half a century long. I marry Helen then—and she marries me—at the moment of impasse and exhaustion. . . . (*POD* 66)

Helen's problem, like that of many of these women, is not unlike that of the Jewish men: harmonizing the sexual side of themselves with the loving side. But Roth's naive Jewish men have something to learn from their dragon ladies. When the still young Professor Kepesh gives Helen *Anna Karenina* to read, Helen brings him up short with the opinion that a real woman would probably see Vronsky as an immature romantic and would prefer taking on Karenin. In *Letting Go* Gabe Wallach's apostleship to Henry James has led him toward a kind of tutorial affair with Libby Herz; when a similar impulse moves him to tout the Jamesian sensibility to Martha Reganhart, the more experienced Martha reacts: "He's virginal. . . . It seems to me that people live more openly with their passions" (*LG* 573). Similarly, in *My Life as a Man* Maureen writes in her diary of her marriage to novelist Tarnopol, "If it weren't for me he'd still be hiding behind his Flaubert and wouldn't know what real life was like if he fell over it. What did he ever think he was going to write *about*, knowing and believing nothing but what he read in books?" (*MLAM* 316). If Roth's novels of the sixties and seventies seem less pat and reducible than the *Goodbye, Columbus* stories that preceded them, it may be partly because Margaret Martinson Williams Roth, whatever else she did, provided a point of view to counter the self-justifying tendencies of the young Jewish narrator-protagonists. Just as Jewish voices and subjects had given Roth's short fiction an authenticity his student stories had lacked, so the threat of being unmanned may have given his novels an edge his previous innocence could not have provided.

Gabe Wallach concludes his narration of *Letting Go* (1962) with this observation in a letter to Libby Herz: "It is only kind of you, Libby, to feel that I would want to know that I am off the hook. But I'm not, I can't be, I don't even want to be—not until I make some sense of the larger hook I'm on." Peter Tarnopol concludes his "True Story," liberated from Maureen and told off by his father for never having been able to take anyone else's advice or help— *not even at age four!*— by turning toward the still dependent Susan McCall, whom he would soon abandon. "Oh, my God, I thought—now you. You being you! And *me!* This me who is me being me and none other!" *Letting Go* was published the year Roth separated from Maggie; *My Life as a Man* was published half a decade after her death. Yet, the letting go of Maggie would be a long—and fruitful—process. It was still not complete at the end of *The Facts*, twenty years after her death. And still five years later, a horrified invoking of Maggie would be a feeble way of trying to ward off yet another incarnation of her in *Operation Shylock*. In stature and build she even reappears as the beloved mistress in *Sabbath's Theater*.

But even in the novels of the sixties and seventies, it had begun. For all her recognizable influence in the tough females of these books, none of them is unelaborated Maggie. Nor does the evidence by and large suggest that Roth underwent the specific conflicts of most of his protagonists, however much psychological mileage, the novelist's fuel, he may have gotten. In Helen Baird of *The Professor of Desire* there is a softening of the hardened adversary, one who can admit to Kepesh years after their divorce that, for reasons she had not understood, she had purposely burned his toast and ruined his eggs in the years of their marriage and who can now tenderly apologize for doing so. And in Claire Ovington, the other gentile woman whose love rescues—for the nonce— the impotent Kepesh, there is the blonde (whom he objects to hearing called just a blonde) who has overcome by force of personal discipline the effects of having witnessed parental strife and parental drinking and who is actually whole, not just a repressed volcano. At the end of his quest, Kepesh has not settled, only temporarily intellectualized, the conflict between the nice Jewish boy and the Jewboy. He is no more at rest than Wallach or Tarnopol; indeed, the reader who knows him fated to become the breast of Roth's earlier novel knows better than the self-analytical Kepesh how unsettled he really is. What Kepesh has lost is not Claire, but his former animal desire for Claire. To live with her without overwhelming desire—which he may have had only for the forbidden—is a fear that dogs him. Kepesh, child of a borscht-belt hotel owner, had been brought up on myths of hotel lotharios to quest after female flesh—the great unkosher act—and had become accustomed in his twenties—before ruining a lovely, innocent girl—to have those desires not only satisfied but exceeded. The reader is moved to wonder, in sympathetic uncertainty, whether Kepesh can find comfort in what remains behind, in thoughts that look through the death of desire, in years that bring the philosophic mind. Kepesh is also left on the hook, as Roth leaves unresolved the question of what constitutes a man who can only half obey the first biblical commandment on marriage: not just to leave his father and mother, but to cleave unto his wife and be with her one flesh. Roth's uses of the Maggie phenomenon, autobiographical but not autobiography, should be kept in focus in any evaluation of the novels of the sixties and seventies. It must be significant that—after all the turmoil of his unwilling marriage to her in 1959, of his struggles with her afterward, and of his separation from her in 1962—he dedicated his 1962 novel, *Letting Go*, "to Maggie."

But perhaps the most potent autobiographical influence that would endlessly recur in Roth's fiction was Weequahic. Not just its physical appearance and settings—the white, art deco high school building with the elementary school next door on Chancellor Avenue, or Unterman Field behind the school, the then sandlot ball field with crude wooden benches since formalized and given its own handsome entrance and grooming—but the *idea* of Weequahic. For to Roth Weequahic answered any longings that Zionists would associate with Israel. It was a haven for those Jews who had to escape from Europe into a Jewish homeland. And for Roth it was a better Jewish homeland than Israel could ever become because it survived under a constitution that had solved the problem of pluralism. For all Roth's calling to account of WASP and establishment America, he never lost admiration for its principle, which he had seen splendidly embodied in his native neighborhood. When Nathan Zuckerman in *The Counterlife* recalls his first visit to Israel (a loose use of Roth's first trip there in the early sixties to participate in panel discussions on the meaning of being Jewish), he resists the suppositions of a long-time pioneer—and of Ben Gurion—that he will stay for good. He celebrates Newark, Chicago, and New York as true Jewish refuges and concludes,

> . . . I could not think of any historical society that had achieved a level of tolerance institutionalized in America or that had placed pluralism smack at the center of its publicly advertised dream of itself. I could only hope that Yacov [an Israeli of the pioneering generation]'s solution to the problem of Jewish survival and independence turns out to be no less successful than the unpolitical, unideological "family Zionism" enacted by my immigrant grandparents in coming, at the turn of the century, to America, a country that did not have at its center the idea of exclusion. (*C* 54)

While it is necessary to separate Roth from his characters and their absurd situations, which he creates to explore issues of freedom, art, and Jewishness, it is not necessary to separate him from his background. All his protagonists share that and use it as the anchorage from which they move out into the world.

Chapter 4

Duty before Rage

Roth's novels from *Portnoy's Complaint* (1969) to *Professor of Desire* (1977) would incur public wrath against protagonists seen as pleasure-seekers; but there was little to upset the public in the two novels that preceded *Portnoy*. In these first novels Roth presented the misadventures of would-be solid citizens, 1950s earnest strivers determined to accept responsibility. Only after exploring their failure could he turn to 1960s protesters demanding personal fulfillment. Unlike Alex Portnoy and his successors, who try to shake off imposed responsibilities, Gabe and Paul of *Letting Go* (1962) and even the much complaining Lucy of *When She Was Good* (1967) embrace those responsibilities as their destiny. Theirs was the age of responsibility. *Ir*responsibility would have to wait in line until Jews could aspire openly to be bad.

As Roth would come to learn, the journey from being good to trying to be bad was not a straight path. There was a necessary detour. Somewhere between *being good* and *being bad* was *doing good*. Only out of the futility of that stopover could there come a license to continue the hopeless journey. In the fifties being good meant being a boy, *doing good* meant being a man.

Partly it was the age, the prolonged aftermath of the war. The main tasks were rebuilding the world and getting out into it. Family men with gray flannel ambitions had to set up a responsible social structure before their children in the sixties could have the luxury to despise it. And for young men starting life in the fifties—and perhaps having to measure up to their older brothers who had fought the war—being mature, being responsible showed best in their ability to head their own households. For educated Jewish young men, there was also the obligation to repay family sacrifices by getting some of the public rewards parents, in pursuit of security, couldn't pause to claim. Yet even this happy obligation was often loaded with impossible freight. As grown-up as they might wish to seem to their fathers, they could almost hear the old man reminding them, "When I was your age, I was older than you." That doomed point of view of the striver might recommend itself as fiction—to the right novelist.

After the success of *Goodbye, Columbus*, despite distress over some of its themes, the reading public expected of Philip Roth a solid novel in the traditional sense, a big book to prove that the talent he had displayed in short stories and a novella could be harnessed to explore the great world. And Roth's intention was to deliver just that. His later characterization, "serious in the fifties," would apply also to his working its material in the early sixties. Perhaps it would have been hard for Roth to be other than serious, considering his marital difficulties; but, beyond that, the tone of the age itself suited perfectly this stage of his career. A writer young and serious inevitably must try his hand at a novel long and ambitious. *Letting Go* (1962) would establish Roth as a novelist.

Letting Go has little comedy, though some strong strands of irony, and Roth worked hard at raveling its contrasting tones. Gabe's final note to Libby, written from abroad after a breakdown, may suggest why. Like his protagonist, Roth was of several minds toward his material and not yet ready to get "off the hook." Roth's primary artistic problem (not Gabe's) involved at least two of these mind sets. His objective was destructive—demythologizing *doing good* as the road to manhood by exposing the strewn wreckage of a do-gooder—but his art required something constructive, a sympathetic journey into the psyche of his well-meaning protagonist.

Roth's strategy was to divide the young seeker into two, two young Jewish men who take on two troubled gentile women. Both Jewish men are their parents' only children. One is a natural-born sufferer already feeling the consequences of his own precipitate action; the other treads safely at the edge of entanglements but eventually plunges into one danger to undo a harm his meddling has partially caused. Neither self-victimization nor dalliance are ready-made examples of a sympathetic psychology. What might be likable in Paul Herz and Gabe Wallach could be their attempts at self-comprehension.

Their Jewishness complicates but does not instigate their quest for personal freedom. Paul's marrying Libby is a response to flattery: her regarding him as a mentor, as more than a mere boy; but he does not understand the dynamic of her habitual seeking for saviors. She will offer worship in exchange for pity, a charter to reclaim her for compliance with her modest, but anchoring, wishes. And both Gabe and Paul are susceptible to this seduction by fragility. Moreover, having already begun to let go of old ties, they need but new ones of their own choosing to confirm their manhood. As for deeper rootedness, they have put their faith in literature and academia as an alternative to the religious tradition of their youth, much as their predecessors of the thirties had done with communism.

The settings are out of Roth's graduate-school life, the Iowa Writers' Workshop and the University of Chicago. Gabe Wallach, the primary narrator and consciousness, is a well-off, Harvard-graduate son of a Central Park West dentist, who meets Paul Herz, a Cornell graduate, and his young wife Libby at Iowa. Paul, after his marriage out at age twenty because he was "fed up with being a boy," has been cut off by his lower-middle-class Brooklyn Jewish family, even though Libby has undergone conversion. Her Catholic family has also rejected her, having refused even to pay tuition for her last year at Cornell, from which she has dropped out to marry Paul. The Herzes pinch pennies in temporary campus housing originally built for veterans, the kind romanticized in Hollywood movies of the day.[1] Paul is prematurely old, in spirit a victim. Libby is of a nervous constitution, her once-flattering dependence now frazzling to Paul, who has lost sexual interest in her. By the time we meet the Herzes in Iowa, Libby has become merely his burden, but being burdened is still his badge of manhood.

Gabe Wallach's reactions to people are also shaped by an inherited sense of responsibility. His widowed father is generous but clingy; his mother had been overassertive. In a deathbed letter to Gabe, she confesses that her past efforts to help members of the family—her desire, that is, to be "Very Decent to People"—had sprung from a tendency to manipulate, and that, as a result, "Whatever unhappiness has been in our family springs from me." Gabe's promise to himself on reading the letter is never to do "violence to human life, not to another's, not to my own."

The letter and the promise open the novel, as part of Gabe's retrospective look at his Iowa City graduate days, now that he is a young instructor at the University of Chicago. As he remembers it, he had left his mother's letter in a copy of Henry James's *Portrait of a Lady*, which he had lent to Herz, where it had been read by Libby. (Thus, for the first time in a Roth novel, but not the last, the ironic lesson of the master is "the unaccountable uses of art.")[2] Suspended between the letter from his mother to Gabe and the concluding letter from Gabe to Libby is the novel, a series of explorations of freedom and identity. In a number of personal relationships Gabe veers between risking intimacy and withdrawing to safety. The question beneath the plot is whether the self is to be found in involvement or detachment. It is a question the novel does not answer, part of the "hook" Gabe is still on at the end.

Gabe wants to remain innocent of the tendencies of his parents, to be neither pushy like his mother nor compliant like his father. He will not get too close to his widowed father, despite the paternal need for some closeness, because Gabe instinctively equates intimacy with surrender of his self. In like manner, he keeps his other relationships controlled at arm's length. Ironically, in trying to navigate between Scylla and Charybdis, to be neither manipulator nor manipulated, he too follows the path of being "Very Decent" and very destructive. The women he meets are mostly Gentiles in some financial need, involved in higher education despite the wishes of their working-class families. They are susceptible to the kindness of softly brought-up teachers. As a Jew, Gabe is sufficiently outside as not to be associated with the corrupt academic establishment (Roth takes some nice potshots at the intellectual conformism of the day) and thus appears an ally to these beaten-about women. Financially independent, he is in a position to help some of them, but he is not sought for money, nor is he in any way the stereotype of the rich Jew trying to buy in. The burden of Gabe's independence is responsibility—of a rather symbiotic kind: in helping others out of trouble, he helps himself to vicarious living of their lives. And it is the rough, emotionally deprived side of their lives that in great part moves him, attractively American even while pitifully brutal. Empathy, however, can carry Gabe only so far: after raising in others hopes he is emotionally unprepared to fulfill, he withdraws to the safety of his contrasting station.

In his relationship with the Herzes, begun in Iowa, he acts as savior: lending Paul a car, listening to Libby's sad tales, even (at Paul's instigation) almost relieving Paul of the burden of being Libby's lover, later getting Paul a job at the University of Chicago, attempting to reconcile him with his Brooklyn family, and, in his last exhausting act, getting the Herzes an adoptive child. In this last episode, which Gabe makes his own trial of commitment after numerous disengagements (from lovers, from his father, and from the Herzes themselves), he undertakes the adoption effort with a zeal—and with physical risks—that might more properly be expected from Paul. Gabe acts almost as if he were fulfilling his own desire for paternity. Indeed, he regards his success in a fairly reckless endeavor as having passed a test of manhood, explaining to himself that

> [t]ill now everything had been by way of imitation. Bumbling toward a discovery of his nature, he had made the inevitable errors of a young man. But he was ready now to be someone's husband, someone's father (*LG* 533).

The irony is that none of this makes things right between the Herzes. Paul Herz sees his new paternity as the confirming duty of a fatefully settled man, settled beyond illusions of happiness, confirmed in notions merely of duty. Gabe's manipulations of their life have been, like his mother's, only interferences.

So also of Gabe's other relationships. Sexual attraction draws him to women, but when they open up enough to expect giving on his part, he withdraws. At first this is humorous, as in his tossing off of the kittenish Marge Howells. But with Martha Reganhart he ventures into romance with a woman of fairly good sense and proportion, and with a wit to match his own. She is more mature than he, but more in need. She knows that she shouldn't trust starry-eyed men, should be wary of falling in love with Gabe: ". . . a woman at least realizes there are certain rotten things she's got to do in life and she does them. Men want to be heroes. They want to be noble and responsible, but they're so soft about it" (LG 68). When she does fall in love with Gabe, leaving a potentially safe relationship with an older, also Jewish, man who loves her and who will finally pick up the pieces, she looks in vain for the commitment Gabe had implicitly promised. But her children annoy him more than amuse him, and his willingness to serve their needs is no more than a well-intentioned pledge of honor he cannot fulfill. Ironically, Gabe's withdrawal from the relationship comes as Martha's children are being returned to the care of Martha's remarried husband. Gabe, having no responsible role to play with Martha except adult to adult, must face his unreadiness to exercise that true freedom, and he begins to fathom the destructive effects of too easily pledging to solve other people's life problems. At the same time he sees how his withdrawal from his own father leaves the old man susceptible to the attractions of a slightly alcoholic society woman: Gabe's refusal of love for fear of what it might demand from him—as well as of how it might, in his mother's vein, cause him to interfere—gains him nothing but alienation from his own people.

In dividing his Jewish seeker for a place in Middle America into two characters, Roth shows two grim aspects of altruism: self-obliteration and self-removal. Paul Herz knows that what his family wants is for him to be good, to be a Brooklyn boy at least in soul, to marry whatever his generation's equivalent of his mother would be, and to be a lawyer or something equally respectable, as judged by family visits, a well-furnished home, affiliations. Paul, however, chary of his father's example in multiple business failures, wants to be a novelist, to break loose and explore his own soul and his own values. From his earliest years he has been a collector and filer of applications that would take him away, and his Cornell education is entirely the result of his own enterprise. But his defiance in marrying out exhausts his reserve of self. He falls back on inbred responses, his having always been made to feel obligated rather than entitled. As James Atlas puts it

Paul's quest for what he calls "manliness and dignity" prompts him to marry because he feels he ought to; to quit school and go work in a Detroit automobile factory; to give up his literary aspirations and consider becoming a high school teacher. The grim, cramped existence he sentences himself to is a form of secular ordination: You promise to deny yourself pleasure? Then today you are a man.[3]

Gabe, who remains single and follows more closely his original career course, seems more independent than Paul; yet he also yields to the will of women when it comes to where and with whom he will live, though he pulls away when those ties threaten to become fixed. His acts of self-denial are for the self-approval he can find in the mirrors of other people's eyes. His need is to be thought ethical, to think of himself as ethical. In helping others he collects counterbalancing obligations, so that when he pulls out he is even. But mostly he offsets his failures to carry through by analyzing his failings—the intellectual's sin of letting knowing replace doing. Needing to have it both ways, to be innocent and guilty, he exonerates himself by indictment.

Gabe and Paul compromise with their self-interest because they have never been brought to see the self as something positive, which must be identified independently and served before it can be given in service to anything or anyone. For both, a self is identified in its sacrifice, not in its fulfillment, happiness, or independence. Manliness in *Letting Go* is a grim business.

In allowing himself the scope of a long, nineteenth-century novel, Roth could develop independent strands of the story, rich in landscape and character, and then weave them together later on. The Jewish settings, self-contained episodes, stand as background references for the main narrative line and as commentaries upon the Jewish covenant. Paul's story is told partly in flashbacks to Jewish settings in Brooklyn and, to some extent, Detroit—where the Herzes had spent a miserable winter—and partly in Gabe's more immediate accounts of university life in Iowa City and Chicago. Gabe's own German-Jewish settings, visited on his trips east, are Central Park West and the East End of Long Island—a social stratum well above Paul's. Roth chronicles the Herzes' early married years, including the experience of a seedy abortion, in a Jewish Detroit slum where two old Jewish rooming-house neighbors impinge upon their lives. Neither Levy, who has a sordid scheme for swindling Korngold out of his hoard of wholesale underwear, nor Korngold, his fellow sufferer in life's harsh underclass, are helpful models to Libby of what a Jewish life might be. Roth refuses to grace their grubbiness with either philosophy or a "Magic Barrel" other-worldliness. Nor does Paul's family represent any positive Jewish values for Libby: "I thought it would be *exciting* to have Jewish in-laws. . . . But not them. They don't want to be happy. They want to be miserable, *that* makes them happy" (*LG* 53–54). And when at Libby's urging the would-be-savior Gabe visits the Brooklyn environment of the Herz family and friends, that environment is both believable and drably predictable, though to Gabe, who has cut himself off from Jewish culture, almost enviably so: hearing the Jewish accents and clichéd values of Paul's old friends, he asks himself, "How do you keep life going exactly as it was when you were ten years old? That day I wouldn't have minded arranging such a life for myself" (*LG* 181).

The whole business of letting go—not only parents' letting go so that children can mature and lovers' letting go so they can extend illusions of independence but children's letting go of a whole heritage in order to swim beyond the last rope in a wider cultural sea—is debilitating and problematic. And the consciousness of origins does not fade; these Jews are ambassadors despite themselves. In Gabe's getting a gentile baby for the Herzes to adopt, compensating for the ruinous effects of Libby's early abortion instigated by Paul, there is the faintest consciousness of a Jewish savior showing this converted *shiksa* that her earliest hopes of Jewish salvation were not vain. Moreover, since the idea of the adoption was Martha's—to help a fellow waitress out of the consequences of an unwanted pregnancy—Gabe's benevolence is also a way of showing Martha, on the eve of his abandoning her, that he is not a complete bastard, that, like the other Jew into whose arms he has driven her (Sid Jaffe, the *pro bono* lawyer in the abortion case), he shares a heritage of responsibility. Their Jewish manliness is not the macho model of gentile America. Yet, Gabe is incapable of owning up completely to the havoc his coasting can cost or to his fear of chaos under the tough gentile life. He deftly blames Martha for a good share of his breakup with her. And when near the end he realizes he misses her and entertains thoughts of sliding into another uncommitted liaison with her, he clears his conscience with a typical Gabe waffle. Seeing her broken car door, he muses:

> *Everything she has is broken* . . . But the thought no longer filled him with fear and distrust. It was not that which had been building in him in the long ride up from Gary [where he has been securing the adoption]. Forgiving himself, he forgave her. (*LG* 562)

Paul Herz, too, finally succumbs to his sense of heritage. His last acts of defiance had been a refusal to visit his dying father in the hospital and a delay in getting to the funeral, so that he missed it by minutes. Now, guilt over his father's death and the embrace by his family overcome his will and stoop him further into his father's image. After not seeing his parents or entering a synagogue for six years, he now takes to attending synagogue daily, supposedly to honor the memory of his father but more to escape the company of Libby by a means she can accept; and he invites his mother to stay with them in Chicago. He bolsters the shaky marriage in the bunting of Jewish tradition, for which play-acting Libby is all too enthusiastic, hers being the zealotry of the apostate. Gabe, outside but evaluating this charade, draws very little wisdom about himself:

> . . . alone, he found himself contemplating the hardest fact of the Herzes' life: the husband did not make love to the wife. *Still* . . . ? No sooner did the idea come into his mind than he pushed it right out. He had not been put on this earth to service the deprived, whatever the deprived themselves might think. Whatever *he* might think! He could not fathom yet his soft heart. It was an affliction! It was not soft at all! *He* was soft—the heart was hard. (*LG* 538)

Part of Gabe's hook is to be a man in control of brain and heart, not a plexus of reactions to parents and to needs for parenting.

But that is the world of *Letting Go*, and the more operative parental conflict is with fathers. Paul's life is a cycle of breaking from and returning to the footsteps of his father. Gabe's fight against complying with women's wills is about not replicating his father's weakness. He wants, and wants not, to be a father. Martha must finally tell Gabe she "can't afford" him. Martha's problem in avoiding abuse is to find the father dimension in a solid man. She settles for Sid Jaffe, who will get her daughter back and save the girl from having to witness more abusive paternal behavior. While living with her father, the child has bizarrely pushed her little brother to his death from a double-decker bed. She will need a kind of fathering that only a mature, selfless man like Sid can give her. Martha determines to take this course even though to the very end it is Gabe who moves her soul and stirs her female responses:

> . . . I'm going to have an orderly life—do you hear? Don't ever try to get me in bed again, you! And don't worry about my conscience. Worry about your own. I'm not playing it safe. I'm using some sense for once. I've let go and let go and let go—I've let go plenty. I've had a wilder history than you, by a long shot. I've got a right to hang on now. Don't ever get in bed with me again. Ever! (*LG* 576)

She chooses not a lover-husband but a father-husband.

Fathering is everywhere an issue. Old Korngold, whose well-off son has broken away, wishes vainly to establish a fatherly relationship beyond that of pensioner. Harry Bigoness, the husband of the young waitress who is giving her out-of-wedlock child up for adoption, is himself an out-of-work father of three children by a previous marriage. Inept and pitiable, he has accepted the responsibility of fatherhood after being abandoned by his first wife, the infant children's mother. She had let go—freedom as total irresponsibility. Now Bigoness wants his second young wife, Theresa, to share the burden of parenthood without adding the product of her indiscretion—of *her* botched letting go—to his load. Theresa, letting go of her own baby to the Herzes, will be dragged at age twenty into a penal-colony motherhood of puking stepchildren, the very existence Herz had tried to spare Libby at that age, the very existence to which he is returning as a failed writer and failed college teacher six years later—to be the legally confirmed father of someone else's child. And Libby's rejection by her father hovers over all the decisions of her adult life. Jewish men trying to be more manly than their fathers and gentile women needing the paternal security missing in their childhood abound in *Letting Go*. Here, the conflict is seen mostly through the eyes of the Jewish man. The gentile woman's view would be studied in isolation, but with a vengeance, in *When She Was Good*.

To reread *Letting Go* with the hindsight provided by *Patrimony* and *The Facts* and by Roth's novels of the seventies and eighties is to look through a reverse telescope across hills and valleys. Responses of the first critics seem remotely rooted in the values of the age itself. Two decades later, after the tumultuous sixties and the loss of innocence in the seventies—after assassinations, defeat in an unjust war, drug and flower-child reaction, burning of American cities, Watergate, genuflection to ayatollahs and terrorists (the Jews all this time being shifted from victim to victimizer), and after Roth's renderings of the responsive whines and ejaculations of the age—readers could hark back to *Letting Go* as part of a longing for pre-Oswald America. In 1982, when the novel was reissued in paperback, its sobriety and solidity in contrast to Roth's more recent effusions prompted appreciations of the pre-*Portnoy* Roth. In the nineties, having heard Roth declare patrimony to be acceptance of the father in the self and the American family to be the true Zion, one may see *Letting Go* as just a natural step in this writer's quest.

Both praise and blame from the earliest critics acknowledged Roth's comparative youth—he was twenty-nine when this second book was published. Praise was for Roth's ear for dialogue, his eye for detail, and his seriousness of purpose; dissenting criticism scored self-importance, moral weakness of main characters, excesses of detail, and the unmitigated "greyness" of the life presented. Critics could also fault Roth for falling into traps he had himself identified in essays and forums. John Gross, for example, denying Roth any of Bellow's or Malamud's ability to abstract from Jewish experience "a metaphor for twentieth-century man: rueful, displaced tragi-comic," placed him, rather, among "slick professionals like Irwin Shaw, Jerome Weidman, or even Herman Wouk." Indeed, Gross added, Roth "takes a big risk . . . when he lets one of his characters talk about *Marjorie Morningstar*."[4] A year earlier, in "Writing American Fiction," Roth had outrightly dismissed Weidman and Wouk, among other authors, and *Marjorie Morningstar* among other novels, as failing to "imagine the corruption and vulgarity and treachery of American public life any more profoundly than they imagine human character—that is, the country's private life" (*RMAO* 122). To these Roth had contrasted several serious writers of his age, among whom, one assumes, he numbered himself. Being included among the slick writers must have surprised Roth, for he surely thought that leaving Gabe Wallach on "the hook" at the end of *Letting Go* was refusing to fall into the easy resolutions of those lesser writers, whom he grouped with "Broadway's *amor-vincit-omnia* boys." And the painstaking but engaging work he had produced (Gross grants him his gift of "readability") was intended to explore a subject he regarded as anything but slick. A generation's trying to live by its parents' definition of manhood, when the conditions and possibilities of life had changed, was to Roth every bit as serious and as relevant to Jewish life as the rueful, tragi-comic metaphors for modernism that Gross and others in 1962 seemed to prefer. In another early review, Nat Hentoff expressed impatience with a "hollowness" in the novel. Hentoff sees the work as but the usual dues-paying plaints of youth against parents— "mainly a tour-de-Werther"—to be gotten out before moving on:

> In *Letting Go*, [Roth] has not so much criticized or explored this society as he has sent it his letter of resignation. But having no other place to go, he has deferred sealing the letter in the sense that other works are surely in progress.[5]

The paying of dues it may have been, but not to clichés; rather, to a view of manhood that had to be got by: self-sacrifice as a way of doing good takes a lot more down with it than self. But whether the dues are paid depends on whether one sees Roth inside the novel speaking for the characters or outside the novel putting them through the disillusionment. Critics, bound by their times, would see it both ways. Between Gross's wanting characters ruefully alienated and Hentoff's declaring parent-child alienation old hat, and what with Hentoff's seeming insistence on some resolution of conflicts rather than leaving characters on "the hook," the early sixties appears to have been impatient with youthful grimness both for not being grim enough and for being unable to kick off its weighty shoes and dance itself into sprightlier moods.

But this puzzling tendency to find in Roth quite contradictory faults emerged more generally in the criticism, echoing, however faintly, a babble that had erupted after *Goodbye, Columbus* and one that would boil up again over the next few decades. What muted the criticism here was a tendency to be kind to the author of a first novel, one who, most agreed, was a genuine writer. The anonymous reviewer in *Time*,[6] who assured that "on every page the reader knows that he is in the presence of a writer," concluded that "*Letting Go* must finally be counted a failure, although it is a failure of a quality few writers could achieve." Orville Prescott found the novel ". . . further proof of Mr. Roth's astonishing talent . . . clumsily constructed . . . , but . . . morbidly fascinating,"[7] finally declaring that it "seethes with life" and that "Philip Roth . . . is probably the most talented novelist under 30 in America." Granville Hicks called it "the kind of bad book that only a good writer could have written,"[8] while *The New Yorker*, in its brief roundup fashion, called it "a frequently imposing failure."[9] If there was consensus in these generalized views, there was anything but consensus in the particulars. The specific points of failure, and of success, divided these reviewers. Somehow agreeing that disapproval was apt, they could not agree on what they disapproved of. The *Atlantic* critic faulted Roth for tending "to bring minor characters unnecessarily into the foreground of the action," while *The New Yorker* critic found the "most impressive characters in the book" to be "its eccentrics, misfits, and marginal neurotics." *The New York Times*'s Prescott agreed that besides the study of its main characters,

> "Letting Go" is a harshly satirical account of many other characters in many different walks of life. Mr. Roth is amusing and touching and shocking by turns. He writes with a fine combination of sympathy and mockery about middle-class New York Jews, Gabe's and Paul's relatives. He is savagely satirical about academic opportunists. He is adroit and amusing in his thumbnail sketches of American types: loathsome old men washed into a dreadful rooming house by a tide of misery; an abortionist; a Negro hipster; a pregnant girl of 19, mentally subnormal; a bellicose, suspicious, ignorant and dishonest factory worker out of a job.

but, Prescott believes, Roth should not have embarrassed his reader with all this personal, closed-door nastiness. Roth, to Prescott, "has absolutely no taste or sense of restraint at all."

The same newspaper's Sunday review, by Arthur Mizener, found that the book was "rich in those minor figures at the edge of fantasy that constantly amuse and astonish us and are almost convincing," that Roth "is particularly good with nitwits . . . [and] . . . very good indeed with children,"[10] but the *New Statesman*'s Gross found all this to make its length, "over 600 pages, . . . a couple of hundred too many." *The Spectator*'s John Daniel found that the "work crackles into life only when Mr. Roth lets go the agony and seizes the farce," when he gives in to his "zany streak," but *Time* assured its readers that "Roth refused to use in it the skill at satirical pastiches that had glittered so brilliantly in *Goodbye, Columbus*" because, quoting Roth himself, "I had done that. Why do it again?" Roth's own future path toward wild satire was apparently obscured even from him.

Libby Herz divided the critics, as indeed—and perhaps because—within the novel she evokes Gabe's contrasting responses. The *Atlantic*'s Barrett saw her as heroic. And the *Time* reviewer declared that "Libby runs away with the book. Perhaps *Letting Go* should have been her novel: certainly the narrative comes fully to life only when she is present." But Hentoff called Libby a ". . . neuresthenic wisp of a lapsed Catholic wife . . . one of the most accurately outlined *kvetches* in recent fiction," yet found "her exasperating verisimilitude . . . one of many indications of Roth's sure, surgical perception of the surface of our discontents."

About its central story, also, critics disagreed. Just whose story was it? To William Barrett in the *Atlantic*, it was the Herzes' story, Gabe interesting only as the marginal friend who tries to influence their lives, which are "too threadbare and starveling to carry the weight of a saga." To Barrett, Paul Herz is "the melancholy and rabbinical Jew . . . [with] . . . a penchant for getting bogged down in troubles. Yet at the end it is Paul and Libby who have won through to some human solidity. . . ." John Daniel also called it a saga, but identified as its hero "Gabe Wallach, Jewish, rich, blundering, indecisive, guilt-ridden, and introspective . . . [who finally] . . . learns not to meddle, to let go." Most saw the protagonist divided, with Gabe predominating. Yet as to just what Gabe's conflict is, or how worthy it is in any case, the reviewers were at odds. Orville Prescott's pronouncement on Gabe was, "Not having serious troubles of his own, he felt guilty." John Gross agreed: "He's altogether too spruce, too well-fed . . . a busybody with time on his hands." Arthur Mizener more generously called both heroes bumblers, but in a world of their own. The *Time* roundup tossed off the "hero" Gabe as "a tedious young English instructor who looks within himself and finds the world empty," but Mizener, among others, took on the emptiness of that world as an issue on which the novel needed to be judged. Several reviewers saw Jewishness in this novel as at least a corollary of Roth's vision of the larger world (though the *Atlantic*'s Barrett must have known little of the subject to have seen Paul as "rabbinical"). These critics may not have been blind, but this elephant may have been more puzzling in 1962 than any one of them could fathom. Certainly Roth builds in ambiguity, perhaps nowhere so much as in the meaning of the title.

Irving Feldman reads the title as part of Roth's "contemporary" vocabulary, a "moral vocabulary" that masks "the self-consciousness implicit in [his two protagonists'] difficulties of 'feeling': don't clutch, don't push and pull, and let go—that is, fail, in order to seize the day."[11] Arthur Mizener reads Roth's meaning of the term "letting go" as following the dictates of the heart, "the only way to fulfill one's nature and therefore the only way to be alive." But, Mizener reminds us, it is a dangerous course, because as Roth had implied in the Yiddish proverb he had used as an epigraph for "Goodbye, Columbus," "the heart is [but] half a prophet." When Martha shouts that she had "let go and let go and let go," that she had had a "wilder history" than Gabe and had a right to "hold on" for a change, she is saying that that feeling of being alive had come at a price. Mizener, ignoring that passage, makes Roth an advocate of such letting go. He notes that the "Herzes [first] . . . commit themselves without reservation to living wholly by the dictates of their feelings; they are tortured endlessly by the world, but they are wholly alive." And Mizener thinks Roth in accepting that kind of letting go as a guide to life—he ignores its consequences to Paul and Libby or Martha's compromise—

> has stacked the cards against good sense, has caricatured ordinary human-
> ity with a subtle violence, in order to suggest that such [ordinary] people
> are at best sterile and at their usual worst malign, and always dead, and
> that only the life committed to the demands of the private sentiments,
> unrestrained by any other considerations, is worth anything.

It is a sweeping indictment, dividing the book into a heroic few who have the guts to pursue the "demands of the private sentiments" and all others who are in Roth's alleged view just dead.

But Mizener finds Roth's use of Jewishness paradoxical: On the one hand, he notes Roth's "almost automatic assumption that no one is quite human who does not feel all the obligations of passionate, selfish, demanding love of the kind he regularly ascribes to Jewish families." (How, the reader might ask, can this square with Mizener's having called it "dead," "sterile," "merely malign"? Isn't "passionate, selfish, demanding love" life-affirming, even though obligatory?) On the other hand, Mizener sees something representa- tively American in the Jewish life that Roth uniquely captures—his "special country"—in descriptions like that of Brooklyn's Doris: "We get Book of the Month, we get *Harper's* and *Look*, we belong to the Play of the Month . . . we go to Temple lectures." To Mizener this is American, not in its accents or its greater intensity, but in its "almost Victorian belief in the natural obligations of family love, its acute awareness of social position and class symbol." The para- dox, then, is that Roth and "to a large extent . . . his whole generation"—and Mizener includes Bellow, Swados, Styron and even Kerouac—share a

> sense of life . . . oddly self conscious and limited, . . . almost exclusively
> personal. There is [Mizener says] a great deal about the public life in

these writers, but they always see that life as an unjustifiable, inexplicable—if immovable—obstacle to the realization of the private self, which is inexhaustibly queried, analyzed and suffered over by everyone in their books, as it might be in some incredibly brilliant soap opera or undergraduate short story.

Contemporary critics were hardly content to let this paradox stand. In Mizener's view, Roth resolves it on the side of the personally selfish by refusing to send Gabe and Paul to the woodshed until they might realize how insignificant their personal *kvetches* really are. But Mizener also sees a generation of writers using human character—what Roth called "the country's private life"—to obscure rather than explore American public life. In his essays Roth had argued not for a new sociology, or a balanced history of his times, but against soap opera writers' failing to "imagine the corruption and vulgarity and treachery" of that public life. For Roth a subtle part of that treachery, along with the more obvious red-bating and quiz-show scandals, was the emptiness of an older generation's promises of freedom. It had educated his own generation to soar and then trapped it in an aviary of conformity. Roth may well have thought that looking closely at the traps restraining Gabe and Paul was a way of exploring a public theme. Critics, though, wanted more than exploration. John Gross places Roth, for his "high-gloss prose," among the "slick professionals" of the soap operas (though he would not, with Mizener, include Bellow) for, he declares, in *Letting Go* "public themes are nowhere confronted." Nat Hentoff finds in the novel a hollowness of intent, a self-indulgent realism "seen only as narrow shades of failure." To Hentoff, Roth's challenge posed in "Writing American Fiction" is not met. "If Roth does indeed believe that it has become impossible to live a rational, resilient, self-willed life in America, his writing, then, is primarily an act of terminal narcissism because his vision is not tragic but is rather laved in grey pathos." Roth had scored the easy optimism of Bellow, Gold, and Styron in their characters' discovery that, as Norman Podhoretz put it, one "can survive and even flourish under such conditions." But Podhoretz sees this novel as an answer that grinds the faces of these optimistic writers in the muck.

> Here, [Roth] seems to be saying, is what life is really like for those who have withdrawn into the interstices of American society; this is what the life of personal relations and self-preoccupation really amounts to; see how mean it is, how narrow, how claustrophobic, how oppressive, and then tell me on what basis you can claim that it is possible for a man living such a life to survive, let alone to flourish?[12]

Podhoretz sees Roth writing not to illuminate but to blame.

Granville Hicks, too, complains about Roth's gloomy perspective. "Roth thinks writers in these days have no business being affirmative—but, on the other hand, none could possibly be regarded as tragic. They go their dull ways and we are dragged along with them." And the *Time* reviewer picks up this greyness, "the novel's uncertain mood," and ascribes it to Roth's unsuccessful attempt

> to deal with the 20th century's grey plague—a paralysis of the apparatus that detects meaning in life. Greyness of spirit is what one writes about these days: fair enough. But the author's view of things must not be greyed. And in *Letting Go* after a few fine satirical flashes at the beginning, Roth becomes bogged in solemnity whenever he tries to assess his dreary hero.

These critics might have disagreed about whether *Letting Go* addressed public issues, but clearly they were at one in finding Roth unable or unwilling to make a definitive statement about his generation's role as it came of age in the postwar era. If Roth's way of addressing that role in the country's public life was indirectly through portrayal of Gabe's and Paul's bumbling private life, it was, for them, a bumbling way to write a novel.

What these early sixties critics share in assessing Roth's view of the fifties, extended to their times, is the belief that the paradox cannot be maintained. An author may not merely represent, but must rise above, the conflict of self and duty. Paul's defeat in settling, with only a veneer of religious equanimity, and Gabe's being, after 630 pages, only more aware but no more understanding of his malaise are not exemplars of the tragic view of life. Roth made them likable enough to carry the plot and, yes, he loosened their trust—and perhaps that of the readers—in Literature 101 as a guide to life, but he gave them no vision of what at its best a committed life—in this case perhaps a *Jewish* life—might be. On the other hand, Roth seems to have felt that a tragic view of life was too easy, too close to *amor vincit omnia*, to apprehend the paradox of doing good. If there was tragedy, it might be in the blindness of one inclined to accept myths as guides to living, Lucy Nelson, for example, out in the heart of the heart. But in 1962 Roth was still trying to square the myth of opportunity with the devilish dues required to sign on to the American dream, especially for a Jew. A novelist's task, he apparently believed, was to turn and turn the problem so as to expose its dimensions, not necessarily to solve it for an age that had not solved it itself. Irving Feldman considered those dues and that age in his 1962 *Commentary* review:

Why, in seeking to engage his characters, should Roth put it that freedom comes from responsibility and not responsibility from freedom? Maybe the answer is, 1956: Only careers in domesticity open to talent. Similarly, *Letting Go* shows a healthy but constricting determination to avoid the other sentimentalities—of individualism, of love, of identity-finding, of availability. But, then, what excitement and openness has life to offer in 1956? or in 1962?[13]

Later, as the sixties ended and the seventies unfolded, after *Portnoy's Complaint* had raised anew the question of what is meant by "a Jewish novel," critics themselves began to line up, as it were, in the camps of Paul or Gabe, defining Jewishness as self-sacrifice or as a detached ironic perspective on American life. That dichotomy has never ceased to exist. Stanley Cooperman, summing up Roth's achievement after half a dozen books in post-*Portnoy* 1973, considers *Letting Go* Roth's finest work because of its "moral judgment and personal commitment . . . without . . . [which] . . . vision the realist is blind." He concludes that "*Letting Go* is a major American novel not in spite of its Jewishness, but because of it."[14]

By 1982 James Atlas, reconsidering the novel as "A Postwar Classic,"[15] could praise the very weightiness of theme, character, and description that earlier critics had faulted. *Letting Go* reminds Atlas that there was an age, before the social loosenings of the sixties and seventies, when people trusted art to set values for life. Roth's later characters, of the seventies and eighties, would feel betrayed in trying to use James or Flaubert as guides to living, but "*Letting Go* was written from within that era, when irony was a literary term, not an attitude toward experience, and when literature was more authentic than life." One might argue that if it was a naive age, it was also an innocent age. If the youth were too susceptible to myths, they at least had motive for starting out in the world. Gabe might use Henry James as a veritable Pandarus—talking literature gets women into bed—but at least he has a vision on which life can work its revision. It is Roth's critique of doing good that these young men are guided by their myths. As Atlas puts it, "Unlike the protagonists of Roth's later novels, who are always protesting the discrepancy between the great themes of literature and their own sordid experience, Gabe is still a prisoner of his own limited ideas about the world." But to understand how Gabe and Paul are locked into their condition, Atlas believes, it was fitting for Roth to spell out those ideas and that world in detail. Part of Roth's achievement, he believes, is realizing what Hentoff had called "the novel's achingly accurate background" and what Gross had complained of as "a great deal of superfluous description." According to Atlas, "The world it brings to life is so various and thoroughly imagined, the narrative strategies it employs so sophisticated, that a reader new to Roth would have no idea where it belonged in the chronology of his work." It was, Atlas avers, too "dauntingly precocious" to be taken for the work of a twenty-nine-year-old writer. As to the earlier charge that Roth had given all up to greyness, Atlas now puts that greyness in perspective:

> The worlds depicted in this novel may seem cheerless and old-fashioned at times, just as the social and ethical constraints under which Roth's characters labor may seem, in the postliberated 1980s, to belong to a remote era, an era when moral compulsions one scarcely understood could determine the course of one's life. But those compulsions hardly died out when President Eisenhower left office. They were just more openly resisted, with the impassioned, willfully hedonistic protagonists of Roth's later novels in the vanguard. As it happened, the freedom they seized with such urgent zeal was to prove no less traumatic than the prohibitions imposed on the characters in *Letting Go* by family, custom, community—as Portnoy discovered when he sought to defy the stultifying beliefs and attitudes that had been crammed into his head.

Atlas concludes that "*Letting Go* is a precursor to these novels, a symptom of Portnoy's complaint." But he finds it "one of Roth's maturest achievements and . . . among the masterpieces of postwar American literature." Although lost in the cacophony that followed *Portnoy's Complaint*, it was worth reading to regain a generation's foothold in solid ground that had since slid away.

Today, one can see the ambivalence in Roth's treatment of that age of innocence as commentary both on his life and on the zeitgeist. Dedicating the book to Maggie and leaving her, whatever the precise order of those events, is perhaps emblematic of the problem. To have Paul remain with Libby, but with totally lowered expectations, and Gabe escape to Europe, but in a state of nervous exhaustion, was to sum up the dismal choices for himself and his generation. Personal freedom was still bound by a social contract, albeit a loosening one. Manhood, which would soon be defined as capacity for choice, was still defined as capacity for obligation. Even the act of defining oneself, soon to be some overt defiance of social norms, was still a process of inclusion, of identifying one's niche. This was a year before the Kennedy assassination, two years before the advent of the Beatles, several years before the liberalization of the divorce laws, a decade before *Roe v. Wade*. Institutions—from the government to the senior prom—were still comfortably in control. The first person was mostly plural, as it would be mostly singular a decade later. If the 1990s is a decade of striving to come together, of assimilating the lessons of 1960s-to-1980s individualism to renewed needs for social contract, then *Letting Go* may be seen as documenting a generation's premature attempt to have it both ways.

Social contract for Jews has an additional dimension besides its resistance to separateness; they are part of a people that sees itself as having covenanted with God for a specific place in the world. No matter that one is not a believer, the contract is in the flesh. Inherent to the venturings of Gabe and Paul is the primary conflict of biblical Judaism: how to be a blessing, a light unto the nations, when not yet confirmed in its own identity. That burden of chosenness, endlessly denied, ties these characters through primal sympathies to the unaccommodated immigrants that preceded them. James Atlas pointed out in the 1980s that "Roth's impatience with [Gabe's] pompous father is tempered, as it so often is where fathers are concerned, by affection for that older generation, so naive yet so sure of its own values." After *Patrimony* and *Operation Shylock*, *Letting Go* can be seen as first steps out on a path that would circle back home.

But in the fifties to early sixties, part of the "hook" Gabe is on, exiled off in Europe, is not knowing where he belongs as a Jew. To youth who rebel against parents and against the culture they associate with those parents, anywhere else they can be—the American heartland or the Europe of undergraduate study—may seem a refuge, until it is discovered to be merely a place of exile. Roth's next young Jewish pilgrim will discover that even Israel can be exile.

But that would come two books later; Roth's next novelistic venture would concern a gentile woman. A mixture of vengeance and expiation, it would take five years in the writing and, one may assume from Roth's comments on the period in his own life, hours on the couch. *When She Was Good* is a better novel than its immediate critics gave it credit for being, but its failings, well described,[16] could not at the time be associated with Roth's ambivalent relationship with Maggie. Without knowledge of Roth's personal connection to the materials, most critics saw it as a mere misstep: a self-assignment to try writing about gentile America. Still, its main failing will reveal itself to anyone reading it after a novel reflecting actual experience of small-town life in the forties and fifties, say *Rabbit Run*. Roth may have known how Maggie sounded when ranting about family betrayal, but—notwithstanding some weekend trips to Maggie's hometown, his meeting her mother, and his brief encounter with her grandfather, which obviously gave rise to the Daddy Will narration (*Facts* 144)—Roth did not really know how these Gentiles sounded in their everyday conversations, in their sectarian bickerings, in the small talk that might reveal life rather than just echo clichés of Middle America. Liberty Center, for all its obvious symbolism and forced thesis, is not Mt. Judge, Pennsylvania.

Roth thought he had gotten down quite well the small-town gentile sound. He agreed with those critics who praised the narrative voice in *When She Was Good* as being accurate for Middle America. And for Roth, here as elsewhere, the question of voice was not just one of virtuoso mimicry—being the

Rich Little or Dana Carvey of fiction. It was rather a way of exposing how his characters "experience themselves," a term he used in defending his practices from "Epstein" to *Portnoy* and beyond.

> *When She Was Good* is, above all, a story about small-town Middle Westerners who more than willingly experience themselves as conventional and upright people; and it is their own conventional and upright style of speech that I chose as my means of narration—or, rather, a slightly heightened, somewhat more flexible version of their language, but one that drew freely upon their habitual cliches, locutions, and banalities. (*RMAO* 18)

Whether or not Roth brought it off—whether we hear in it the voice of anyone Alex Portnoy might call "Thereal McCoy"—Roth kept shifting his emphasis during the writing, away from folkways toward fixation on his nemesis. That shift can be seen in the changes of its working titles: *Time Away*, *In the Middle of America*, *Saint Lucy*, and finally *When She Was Good* (*RMAO* 35). Roth was not yet ready to spell out this provenance when he analyzed the novel's voices in 1974, but the issue of the book was more than the sound of Middle Westerners.

When She Was Good is Maggie's complaint—and avowal. Why Roth saw fit to give it utterance after he had separated himself from all involvement with her except that dictated by the alimony courts may stimulate some psychological speculation (Roth was still speculating in the Zuckerman letter to him at the end of *The Facts*, 1988), but part of the answer must be that he thought it a good story, a story that could suggest not just why Maggie had been such a plague to him but why one like Maggie must necessarily be a plague to herself. In telling a story based on her early life and first marriage—and in fictively killing her off before she could break loose and meet one such as himself—Roth may have been trying at once to cast her out of his system and to rescue some narrative capital from the disastrous half-dozen years of their relationship. At the same time, in seeking for something sympathetic in his protagonist, he may have been rationalizing her long, seemingly irrational hold on him. It is a story about a woman brought up in a family striving to be decent, but against a dark strain of abuse in their own history that emerges in her parents' generation with an alcoholic father and an abuse-accepting mother. Neither parent is as pat or bad as Lucy sees them; and her judgment of them, and of her fear-ridden grandfather, rigidly devoted to decency, who fails to hold them together in the face of her extreme reactions, leads her to seek elsewhere: first in a flirtation with Roman Catholicism, then with an attempt to make a strong, upright husband out of the simple lout she chooses to work her will upon. When all fails, she follows Anna Karenina and Emma Bovary into desperate moves leading to her untimely death.

Roth wrote the novel mostly in New York, where he was now living a good part of the time with Ann Mudge, the prototype of the socialite Susan McCall in *My Life as a Man* and perhaps the immediate stimulus for attitudes he would ascribe to the "Pilgrim" in *Portnoy's Complaint*. He was financially at loose ends because of the alimony to Maggie, unable to earn enough to feel himself his own person, but able to spend social time with many New York literati, including Robert Brustein and his friends in the theater circles. Stanley Kauffmann's recollection is of a first rate raconteur, especially a master of stand-up comedy with a Jewish flavor, who had his parlor audiences bladder-weak with laughter. While writing the book without Jews, Roth was once again living in the center of American intellectual life, no small part of which was secular Jewish, and absorbing flavors that could not be included in the novel set way out in Liberty Center. Roth's dedication of that novel was to his brother, six friends, "and to Ann Mudge: For words spoken and for deeds done." He was seeing Ann steadily—separated, but not divorced, from Maggie. Whether or whatever he might have thought of other legal venues, New York law at that time gave him no prospect of freedom from the woman whose early life story he had reworked into the fiction of *When She Was Good*.

Post-*Portnoy* criticism would tend to see Lucy's novel as an anticipation of Alex's, inasmuch as "both books explore the problems that result when the desire for personal autonomy comes up against the restraints of the family, from which the individual needs both autonomy and sanction."[17] But Lucy Nelson doesn't just indict her family or seek to fly from it, she first strives to reform it, to do good. Unlike Alex, she has no desire to achieve badness; rather, she wraps herself in delusions of righteousness. What she may lack that Alex has, that Gabe and Paul had, that all Roth's Jewish protagonists will have, even if unconsciously, is a heritage of chosenness. Consequently, she must choose herself as an agent of superior morality, and must define that superiority, since it has not come to her with her mother's milk. The psychological burden is too much for her, and she becomes instead a bitch, "a Midwestern Medea who embodies the horror of the Protestant ethic run amok."[18] For many of Roth's readers, this treatment of Lucy would confirm hints, begun with Brenda and Libby, of Roth's misogyny.

By 1967, the year *When She Was Good* was published, Roth was widely considered a Jewish writer, so the novel received some critical attention in the Jewish journals, but not much in pulpits or in mainstream organizational circles. Critics, remembering essays such as "Some New Jewish Stereotypes" and "Writing about Jews" anticipated Roth's return to the subject of Jewish-American life. He was only thirty-four and had hardly exhausted in fiction the implications of his forays into criticism. But 1967 was also a turning point in Jewish history. Israel's victory in what came to be known as "The Six-Day War" would at once give Jews a new pride in their ability, and right, to assert themselves in the world and would deprive them of their long-standing status as victims entitled to silk-glove treatment. It would also begin the decades-long propaganda war to paint them as racist abusers of another minority population, though that theme would take some years to develop momentum. Meanwhile, Jews in droves had been coming out of the professional closet and being overtly Jewish. Even Middle America now knew that some of its most broadly American entertainers—Jack Benny, Phil Harris, George Burns, Danny Kaye, Jerry Lewis—and he-man actors like Kirk Douglas and Jeff Chandler, not to mention old favorites like Edward G. Robinson, Melvin Douglas, Paul Muni, and Edward Arnold, as well as most of the writers of their favorite songs, were Jewish. Sammy Davis Jr. and Elizabeth Taylor had actually converted. After Milton Berle and Sid Caesar had begun to use Jewish variants of typical American material—Berle's twists on Red Skelton's slapstick and Caesar's skits of movie sagas had been heavy on *shtick*—Jewish stereotypes became a staple of television comedy. And in the persons of Phil Silvers, Jackie Leonard, Buddy Hackett, and Don Rickles, whose abusive "pushy" styles almost dared gentility to object, there was the complete, 180-degree turn from the hidden Jewish identities of the earlier comedians. Malamud's notion that the Jew is like everybody else "only more so" became what Albert Goldman called "the Jew as Everyman."[19] Whatever Roth's next project might be, he could perhaps anticipate less sensitivity to uses of Jews than had greeted *Goodbye, Columbus*.

This new Jewish security had not set in overnight. Even the transition in image of Israelis from wimps to warriors had begun some half-dozen years before with the popularity of Leon Uris's *Exodus*: novel, film, and song ("This Land Is Mine"). In 1961, even as Roth was concluding *Letting Go* and his marriage to Maggie, he had considered *Exodus* in "Some New Jewish Stereotypes" and had scorned the easy shift from victim to victimizer foreshadowed in the new Jewish pride. Inflicting death, even in self-defense, he pointed out, diminishes a moral heritage. Roth also scored the other, countervailing, popular myth, that of universal Jewish joviality and warmth, as spread by such as Harry Golden (*For 2c Plain, Only In America, Enjoy, Enjoy!*). The price of Golden's assertion that Jews had always felt at home among their Christian neighbors was also too high. By allowing Gentiles to comfort themselves that Jews had not suffered in the new world, the myth let them acquit themselves of having blocked Jewish access to American opportunity. Nor did Jewish experience of themselves in America, Roth knew, justify Golden's overblown assertions of warmth.

Indeed, countering the benefits of such warmth, Roth posited the anxieties of asphyxiation. He relates the experiences of his Jewish students at the Iowa Writers' Workshop, whose complaints about their overprotective families anticipated Portnoy's. These students shared not only Alex's complaint but also his forbidden desire—to be bad! Exploring that desire would create the eruption that came to be known as *Portnoy's Complaint*.

Chapter 5

The Alex Perplex

To be bad! Neil Klugman had flirted with the idea and gone back to the library. Paul, Gabe, and Lucy never got to first base with it; duty, in an age of duty, had pulled them down. It was an American ideal that traced at least to Huck Finn's glorious refusal to be civilized, and it was the underside of niceness that all "nice Jewish boys" could spot down the block or across the fence or tracks, where unparented gentile kids roved unencumbered by expectations of A's or Hebrew school or even homework.

To reveal this underside of the Jewish psyche, Roth would need release from the artistic and emotional restraints under which he had always practiced his craft. No simple matter. The writing of *Portnoy's Complaint* (1969) was a complex and indirect undertaking, a coalescence of awarenesses and events within the writer and within the age. *Portnoy*'s multiple-stage process of gestation Roth would analyze in a series of interviews and responses to critics published mostly in *Reading Myself and Others* (1975); but the shocks that induced its birth he would not disclose until *The Facts* (1988). What should become clear to the ordinary reader of these works—and should have been assumed, though it was not, by all critics—is that *Portnoy's Complaint* is no spontaneous ranting by its author, although its final drafting came in a spurt of concentrated energy that helped give it that tone.

The five years Roth took after *Letting Go* to convert Maggie's oral history into *When She Was Good* was the longest time he would ever take between published novels. But during that time he was also trying out stories, in different forms, based in his own background. The strain of maintaining his contrived Middle-American tone in the novel in progress could be relieved by some free use of his adolescent wisecracking tone in these other pieces: that tone he had so studiously striven to replace during years of absorbing the great tradition. And imagining Maggie into Lucy could be offset by imagining Newark's Weequahic boys into their wilder ethnic possibilities. Roth needed, he said, to work both veins at once:

> This continuous movement back and forth from one partially realized project to another is fairly typical of how my work evolves and the way I deal with literary frustration and uncertainty, and serves me as a means of both checking and indulging "inspiration." The idea, in part, is to keep alive fictions that draw their energy from different sources, so that when circumstances combine to rouse one or another of the sleeping beasts, there is a carcass around for it to feed on. (*RMAO* 35)

Early in that five-year span Roth worked up a two-hundred-page manuscript titled *The Jewboy*, based loosely and folkloricly on growing up in Newark, in which he gave free rein to wordplay and *kvetches* (*RMAO* 33–34). Pursuing an interest in drama (that shortly would win him a Ford Foundation grant to study the genre), he also worked up the draft of a play titled *The Nice Jewish Boy*— "in its way a less comforting, more aggressive *Abie's Irish Rose*"—which got as far into production as a 1964 reading at the American Place Theater, the nice, *shiksa*-involved Jewish boy being played by the then unknown Dustin Hoffman (*RMAO* 34). But though the dialogue revealed the surface conflicts of his characters, Roth was not sufficiently at home in stage drama to explore their "secret life," and so he gave up the project. He was now two years into the writing of Lucy's complaint; without knowing it, he was also in the early stages of writing Alex's. But neither the theme nor the form it would take was clear to Roth:

> . . . the struggle that was to be at the source of Alexander Portnoy's difficulties, and motivate his complaint, was in those early years of work still so out of focus that all I could do was recapitulate his problem *technically*, telling first the dreamy side of the story, then the story in more conventional terms and by relatively measured means. Not until I found, in the person of a troubled analysand, the voice that could speak in behalf of both the "Jewboy" (with all that word signifies to Jew and Gentile alike about aggression, appetite, and marginality) and the "nice Jewish

boy" (and what that epithet implies about repression, respectability, and social acceptance) was I able to complete a fiction that was expressive, instead of symptomatic, of the character's dilemma. (*RMAO* 35)

There would first be other stages to go. In 1964 Roth faced Maggie in court for legal separation proceedings (*Facts* 155), and subsequent telephone calls and other entanglements kept the real woman not far from the forefront of his mind. Writing *When She Was Good* continued to be an emotional strain. Its very writing was in part an attempt to exorcise Maggie from his own psyche, but whatever royalties it might bring would not free him from the burdens of her alimony: he had not had a great commercial success in his writing and he saw himself doomed by Maggie's refusal of a divorce and her insistence on claiming social, emotional, and financial rewards from his limited fame. Whatever relief Roth might have gotten on the couch, or in bed, his vocation was that of writer, and his instinct was to write himself free.

After he completed the manuscript of *When She Was Good* in mid-1966, feeling the need to break loose, Roth "almost immediately began to write a longish monologue, beside which the fetid indiscretions of *Portnoy's Complaint* [he later said] would appear to be the work of Louisa May Alcott" (*RMAO* 36). In this manic piece, his monologist delivers a slide-show lecture on sex, the slides being of the genitalia of the famous. Roth did not finish this monologue, realizing that it was "blasphemous, mean, bizarre, scatological, tasteless, [though] spirited" and therefore unpublishable. But, Roth explained,

> buried somewhere in the sixty or seventy pages were several thousand words on the subject of adolescent masturbation, a personal interlude by the lecturer, that seemed to me . . . to be funny and true, and worth saving, if only because it was the only sustained piece of writing on the subject that I could remember reading in a work of fiction. (*RMAO* 36)

This was not an attempt at personal confession, or even a deliberate attempt to explore the subject, rather an emanation from an unpublishable "writer's hijinks" that allowed Roth, he says,

> to relax my guard and go on at some length about the solitary activity that is so difficult to talk about and yet so near at hand. For me writing about the act had, at the outset, to be as secret as the act itself. (*RMAO* 37)

Roth had also embarked on still a fourth piece, an autobiographical fiction about growing up Jewish in New Jersey, to which he had assigned the tentative title *Portrait of the Artist* and for which he had invented another family living upstairs in their two-family house, based partly on families of child-hood friends but drawing themes also from writings of Roth's Jewish students at the Iowa Writers' Workshop—a family he called the Portnoys.

What his Jewish students had written about—what Roth had contrasted to Harry Golden's asserted contentment in his 1961 "Some New Jewish Stereotypes"—was the phenomenon, common in his students' early adoles-cence, of parental smothering: being watched, forever watched, by their moth-ers, and envying their gentile friends their parents' indifference. That indif-ference to the details of a son's life afforded the gentile child opportunity for sexual adventure. As Roth had noted,

> . . . in these short stories the girls to whom the Gentile friend leads the young [Jewish] narrator are never Jewish. The Jewish women are moth-ers and sisters. The sexual yearning is for the Other. The dream of the shiksa—counterpart to the Gentile dream of the Jewess, often described as 'melon breasted.' . . . [W]hat the heroes of these stories invariably learn—as the Gentile comrades disappear into other neighborhoods or into maturity—are the burdensome contradictions of their own predica-ment. (*RMAO* 143)

So many of Roth's students had written variations on this story that he now confidently regarded it as a genuine folktale, "an authentic bit of American-Jewish mythology" that could transform those Portnoys upstairs into some-thing more.

> . . . here were the fallible, oversized, anthropomorphic gods who had reigned over the households of my neighborhood; here was that leg-endary Jewish family dwelling on high, whose squabbles over French-fried potatoes, synagogue attendance, and shiksas were, admittedly, of an Olympian magnitude and splendor, but by whose terrifying kitchen light-ning storms were illuminated the values, dreams, fears, and aspirations by which we mortal Jews lived somewhat less vividly down below. (*RMAO* 39)

Roth's 1974 account of the coalescing of all these elements is pat and entertaining, though not yet complete. He had begun

> to ground the mythological in the recognizable, the verifiable, the his-torical. Though they might *derive* from Mt. Olympus (by way of Mt. Sinai), these Portnoys were going to live in a Newark and at a time and in a way I could vouch for by observation and experience.

This required the first person, dropping the restraining conventions of *Portrait of the Artist*, and releasing

> the Portnoys from their role as supporting actors in another family's drama. They would not get star billing until sometime later, when out of odds and ends of *Portrait of the Artist* I liked best, I began to write something I called 'A Jewish Patient Begins His Analysis.' (*RMAO* 40)

From all this experimentation Roth was almost prepared to fashion the work that, after taking the country by storm, would be criticized for being a mere personal rant. Roth's account concludes:

> This turned out to be a brief story narrated by the Portnoys' son, Alexander, purportedly his introductory remarks to his psychoanalyst. And who was this Alexander? None other than that Jewish boy who used to turn up time after time in the stories written by those Jewish graduate students back in the Iowa Writers' Workshop: the "watched-over" Jewish son with his sexual dream of The Other. Strictly speaking, the writing of *Portnoy's Complaint* began with discovering Portnoy's voice—more accurately, his mouth—and discovering, along with it, the listening ear: the silent Dr. Spielvogel. The psychoanalytic monologue— a narrative technique whose rhetorical possibilities I'd been availing myself of for years, only not on paper—was to furnish the means by which I thought I might convincingly draw together the fantastic element of *The Jewboy* and the realistic documentation of *Portrait of the Artist* and *The Nice Jewish Boy*. And a means, too, of legitimizing the obscene preoccupations of the untitled slide show on the subject of sexual parts. Instead of the projection screen (and the gaping), the couch (and the unveiling); instead of gleeful, sadistic voyeurism—brash, shameful, masochistic, euphoric, vengeful, conscience-ridden exhibitionism. Now I could perhaps to begin. (*RMAO* 40–41)

The birthing of the novel, however, was attended by two unexpected events; one would provide Roth with a sense of destiny about himself that would surface again two decades later, and the other would both provide the final thrust into publication of *Portnoy's Complaint* and hover at the edge of Roth's fictive imagination for the next half decade. The first event was an attack of appendicitis that brought him to within two hours of death, left his stomach filled with poisonous pus, had him delirious from peritonitis, and kept him in the hospital for most of two and a half months; he had, as Albert Goldman would put it, "wrestled the *Malekhamoves*—the angel of death—to a fall" and felt prophetically charged with new life. That and his convalescence in Florida, shared time with Ann Mudge that did not allow him to write, exacerbated his itch to get back to *Portnoy*, parts of which he had brought out in periodicals. But over the project hung another cloud; the enthusiastic responses to episodes already published had sparked speculation in publishing circles that the whole work, if it were finished and brought out as a book, would pay handsome royalties. Maggie was now working in publishing, resentfully drinking, and positioning herself, through phone calls and legal inquiries that Roth had heard about, to make herself known as his muse and to turn a considerable portion of any royalties into alimony. The prospect of a custody battle over the as-yet-unborn novel was enough to protract the labor. It might take years or leave the fetus stillborn. The other event, which Roth would fictionalize six years later in *My Life as a Man* but not disclose to the public until twenty years later in *The Facts*, was Maggie's sudden death in a car accident in Central Park.

The conflict of Roth's feelings at the latter piece of news one can only begin to imagine. Commanding his responses into order and out of guilt would preoccupy Roth personally and fictively for at least two decades. But the immediate practical effect was liberation, the end of the waking nightmare. She was out of his life, and he, despite wishes and fantasies, was guiltless of her blood. Anything he published now he would own himself. No court could limit his activities. After the funeral (Jewish, at her obsessed request) and the partings from her now grown children, for whom he had done some parenting a decade before, he returned to his manuscript and within a few days made hasty reservations to lose himself in the Yaddo artists' colony at Saratoga Springs (he had gone there two years before to finish *When She Was Good*)[1] so as to bring to publishable light the text of *Portnoy's Complaint*. He went by bus—a car might, at flagging moments, tempt him out of the concentrated discipline of staying in his cabin at his typewriter—and he was at work from the time he left the Port Authority bus terminal, "rereading on the long trip up the thruway the rough first draft of the last two chapters of [his] book" (*Facts* 156). His sense of freedom, converted to total concentration, allowed him to work in isolation "twelve and fourteen hours a day until the book was done, and then [he] took the bus back down, feeling triumphant and indestructible."

Roth provided his accounts of the writing of *Portnoy's Complaint* long after publication, to answer that strain of criticism that would equate him with his protagonist and the novel with a transcript of his therapy. But the experience, he has said, liberated more than his unwritten life; it liberated him as a writer

from an apprentice's literary models, particularly from the awesome graduate-school authority of Henry James, whose *Portrait of a Lady* had been a virtual handbook during the early drafts of *Letting Go*, and from the example of Flaubert, whose detached irony in the face of a small-town woman's disastrous delusions had me obsessively thumbing through the pages of *Madame Bovary* during the years I was searching for the perch from which to observe the people in *When She Was Good*. (*Facts* 157)

From now on his characters could sound like the Jews among whom he had been most comfortable in his youth and like those popular comics now teaching rising inflection to the general population. The most endearing among these, for Roth, had long been Henny Youngman, whom he had seen on stage at the Roxy when he was ten. Considering in 1973 whether he still viewed himself as a disciple of Youngman, he concluded:

I do now. Also of Jake the Snake H., a middle-aged master of invective and insult, and a repository of lascivious neighborhood gossip (and, amazingly, the father of a friend of mine), who owned the corner candy store in the years when I much preferred the pinball machine to the company of my parents. I am also a disciple of my older brother's friend and navy buddy, Arnold G., an unconstrained Jewish living-room clown whose indecent stories of failure and confusion in sex did a little to demythologize the world of the sensual for me in early adolescence. As Jake the Snake demythologized the world of the respectable. As Henny Youngman, whining about family and friends while eliciting laughable squeaks from the violin (the very violin that was to make of every little Jewish boy, myself included, a world-famous, urbane, poetic, dignified, and revered Yehudi), demythologized our yearnings for cultural superiority—or for superiority through culture—and argued by his shlemieldom that it was in the world of domestic squabble and unending social compromise, rather than on the concert stage, that the Jews of his audience might expect to spend their lives. (*RMAO* 81)

Whether the liberation was into a discovery of his own voice and subject or out of the bonds of social contract with his people would be a subject of debate among critics for almost the rest of Roth's career. Put another way, would Roth now be using the voices and anxieties of Jews to probe their, or America's, repression or to denigrate Jewish ethical values? Should America feel for Portnoy or revile him and his author as turncoats?

Alex Portnoy wants to be bad and to be guilt-free. He manages neither. Sexually violate and curse as he may, his soul belongs to those who owned his first years; and Sophie and Jack stand for goodness. How far can he distance

himself from them when his only outlet is Dr. Spielvogel, sitting silently opposite the couch, and when all his words are but a preface to dubious action? Any
healing (highly unlikely) will have to take place after the novel has concluded.
Behind Spielvogel looms Sophie, "the most unforgettable character," as the
Reader's Digest would put it, Alex "has ever met," her original female musk
Oedipally perfuming—and endowing with moral sanction—every woman he
will meet from his first-grade teacher to the Israeli who finally wrestles him
into humiliated submission. Jack, his unworthy Oedipal rival, is a nebish with
heart—but away from Sophie able to move policies and agents—who wants
for Alex opportunities beyond the eighth grade and a company desk. The insurance company for which Jack sells policies to the blacks of the inner city is
located off in Massachusetts, where the pilgrims still hold sway; on his company
stationery a picture of the Mayflower underscores the awareness that Jack and
his crew of customers have yet to land in the real America. In hopes that his son
can complete the journey, he sacrifices in heat and spikes of light. But Alex
can move past his father only in paroxysms of guilt, alternately ranting and
weeping. "Doctor, what should I rid myself of, tell me, the hatred or the love?"

At thirty-three, now Assistant Commissioner for Human Opportunity
for the City of New York, Portnoy spends 274 pages poring over the causes and
effects of this ambivalence toward parents. He rehashes his attempts to free
himself through sex, reiterating its failure to bring pleasure or release. He is
"torn by desires that are repugnant to [his] conscience, and a conscience repugnant to [his] desires." To free himself from goodness, from being the "nice
Jewish boy" that his job description appears to underscore, he would be secretly
bad, sexually licentious, except that the shame such behavior engenders only
intensifies the problem. He wants "to be bad—and enjoy it!" But he can't, at
least not without help. Desperately he prays to the deity Spielvogel: "Bless
me with manhood! Make me brave! Make me strong! Make me *whole*! Enough
being a nice Jewish boy, publicly pleasing my parents, while privately pulling
my putz! Enough!"

Why this need to "put the id back in Yid" at age thirty-three? Perhaps
because he had not satisfied other needs earlier, especially the adolescent's
defining need for separation and privacy. Alex's only chance for that had been
the one venue from which he could close out his prying mother, the bathroom
(though his family did not accept the closing even of this door). Another adolescent need, to be one of the guys, he could fulfill by swapping fantasies on the
corner and then playing them out in that bathroom. The danger of discovery and
the realization that what he was doing flew in the face of tribal taboos gave the
activity zest and himself identity.

Unable to stand up against Sophie, Alex had thus learned in youth to
substitute masturbation for assertion, to drown out her carping plaints with a

sexy blonde voice in his head urging on "Big Boy." Then in adulthood, as he exchanged this fantasy Gentile for the real-life women he met, he reduced them similarly to stereotypes: "The Pumpkin," "The Pilgrim," and "The Monkey" were all the forbidden *shiksa* in her respective guises as Middle-American wholesome, old New England establishment, and blue-collar ex-hillbilly. Among them, in Alex's recountings, only the Monkey approaches a rounded character with needs and capacity to love. But sexually liberated, nearly fulfilling Portnoy's fantasy, she is the most threatening. Her being almost illiterate (though a highly successful professional model) and slightly whorish affronts the Jewish parents buried within him. Sophie with the breadknife lingers in the back of his mind ready to castrate as once she would cut him bread and wave away constipating French fries. Alex must cast his Monkey off. After taking her as far away from Sophie as possible, he leaves her on the ledge of an Athens hotel, threatening to jump, while he flies off to Israel, to another mythic bosom. Portnoy's assertions of penile prowess—his personal myth of the battering ram that could break down barriers—have left him alienated and lonely. "How have I come to be such an enemy and flayer of myself? And so alone! Oh, so alone! Nothing but *self*! Locked up in *me*!"

Alex's only happy memories of his Jewish boyhood are not of solitary but of participatory activity. His most religious experiences, though, had nothing to do with *shul*. Flying into Israel, in the chapter ironically titled "In Exile," Portnoy daydreams of what had been for him the perfect Jewish homeland, the Weequahic neighborhood field where on Sunday mornings he had watched the "men" play softball. They were Jews of every station, and teachers of the art of kibitzing, and he had supposed that he would always be there, even when grown, to complete his Sundays after *his* participation with *his* own wife and children and family meal and radio shows, in a Jewish national home where he would be totally American. Alex was too young then to ask whether this ball field was any different from those that had nurtured the heroes of his bubble-gum cards. But the "men" were communal parents. His own father had not played, had been able only occasionally to be a spectator; but through membership in this circumcised Weequahic tribe, Alex felt connected to the larger Jewish peoplehood.

Alex's apprenticeship for being one of the "men" was served in two illusory worlds of safe haven, a sunny world of center field and a misty world of fat and sweat. On weekdays after school Alex had played baseball, the most self-defining of team sports, and once a month he had gone with his father to the Turkish baths. These totally male spheres, with their initiations and ceremonies, had provided respite from the suffocation of Sophie. Baseball represented the opportunity for individual grace. Unlike other team sports where one could be lost in the huddle or the whirl of bodies, baseball focused instant after instant on the solitary player. The grace of the ball player is a common theme in Roth, beginning quite early. In "You Can't Tell a Man by The Song He Sings," the sixth story in the *Goodbye, Columbus* collection, it is relative prowess in baseball that distinguishes the doer from the talker among school-yard kids, and in "Recollections from Beyond the Last Rope" Roth mused on the ball player's poise and sense of control, which he as a child had practiced in his cellar winters at Newark to impress the girls of summer at Bradley Beach.

> I practiced not only throwing but standing, waiting, retrieving. I knew exactly what I wanted to look like; and it was some years after I'd stopped vacationing at Bradley that I saw in Florence what I'd had in mind—it was Michelangelo's David. He would have knocked the girls at Bradley for a loop. Imagine that what he is holding up to his breast is not a sling, but a glove; imagine in that throwing arm, loose but ready at his side, not a rock but a baseball; see the way each joint picks up the weight from the one above; see how he peers down for the signal beneath those brows. See all that, and you'll see what I was trying for in my cellar all winter long. (45)

That same sense of poise and control Alex Portnoy had known in center field. There everything was clear. He knew who he was and what he had to do; practice let him do it without endless thinking about moral consequences. And since Sophie knew nothing about its mysteries, there was no question of pleasing or disappointing her, or need—or opportunity—to disappear within the team. "Is it me?" was not at war with "Is it us?" A center fielder had sovereignty over his life. Portnoy tells his doctor, "there are people who feel in life the ease, the self-assurance, the simple and essential affiliation with what is going on, that I used to feel as the center fielder for the Seabees." Those people, at ease under spacious skies, were Americans.

Another escape into a purely male world had been Portnoy's monthly visit with his father to the local steam baths, a return to a primeval pre-Portnoy era, "some sloppy watery time, before there were families such as we know them." Here Jack is relaxed, in charge of himself; and Alex not only feels the warm physical bond to his father in a "natural" domain "without *goyim* and women" but also ". . . lose[s] touch instantaneously with that ass-licking little boy who runs home after school with A's in his hand. . . ." Like the ballfield, this haven from oppression remains a dream, a time out from his two nemeses. Not only from women, tainted by Sophie, but also from *goyim*, tainted by Jewish suspicion: for beyond the bounds of Weequahic, in headlines and table talk, is gentile America, and Gentiles make the country unkosher. Alex may continually assert to Spielvogel that he is more than a "nice Jewish boy," that he *"happen*[s] *also to be a human being!"* but neither principled egalitarianism nor all his familiarity with the America of movies and radio can make "natural" the Gentiles his parents have taught him to distrust. Interludes in the bath house could expunge them from consciousness, but afterward—and long after—it was he who would be the alien. Seeing himself at the mercy of the *goyim*, he could approach them only obliquely through their daughters: he could *"conquer* America" by debasing "Thereal McCoy" or her nicknamed variants.

But it is he who is subdued—as a man, as an American, as a Jew. He runs to Israel to see if he can regain two out of three. He finds that he cannot. If America was "Thereal McCoy," Israel is Sophie (or Naomi, the soldier who looks like her), taboo and therefore impregnable to conquest by sex. Naomi's rejection, first driving him into a frenzied attempt at rape, leaves him impotent. Portnoy recoils, no more at home in Israel than in New York or soon-to-be-*judenrein* Weequahic. The Jew in him, cultivated by fear, had prevented his entering fully into America; the American had all but eviscerated the Jew. Powerless to assert a self, he is unmanned. The obscenity of his situation leaves him on the couch unpacking his heart like a whore with words. What words can they be but obscenities?

If this sounds as grim as the conflicts of *Letting Go*, perhaps it is because the sound so far described is incomplete. That novel had presented the anguish of young men trying to achieve manhood by doing good; this, of one trying hopelessly to achieve manhood by being bad. For a Jew of their upbringing, the second quest is harder because it is perverse. And being perverse, being a total inversion of normal expectation, it is comic. To have to try, to strive, to be bad is on the surface absurd, yet for Jews of this upbringing—and for many readers—licentious behavior would have required a willful effort (that some were putting forth). What made a whole country laugh was an absurdity recognizable. Not the daring (for its time) language, not just the "Jewish joke" in which Portnoy complains of being trapped—even though the novel ends in a punch line. This is a comically absurd novel because Portnoy's moral anguish threatens the reader in a way Gabe's did not. The reader shares Portnoy's surrender of illusions about a higher moral plane, about sacrifice being noble. That illusion had been stripped away between 1962 and 1969. (Roth would come to speak of the sixties as "the demythologizing decade" [*RMAO* 86].) Along with Portnoy, the reader must also flinch; and among the legion of theories about what constitutes humor, laughter as a way of handling pain has some application here, as much for the reader as for poor Portnoy. Roth would say a few years later that in this novel "comedy was the means by which the character synthesized and articulated his sense of himself and his predicament" (*RMAO* 75). It was also the synthesizing means for the reader. Roth's conversion in discipleship from James and Flaubert to Jake the Snake and Henny

Youngman was also attended by a new respect for Kafka's sense of "guilt . . . as a comic idea" (*RMAO* 22). Burlesquing remorse and victimization might, by its very excess, render the most painful self-recognition bearable. Mixing the burlesque with passages of awakening sexuality and adolescent burden could render a complaint like Portnoy's sufferable in howls of resignation. The less curable, the more likely such a disorder is for Kafkaesque treatment, whose very essence is hopelessness. And Alex's monologue—Roth's novel—is only an introductory statement, the opening exposition of patient to analyst. Nowhere does it proceed into the treatment itself, still less near to a cure.

Nor was the sickness just some exotic Jewish complaint. The fictive dictionary definition of **Portnoy's Complaint**, which precedes the title page begins; "A disorder in which strongly-felt ethical and altruistic impulses are perpetually warring with extreme sexual longings, often of a perverse nature." The bedrock of this comedy was an inconsistency between ethics and longings felt throughout American society. In the 1960s not only liberated Jews were trying to live by a fate-thwarted conflict of codes; so was the nation. Camelot, as the Kennedy administration had been dubbed, called into service idealistic young men like this Assistant Commissioner for Human Opportunity to uphold the family—those home movies out of Hyannisport and the White House—and pour their energies sacrificially into civic amelioration. But Camelot also offered them partying at night, glamor and movie stars, the license to experiment with forbidden sexual pleasures, the right to fulfill their most primitive instincts and passions. Like King Arthur's "city built to music" it depended on a harmony of idealism and trust, and when the music stopped, shattered by assassination, divisive war, and the cynical foreclosures of the new Mordreds, it left not only the best and the brightest but a whole once-idealistic nation suspended in anger and impotence. Needing defenses against the compromised notion of good, the young had begun celebrating the natural life. A capacity to experience that life to the full might be a proof against the despairing consequences of their parents' values. There might be hope in the joy of badness. Comedy is built on tensions of inconsistency, comedy of the absurd on thrashings amidst hopelessness. America in 1969 knew Portnoy's basic conflict. You didn't have to be Jewish to feel the schizophrenia of the age.

After Roth returned from Yaddo, as he tells in *The Facts*, his agent arranged for a landmark contract with a huge advance from Random House. From the receptions to those episodes earlier published in *Esquire, Partisan Review*, and Theodore Solotaroff's incipient *New American Review*, the book, he knew—and publisher Bennett Cerf knew—would be a blockbuster.

Indeed, the sensation caused by this publishing event has never been duplicated. It was the perfect emblem of a turning point in American history from which there would be no going back. This was February 1969. Hippies, flower children, the Beatles, rebellion against the older generation were the order of the day. Major elements of that rebellion were freedom of language and openness about sex. The cover once off, the subject would never startle so again, nor would its language. Nixon had been in office less than a month. The events of the election of the previous fall had left the nation angry, the generations at war. *Portnoy's Complaint* would be a national cathartic (a function, though, that would cast a shadow over the novel's status as a work of literature). Even the anticipation was part of the event. Review copies were out to the periodicals (as is usual) weeks before the February 21 publication date, and reviewers were now jockeying to be first into print. Geoffrey Wolff, writing in the February 10 *Washington Post*, spoke for many when he said that "Roth has composed what for me is the most important book of my generation." In the February 7 *Life*, the nation's family magazine, a review by Albert Goldman prepared America for Alexander Portnoy with a long piece largely about his creator. Its two-page opening spread, seven eighths occupied by pictures of Roth and, as his shadow, Franz Kafka, was introduced with the announcement, "'Portnoy's Complaint' by Philip Roth looms as a **Wild Blue Shocker** and the American novel of the sixties." The opening portion of Goldman's article was not a piece of criticism but a piece of history:

> The publication of a book is not often a major event in American culture. Most of our classics, when they first appeared, met with disappointing receptions, and even the much-balleyhooed best-sellers of recent years have rarely cut a great swath, outside the lanes of publicity and journalism. But this year a real literary-cultural event portends and every shepherd of public opinion, every magus of criticism, is wending his way toward its site. Gathered at an old New York City inn called Random House, at the stroke of midnight on the 21st of February in this 5,729th year since the creation of the world, they will hail the birth of a new American hero, Alexander Portnoy. A savior and scapegoat of the '60s, Portnoy is destined at the Christological age of 33 to take upon himself all the sins of sexually obsessed modern man and expiate them in a tragicomic crucifixion. The gospel that records the passion of this mock messiah is a slender, psychotic novel by Philip Roth called *Portnoy's Complaint* (the title is a triple pun signifying that the hero is a whiner, a lover, and a sick man). So great is the fame of the book even before its publication that it is being hailed as *the* book of the present decade and as an American masterwork in the tradition of *Huckleberry Finn*.

Apparently, Jewishness had arrived: for all America, 1969 could be 5,729 and sexual adventurers could be circumcised. Goldman's article went on to tell that parts of the novel had already been passed around at fashionable parties where guests had been invited to read sections serially at table, "Portnoy" being the password of the day, and compared the publisher's final cutting and binding of pages to the secret cutting of heroin for injection into the national veins. What with book club contracts and advances on softcover and movie rights, the novel had "earned almost a million dollars prior to the first press run." That run of 150,000 copies would be tripled and 420,000 hardcover copies sold within a year. *Portnoy's Complaint* would give Roth financial independence and the opportunity to write about whatever he chose for decades.

Yet for Roth's career as a writer all the personal fame and notoriety was less important than the responses of serious critics and of the organized Jewish community. And the Jewish reaction was important more for the material it would give him than for any immediate concern about pleasing a constituency. The popular media quickly identified Alex with Roth, and the talk was as much about masturbation as Jewish mothers and more about both than about ethical angst. Jacqueline Susann quipped that she would invite him onto a talk show but she would not want to touch his hand. (This from the author of *Valley of the Dolls!*) The press had him secretly engaged to Barbra Streisand, whom he had never even met. Nor was engagement what Roth sought. He shortly broke off the relationship with Ann Mudge, despite her having seen him through nightmares of marital war and peritonitis delirium. It was not just that she was unable comfortably to introduce the arch-Jew into her patrician WASP family or that she shared with Maggie, for all their social differences, a reaction against her origins that made Philip a cause as much as a person (*Facts* 133, 158). He was determined, for the foreseeable future, to give no more hostages to fortune. Not even Streisand could have stood a chance.

The literary and pulpit reactions to *Portnoy's Complaint* were mixed but never mild. It seemed as if everybody bought the book, everybody laughed, and then everybody sat down to decide whether, having bought the book and having laughed, they had acted correctly. Part of that decision would depend on age. When Wolff spoke of the novel as "the most important book of [his] generation," he was speaking roughly for Roth's contemporaries. So did some of the younger rabbis, at least those of a somewhat liberal persuasion. Rabbi Eugene Borowitz, a few years Roth's senior, finessed the issue by neutering high praise with an observation: the titled complaint, in its psycho-medical sense, while astonishingly true for his and Roth's generation, was quickly becoming a piece of history, no longer affecting Jewish children because they were now being spoiled rather than repressed.[2] Borowitz does not use these as relative terms—as if "spoiled" were not what Roth's Jewish Iowa Workshop students must have seemed to their unwatched gentile friends—rather, in his zeal to affirm Roth's "moral earnestness," Borowitz treats a cultural heritage as if it could transform itself overnight by adopting new child-rearing fashions. But beyond changing fashions was burgeoning size: the very numbers of the young fostered both change and continuity. The sixties baby-boomers were a larger group than all who had come of age in the preceding several decades combined. Not only were they overwhelming their parents with a culture of their own, but their ways of assimilating the traditions of their parents were often obscure, even to themselves. They protested too much to acquit themselves entirely of being papa's and momma's continuators. In 1992, playwright Donald Margulies, considering the forces that contributed to his writing *Sight Unseen*, testified:

> I was 15 when I first read "Portnoy's Complaint" and for all the wrong reasons; I was scanning for tales of sexy shiksas, but what I found were stunning insights into what it meant to be a Jew and a man. Even though he was nearly a generation older, Roth and I seemed to have grown up together, surrounded by many of the same relatives, sharing many similar experiences. He opened a window for me and let fresh air into a stuffy Brooklyn apartment and gave me (and still gives me) the courage to write what I know.[3]

The children of Borowitz's readers, it seems, had not been so unaffected, or so homogeneous, after all. But in 1969 it was grownups, ranging in age and affiliation, who were voicing official opinion.

Surprisingly, many rabbinic and other Jewishly affiliated reviewers knew Roth's critical essays of the early sixties and were prepared to parry them. His insistence that a novel is not a position paper and that mature readers do not require clichés of Jewish saintliness was to them smoke and mirrors. These spokesmen would identify Portnoy's vilifications as Roth's deep-harbored anti-Semitism. In supposed essays in criticism, many argued circularly from premises accepting such identification to conclusions proving it. The conflict for these makers of opinion was often that the literary distinction was a luxury a culture under attack could not afford, and this Jewish culture, now under attack from its own children, would eventually be under attack from traditional enemies who would use against it this testimony of one of its own sons. Some of the less fearful dismissed the book as a mere collection of gags, asserting that the motive for trying to satirize Jewishness, if it was not anti-Semitism, was vulgarity, the venting of low impulses in comic *shtick*. Any work this frenetic in its accusations of Jewish practices, they said, could not be respectable literature; and Alex's anguish belied Roth's alleged artistic distance. Many, in many moods, identified the problem as *galut*—the Diaspora. But swept up in Zionist solutions, Jewish leaders often declared the remedy to be *aliyah*, missing the satirical reference to Israel as "The Exile" for an Americanized Jew. The least accusatory detractors just felt that Roth lacked an abiding faith in the peoplehood of the Jews and that perhaps his satire had consumed itself and could be considered done (Already!).

As to the argument that *Portnoy's Complaint* posed an external threat to the Jewish people, it had at its core an analogy. Portnoy's lusts for *shiksas* were precisely what the traditional anti-Semite said all Jews felt, what the Aryan accused the would-be-defiling Jew of trying to perpetrate. Marie Syrkin raised the decade-old Julius Streicher and Joseph Goebbels references (they had appeared after *Goodbye, Columbus*) in her *Midstream*[4] review:

> . . . under the cartoon of the Jewish joke leers the anti-Jewish stereotype. Portnoy polluting his environment is one such. When he graduates to the fascination of female "apertures and openings," his penis never loses its Jewish consciousness. Like Julius Streicher's satanic Jewboy lusting after Aryan maidens, Portnoy seeks blonde *shikses*. . . . [In the] baleful stereotype . . . [which] . . . emerges from under the banter . . . [t]he dark Jew seeking to defile the fair Nordic is standard stuff. . . . [T]here is little to choose between [Goebbels'] and Roth's interpretation of what animates Portnoy. In both views the Jewish male is not drawn to a particular girl who is gentile, but by a gentile "background" which he must violate sexually.

Syrkin quotes raunchy text (with dashes in place of the four-letter words) to support each claim. She scores the "Jewboy," but does not assess the "Nice Jewish Boy" at war with him. But her main fallacy is the one inherent in all reasoning by analogy: the analogy goes only so far and then the two subjects being compared part company. The parting here comes at the point of motive. Streicher's and Goebbels's motives, we may say (at least for these purposes), were clear. But Roth's purpose in giving these thoughts to Portnoy is the bone of all the critical contention that was emerging. Portnoy, here before Dr. Spielvogel, is not proud of these urges. They are part of his sickness. He would rid himself of them as well as he would rid himself of the parental inhibitions that have magnified them in his unconscious. That his whole background has made him anti-*goyish* is also a serious problem. He laughs over his having been an investigator who helped expose the WASP hero of the quiz-show scandals:

> Yes, I was one happy yiddel down there in Washington, a little Stern gang of my own, busily exploding Charlie's honor and integrity, while simultaneously becoming lover to that aristocratic Yankee beauty whose forebears arrived on these shores in the seventeenth century. Phenomenon known as Hating Your Goy And Eating One Too. (233)

Syrkin extends her accusation of Roth to embrace Portnoy's sick glee in recollections such as this. To have Portnoy admit to these vindictive feelings and to sharing his father's exhortations about the absurdity of the whole Christian premise—feelings shared by a huge proportion of his Jewish readers!—is from Syrkin's point of view dangerous to Jewish life in a pluralistic society. (To the dedicated labor-Zionist in Syrkin, the reminder about the Stern gang was not very helpful either.[5]) Yet in assigning to Portnoy thoughts that resemble Nazi stereotypes Roth needed no more vicious a motive than a wish to underscore a main conflict of Diaspora life: that the conditions of living as a minority create urges to assimilate into the majority and that guilt over those urges creates anger directed against what is seen as the oppression of the majority. That aspect of being "bad" is part of Roth's subject, not as an endorsement of enemy propaganda but as an issue of identity and freedom.

Perhaps the most outright condemnation on grounds of comforting enemies came from Gershom Scholem, writing in Hebrew in *Haaretz*.[6] Scholem begins with the premise that "anti-Semites [having] long dreamed of defaming the Jew by producing literature intended to reveal his degeneracy and corruption, particularly in matters of sex," but failing for want of "authentic knowledge of the Jewish way of life," are now handed their model by "a brash young Jew who knows that way of life in all its essential atmosphere, and does their work for them."

> Here in the center of Roth's revolting book . . . stands the loathsome figure whom the anti-Semites have conjured in their imagination and portrayed in their literature, and a Jewish author, a highly gifted if perverted artist, offers all the slogans which for them are priceless.

Scholem will not be deterred by arguments about literature.

> Let the Pollyannas not tell us that what we have here is satire. . . . The fact is that the hero of a best-seller, avidly acquired by the public, proclaims (and lives his proclamation) that his behavior is shaped by a single lust which becomes the slogan of his life: to get "*shikse* cunt."

For this, "the book for which all anti-Semites have been praying," Scholem says, all Jews except "the author who revels in obscenities" will pay.

> I daresay that with the next turn of history, not long to be delayed, this book will make all of us defendants at court. . . . This book will be quoted to us—and how it will be quoted! They will say to us: Here you have the testimony from one of your own artists . . . an authentic Jewish witness.

This is the man whom you have summoned to the dialogue between Israel and the Diaspora. This is the man whose hero finally complains about the *chutzpah* of the kibbutz girl, the Jewess emancipated from the oppressive nightmare of Judaism, because she will not do him the honor of serving as his Jewish *shikse*. This is the man who pours out his heart to the public, whom he mockingly calls by the name of his analyst, Dr. Spielvogel.

"I wonder what price *k'lal yisrael* [the world Jewish community]—and there is such an entity in the eyes of the Gentiles—is going to pay for this book. Woe to us on that day of reckoning!"

An American reader might well have wondered whether Gershom Scholem was serious. An Israeli psychiatrist found his fears "more ridiculous than any one of Portnoy's absurd fears or all of them put together . . . [for] . . . [t]he Goyim who want to hate us will, with or without Portnoy, never run out of ammunition. . . ."[7] But Scholem was deadly serious. Whatever he might say elsewhere about trial of the Jewish soul by sin in a mystic, remote age, this book and this man, he avers, is a contemporary threat. To Scholem it is hardly a novel; it is a tract. Portnoy and Spielvogel are mere devices for Roth's spewings into the public ear. Scholem does not even read the book as an American phenomenon. Or if he does, he reads America as vulnerable to—or possibly responsible for—all the effects to come of the Nazism he had known in his own life in Europe.

When respondents to the *Haaretz* piece objected that Scholem's article confused literature with history or that these were an aspect of Diaspora responses that it was well worth knowing about, Scholem reiterated his position. He had been talking, he said, about the effect of the book—worse than *The Protocols of the Elders of Zion* because insider evidence—for which "the Jewish people are going to pay a price. . . ." Toward the end of this defense of his earlier remarks, he includes a quotation (changed slightly in its double translation back and forth across the ocean) from Roth's "Writing About Jews" and curiously mixes a concession to literature with a sense of doom.

> I recently read that Roth's book has now appeared in German translation. Marvelous news indeed!
>
> It is quite correct that we need hide nothing for fear of, "What will the Gentiles say?" I have repeated this obvious and simple truth in some of my articles condemning Jewish apologetics. But we have to know and acknowledge that for speaking such "truth", even this kind of "truth from America", the full price will have to be paid. He who states this fact should not be blamed for doing so.

It is impossible to know whether Scholem's jeremiad has had any prophetic merit. It does not seem so. The very pursuit of the question would require investigative techniques that Kafka could hardly imagine. There seemed to be no sudden surge or overt demonstration occasioned by the publication of the novel in Poland in 1986 as "Kompleks Portnoya," whose 50,000 copy first printing sold out immediately and won for its translator, Anna Kolyszko, the annual award of the Polish Translators Union. Nor was there any reaction but laughter and praise when an avant-garde Lodz theater presented the translation as a play—here Portnoy unshaven in hospital pajamas delivering a ninety-minute monologue—to a "captivated" audience in 1988.[8] Whether anti-Semitism (as distinguished from traditional Jew hatred on grounds of religious objection) is prompted by behavior or competition from a threatening Jewish presence[9] or arises as an echo whenever there is social unrest even in the relative absence of Jews,[10] it tends to be ignited by effects other than those of fiction. And the new nationalisms need no *Portnoy's Complaint* to justify their surging xenophobia.

The rationale of the less frightened but merely revolted critics was that the vulgarity proceeded from infectious self-hatred. Syrkin's review embraces both objections. Alongside its concern with a clear and present danger, it is representative of many reactions of the Jewish reviewing core in its shifts of grounds within standard terms of literary criticism. Syrkin reasons frequently by definition. She identifies a category that the novel is allegedly striving to fill and then shows how it fails to meet the criteria for that category. She calls the book bad satire because it cannot make up its mind; she calls Alexander Portnoy "unconvincing" as an emancipated Jew because—she blithely generalizes—"an emancipated Jew does not invariably refer to gentile girls as *shikses*; his vocabulary and imagination are more flexible." She posits a restricted category called "human being" and denies Portnoy membership because "no trace of any intellectual or social concerns is permitted to smudge the contour of Portnoy as sketched by Roth." That Portnoy is speaking in pain in an analytic first session, unloading his whole Complaint, does not influence Syrkin's appraisal:

> His scholastic excellence and the post he occupies do not serve as amplifications of his personality; instead they are further Jewish demerits hung on him like tags: Jews may be smart students and be interested in social causes but beware what is within. Roth's scalpel exposes not only the dirt behind the respectable facade of the Jewish family, but the wretched creature cowering behind the much-touted Jewish intelligence and devotion to liberal causes. At any rate Portnoy never voices an idea or expresses a generous emotion. A total phony, presumably, and a rebuke to all those Jews who get high grades and profess to be socially involved.

Is the book, then, in Syrkin's view, an attack on the phoniness and hard-heartedness of Jewish intellectuals? Even Syrkin acknowledges that that is not its intent, just its effect. But, she asserts, Roth's intent to make Portnoy's condition a "disorder" (in the words of the fictive medical definition of the **Complaint**) fails its own test of complexity:

> Where is a single scene in which the patient suffering from this conflict [between strongly felt ethical and altruistic impulses and extreme sexual longings] appears as an ethical or moral being? The reduction of Portnoy to a series of compulsive sexual practices dehumanizes him, and the author's chief way of redeeming his hero from anonymity is to label him "Jewish."

But, one may ask, how does someone "appear as" an ethical or moral human being in a complaint? Only through the recounting of deeds, hopes, fears, impulses. All his life Portnoy had done his homework and followed the rules, and now he has seen others who had flouted them achieve success and fame. What, if not "ethical impulses," is it that keeps him from enjoying being bad? Syrkin's only answer is that when he cries out that he has become "'the son in the Jewish joke,' he is chanting Roth's themesong."

Another category Syrkin raises is the false comparison some critics have made with Bellow's *Herzog*. She has known Herzog, and Portnoy is no Herzog. One is a "human being" presented with "rich humor"; the other a "caricature" in a "farce." When Portnoy gets his comeuppance from the Sabra in Israel, Syrkin sees him writhing "unchastened" on the floor. Her proof is Alex's own words: "Ow, my heart! And in Israel! Where other Jews find refuge, sanctuary and peace, Portnoy now perishes! Where other Jews flourish, I now expire!" A less angry Marie Syrkin might have seen a kind of chastening here. She knew her English literature well and could quote at length from the poets. Surely, had she no program of her own, she would have recognized the echo of Byron's Childe Harold pronouncing on his exiled self in the third person. And perhaps in that and in other variations of tone she might have begun to see something else going on besides Roth's chanting his theme song, perhaps Portnoy's author faintly mocking him, taking him less seriously than Syrkin's righteousness would allow. In failing the novel for not *being* another *Herzog*, Syrkin never raises the question of whether Roth *intended* another *Herzog*. Clearly he was limiting himself by the form of the introductory analytic session—and its controlling anger—to a narrative point of view that could not explore the many sidedness of character and situation that *Herzog* encompasses.

As to the range of Roth's intents, Syrkin is easily guided by her own responses. And in this she is typical of many critics over the years. If Roth presents a double point of view on any subject, they will type him with the more stridently expressed side and see any characters who oppose what they take to be Roth's point of view as mere surrogates for themselves. Syrkin sees such inclusion as a deliberate debating point, not as part of the fiction. In this case, she decides, Roth is warding off anticipated criticism by putting the obvious accusation of Portnoy as a self-hating Jew into the mouth of the sabra, giving Roth the appearance of being above the battle. As if there were no sound fictive reason for having Naomi seal the doom that sends Portnoy packing to seek Spielvogel, Syrkin reads the episode as a strategy in Roth's war with her and her colleagues. They cannot seize on Naomi's words since "[t]o quote Roth against Roth would be a reductio ad absurdum." But Syrkin can expose the stratagem and reduce the reductio.

Syrkin also scores what she sees as Roth's obvious intent to shock in introducing into literature all the four-letter words that Syrkin apologizes for being unable to quote. Having declared the motive, she pronounces its failure: the language is not new. Witness Joyce and Lawrence. What is new is its obscene use. *Ulysses* had been cleared of obscenity charges because the words in question were not used as "dirt for dirt's sake." Lawrence had used them in *Lady Chatterly's Lover* "romantically rather than obscenely." Syrkin's own last words on the subject are an attempt at a literary distinction.

> Intense sexual passion circumstantially described is not obscene, as any number of literary works demonstrate. Obscenity is achieved when the writer shows not human beings animated by emotion but merely organs in friction. This contemptuous dismemberment of personality Roth aims for and achieves *ad nauseum*.

"Merely organs in friction" may be the distinguishing feature not of obscenity but of pornography. Certainly in obscenity intent is also an issue. And Portnoy's graphic re-creations for his analyst have something to do with verifying his need for help. But even the pornographic does not apply. Roth's purpose is hardly titillation: there is not a passage in the book that Portnoy, himself, would take to the bathroom. And only the most unsympathetic reading would find Portnoy, or the Monkey, never "animated by emotion." If Roth is writing out of contempt, one may ask of what he is contemptuous. Syrkin's cryptic answer is, of "the sty under the abstention from pork," that is, of all that keeps Jews from assimilating guiltlessly into the gentile culture. But that is the whole issue of Diaspora, and one Jew's questionings may be another Jew's vilifications. Nowhere does Syrkin acknowledge that Portnoy sees his flight from Jewish compunctions as trying to be "bad" or that its opposite, the "good" from which he would fly, has him hooked.

In Syrkin's and others' reviews Roth's failures to satisfy imposed categories of critical judgment become reductions of the novel (and its unique mode) to everything from mere failed first draft,[11] to a series of stereotypical stand-up gags, to a comic strip, to an attempt to normalize Jews by a "paradoxical effort to help the Jews by reviling them."[12] Critics regularly accuse Roth of misrepresenting Jews because Sophie would not intend the breadknife to threaten castration or because Jack, as presented, would never be unfaithful with a secretary—ignoring the fact that these are clearly Alex's fantasies, about which not accuracy but anxiety is the issue in an analysis. Portnoy is called a failed *schlemiel* because he does not conform closely enough to the tradition of *schlemiel*dom. He is said to draw upon the Sabbatarian tradition of rebellion in the Jewish community, "the impulse to violate, to light fires on the Sabbath, deny the existence of God, destroy the purity of the family, the desire to expose and destroy rather than to create and revere." But, the accusation continues, he is no Sabbati Zevi, his world no *Satan in Goray*, because he is just an imp, not to be taken seriously. "Indeed," says this last analysis, "if we take him seriously, we are lost."[13] Even the defense that this whole monologue is a therapeutic session with requirements of its own evokes analyses of the analysis to prove that that will not do. Okay, says this line of argument, there are works where we are tipped off that we cannot trust the internal narrator's accounts. "[W]e can trust his report of what happened but not his interpretation of what it means. In *Portnoy* . . . the reader is never given an objective view of events from which to measure the narrator's version."[14] Such a reading, that misses the fixation in Portnoy's hyperboles or the love-hate in his accounts of his parents, has either very fixed criteria for the device of the known-unreliable narrator or is too put off by the subject to allow itself to do the reader's job. Roth gives the book only one narrator—though he modulates that voice in moods created by the memories—but the reader is never intended to take Portnoy on face value. Certainly Spielvogel doesn't. The reader has a role to play. And even if Alex's analyses are wrong, does that render him without any meaningful complaint? Experts from Bruno Bettelheim[15] down were tempted to analyze Alex's analysis to show that from this or that school's perspective, he was not so sick—maybe just spoiled by an immature author, or by an author needing to make *aliyah*.[16]

One did not have to be a psychoanalyst to hold the point of view. It was shared by many in the lay core of traditional Jewish opinion makers. For Trude Weiss-Rosmarin, the book was just immature filth. Weiss-Rosmarin, editor of *The Jewish Spectator*, had a long-held set position. She had written at the time of the publication of *Goodbye, Columbus* that the question: Who is a Jew? akin in many ways to the predicament of modern man's uncertainties of identity, is a product of "negative identification" that comes from the fragmentation of *galut* existence.[17] She was impatient with Americans who sought or fought this fragmented Jewish self when they perhaps belonged in Israel. In her non-review of *Portnoy's Complaint*, what she calls a "no-book," she begins by telling she did not really read it. Her tone is almost self-exonerating, as if to have really read it were to have been an accessory to some crime. She says she speed-read twenty pages and found it boring, with its juvenile repetition of four-letter words, conceding that she might have liked it in her teens, but assuring that she is not given to vicarious titillation or to being "a voyeuse of the Peeping Jane type."[18] She goes on to aver that "I am not doing therapy so why should I be privy to *Portnoy's Complaint?*" She draws a contrast between the sexually starved who reduce sex to a certain four-letter word and the sexually sophisticated who can appreciate "The Song of Songs" and mentions a rabbi friend who was unable to review the novel from the pulpit because he considered it "disgusting." Roth, she goes on, "speaks for a certain segment of alienated Jewishly ignorant Jews who write and teach." In contrast, she draws on a leading critic to raise another question:

> I do not think *Portnoy's Complaint* will become *the* definitive statement on "the Jewish condition of the modern Jew." After all, as Alfred Kazin concluded his review of this no-book, if "the complexity and moral depth of Jewish experience, which may look reducible to a mother, a son, a shriek, a cry" were just that, "as a subject it would have been exhausted long ago."

Weiss-Rosmarin's editorial dismisses the novel but not its social effect. Seventeen years later, collecting the fifty most telling editorials, one each from fifty years of *The Jewish Spectator*, she reprinted it as her most significant editorial of 1969.[19]

Kazin's question was introduced by "if." But Roth did not intend to reduce or exhaust "the complexity and moral depth of Jewish experience"; he intended merely to show a dimension of it elicited by the new freedom—and perhaps to portray the frustrations of any psychological entrapment. He well knew that "freedom" was no mere absence of legal or physical restrictions, that the "hook" one might still be on can cut far deeper into the flesh. Roth would continue to explore the effects of feeling trapped in his next few works of fiction.

Debate within Jewish circles—magazines to pulpits—was almost as feverish as sales of the novel. Like a giant Rorschach test, it allowed the passionate reading in of every mind set. Rabbi Borowitz's review could have stood in part as an answer to Trude Weiss-Rosmarin's. He calls *Portnoy's Complaint* "one of the great moral documents and Jewish books of our time" for its portrayal in modern terms of the traditional problem of "the *yetzer hara*, the urge to do evil," always associated with sexuality. And though the traditional rabbis would have objected to Roth's *nibbul peh*, his filthy mouth, it is for our time honest language:

> To use euphemism or be delicate would simply reinforce the old cerebral defenses. We do not lust in detachment. . . . The gutsy language makes the book a visceral experience . . . [of] a universal malady of civilization, the inability to integrate a schizoid yetzer.

The humor, Borowitz asserts, is right as a device to make one not just "crack up" but "crack open," a "very Jewish" use of humor that "heals more than it hurts." And it is fitting, not insulting, that Portnoy is Jewish, for

> who better than the Jew should serve as a symbol of mankind's aspiration to morality—more, mankind's obsession with morality despite what nature and history have taught! [Alex's] . . . commitment to the ethical...is as strong as his sexuality for it derives from centuries of doing mitzvot. [Finally, Portnoy's] sense of Jewishness/community [is] one of his human ideals . . . he loves his Diaspora Jewishness and sees it as a key means to his humanization. [In short,] . . . here in the guise of humor, much of Judaism's most serious message about being a man has been given modern and effective voice.

Rabbi Borowitz did not remain unchallenged by pulpit rabbis. Rabbi Arthur Lelyveld, who saw Borowitz "playing Akiba to Philip Roth's Bar Kochba," could not buy the characterization of the book as uniquely Jewish or profound.[20] "Oedipus and Electra were not Jewish." Portnoy, says Lelyveld, may be a stereotype, but he is not a type. Nor will it do to say that Portnoy is no more intended to be typical of Jews of his class than Emma Bovary of Frenchwomen of hers (an argument that Roth had made about some of his earlier protagonists). Portnoy shares, rather, the faults (as Lelyveld sees them) of Shylock and Fagin who "are *less than true to life*" because they are "besmirched by the prejudices of their time." This interesting statement, fraught with contradiction, contains a premise that has been advanced and countered endlessly in Jewish critical writing. It is the chicken-and-egg game of all social stereotyping in literature.[21] Certainly the besmirching effects of anti-Semitism in Shakespeare's and Dickens's days were part of their characters' reality, gave them the distortions of point of view that their authors observed. In an analogous example, though the taint of bastardy did not make every bastard in Shakespeare's day act like "a bastard," it made enough of them do so to allow Edmund's "Now, gods, stand up for bastards!" to ring true in *King Lear*. If

Lelyveld means that the writers themselves were so blinded by prejudice that they could not compose believable characters, then he is declaring Shylock and Fagin to be grotesques that have brought down the works containing them—patently not so. But Lelyveld denies and affirms the "Portnoy type" all in one statement:

> One can find Alexander Portnoy "hilarious" or revealing of a repressed self, only if one is able in some way to identify with him. I have great pity for those who do so identify with Alexander Portnoy. They have evidently failed to find in their lives that genuine meeting with another which is true relationship.

The logic here is a double bind. The "way" that fiction creates identification is by drawing on elements already within readers. Men can identify with oppressed women because men have experienced similar powerlessness as children. But to Lelyveld, Jews who identified with Alex Portnoy were displaying not capacity for sympathy but failure of living. In equating "identify" with "being identical to" and gilding the equation with a show of pity, Lelyveld wishes away a significant part of his congregation. But, then, older critics were quicker to deny the believability of Alex Portnoy than Alex's peers. Like Weiss-Rosmarin and, (in some respects) later, Irving Howe, Lelyveld's declared reactions "progressed from shock and disgust to compassion and finally to boredom." What is even less understandable is Lelyveld's declaration that neither Portnoy nor Spielvogel can be real because they are comic figures or that guilt as a comic idea cannot work because the suffering character is driven to turn against his true Jewish self in asserting that he is "*also a human being!*" Lelyveld finds himself, as defender of the faith, compelled to reason that "[e]xposing self-hatred as a neurosis, the book also characterizes Jewishness as a neurosis." Such zealous refusal to separate the book from the character might be expected to elicit declarations like Lelyveld's next lines:

> At this point I must respond with every fiber of my chauvinist, separatist being. I have no will to be just like everyone else—whatever that means. I want to identify with Jewish triumph, with Jewish wisdom, as well as with Jewish suffering.

"I want" is the cry of Portnoy, and also of Tarnopol and Kepesh and a few more of Roth's protagonists to come. The rabbinic "I want" and Alex's "I want" are both recognizable cries in the real world, but they do not meet on the plane of literary criticism. Roth has not said "I want." He has said that "Portnoy wants," as, had he chosen to write a novel about the frustrations of being a rabbi in 1969 America, he could have had his suffering hero declare "with every fiber" of his being that *he wants* his congregants to know their heritage and forget their petty complaints. Or he might have had his wild-eyed rabbinic hero excommunicate everyone he considered Jewishly ignorant and found himself mumbling to God about his principled unemployment. But would such a rabbi have been more Jewish than Portnoy?

Lelyveld is missing something else in his reading of Portnoy's outcry. Alex, this professional assister in "humane" affairs, equates "Jew" with "humane." When he asserts that he is not just a Jew but also a "human" being, he is partially contrasting "humane" and "human." The "humane" side of him has kept at bay his "human" needs, whose visceral dimensions emerge from beneath his repressions unsatisfied and shaming. At thirty-three Alex should be able to balance—and satisfy—both dimensions as a man.

Five years later, another rabbi, Robert Saks, wrote an essay on Gershom Scholem's *Sabbatai Sevi*, focusing on its discussion of "the paradoxical concept of holiness coming out of sin."[22] Saks, apparently unaware of Scholem's own pronouncements against *Portnoy's Complaint*, reminds his readers that Scholem defines Judaism as a religion encompassing wide varieties of conduct, the belief *of* Jews not just a belief *for* Jews. For Scholem a Jew is to be defined in large part by one's sincere belief that one *is* a Jew. In his own work, Scholem thus treats cravings and appetites not as drives foreign to Judaism, needing only to be repressed, but as indicators of a striving for holiness. Saks, interpreting Scholem on this conflict, says, "In Sabbatian terminology . . . where the holy spark of peace and freedom from craving is hidden in a shell of longing and temptation, a person should enter the shell—do the forbidden act—and thus break the shell's power from within." In this regard, says Saks, *Portnoy's Complaint*

> can be read as a satirical comment, from a Sabbatian perspective, on Jewish law. Portnoy is a Jewish boy with a healthy libido, the son of the most repressive of Jewish mothers. Roth, I believe, makes it very clear that the Jewish Mother, the Jewish God, and the Jewish laws are of one mold for [Portnoy].

To prove his point, Saks quotes Alex's diatribe on the dietary laws, concluding with Alex's speculation that maybe in breaking them, he found the wherewithal to break a sexual taboo:

> Now, maybe the lobster is what did it. That taboo so easily and simply broken, confidence may have been given to the whole slimy, suicidal Dionysian side of my nature; the lesson may have been learned that to

break the law, all you have to do is—just go ahead and break it! All you have to do is stop trembling and quaking and finding it unimaginable and beyond you: all you have to do, *is do it*! What else, I ask you, were all those prohibitive dietary rules and regulations all about to begin with, what else but to give us little Jewish children practice in being repressed? Practice, darling, practice, practice, practice. Inhibition doesn't grow on trees, you know. . . . (79)

Saks ends his essay shortly after this quotation, letting it speak for itself without analysis. His Jewish readership would know the echoes: practice, practice, practice was to make them all Yehudi Menuhins or Artur Rubinsteins; what didn't grow on trees was money—controlling echoes applied to the very subject of control. Portnoy's point, of course, is that the sinning didn't work. The floodgates once opened, further practice in the forbidden didn't inure him to guilt but only pushed it under awhile until it returned to overwhelm him. "Why is a little turbulence so beyond my means? Why must the least deviation from respectable conventions cause me such inner hell? When I *hate* those fucking conventions! When I know *better* than the taboos!" (124). Roth presents the irony of supposing one can reason himself into freedom. Saks thinks "a satirical comment, from a Sabbatian perspective, on Jewish law" can illuminate the Sabbatian danger: Portnoy is within "the shell of longing and temptation"; it remains a question whether Spielvogel can help him break its power from within. For twentieth-century American Jewry a next question might be: if Portnoy can break the power, will the longing, the temptation, and the suffering have been worth it? It is a question only for one who takes the book seriously.

Critics implicitly debated whether *Portnoy's Complaint* is a Jewish book. One answer is an implication of Scholem's distinction of a Jew. If Alex's sincerity *is* his authenticity, then he is every bit a Jew and his problems a Jewish problem. His being Jewish does not turn on the extent of his knowledge of the tradition, but on his personal response to whatever he knows of the tradition. His father, as Sanford Pinsker points out, embodies the conflict too: ". . . Jake Portnoy speaks for thousands when he takes his brilliant, rebellious son to task:

Tell me something [Jake demands], do you know Talmud, my educated son? Do you know history? . . . Do you know a single thing about the wonderful history and heritage of the sages of your people?

Alexander, indeed, does not, but then again, neither does his father. And for all the passionate denials, neither do most American Jews."[23]

Pinsker is, of course, right. Nonetheless, the "passionate denials" of their ignorance by American Jews are a form of self-identification, even if their tradition is largely a set of echoes replayed as origins. American-born Jack Portnoy (Alex calls him "Jake" only when fantasizing the old man's independence of Sophie—for example, *shtupping* his *goyische* secretary) had gotten through the eighth grade, without Talmud, on the bounty of the State of New Jersey. What he knows as Jewish, and has passed on, includes a respect for learning of all kinds. Roth, giving Jack that ironic cross-examination of his son, does not let young Alex respond by questioning his father's authenticity. Even on Spielvogel's couch he recounts the episode more in anger than in a reasoned challenge to his father's Jewishness. Jack Portnoy's respect for the learning he lacks is part of his personal identification as a Jew. Part of Alex's conflict with his father is his guilt about the old man's uncompleted emancipation. Grateful for his sacrifices but ashamed of his relative lack of education, Alex feels responsible for completing that education and bringing its benefits home: ". . . in my liberation would be his—from ignorance, from exploitation, from anonymity." Here is some of that ethical striving and moral conscience, indeed, the generous emotion, that Marie Syrkin denies.

Portnoy's sense of responsibility for helping his father to continue learning is part of the inverse Diaspora heritage (Roth owns up to the same feelings in *Patrimony*). It need not be demeaning to father or son, provided the father has dignity in his home. But Alex's counter-feelings for his father arise from another aspect of their transformed heritage. The father's achievements outside the house pall next to the mother's need for recognition of her accomplishment. In their Jewish value system, that accomplishment is Alex, the only son. Departing from his own family model (Roth has an older brother), he makes Alex's one sibling an older sister. This choice of personae, which allows Alex in the bathroom to obsess over her drying underwear, also leaves the boy with the burden of being Sophie's major project. He has to be good and be brilliant and be more. Two generations back, in *shtetl* society, women earned much of the living keeping store or sewing dresses, and men spent much of their time in respected study. But women no longer had outside occupations or large families to diffuse their energies, and among men study for its own sake was no longer respected. Alex's brilliance could have value only to the extent that he became somebody in the world and brought dividends, including children, back into the home. Implicit in Alex's complaint is resentment about the reduced role of the father created by the new Jewish need to gratify a home-centered mother. (From the Freudian standpoint one might say that Jack is not competitor enough.) But Alex also resents the burden of goodness that the new focus has placed on the son, the burden of being the superachiever.[24] Being watched so, he feels emasculated. Roth lets the overwrought Alex sum up this trap in his burlesqued detail of Ronald Nimkin, the fifteen-year-old pianist-suicide, who had been dubbed by the women in the building "Jose Iturbi the Second," found hanging from the bathroom showerhead with a note pinned to his well-laundered shirt:

> *Mrs. Blumenthal called. Please bring your mah-jongg rules to the game tonight.*
>
> > *Ronald.*

At the same time, Alex resents Jack's having been reduced and made ridiculous. How easy, and how betraying, to go beyond him. This was, indeed, a Jewish subject.

That Jewish America, outside the closed world of yeshiva orthodoxy, was as ignorant of Talmud and the Jewish sages as were Jack and Alex Portnoy may account for the pious tones of some of the reviews and sermons directed at the book. More musing tones were not available for use with this audience. Congregational ignorance had taken some of the old-world play out of rabbinic communication. Irony requires a knowing audience; the cryptic remark requires freedom from misunderstanding. Without that common wavelength between rabbi and congregation, reasoning with becomes talking to; parable becomes preachment. Sermons on the trendy *Portnoy's Complaint*, the prerogative of senior rabbis, tended to be negative because most senior rabbis were looking for moral content and finding it in the short passages rather than the whole text. These defenders against the new liberation were unlikely to find, under apparent insults to Judaism, satire on goodness. Rushing to keep up with the hubbub about the book, many noted its surface for the sake of the sabbath sermon. But few could identify Roth's subject. They could address the problem of values, the problem of assimilation, the problem of self-hatred, even the problem of sexual freedom, but they could not address the *problem* of goodness, except to deny it existed.

But goodness was being devalued all around, evoking cynicism to conceal its loss. For more than another two decades America would openly expect not the best but the worst from its politicians, its athletes, its parents and children. Psychiatrists and evangelists would be seen as Mercedes-Benz charlatans; athletic heroes, as cool millionaires; captains of industry, as leveraged buyout artists. The corrupting octopus of the 1980s, BCCI, would embrace governments at all levels and on all points of the political compass. "Ozzie and Harriet" would have long given way to "Married with Children"; the hit song of the late eighties would be Michael Jackson's "I'm Bad," with only a pale afterflash of the ironic inversion in that term long understood in the black community. But in 1969, after Camelot, the idea that goodness could be a burden felt intensely by Jews was an idea less worthy of ironic reflection than of pulpit denunciation.

A few Jewish periodical reviews saw the book as more than a rant or psychological case study or confession, saw it as comic parody of that mode or even allegory, which requires, for heightening, the typecasting other critics condemned. Helen Weinberg saw it as an allegory of the Jew in Diaspora America, of

> . . . the restlessness, the near-feverishness, the anarchistic itchiness of the young American Jew, burdened with the remnant of an authentic tradition of justice, law, reason, and righteousness, while forced to live in the mad, illogical, meretricious world of American culture.[25]

Taking seriously Roth's view that fiction cannot outdo the wild American reality, this view sees Roth's sensibility naturally turned to satire—not the objective, distancing satire of the eighteenth century, but one that had to be peculiarly subjective to get at an elusive unreality partly created out of the satirist's inner self. Put another way, this is not the satire that can stand aside and sneer at the unworthiness of institutions to fulfill their own ideals. This is satire in which the victim rages at the victimizer who has become the victimizer partly through the licensing admiration of the victim. Part of Portnoy's "Complaint" is the lover's complaint, satire of which goes at least as far back as Chaucer's "complaint to his empty purse," but the other—sorrowful—side of the lover's complaint is also to be found in Alex's compassion. Unlike Syrkin and Weiss-Rosmarin, Weinberg finds that

> [t]here is as much compassion as there is anger in his complaint, though the anger is noisier, more attention-getting; and, since the total thrust of the book is comic and satirical, the anger is more in keeping with the wished-for final tone. But the compassion is undeniably present and cannot be avoided: the scenes in the mother's hospital room; the private discussion between Alex and his sister about the Jews of Europe; on the baseball field; of the hours of a brief feeling of real love during the love affair—all of these scenes, and several others, reveal Portnoy's deep tenderness toward all that appears to enrage him the most. His compassion—or "suffering" in the broad sense—is what really threatens him. He is likely to lose his free self if he loves the Jews, or his parents, or his girl friends too much. And so he does not love them, and is angry with himself and them.

Satire on goodness cannot be Swiftian satire. Who but a devil would really have moral objections to goodness? But the impotence of goodness to overcome the paradox of America is an impotence legitimately expressed in self-mocking rage. That paradox, so heightened for the Jew, is an integrated self to be created out of the WASP and the transported European-Jewish senses of self without mutual denigration. To get a handle on it, one would have to be comparatively, perhaps enragingly, secure.

Alexander Portnoy is not secure, and many of his grievances are myopic: The Jews are not the only conscience- or custom-repressed group in America. The *goyim* are not one homogeneous mass. Venturing outside one's ethnic group for sexual adventure or proof of individuality marks a wider American conflict than just a Jewish one. Not only Jews value education and intellect. Self-mockery and invective are not exclusively Jewish arts—as Alex might have learned had he attended an Irish, Italian, or Puerto Rican softball game. With one or more of these conflicts most people everywhere can identify. Their peculiar combination may constitute a Jewish syndrome, but it is the Jew's belief that it is only his problem that makes it a Jewish subject. And that belief is a reality. Goodness wed to exclusivity needs to be examined—best through the permissive light of satire. Roth, unbound from Jamesian sobriety, was secure enough to examine it. But Roth had no intention of, or illusions about, making the psychoanalyst's couch a new subgenre of the novel. He could take liberties in the form but once. Some of its tones might apply to fiction dealing with entrapment and to satires in different forms, but as a mode this novel of the couch could neither pass nor fail tests of comparison. For Roth's future considerations of the American-Jewish problem, the reaction of the Jewish establishment to *Portnoy's Complaint* would be more interesting than Roth's limited attempt to portray the demigods of Weequahic.

Chapter 6

ABSURDITIES:
THE POST-PORTNOY SEVENTIES

Nothing is never ironic, there's always a laugh lurking some-
where.

—*Alexander Portnoy*

Within *Portnoy's Complaint* can be found the seeds of Roth's writing for the next decade and beyond. Its comic core is absurdity: Alex's doomed quests to liberate himself, first sexually, then narratively. Its main struggles are to extract restraint from restriction, liberty from license, and a self from a set of countervailing demands. Its chief experience of self is humiliation, the humiliation of having to justify desire to conscience and conscience to desire. These elements, which will survive the novel's merely temporal allusions—even its jokes and wisecracks—would remain the marrow of Roth's later fictions.

The humor of absurdity, which Roth would continue to wield, is the humor of double vision: his strivers rebut themselves; shadowy counterselves stalk the selves they would project. In trying to achieve some promised but dubious end, Roth's characters often find themselves transfixed, unable to go forward toward happiness or backward toward safety. Their nearest approach to heroism may be their compulsion to tell their stories right. But their self-deflating double vision, intensified in all Roth's fiction from *Portnoy* on, keeps them nicely in doubt. That double vision is characteristically Jewish. So is the need to construct lives with the mortar of words.

Roth's characters often find themselves in absurd situations, stuck in predicaments they could not foresee or subject to cosmic or cultural forces to which they can make no appropriate responses. The seeming promises of America may be at odds with their Jewish skepticism or, even worse, with their inbred concern with virtue. The Jewboy may be at war with the nice Jewish boy. In response they experience an abeyance, or impotence, of will. Their feelings become constrained, their personalities distorted. Those constraints and distortions are the vital subtexts of *The Breast*, *My Life as a Man*, *The Professor of Desire*, "On the Air," "Looking at Kafka," and the Zuckerman novels. Some of Roth's characters protest the absurdity; others recognize it as the human condition. Collectively, they would irritate many Jewish critics of the seventies and early eighties; but as Sanford Pinsker has said, "satirists make few friends,"[1] and the absurdities underlying conflicts of identity are discomforting to those who must live close to them.

In *Portnoy's Complaint* the underlying absurdity is glimpsed only spasmodically as Alex, the flailing analysand, shifts his targets. But some of his passing accusations, with their Jewish takes on modern life, are seeds of entire works to come. Roth's fiction of the seventies would focus on the siren song of gentile America, on manhood, on desire, on personal identity, on political control through manipulation of language, on the marketing of fake heroism and the subversion of culture, on the guilt of Jewish safety in America, all subjects probed by a Jewish sensibility, all of them already touched in Portnoy's monologue.

Alex's reliance on the psychiatrist as his confessor and surrogate parent also plays itself through, and out, in these novels—not always to the benefit of their author's reputation. If any reaction to *Portnoy's Complaint* was applied as whole cloth to *The Breast*, *My Life as a Man*, and *The Professor of Desire*, it was a certain readership's disgust with psychoanalysis as exoneration. Even though the psychiatrists in these novels are studies in serious practice—no mere clichés or cheap jokes—and even though these novels of unburdening have since been credited with addressing universal issues, many readers initially viewed them as Rothian solipsisms. Although none of them can be called a novel of the couch, they all use psychoanalysis as a stage in their protagonists' battle for personal control. Yet the "talking cure," especially when it addressed problems readers identified with Roth, seemed to many not so much material in a novel as the aired hangups of its author.

But those embedded Jewish issues of *Portnoy's Complaint* that continue to reverberate through the novels of the seventies are ways of testing American society. One is response to the Christian majority. Alex, who had always mocked Christmas, tells Spielvogel how, as a small boy, he had "turned from the window out of which [he] was watching a snowstorm and hopefully asked,

'Momma, do we believe in winter?'" Integrity, for Alex, is absurdly frozen between the American and the Jew. And at seventeen, while visiting "The Pumpkin"'s family in Iowa during Thanksgiving break, Alex cannot decide whether her father's being polite to him owes to his having been forewarned that Alex is a Jew or to his not yet knowing. At the moment, the question exists only in Alex's head, sparked by guilt at defying his own family in being with hers; still, his paranoia is not baseless: he knows that his Jewishness, whenever it surfaces, will evoke reaction.

What Alex does not acknowledge is that reaction cuts both ways. Later in his student life, thinking "The Pumpkin" pregnant and planning an idyllic marriage, he turns to her, ironically he thinks, and asks, "And you'll convert, right?" When she answers, "Why would I want to do a thing like that?" he becomes totally and unexpectedly indignant that she would not want to join him in the state he would soon decry as the bane of his life. After the false pregnancy passes, her refusal to convert, more than anything else, leads to his breaking off the romance. Portnoy's anger at Gentiles bursts easily into abuse. He recalls pictures in their houses "of Jesus flowing up to heaven in a pink nightgown . . . [a dream of] . . . base and brainless schmucks . . . who . . . worship somebody who, number one, never existed, and number two, if he did, . . . was without a doubt The Pansy of Palestine." But these pictures are pitted in Alex's soul against his "earliest movie memories . . . of Ann Rutherford and Alice Faye, America . . . a *shikse* nestling under your arm whispering love love love love!"

Portnoy's reviling a part of himself that he cherishes while trying to win acceptance in a culture he scorns is part of the absurd underpinning of that book. Such absurdity would be elaborated into major conflicts in the works of the seventies. The conflict between Jewish scorn of Gentiles and the mythic Americanization of Jews through radio and movies is the theme of "On the Air," the very next fiction (1970) after *Portnoy* that Roth would publish. As shall be seen, "On the Air" takes absurdity to surreal heights, exploding in *Grand Guignol* fashion the myth of Jewish safety in America.

But it is more than the anger in *Portnoy's Complaint* that Roth would expand into later fictions. Reading Freud on degradation gets Alex to consider people who frequently fail to unite the "two currents of feeling . . . the tender, affectionate feelings, and the sensuous feelings." Freud, he notes, says, "Where such men love they have no desire, and where they desire they cannot love." Loss of desire in the presence of love and its converse are the subject of *The Professor of Desire*, where Kepesh's determination to be, like Byron, "studious by day, dissolute by night" or, like Richard Steele, "a rake among scholars, a scholar among rakes" stems from his fear that his Jewish heritage has left him with capacity for love only at the cost of desire. This absurdity is the price to any sensitive male for trying to live the American myth of sexual anarchy. For the Jew caught in the middle it is devastating.

Roth makes David Kepesh such a Jew. He has been brought up, not in an urban ghetto, but in a Borsht Belt hotel, where old-world morality vies daily with new-world liaisons and deflative shtick. What Kepesh knows of real love he knows only from his parents; and as a son he associates their feeling for each other with an age when the heyday in the blood is tame. But he considers passion his generation's birthright; it is the vehicle for, and a defining element of, his rightful happiness. At first, giving himself over to passion, he almost destroys one lover and dehumanizes others. By the end of the novel, when Kepesh is genuinely in love, his sense of diminishing desire in the presence of that love is movingly counterpoised to his tenderness for his postlibidinous widowed father. Kepesh is a professor and a writer. His discourse on his conflict is the text of *The Professor of Desire*.

In his recounting of events, which is more reflective than narrative, the still young professor adopts an elegiac tone to lament his loss of heat, but he cannot explain that loss rationally. Reflecting on his old escapades with the totally sensual Birgitta makes him feel compromised in his present desireless love for Claire. Were he an older man, he might see desire differently, as some biological process given the young to continue the species, out of which affection might emerge as a dividend. The transience of desire might then be justified by an abiding love such as he has seen between his parents. But Kepesh is of an age and a disposition still to value desire for itself, and where he feels compromised he feels no compensating comfort. Vaguely fearing "transformations yet to come," he is moving unwittingly toward the predicament Roth had already given him in *The Breast*. In the last movement of the book, when he is sharing a peaceful summer in the country with Claire, the added presence of his father and a Holocaust-survivor friend juxtaposes the two worlds between which Kepesh stands: the inclusive tribal world that the younger Roth protagonists had struggled to escape and the longed-for but ironically self-alienating world of total freedom, wherein sexuality, the only human nexus, becomes the defining issue in human happiness. Kepesh's whole bifurcated life has been an attempt to have both. But his attempt now to harmonize these conflicting impulses in wistful contemplation holds a danger: by analyzing his lost desire (for the benefit of his reader) and by teaching a course on the subject—becoming a professor of desire—for his students, he chances finding satisfaction in story rather than in living. He may be glimpsing the ultimate patrimony of his senior years, memory replacing desire. But until then, for Kepesh, no longer to profess desire is no longer to assert a self.

Kepesh's position is doubly ironic. First, even as he is planning to publish this analysis of his growing impotence, he is aware of how paltry his problem is compared to the politically imposed impotence of iron-curtain writers to publish anything this personal (trapped in the political aftermath of the war that had ended European Jewry, they reflect a special guilt for safe American Jews). Second, profound as his analysis may be, it cannot account for what is to happen to him in *The Breast*.

That earlier novella, transcending Portnoy's anguish and Kepesh's despair, does finally harmonize erotic and intellectual inclinations but in nightmarish circumstances. *The Breast* has been derided as a silly imitation of Kafka's "The Metamorphosis" or Gogol's "The Nose." It is not; it speaks to a different order of absurdity: the requirement to choose where there is no choice. The Kepesh of *The Breast*, bewildered and susceptible of hysterics, has the feel of a victim from the start, yet a civilized victim, perhaps the arch-Jewish victim. Ultimately, his story is one of will and cultivation.

In *The Breast* the issue is not whether it is possible for a man to be transformed into a female breast, but whether, given such a transformation, the sufferer can extract meaning from his life. Kepesh can no more wish away his predicament than one can wish away cancer or aging. And it is not a random affliction but an absurd commentary on his life. He has lived, a secret voluptuary, by trying in his overt life to stifle his passions rather than admit them into some moderating role. Now he is a 155-pound female breast: the passionate aspect of his nature has become the very surface. Like Job, Kepesh will want to know why, and like Job he will not be given an answer—nor will the reader be given the comfort of Job's final problematic restoration.

Kepesh's perplexity at the beginning helps the reader make the one required stretch. As in science fiction, once the reader accepts Kepesh's impossible transformation, everything else in the story becomes not only possible but compelling. The implications of his transformation slowly dawn on Kepesh. The one-time libertine, in becoming the most desired object of libertines, has realized the ultimate pornographic fantasy: being passive and having things done to him; but he sees this extreme as at once infantile and senile, sexual striving consummated in nursing-home helplessness. And in experiencing the most intense sexual arousal without the possibility of climax, he now sees pleasure as valueless unless it can issue in something beyond itself. But while being stroked with these realizations, and moving inexorably toward a discovery of his true self, Kepesh nobly preserves responses bequeathed to him by his culture. *The Breast*, which combines the frustrations of Job with the futility of Koheleth, is about the need to find sanity and civility in the objectively meaningless existential condition. It is the challenge of modernism—to Jew and Gentile alike—that arises from the loss of traditional belief in God.

The several ploys that Kepesh uses to try to explain his transformation, the narrative substance of the novella, are an odyssey of the mechanisms available to a literary man in a physical world. Needing something to believe in, he grasps, first, for a full measure of the erotic pleasure; then, for a psychological denial of his condition; and, finally, for an affirming power in art to have turned the imaginings of literature into physical realities. Forced at last to see the futility of these dodges and to acknowledge the absurdity of his state, Professor Kepesh finally comes to a realization about himself and his ilk: the whole man is not just the framer of words but also the liver of life; he has at least the responsibility of harmonizing what his life of reading and lecturing has taught him with the reality of his present physical condition.

At the end of the story, Kepesh, headless and sightless, compares himself to the stone torso in Rilke's poem, "The Archaic Torso of Apollo." Like that headless figure, whose loins, breast, and shoulders still glow with the lineaments of its original gaze—examining, eyeless, their transfixed viewer—the transformed Kepesh reads everyone who comes in contact with him and now utters, as it were, the words Rilke imputes to the torso of Apollo: "You must change your life." By this point, Kepesh's Quixotic efforts to reverse the outward transformation have moved from the absurd to the sublime. For when, with the quotation from Rilke, he accepts the victory of his defeat, he accepts as well responsibility for living the life he has now been dealt.[2] Self-acceptance, the only resolution of the absurd, takes the doomed Kepesh to a level of maturity beyond that of Portnoy—or of any other Roth protagonist since Sergeant Marx.

The Breast has been accused of lacking subtlety, its symbolism of being as obvious as it is heavy: a man regresses beyond the suckling stage to become the dug itself. But the use of that device for achieving maturity is less obvious. So is its relation to the Jew. Not just that it twits the gentile myth of the "full-breasted" Jewess: the breast for the Jew is the family, the tribal nourishment, the shelter against the wider world. To lose oneself in it is, yes, to revert to an infantile state. But to have to accept that primal part of oneself *and* assimilate to it the teachings of the wider world—Kepesh is a reader of all literatures—is the Jewish challenge for Roth. He has little to say at this time about the numerical survival of his people; certainly his preoccupation with intermarriage subordinates that concern. But just as Kepesh's responses are idiomatically Jewish, so is his predicament vaguely sensed as situationally and ethically Jewish. He has three choices. He can turn inward and pretend that the other world does not exist, or he can attempt to stay in profitable contact with it, taking nourishment, medicine and therapy but nothing else, or he can interact with it intellectually and culturally while acknowledging his permanent difference. He is only as stuck as he lets himself be once he determines that he must change his life.

Between *The Breast* and *The Professor of Desire* came *My Life as a Man*, all three extending private frustrations into wider issues adumbrated in

Portnoy's Complaint. "The Monkey"'s sexual adventuring anticipates Sharon Shatzky's pyrotechnics in *My Life as a Man.* But the response to Sharon by the twice-fictively removed Nate Zuckerman represents a step toward Roth's later, maturer concerns: novelist Tarnopol's reason for having his fictive self reject this tantalizing love slave is not conscience—the spectre of some Sophie and Jack—but his realization that a true mate must be more than body, must be a soul who can share his dedication to the life of a writer. Tarnopol must integrate, not compartmentalize, the antithetical aspects of his soul: not as the scholar-rake, he realizes, but only as the creator-lover can he use writing to liberate him.

Appearing again in this novel is Dr. Spielvogel, no longer just an ear and a punchline but a more active, even somewhat adversarial, figure. Given an opportunity to publish a paper on his patient's condition, he is not above sacrificing Tarnopol's privacy and amplifying his own role in the analytic treatment. Indeed, Spielvogel's role in this work, with its connection to his role in *Portnoy*—linking both novels to Roth's own real analysis and to a paper on neurosis and creativity actually published by Roth's own psychiatrist—has been fascinatingly presented in Jeffrey Berman's *The Talking Cure.*[3] And *My Life as a Man*, reissued in 1994, has been appreciated increasingly as perhaps the most authentic novel yet of the psychoanalytic process. This Spielvogel, no silent sounding board waiting to deliver a punch line, interacts with his patient, identifying Tarnopol's penchant for troubled *shiksas* as the attainable, self-punishing substitute for the unattainable mother. For the writer Tarnopol, whose name is close to an anagram of Portnoy (at least all its letters can be found in the earlier character's name), personal heroes are Kafka and Freud, whom he sees as avatars of Jewishness—preoccupied with and projecting their own repression into their greatest accomplishments for mankind. The very civility of talking out one's problem rather than physically acting it out in violent behavior is to Roth's characters a Jewish response. And the involvement of these Freudian practitioners is Roth's nod to his tribe's civilized way of addressing personal paralysis caused by conflict of culture.

While Spielvogel is more active in *My Life as a Man* than in *Portnoy*, and while Kepesh's psychiatrist, Dr. Klinger, is an active player in the two Kepesh novels, by the late seventies their roles are pretty well exhausted. After mediating briefly some narrative concerns of *The Professor of Desire* (1977), Klinger disappears. Thereafter, any indulging of the unconscious takes place not on the analyst's couch but in altered consciousness incorporated into Roth's narrative plots. The use of the psychiatrist in these mid-seventies novels[4] gives way completely in the Zuckerman novels to the counter-self within the story. Rather than have the character test his longings on an outside, artificial consciousness, Roth weaves in foils, dreams, or fantasy episodes, or he reverses the story by retelling it from an opposing point of view. What might have been material to be analyzed for the Spielvogels and Klingers becomes experience to be synthesized for the reader of the Zuckerman fictions.

Although Roth's critics would lump the immediate post-*Portnoy* works together, they vary greatly in point of view and tone. Each work opening out from a personal concern or episode in Roth's life develops some significant theme affecting the image of American Jews. *My Life as a Man* is a kind of precursor of *The Facts*, a summing up of the problem of the literary Jew's need to be done in by contact with the rougher, less genteel side of the Protestant tradition, preliminary to moving on. It uses Roth's college experience and his career through the mid-sixties, before the fame and infamy, as a way of looking at personal sovereignty and the pull of intermarriage. It is also about guilt and ripeness for victimization, quintessential Jewish subjects. More than any of its predecessors, it is about getting one's story right, about the pitfalls of cozying up to the wrong fictions. Among the temptations to misperceive oneself are those posed by the myth of American openness to Jews.

A reader who skips the prefatory material might see *My Life as a Man* as three separate or loosely tied fictions, might miss Roth's advisory that both parts of the novel, "The two stories in part I, 'Useful Fictions,' and part II, the autobiographical narrative 'My True Story,' are drawn from the writings of Peter Tarnopol." Roth had varied his narrative approaches within single works before: in *Letting Go* he had divided the story between a third-person omniscient voice and Gabe's first-person narration, and in *When She Was Good* he had begun with an overview by Daddy Will before letting the narrative voice settle in closer to Lucy's point of view. But Roth had never simply gone from story to story whose primary details differed and bound them only by a preliminary authorial hint. Abrupt changes of consciousness that the reader would have to resolve was a device of double vision more intensive than those he had previously employed. Roth was looking for a way to achieve maximum openness, only apparent closure. Maybe Tarnopol's "Useful Fictions" were independent creations of Roth, drafts or stages in his writing of the novel; he has spoken about the uncertain life of fictions that—like a Richard Rodgers tune—might wind up in works for which they were not originally conceived. In any case, these false leads for Tarnopol become stages in his discovering his life as a man. Throughout Roth's later career, as his subject turned increasingly toward the fictive nature of truth, Roth would increasingly refract images of the self through different narrative prisms.

My Life as a Man, like the Kepesh novels, continues Alex Portnoy's theme of avenging his Jewish exclusion from the gentile world by conquering the Gentile's woman. But that gentile woman is also a reflection of the Jewish man who seeks her out. He doubts his masculine capacity to be the macho

American; inevitably she proves him right. She is the questioning self taken on to challenge what he thinks he wants by showing him to be as inadequate as he has always feared he was. What makes her attractive is her mystery. These Jewish male narrators know neither the minds nor the psyches of their gentile women, and Roth does not presume to explore the world through female eyes. His subject is the vulnerable, but aspiring, male. These women are that male's projection onto America, part of themselves that they have not settled and cannot ultimately settle with.

My Life as a Man is also a novel about a blocked novelist trying to write a novel. Closest to Roth's biography of any of his books, it has been seen as a novel about three novelists.[5] Nathan Zuckerman, the fictional hero of the two conflicting but "Useful" fictions, "Salad Days" and "Courting Disaster (Or, Serious in the Fifties)," is a writer silenced by a brief catastrophic marriage to a *shiksa* whose suicide leaves him exiled with her daughter. Tarnopol, the author of these fictions and narrator of his own autobiographical novella, "My True Story," is blocked in this short work by his destructive wife and by the compromises of his therapist, who has published a study so closely resembling the circumstances of his novel that any reader of that paper is in a position to guess his *really* true story. Roth, writing daringly close to the bone, is perhaps the third novelist, barely veiled by the Tarnopol persona. Like Fellini in *8 1/2*, Roth was willing to explore his own life in the risky business of trying to discover secrets of his art. Some critics would find its honest vulnerability a high mark of Roth's middle career; others would hear its echoes of earlier plaints as tiresome. It never achieves the transcendence of *8 1/2*, perhaps because its honesty is not yet total—there is the leftover business to be picked up in *The Facts*—or because Tarnopol, more guilty than embarrassed by his past, never finds the shrugging self-exoneration of Fellini's Guido, who is finally at one in the circus of his life with all the haunting characters he has betrayed. The timing of *My Life as a Man* in Roth's oeuvre, after the critical disasters of *Our Gang*, *The Breast*, and *The Great American Novel*, tainted its public reception. Amidst the seeming complaints, absurdity was not yet identified as an ironic Rothian point of view.

Tarnopol's life, that of a Jewish artist testing American freedom, does also mirror Roth's own adult life and writings, his own quest to define "a man." Tarnopol's three fictions roughly parallel Roth's career to the early seventies. In tone and attitude, "Salad Days" reflects the bachelor college and army days that rendered for Roth the materials of *Goodbye, Columbus*. Then, "Courting Disaster (Or, Serious in the Fifties)" parallels Roth's meeting with Maggie and imagines what might have happened if he had not ended the relationship. The burdened tone resembles that of *Letting Go*, and the exiled hero shares a fate akin to that of the exiled Gabe. In the third, and longest, fiction of the book, "My True Story," Tarnopol lives something very close to Roth's real life—including the writer's block that had accounted for much of the first three of the five years it took to write *When She Was Good*.[6] Tarnopol has come through the debilitating fifties, where breadwinning men in a power struggle called marriage exercised responsibility for defenseless women, victimizers chained to their victims. In Tarnopol's view the wives' sole purpose was to stand guard over their husbands, to ward off ideas or people that could threaten change. But he believes that without change there is no growth, and without growth, no freedom. He has also come through a sixties bout of seeming freedom—noncommitment tethered to the threat of a nervous breakdown. At the end, Tarnopol, free of the need for dependent women but without anything like a successful *Portnoy's Complaint* under his belt, hopes he can build a creative life *"being me and none other!"* that is, able to distinguish himself from his surrogates in his not-so-useful fictions and his pathetically true story.

Whether he can achieve this true freedom remains a moot point: Tarnopol ceases to exist with the conclusion of the novel. Reviewers of the later Zuckerman works from time to time felt constrained to state that the later Nathan Zuckerman is not Roth's but Tarnopol's creation, since a character with Nate's name, though of varying parentage, first appeared in Tarnopol's "Useful Fictions." Their suggestion, an acknowledgment that Roth had built Chinese boxes between himself and his character, put too fine a point on the device. Tarnopol is not there. The later novels have no need of a struggling blocked writer as intermediary between Roth and Zuckerman. The absurdities to come would be the absurdities of success.

Not only Tarnopol, but also Kepesh and, later, Zuckerman must decide what kind of life is worth living and what it means to be "a man." "Man" includes "mensch": they must do more than get parents and dependent women off their backs, they must eventually contribute to the world, often amidst isolating conditions. Becoming a mensch takes time. Consistently, Roth's young men start out looking past their own ghetto lives for genteel or literary models on which to pattern their expectations. Their first inclination is to dismiss their backgrounds, not as hateful or embarrassing, but as irrelevant to or hindering of their quest. In college, Nate takes his "Salad Days" tea with his seminar teacher, Miss Caroline Benson, and learns new aspirations—including aspiring the "h's" in "where," "when," and "which." When young (*Ghost Writer*) Zuckerman visits the older writer E. I. Lonoff's Berkshire Yankee farmhouse, it immediately induces in him the thought, "This is how I will live." Feeling something likc the seduction that drew Neal to Patimkinland, these pilgrims are all too willing to forget stories of steerage and stow away on the Mayflower. But their greater quest is to discover themselves and the life they were meant to live. Because they are writers of stories and interpreters of literature, they have endless models for helping them read—or deceive—themselves. And because creating and interpreting fictions are such closely related acts, sometimes interchangeable, their quest for self-knowledge may be self-deceiving. "Is it me?" becomes harder and harder to answer when one has been at home for a while in the great tradition. For Roth's writer-heroes to be at home with themselves and free of the scripting of others, they must find the stories they can enact most naturally. The Jewish element is an important part of those stories, especially the constant struggle between the Jewboy and the nice Jewish boy. The false leads are the fictions they must surrender in order to live the fiction that is true.

As Roth's literary men move out into the world beyond their books, they test their sensed freedom against defining issues of the day increasingly conscious that Jewish concerns transcend America. Where Roth is ahead of most of his readers and many of his critics is in realizing that nothing stands still, that everything changes. When Kepesh pursues passion as the way to happiness, only to find passion cannot survive happiness, he makes that discovery in Prague, where the zeal of revolution has yielded to the paralysis of communism, and where intellectuals are absurdly given meaningless projects to divert their passions. Now not only Jews are paralyzed: a whole nation of Kafkas might have to waste law degrees clerking in insurance offices. This Prague transcends the Prague of Kepesh's reading, fulfills Kafka's worst fears about bureaucratic soullessness. Kepesh may still need it to be a vague metaphor for Kafka's Jewish problem, but it is also a monument to the futility of human desire. It no longer pulsates primarily with mysteries of self, fantasize as Kepesh may about visiting Kafka's ancient whore to unlock its secrets. As a writer, Kepesh can only experience the Communist East as a hardening of metaphor into fact. The maze of the mind has been poured in political concrete, so that his eternal quest to find and write about himself is ironically contrasted to the resignation of writers who know very well their subject but cannot publish it. Complaints about psychological entrapment, a comparative luxury of the West, have a falling echo within the walls of the political prison that is now the East, where knowledge itself is mocked by the system. Here the whole society is locked in what greatly resembles a Jewish joke. For the Jewish joke that had contributed to centuries of Diaspora survival was self-mocking: powerlessness shrugged off in uproarious absurdity.

Prague, which in Roth's own imagination had once seemed a model Jewish ghetto homeland, and which had been emptied of an important part of its culture by the very Holocaust his family had escaped, now stood for the emptiness of Eastern European culture under communism. This public counterpoint to Kepesh's personal conflict—self and culture held hostage to international politics—makes what might have seemed but a small personal fiction resonate briefly with overtones of a political novel. *The Professor of Desire* was not the occasion to wring these absurdities fully; the manic tones of "The Prague Orgy" would do that. Yet, this current awareness of Prague enriches the novel for the reader of the seventies. The mood of the city is absorbed into the elegiac, or wistful, tone (Kafka loosened up through Chekhov, echoing Kundera) of Professor Kepesh's lecture on desire, which is being prepared for safe American students threatened only in their reading. Prague connects past to present to future: the need to bring old written worlds to bear on an unwritten world still to be struggled with. Visitors today to this most culturally vibrant city find no hint of that stifling gloom, but *The Professor of Desire* preserves it as few historians can.

Increasingly in Roth's works Jewishness itself changes—as, indeed, the societies that opposed or welcomed it change. People first stick each other with the old story, creating the wrong expectations, and then face disappointments inherent in their fictions. To Jews, Gentiles are notions formed by limited contact, family myth, and oblivion to change. Gentiles equally misread Jews. Men misread women; women, men. Jewish men and gentile women start relationships under quadruple handicaps of misunderstanding, down to their very language. And if they come from opposite sides of the Atlantic or the iron curtain, misprision is their only certainty. Yet, except for the occasional relief of a daydream, Roth's characters never retreat from engaging their changing world, from making it redefine its culture and theirs by challenging it to offer or withhold itself. If, myopic with myths, they at first respond absurdly, they eventually experience some emerging awareness about themselves and the world. The Jewish man's most common absurdity is in failing to recognize a blinding prejudice against his *shiksa* at least equal to the one he is sure she is leveling at him. The early Rothian hero, self-deceived, reaches heroically across cultures only to find himself impaled on the barricade between them. In the Zuckerman works, where the now exposed hero will have to battle both the tribalists he has supposedly betrayed and the universalists he has sought to join, Jewishness will be redefined against a shifting gentile world that has absorbed some of its tones. Many of these absurdities would be explored in the novels of the eighties, but Jewish sensibility, even as it was changing in the seventies, provided a criticism of America first hinted at in *Portnoy*.

Alex's impossible courting of the rich society girl he calls "The Pilgrim"—both the love and the abandonment—prefigures the Susan McCall episodes of *My Life as a Man* (and may suggest elements of Roth's departure from Ann Mudge). The absurdity of union with "The Pilgrim" is revealed in a reflection that may seem mere petulance. But Alex's speculation touches a linguistic nerve that Roth would lay open for greater dissection later.

Why didn't I marry the girl? Well, there was her cutesy wootsy boarding school argot, for one. Couldn't bear it. "Barf" for vomit, "ticked off"' for angry, "a howl" for funny, "crackers" for crazy, "teeny" for tiny. Oh, and "divine." . . . Then there were the nicknames of her friends; there were the friends themselves! Poody and Pip and Pebble, Shrimp and Brute and Tug, Squeek, Bumpo, Baba—it sounded, I said, as though she had gone to Vassar with Donald Duck's nephews. . . . But then, my argot caused her some pain too. The first time I said fuck in her presence (and the presence of friend Pebble . . .), such a look of agony passed over The Pilgrim's face, you would have thought I had just branded the four letters on her flesh. Why, she asked so plaintively once we were alone, why *had* I to be so "unattractive"? What possible pleasure had it given me to be so "ill-mannered"? What on earth had I "proved"? "Why did you have to be so pus-y like that? It was so un*called*-for." Pus-y being the Debutante for disagreeable. (*PC* 233–34)

Here a mismatch of ethnicities is presented as an incompatibility of language. The device reveals Roth's attention to language itself as an indicator of personality and culture. So much has been written about Roth's mastery of prose and of modes of speech that it is easy to just credit his ear and not appreciate the Orwellian issues of language as communication, or the corruption of communication, that he often raises. But that would be the real issue—beyond simple Nixon hatred—in *Our Gang*.

In that lampoon, not just Nixon's doublespeak, but the tones of the whole country are laid open for dissection. Citizens from all walks of life come forward to confess to having killed President Tricky E. Dixon so they can have their fifteen minutes in the headlines. Their stations are revealed in their voices. Roth's exposure of pomposity on all sides is refreshing: Spiro Agnew's[7] puffed alliterations vie for pretentiousness with the clucking over them of his silenced opponents and with the myth-making activities of the press. Twenty-one years later, in July 1992, the death of Eric Severeid occasioned numerous eulogies for a broadcast journalist who had often told America what it needed to hear, sometimes in very unpopular situations. But there was another side to Severeid's speech, something a little melodramatic, sanctimonious, and not always clear, that Roth captured in the voice of Erect Severehead in *Our Gang*. In its absurdity, the high-toned reportorial acceptance of the great lie is wickedly but hilariously revealed—its gropings for metaphor finally devolving into "blah, blah, blah." The reader cannot choose but laugh—to release himself from complicity.

Our Gang was tossed off in less than two months in response to certain political statements in 1971, a year before the renomination of Nixon and

Agnew and the events that would become the Watergate scandal. It is a lampoon that makes no pretensions to the standards of a novel, and the reader is immediately aware of its sophomoric excesses. Yet its occasional belly laughs trace to Roth's ear for the national babble, the sound of a country that had suspended its values and set absurdity abroad in the land. The theme was Orwellian, but that ear had been sensitized by Jewish cynicism toward the promises, in various tones, of establishment America.

Still other Alexander Portnoy pronouncements contain the seeds of future Philip Roth fictions. Alex's characterization of "Charlatan Van Doren," the quiz show hero, prefigures a theme in *Zuckerman Unbound*. Portnoy exclaims

> Such character, such brains and breeding, that candor and schoolboyish charm—the ur-WASP, wouldn't you say? And turns out he's a fake. Well, what do you know about that, Gentile America? Supergoy, a *gonif!* Steals money. Covets money. Wants money, will do anything for it. Goodness gracious me, almost as bad as Jews—you sanctimonious WASPs! (*PC* 232)

Alex Portnoy's rage is paralleled in *Zuckerman Unbound* in the life mission of Alvin Peppler. This ex-marine quiz-show contestant and twisted victim of a national conspiracy (America's wanting WASP refinement to replace his Jewish grubbiness in the contestant booth) lives only to expose the wrong done him and to triumph as a writer, though he has no talent other than an almost idiot-savant memory. His attempts to use art to avenge mistreatment almost destroy Zuckerman's legitimate life as a fiction writer. Roth would later turn this commentary on art as vengeance inside out in the Milton Appel episode of *The Anatomy Lesson*. In that book and its immediate predecessor, *Zuckerman Unbound*, *Portnoy's Complaint* is very much an issue; through its fictive incarnation *Carnovsky*, *Portnoy* broods over the stories and determines the fate of the protagonist.

Alex's love, baseball, is elaborated to touch many themes in the later works. In *Our Gang*, Curt Flood's suit to create free agency for major-league ball players is used to expose Tricky's doublespeak on free enterprise. *The Great American Novel* uses the pastime as a metaphor for American life. Here absurdity reigns from the dugout bench to the corporate boardroom, and here the homeless baseball team, like a tribe of wandering Jews—never able to get last licks—is, along with its whole history, being written out from the annals of the sport like Toynbee's fossil. *Patrimony* would show baseball to have been a lifelong link between Herman and Philip Roth, as it had promised to be for Jack and Alex Portnoy.

Portnoy's echoes in Roth's later fiction, as shall be seen, include the Jewish neighborhood with its values and taboos. Alex's dream that Weequahic would never change is dashed at the end of *Zuckerman Unbound* in Zuckerman's return drive through that by-then black and seedy area following the death of his father. Alex's scorn of parents' wanting every Jewish boy to become a doctor—those successful sons he calls "Seymour Schmuck, . . . or Aaron Putz, or Howard Shlong"—turns on itself in the middle-aged, almost-defeated Zuckerman's futile attempt to enroll in medical school, to become at last the nice Jewish boy of childhood myth. That irony is but one of the meanings of the title *The Anatomy Lesson*. Jack Portnoy's lecture on Jewish tradition and his invoking of Rabbi Warshaw anticipate Judge Wapter's sanctimonious lecture in *The Ghost Writer*. Masturbation, the most famous activity in *Portnoy's Complaint*, remains a symbol of frustration linking past and present in *The Ghost Writer* and *Zuckerman Unbound*. With this activity young Zuckerman will punctuate his midnight spyings on Lonoff's upstairs room, conjuring Amy Bellette's return to the house, where she will whisper her love—not to Nathan, but to his sanctified host; and with this activity, one novel later, a dubious admirer will anoint a handkerchief and leave it in the letter box of an older Zuckerman to remind the successful author of *Carnovsky*, (*i.e.*, *Portnoy*) of the tenuousness of fame. Finally, Alex's whole trip into "Exile" in Israel, with its hopes and fantasies of escape into Kibbutz life, will be renewed in *The Counterlife*, elaborated into Henry Zuckerman's escape fantasy and his brother Nathan's real or fancied mission to rescue him. Indeed, comparison of Israel and the Diaspora will be the very substance of *Operation Shylock*. In all these works characters sensing the absurdity of their situations attempt definition by trying on fictive selves offered up by their competing cultures.

Mutual mistrust of Jew and Gentile would shade all Roth's works of the seventies and eighties. Generally, he would treat that mistrust as absurd yet inevitable, concealed in intellectual circles under a blanket of civility. But in the nation's workaday life it always threatened to reveal its full potential for horror. Roth would explore that horror most intensively in the 1970 work that immediately followed *Portnoy's Complaint*.

Chapter 7

THE MOST OFFENSIVE PIECE
ROTH EVER WROTE

Hilarious in its spasmodic fits and savage in its nihilism, the story "On the Air" (1970) addresses a self-limiting audience: even more idiomatic than *Portnoy's Complaint*, it requires its readers to understand its Yiddishisms and its allusions to life around 1940.[1] It could not appear in a magazine like *The Atlantic* or *Harper's*, Roth's usual outlets for short fiction, or in a Jewish journal. In these, still echoing with reactions to *Portnoy*, it would only offend. Swiping at sacred symbols in tones sometimes reminiscent of Lenny Bruce, the story mocks everything from the Pope, to apple-pie America, to gentile notions of manhood. But it also mocks the mocker, who in this story is a Jew, and with him notions of Jewish superiority. A story that gives no quarter, Roth might have realized, could expect few friends.

Yet, in a little literary magazine like *New American Review*, under a trusted editorial hand like that of Ted Solotaroff and for the eyes of sophisticated readers, "On the Air" could see the light of publication. Once!

"On the Air"—the title is the flashing sign that notifies studio audiences they are participating in the magic of radio—is divided into sections, and each section heading evokes that radio world: "The Answer Man," "Duffy's Tavern," "Howard Johnson's," "Gangbusters," "Special Bulletin," "The Lone Ranger," "Contest Announcement," and "Now Back to—The Lone Ranger."

The story is set during the late thirties or early forties, when radio served to bring the world close to Americans and seemed to unify them as one culture. It recalls the spirit of those prewar or early-war years when Hitler and Mussolini were more comic than threatening, when the country got its blessings from Kate Smith and Molly (Mrs. Fibber) McGee, and when it took its weekly comfort from the presence of Eddie Cantor (whose time was their time) and "Archie the Manager Speaking, Duffy ain't here. . . ." Looking back from 1970, Roth presents that era as having been a sham—an "on the air " covering up what was off the wall. Trying to live the popular fiction can be tragic. As in Stephen Crane's "The Blue Hotel," a newcomer is victimized by his belief in myths.

The story blasts nostalgia: in spirit, the very opposite of Woody Allen's *Radio Days* or Neil Simon's *Brighton Beach Memoirs*. And the humor—it cannot be read but in convulsions—moves from the light rantings of a foulmouthed *schlimazl* (everybody's most entertaining uncle) to the increasingly dark fears of a Jew who, having stumbled into the anti-Semitic underside of gentile life, is made to face the consequences of his own too-comfortable sense of superiority. The story presents every minority group from the viewpoint of some antagonist: a world of "*goyim*," "*kikes*," "*shaygetzes*," "colored," "Chinks," "homos." Everyone is prejudiced and everyone is outraged at being discriminated against. And as the story shifts realities from the points of view of one to another offended character, it doubles back on the reader and keeps him perpetually off balance. There is craziness in the story, in the best sense of that word: of a writer just unleashing his imagination and following the leads of his own created characters and premises. Roth, manic, is unmatched. That part of his talent that even the moralists grudgingly acknowledged—and secretly revisited even as they obligingly disapproved—is given free play; and what it plays with, as elsewhere, is the lost-and-found line between madness and inspiration, between righteousness and self-righteousness.

The controlling point of view in "On the Air" is located somewhere just off the shoulder of Milton Lippman, Jewish shoe-store proprietor and minor but aspiring talent agent. He is also a patriarch for his wife and little son, their guide into a mainstream America he hardly knows, except as it is presented on radio. His way of conquering the land is to remake it in his own image. For Lippman, America is a land hoodwinked by its "*goyish*" pretension to a culture, a civility, and an intelligence it does not have. And the proof of that pretension is its radio programs. Lippman's assessment starts the story:

THE ANSWER MAN! Some schmuck from Fort Wayne, Indiana, with a deep voice who next year will be selling soap flakes on Helen Trent! This is somebody to look up to? I spit on him! Schmuck, with your answers, you don't begin to know the first thing about *anything*. You want The Answer Man? I'll give you The Answer Man. . . . (7)

And Lippman, who believes that what little good there is on radio is contributed by Jews, knows what a real "answer man" should be:

> Dear Mr. Einstein:
>
> I am writing you with a wonderful suggestion that I know would bring about gigantic changes in the world and improve the lot of Jews everywhere. Mr. Einstein, I am a fellow Jew, and proud of it. Your name is sacred to me as to people of our faith around the globe. That the Nazis chased you from Germany is our gain and their loss a million times over, if they even know what a loss is, and I only hope and pray that you are happy here in "the land of the free."
>
> Here is my suggestion. Why don't you go on the radio every week with your own show? If you would agree I would like to manage you, so that your famous mind would not have to be cluttered up with business and so on. I am ashamed to say this in the same breath with your name, but probably you are aware of "The Answer Man" program which is on every night from seven to seven-fifteen. If you're not, just listen for a minute some night. Children all over America think this fake is "an Einstein" probably, when the real Einstein is something they would faint to hear in person. I would like them to know that THE GENIUS OF ALL TIME IS A JEW! This is something the world must know, and soon.
>
> > Respectfully yours,
> > M. Lippman,
> > Talent Agent (9)

When Einstein doesn't answer, Lippman writes again, deferentially, to assure him that Lippman "can understand how busy [Einstein] must be thinking" (10), and to suggest that another nice Jewish boy with a mellifluous voice, Tony Martin, would be perfect to read Einstein the questions on the radio. Further silence induces Lippman to address Einstein as "Doctor" and to inform the great man he need do nothing, that Lippman will drive down to Princeton with his wife and young son this Sunday morning and that Einstein can signify his acceptance by just waving to them from his window when they arrive on the front lawn.

The rest of the plot involves the aborted trip to Princeton. Passing through the town of Scully, Lippman stops for ice cream and drags his family mistakenly into an adjacent saloon (no Duffy's Tavern) and then into a surreal ice cream parlor (more like Circe's lair than Howard Johnson's). In this nightmare world Gentiles ambush Jews who consider themselves above the smell of whiskey, the violence of bowling, the ribbing of the handicapped, or the senselessness of stopping for ice cream—as Mrs. Lippman puts it—"At eleven o'clock A.M.?"

By story's end, the Lippman family has been abused—mother and child may possibly be dead (one of those not-quite-sure endings that seventeen years later would be perfected for *The Counterlife*)—and a bigotted police chief has gotten his. The chief, first wounded by a misfired bullet, dies when that first bullet is driven into his heart by his own later bullet, ricocheting in ironic reversal off its intended target, the spot between Lippman's eyes that happens to be the bridge of his prominent Jewish nose. The nose proves mightier than the bullet, and the anti-Semitic bastard chief is finally "Jewed down."

By the time the plot has developed that far, however, it has ceased to function, in the ordinary sense, as a plot. The reader is carried on a hysterical tide of recriminations as each suffering bigot inveighs myopically against the forces mistreating him. Distrust shapes differences into torments, turns innocent details sinister, makes Lippman feel unsafe, makes the reader uneasy, even in laughter. And as Roth loosens the reader's grasp of verisimilitude and forces increased suspension of disbelief, he makes the impossible probable. A moronic soda jerker has an ice cream scoop where one hand should be; ice cream comes in such flavors as "penny," "ink," "wood," "glass," "shoe polish," and "newspaper" (this last one kills Lippman's little boy by turning him gray, even to the whites of his eyes); and a police chief weighs his manhood against Lippman's at gunpoint by having them both lower their testicles in a controlled squat onto a scale.

Ethnic hatred, this story seems to say, is not one-sided or even more excusable in the more victimized. Lippman's scorn for gentile America is part of the problem of anti-Semitism. Roth's humor is devastating when it seems to ride comfortably on Jewish biases, especially against the irrational in Christianity. Witness Lippman's broadside at Pope Pius XII:

> And how about that skinny Pope with the glasses: catch this—he raises that pale little hand of his and says some mumbo jumbo, and grown men, truck drivers, athletes, financial wizards, smack their foreheads down onto the pavement in awe. Imagine it—a man in a dress is in charge! A man wearing a *dress*. Because what else is that if it aint a dress, an evening gown? And telling them, "Dominoes chess checkers bingo you're going to live forever Jesus christ." And they swallow it— whole! Now if that is no hallucination, then what is? Only it is *not!* (18)

Irreverent? Yes, but close to the prevailing Jewish view of Catholic obedience, ritual absolution—mumbo jumbo! And the trouble Lippman can get himself into by acting on his feelings is potentially trouble for anyone. Indeed, these biases trap Lippman into paralyzing irrationality of his own. When Lippman sees a row of women in flowered dresses and Kate Smith hairdos sitting on the side of the saloon, fat, husbandless, but with children fresh out of Sunday School, he can only assume that the women are swollen on beer, that their men are all off getting drunk ("what are they up to in their bare feet, those savages . . ."), that their fat little children, "pounds of lard (from *eating* lard)" clutch "Sunday School books telling them how the Jews killed their Jesus Christ," and that the explosive sounds from the next room portend some violent ritual threatening him and his family. Only later does it dawn on Lippman that the explosions are bowling pins being struck and that the women are holding their husbands' shoes while their missing men are in the adjacent "room" bowling in their Sunday league. Lippman, doubly obsessed—with "*goyim*" who threaten and with radio that soothes (it can present the higher truth)—cannot credit the harmlessness of a gentile bowling outing: ". . . he could have sworn afterwards that the room from which the bowler had emerged was a radio studio: rows of people, an audience sitting in silence, looking toward a stage . . . or were they only looking toward the bowling alleys?" (26–27)

Lippman's intolerance is a fear of difference, the challenge to every ethnic group in a pluralistic society. He defends his own by scorning others. So for Lippman the bar was one of those

> . . . dark places where Christians found happiness pouring whiskey into their mouths and passing it on out of their putzes (what fun! to make yourself into a piece of plumbing! to turn yourself from a human person into a length of pipe! what brains that takes, to drink something that is brown and turn it into something that is yellow! what a way to use your time!). . . . (15)

It does not occur to Lippman that Jewish tea may be as brown as gentile whiskey because to him tea (probably in a glass) would be normal, as drinking it in the dining room or kitchen would be normal, as drinking it sitting down would be normal. And through the disarming effect of humor and the cushioning of retrospect, Roth gets his reader to share Lippman's view that civilized people would not drink standing with one foot on a brass rail.

Part of Roth's reason for setting this story back in the forties surely was to play off this jaundiced vision against clichés of nostalgia, but he also gets heightened contrast from the changes in Jewish attitudes toward liquor. In the fifties assimilating Jews could emulate Gentiles by building bars in their suburban houses—with what irony Roth had well indicated in "Goodbye, Columbus," where the basement bar has been unused since Ron's bar mitzvah and bottles have unbroken labels. But in the forties Jews were not yet associating liquor with sophistication. So when the Lippmans first enter Scully's Tavern, the bar they have mistaken for an ice cream parlor, the

> genteel Mrs. Lippman, a mannerly and pretty dark-haired young woman, with little experience of the greater world her husband had come to inhabit, reached with one hand for the back of his coat at the first whiff of beer. With the other hand she made a little cup, a little gas mask, over her child's nostrils. "*Goyim*," she whispered.
>
> "So what?" snapped Lippman—for the child's sake. Yet even he . . . sensed a certain strangeness beyond the ordinary strangeness of these people. (15)

Roth moves the reader into Lippman's head, place of dreams and nightmares, and leaves him intentionally disoriented there. The saloon is not only not a benign Duffy's Tavern, it is more disquieting than normal Jewish prejudice might lead one to expect.

> For instance: the head of some antlered animal, stone blind, hung above the bar; not so unusual, except that the head was no larger than [Lippman's] fist, the eyes as big and as black as his little son's. The animal could have been no bigger than a baby when the head was severed from the body. Then there was the door beside the bar: in the center hung a round target, a photograph of the prizefight champion Joe Louis where the bull's-eye should be. Dangling from the target, aside from the regulation darts, were half a dozen ice picks, some Indian arrows, and a bayonet from some bygone era, rusty and heavy, hanging at a precipitous angle. (15–16)

Lippman notes all these signs of violent perversion on first entering the saloon, and through the rest of the story Roth mixes danger with hilarity. The narrative moves easily back and forth from Lippman's fear of how the majority treats minorities to his dreams of success in putting the whole world on radio: (Hitler, Mussolini, F.D.R., they are all to him potentially the stuff of situation comedy). And in other reversals the vicious characters garner sympathy by accurately indicting Lippman for his prejudices about them—suddenly dropping their hick accents like radio actors objecting to the thinness of their parts or adopting mock comic tones faintly reminiscent of radio characters. When the Chief—having ". . . plunged the revolver directly into Lippman's mouth . . ."—withdraws it with a curse and ". . . wiping it beneath his arm . . ." says, "'Don't start spitting into the barrel, will you? This is a precision weapon and you're not supposed to *wet* it,'" one can hear echoes of that ubiquitous tormentor—sometimes the store manager, sometimes the railroad station master—on the Jack Benny program. And when Lippman, in response, gasps that his child has been poisoned, the same Chief, now in Fibber McGee tones, sighs, "'Reckless Accusation, eh? Reckless Accusation Against Christians. The age-old crime, right here in our little town. . . . [the capitalized indictment certifying an almost capital crime]'" and then switches back to the Benny-tormentor voice, "'Boy, you certainly know how to ruin a revolver, don't you? . . . I mean, the cardinal thing about any weapon is *to keep the thing dry. A child* knows that much. . . .'"

The reader is never sure how safe laughter is. When Lippman finally comes to harm, it is not in the bar, where the reader is most moved to anxiety, but later in the ice cream parlor, where quaint locals turn out to be plaguing demons. The Chief, Lippman comes to realize, is the bartender now transformed for at least the third time. When first described, he was a "strongly built young man, with magnificent biceps and a blond Heinie haircut, wearing white bell-bottomed trousers and an armless white undershirt" seen throwing kegs of beer down into a cellar to a "Negro" dressed in Joe Louis boxing shorts. Slightly later he has aged, tortured by having to listen to ten years of mispronunciation from two Chinese kitchen helpers, so that he has scars behind his ears from seven mastoid operations they have put him through—the wages of tolerance! Now, in the ice cream parlor, with Lippman at the end of a pistol pleading for his child and his wife, with the Chief roaring back, "'Oh, you people with your children—and your wives!'" Roth pulls the rug from under the reader again. Lippman thinks, ". . . wasn't this the bartender from that saloon? But if so, where were those scars?" And when, shortly before the final massacre, Lippman desperately tries to adjust these perceptions, he erroneously concludes that

> . . . this was a joke! And a bad joke! *Obviously* it was a pistol full of blanks! *Obviously* this "Chief" was the bartender—and obviously those scars back of the ear had been so much makeup, that mastoiditis so much malarkey! And the ice cream—had they given Ira a "Mickey Finn," or had the boy simply succumbed to his panic? But—if this Chief was such a joke, and this gun such a little toy, why was Lippman allowing it all to happen? What about his wife! his child! and Einstein! What if Einstein was getting up a lunch for them this very moment? *That* could be too! (35)

Lippman, overwrought, cannot tell reality from his own imaginings. And the reader, seeing largely through Lippman's eyes, is similarly disoriented. It is a technique Roth often uses when not so much plot as identity is at issue.

Lippman's quest for Einstein, as in all good quest stories, has been an occasion for self-discovery. Just as the yeshivah in "Eli, the Fanatic" forces Eli to face the assimilationist he has become, so Scully's Tavern and ice-cream parlor (Scully turns out to be the proprietor of both) forces Lippman to face the facile bigot he has become, the man whose easy scorn is really fear.

But facing is not the same as seeing. Lippman cooks his brain up into a feverish state and denies his own implication in any unkindness. All he wants to do with the Gentile world, since he cannot live by just leaving it alone, is convert its unpleasant side to something pleasurable, something entertaining, and show his son that he need not be afraid. Like the questing Eli, who must continually do double takes, Lippman is a man whose vision is being tested. But while "Eli, the Fanatic," seems to have a palpable design upon the reader, "On the Air," in which right and wrong are more elusive, intentionally leaves the reader in uncertainty. After all, where physical violence was concerned, Gentiles *were* more likely to abuse Jews than Jews to abuse Gentiles.

But verbal abuse and physical abuse are sides of a coin, and in this story the coin is frequently flipped. The old Chief (the transformed young bartender) invites Lippman to blow his gentile brains out (he actually places the gun in Lippman's hand) if Lippman is "so sure [he, himself] has committed no crime, if it seems to [Lippman] that Reckless Accusation Against Christians is some sort of trumped up charge . . ." (35). And like Lippman on Gentiles, the Chief has a certain skewered knowledge of Jews:

> Oh you Chosen People, . . . or do you pronounce it like in Chanukah, with a *choff*? Not so dumb, after all, am I? Aahh, who doesn't understand your God damn alphabet? You think we don't know the secrets you write on the outside of those salamis? You think we don't know the messages you send each other right on the butcher's window? "Aleph, bays, gimmel, daled—chess, tess, kiss mine ess!" Aahh, you Chosen People make me sick, if you want the truth! You stick your balls up over a pawnshop and that's the last you ever see of them! (35–36)

And that final image leads to the test of manhood that precedes the bloody ending.

But the reader who has been enjoying Lippman's *schlimazl* story—indeed, enjoying Lippman—knows, despite himself, that Lippman *is* guilty of reckless accusation against Christians, even if that guilt is only lower-cased. And Roth knows that is the kind of knowledge one can bury when it is about a friend. This *schlimazl* is also sympathetic because he dreams, strives to be *someone* in the world. Indeed, there is in his striving and in the philosophy that supports it something of the soul of an artist and perhaps, in his chosen profession, something peculiarly Jewish. Roth uses these sympathies to abet the reader in glossing over the crime. At the same time, he uses the bartender-Chief as Lippman's doppelganger, the secret sharer of his victimization.

What redeems Lippman, despite his limited vision, is his sense, albeit misguided, that he can change the world, that he has chosen a noble profession. A talent agent both discovers and exploits the need for his services, carrying his skills in his head—a classic Jewish occupation. Lippman, insecure in a gentile world he considers phony, comforts himself that nothing imaginable is impossible. He can live in this world by imagining bigger and making his dreams happen. As he puts it, "What you could imagine could also be so. What was not could become!" (16). Precisely when he arrived at this philosophy, he isn't sure. "Seeing 'The Diving Horse' in the show at The Steel Pier in Atlantic City had something to do with it . . ." (16) (though his wife thinks it more likely that he has taken a whack on the head from one of his shoe boxes).

> [I]f somebody once thought up the idea to have a big white horse jump from fifty feet in the air into a tank of water—if that, why not this? When that other fellow came home to his wife in Atlantic City and said, "Honey, I am going to buy a horse and teach him to jump from a diving board with a girl in a bathing suit on his back," would anyone ever have thought that one day people would start out on vacation trips from all over the country to drive to New Jersey to pay to see such a thing? To applaud and applaud and then go home and talk about it for the rest of their lives? No. Oh, no! (17)

A Lippman of loftier ambition might have said with Herzl, "If you will it, it is no dream!" A Keatsian Lippman might have compared his imagination to Adam's dream: "he awoke and found it truth." But this Lippman, who when he runs off at the lip celebrates accumulation of facts as brain power, is pursuing the American dream "(fearless[ly] for the sake of his child)" yet anticipating (and by that anticipation, precipitating) the American nightmare. Still, for some moments the reader is tempted to savor his logic: sometimes whacko ideas, like the diving horse, are sheer genius.

In fact, so far Lippman's only success as a talent agent has been to represent two young black tap dancers—shoe shine boys who worked outside his store, whom he has renamed The Famous Brothers, Buck and Wing. And his dedication to them has been as much in teaching them genteel ways as in getting them work: his great accomplishment, to get them to stop saying "shee-yit" and—against every law of nature—to eat watermelon with a knife and fork. Lippman sees his talent for spotting entertainment as a calling, a gift he repays by giving back to society. "'What if—' Lippman had thought, and that was how the whole [Buck and Wing] thing began. He had cleaned the lice out of their hair and made them stars. And it had begun only as *an idea in his head* . . ." (16). Lippman does not overrate his single accomplishment.

> By comparison to [the creator of] The Diving Horse, Lippman was a very small-time genius, so far. All he had set out to do was to take two [tap dancers] and teach them to do it without saying "shee-yit" every other word out of their mouths. . . . What it had taken him in blood and sweat just to get them to say "Good evening, ladies and gentlemen," without fifty shee-yits in between! But still, it was not so very much compared to teaching a brewery horse to take a dive, a leap, into the blue! (17)

Yet in his misguided way Lippman has a heroic vision. For him the whole world is a stage—or a radio studio. He is almost intoxicated with possibilities the rest of the world is missing. Roth interlaces Lippman's rhapsodies with themes that would obsess his artist-heroes of the seventies and eighties, Tarnapol, Kepesh, and Zuckerman: the differences between appearance and reality, the relationship of art to life, mimetic theory—trivialized, of course, by Lippman's limited sensibility and submerged beneath Lippman's discomfort in America. Lippman almost echoes Roth's own famous statement about the imagination being no competition for the realities that life is constantly tossing up:

> Oh, Jesus—the things you could make in this world! The things that were already *made*! The acts they were just *giving* away! For nothing! Gratis! Step right up, ladies and gentlemen, and pay *nothing*! Of which ten percent, Lippman's commission, was of course nothing too. Hitler, for instance—that little nut over in Germany thundering and howling at those millions of German people, and them saluting and cheering him back, goose stepping for him all night long from one end of the country to the other, and all the time all this goose-stepping and *sieg-heiling* is going on, all the time the torches are burning and the millions are on their feet roaring, all the time in the middle of that face *there is this little moustache*! Hitler! What an *idea*! Or that Mussolini character—with a neck on him like Two-Ton Tony Galento, with a collar on him made of his own thick flesh, and *he* is in charge of all of Italy! With *that neck*! Oh, just think about the big headliners and you could (in a way, in a way) die not to be handling them! "The Adolf Hitler Show." "The Benito Mussolini Comedy Hour." (17–18)

This ecstasy over his role in life and his reading radioland into reality lead Lippman into his perhaps fatal misjudgments. But there is another element connnected to these illusions. Lippman, with his immigrant traces, is unsure of just who he is and needs to secure a place for his son in America. The hunky-dory radio world gives him roles he can assume to assure his son that he belongs. When he decides to stop for ice cream in the town of Scully—the name both of Stephen Crane's hotel owner and of the proprietor here—it is because he is attracted by a wayside sign. "'Ha!' shouted Lippman. It was just his delight coming out. 'So how about it? Who wants any flavor known to man?'" But not just his delight is coming out. Roth interjects, "These remarks were directed . . . to the little boy" (14).

As Lippman proceeds ever further into barely imaginable dangers, he does so largely to impress the child, or to egg the boy on to responses of bravery. The child hides at key times under his mother's skirt, so that she appears to have four legs, two in brown and white saddle shoes. The various bar and parlor characters try to coax him out. And Scully, the man for whom the town is named, sits—benignly it would seem—on the side reading his newspaper and watching things happen. Scully's is the real America, the trap-filled promised land for most Jews in the late thirties and early forties, before knowledge of the Holocaust shifted hopes to Israel. Lippman, the recent immigrant—accommodating like the patriarch Isaac—is trying to secure his place, so his son can "dwell in the land of his fathers' sojournings." But the American dream—how soothingly do the Chief and the soda jerker call to little Ira hiding beneath his mother's skirts— inveigles to destroy. That they tempt him with "penny," "shoe polish," and "newspaper" (ice-cream flavors suggestive of wealth, assimilation, and fame), that "newspaper" turns Ira's body gray (does that mean neutral, neither Jewish nor American?), and that Ira is approximately of Roth's generation may seem like heavy and apparent symbolism. But not to the reader caught up in the black comedy of the scene as it is unfolding. Any symbolic meaning occurs to the reader, if at all, in speculation after the reading is over, prompted by Roth's final ploy of leaving the whole plot unresolved—soap opera fashion. Now, as the son writhes and perhaps dies, the reader watches helplessly through the father's eyes. If Roth is looking at the problems of his own generation as brought on by those of his father's generation, it is not without some sympathy for the agonies of the father.

And the sympathy is even more profound because it recognizes the igno-rance at the base of Lippman's prejudice and the desperation of the man to have all seem well. What drives Lippman to subject his wife and child to dan-ger even after his initial suspicions in the bar is his insistence on treating the real world as though it were the radio world. When he first approaches the bartender (still young with the "Heine" haircut) Lippman gleefully assumes the accent of Mr. Kitzel of the Jack Benny show. And when the bartender seems not to understand him, Lippman sees only the comic possibilities, but from the comfort of his own uncritical ethnic bias:

> Oh, now this does beat "Duffy's Tavern" a thousand times. This guy is rich! A real muscle-bound *goy!* A stupid *shagetz par excellence!* And what about those women, cleaning sawdust out from between the folds of their flesh. Priceless. Perfect. How about a program starring this whole lot—call it "The *Goyim*"! And use that garbageman, too. Sure! A colored singing group, like the Ink Spots or the Mills Brothers. Wait a minute! "Joe Louis—and the Garbagemen!" What if he could get the champ to carry a tune! Dear Joe Louis, Champion of the World, My name is Milton Lippman, agent to Albert Einstein—. . . . (22)

But Kitzel, with his high-pitched "Pickle [peeikel] in the middle [meeyiddle] and the mustard [mushtard] on top," has a stereotypical Jewish accent more vulnerable than charming. And not only does the bartender take unkindly to the put on, pretending not to be able to understand Lippman and generalizing him into "you people," a category extended to Italians, blacks, and Chinese, but it gives him the opportunity (first vaulting the bar and grabbing Lippman by the shirt) to score all immigrants and to declare that the only saving grace in America is "those girls," the fat wives of the bowlers, whom he proceeds to lead in singing Kate Smith's theme song, "When the Moon Comes Over the Mountain."

The answer to Lippman's Mr. Kitzel is the bartender's Kate Smith, offered with ample praise of her manager, Ted Collins, who was the real combination radio talent scout and impresario, living as a millionaire off his one great discovery and promotion, Kate Smith. The nonchalance Lippman has assumed for the sake of his son draws only diatribe from the bartender. But Roth follows his own manic music. He mixes perspectives (at one point the narrator, sounding like Lippman, says, "and get this"). He allows anachronisms (in the forties Lippman would not have named a singing group "Joe Louis—and the Garbagemen"). Roth even parodies other works about dreamers (Lippman composes Herzog-like letters in his mind). All of this blurring and mixing and carrying the reader along on a tide of emotion serves a purpose seemingly at odds with the narrative point of view. The hyped-up narration set in the forties gives us Lippman, but the effect of the narration, read in the seventies, is on the generation of his son—and of Roth's major fictional protagonists. To some extent, all this confusion represents the loving sins of the fathers that would be paid for emotionally by the children of Roth's generation. But the mixing of narrative perspectives also allows the reader to withdraw from Lippman at the very end and view him as a comic soap hero without a grounding in anything substantial.

What is it that Lippman is proud of in his own heritage? He tells nothing about himself to indicate whether he is an observant Jew, but the negative evidence suggests that he is not. Among his oaths are none that come from prayer ritual or suggest that his fears are based in some avoidance of religiously prohibited behavior. Yet he is of a worshipping disposition. His letters to Einstein are reverent. And, of course, for a whole generation of secular Jews it was a point of pride that the seminal minds of the twentieth century were associated with Jews: Einsten, Freud, and Marx—even if those three giants were ambivalent about reciprocating that association. Lippman's allegiance is not to Judaism but to Jewishness. He honors God as a creative force, but not as a repository of morality or enforcer of codes of conduct. As in most of Roth's fiction, this protagonist is a secular Jew whose knowledge of his own religion is general and ethical rather than specific and ritualistic. His responses are tribal: he sees all Gentiles as one religion, summed up in the word *goy*. In response to the "Answer Man" Lippman declares, "You are just another sure-of-himself *goy*, and the truth is that you are a fake, just like the rest of your religion!" (8). In contrast, everything Jewish is good.

> . . . We already have got the best comedians of all time on the radio—Jack Benny! Eddie Cantor! George Burns! Georgie Jessel! Henny Youngman! We have Mrs. Nussbaum on Fred Allen, on Benny we have Shlepperman and Phil Harris and Mr. Kitzel—we have, in straight drama, "The Goldbergs," and on Sunday we got "The Eternal Light" and "The Barry Sisters" both! And who's the funniest on "Can You top This?" Not that *goy* Senator Ford! To tell you the truth, he puts me to sleep with those so-called jokes about morons and idiots. Dopey Dildock—he thinks the *name* is a joke because its got "dopey" in it. Big *goy* joke. No, the best is Harry Hirschfield, and second to him is Peter Donald! Two Jews. And in singers who do you have to top, for an all-around beautiful voice, who do you have better than Tony Martin? I'm talking about a real voice, someone who when he puts on a dinner jacket and opens that mouth gives a person gooseflesh. (8–9)

The absurdity of this list—some of the clearly Jewish characters he mentions, Shlepperman and Mr. Kitzel, are butts of gentile humor and most of the others are Jews not known as Jews, Jews who pass for Gentiles in the broad American consciousness—makes Lippman's chauvinism feeble. It also makes his argument for Jewish superiority patently fallacious.

But the idea of God as creator moves Lippman, moves him to see man's noblest calling as presenting God's universe. That the material is all there already, that all the foibles of political leaders and the physical attributes that make them dramatic are God's doing is Lippman's crude embracing of mimetic theory. Lippman need only hold, as it were, the mirror up to nature. Not only does Lippman defend himself against the accusation that his imaginings are tasteless—"our own dear and beloved F.D.R. . . . with that big cigarette holder and his Mandrake the Magician cape" and Mrs. Roosevelt with "those teeth." "What a character, what a radio personality she could become. Bigger than Baby Snooks" (18)—but he renders his defense in sentiments that might have come right from Alexander Pope— the talent scout as poet, his the true wit that dresses nature to advantage: "People don't notice the unusual things that happen in life until somebody that does comes along and points them out. And that is all I do, and is nothing I will 'be ashamed of.'" (19) Roth injects, in Lippman's distinctive tones, a fervor not unlike that which Robert Browning gives his own "lip man," Fra Lippo Lippi.

> It wasn't as though *he* had put the Pope in a dress. It wasn't as if *he* had given Mrs. Roosevelt those teeth. Lippman was only pointing them out, that they were *there*. "God," he announced to his wife, "God is the Greatest Talent Scout of Us All!" (20)

The comparison with Robert Browning is not so farfetched. Browning's dramatic personae, set often in past ages, were created largely in reaction to critics' reading his life into his narratives. Of course, Browning's style and narrative purpose are totally different, and Fra Lippo Lippi was no merely would-be painter; yet, for Lippi as for Lippman God is the great creator; painters, like talent scouts, his mere mirrors:

> . . . we're made so that we love
> First when we see them painted, things we have passed
> Perhaps a hundred times nor cared to see;
> And so they are better, painted—better to us,
> Which is the same thing. Art was given for that;
> God uses us to help each other so,
> Lending our minds out. (300–306)

And Lippman, too, servant of taste, is glad to make the loan.

What God does for Lippman in creating such a world is permit him to aspire. Somewhere in that created universe is the place that Lippman alone can discover as the arena for his talents. And he thinks that in his present inspired state it has been shown him what he can do to be somebody.

Ah, what a world—Eleanor Roosevelt's teeth, Hitler's little moustache, Mussolini's thick wop neck, the skinny Pope going shopping for his dresses—"Oh, that's you, Pope, that dress is definitely *you*"—oh he could *plotz* from the acts that they were giving away *for nothing*. Ah, but Einstein, Einstein would be his—Einstein with that great hair on the outside and that brain on the inside! Who is Einstein? I'll tell you who—he is the Marx brother who quit the act and went to medical school! ... But if I tell *him*, will he laugh? Will he see the humor? Oh, if he can see the humor, we're in business! Because that's what people love the most in life—that is the truest thing there is, a good laugh! Imagine—if he could get the famous Einstein to crack a few jokes, *and still be a genius!* (18–19)

Lippman packaging Einstein, making the world know the great genius, with some trimmings of humor so he can go down more easily, will help the world, will help the Jews, and will help himself by fulfilling his creative purpose in life.

Art, then, man's imitation of God in being a creator, is the focus of Lippman's real worship. In that regard he is not atypical of the protagonists Roth would create as he moved further into the seventies and eighties. Lippman is, of course, more absurd, and to that extent less likely to complicate a reader's response with questions of biography, but what Roth is up to in "On the Air" makes it very much a Philip Roth story. It concerns how to live—with what value system—in that kind of pluralistic society that modern social philosophy tells us should be the aim of democracy, in a world of competing ethical and religious views, at a time when the prayer book idea of God is untenable for growing numbers of people. It weds the problem of modernism to the problem inherent in the entire history of Judaism beginning in the Bible itself: the problem of how a people that separates itself to develop its own (higher) ethic—"be thou a blessing"—can fulfill its mission to transmit the blessings of its ethical development to the other peoples—"and in thee shall all the families of the earth be blessed"[2]—without coming into assimilative contact with them and without despoiling its own ethic by nurturing illusions of superiority. It presents man as more and more removed from any certainty and therefore grasping for associations that can anchor him safely in the world. And as in many a Roth story yet to come, it presents a creative person rejecting a false world and substituting his own truth, only to have that truth seen as also false. In this case Lippman is even unable to know what he knows, to be sure of what he sees and hears, and Roth makes the reader also uncertain, increasingly aware that what he is experiencing and being entertained by is not reliable information. Moreover, it is not linear plot narration that Roth is practicing here or that he will be practicing in the stories immediately to come. Rather it is narration from shifting points of view, a method for which Roth's special talent for presenting character through speaking voices is particularly suited.

Roth does not end the story with the bullet killing the Chief in some comic or poetic justice. No sooner has the Chief been "Jewed down" by his own bullet, than the story shifts again. The narrator jumps in with a radio voice of the kind that poses questions at the end of a serial soap opera. They are questions that serve up ambiguities on every level and that give this fiction itself the paradoxical quality of modern life, in which fiction is fact and reality factitious.

> What next? Bewildered momentarily by the impact of a .38-caliber bullet on what was, in certain ways, only a nose, Lippman did not at first realize that he was still missing a wife and a child. What had become of those two while he was being held prisoner by Scully, The Chief, and Scooper? And who is this "Scully" anyway? Why is he one thing one moment and something else the next? Why is anybody for that matter? What did The Chief mean when he called Scully "Mr. International Ice cream Cartel"? Anything whatsoever? And what use will Lippman's nose be to him now that he knows it is bullet-proof? Will it prove beneficial in his search for his wife and his child? Will it be good for business? What humiliations have Mrs. Lippman and the child been forced to submit to? Or could it be that they are safely in hiding somewhere— could it be, in fact, that the clever child was only *pretending* to be poisoned by the ice cream, and has taken the occasion to elope, as it were, with his beloved mother? And what of Einstein? Will "Can You Stump Einstein?" remain no more than a program in Lippman's imagination? How can he proceed to Princeton, where the famous scientist may well be awaiting his visit, while his child is at large with his wife? And then, too, there is the small matter of a ritual murder rap. What of that crowd gathering around The Chief's dead body, those angry citizens of Scully muttering amongst themselves, "Yep, Jewed him right down—in cold blood!" For the startling conclusion to this latest adventure in the life of Milton Lippman, Talent Scout! tune in to this same wavelength tomorrow—till then, to all those out there "Beyond the Pale," good night, brethren, and sweet dreams! (48–49)

But there is no conclusion, startling or otherwise. All is open-ended. There are only dreams, mocked by the radio voice. There is nothing "Beyond the Pale." "The Pale (of settlement ?)" has traveled with the Jew into the New World. No escape into Scully America is possible. The Jew may puff (for his

son). He proposes. Scully disposes. And all solutions—Freudian (the son elop-
ing with the mother), Einsteinian, or Marxian (resistance to Mr. International Ice
Cream Cartel) are just so much soap. "Why," the announcer asks, is Scully
"one thing one moment and something else the next? Why is anybody . . . ?" An
ironic question for an American Jew. When he does not even know who he is to
start with, Roth implies, a Jew may try to be "something else" only at his peril.

———————

Postscript: In *The Counterlife* (1987) Roth is exploring, among other
things, the question of identity. Again it is how somebody can be one thing at
one moment and something altogether different at another. Again Roth's touch-
stone is the Jew, the Jew whose parents or grandparents escaped to America and
the Jew who remained in Europe to be trapped in the Holocaust. In *The
Counterlife*, set in 1978, we meet one such European Jew now escaped to
Israel, the Kahane-like leader of a West Bank settlement. His name is Lippman,
first name—not the American "Milton," but the Israeli (and centuries-old traditional) "Mordecai." Here is Roth's description: "Lippman's very looks
seemed to be making a point about colliding forces . . . his nose had been
smashed at the bridge by something that—more likely someone who—had
tried and failed to stop *him*."[3] Mordecai Lippman would be about a decade
younger than Milton. He is from Berlin, and he saw the death lurking behind
Hitler's funny mustache. To him Gentiles are not *goyish shmucks*. They are
mostly advocates of causes inimical to his, and, therefore, quite simply, enemies. In the novel Nathan Zuckerman is trying to rescue his brother Henry
from Lippman's influence and momentarily finds himself walking alone with
Henry down a street of the settlement. He thinks about the last time the brothers were alone and intimate, at night in their little Newark apartment "way
back [in] the early forties" when their only light was the one "shining from
behind the dial of the Emerson radio on the small night table between the
beds."

> I was remembering how, whenever the door creaked open at the begin-
> ning of another ghoulish episode of "Inner Sanctum," Henry would fly
> out from beneath his blanket and beg to be allowed to come over with
> me. And when, after feigning indifference to his childish cowardice, I
> lifted my covers and invited him to jump in, could two kids have been
> closer or more contented? "Lippman," I should have said, when we'd
> shaken hands for the night at his door, "even if everything you've told me
> is a hundred percent true, the fact remains that in our family the collective
> memory doesn't go back to the golden calf and the burning bush, but to

'Duffy's Tavern' and 'Can You Top This?' Maybe the Jews begin with
Judea, but Henry doesn't and he never will. He begins with WJZ and
WOR. . . . Why won't you let my brother go?"[4]

Nathan Zuckerman reaches back for the sweet comfort of a world that
never was except as part of the American dream, the world of "On the Air." It
was a world that had been provided for him by his father, of Milton Lippman's
generation. Mordecai Lippman, by contrast, brooks no illusions. As real and as
threatening as Scully and the Chief, he has come through the Holocaust bearing
the mark of Milton Lippman's personal nightmare. Perhaps Roth decided,
years later, that one way of looking at what he had been writing about in "On
the Air" was the little horror in the American experience that could turn a
Milton Lippman into a Mordecai Lippman.[5]

Chapter 8

WATERSHED

Try mentioning *Commentary* to Philip Roth, even to broach an objection, and he will cut you off curtly with "I don't read that magazine." He once did. He also once published in it. But changes in editorial policy during the sixties and a landmark essay in the early seventies forced a rupture. So strong was the influence of *Commentary* that its withdrawals of favor can be seen as a watershed in Roth's standing with the Jewish intellectual community. The succession of Norman Podhoretz to editor in 1960 portended changes in the magazine's politics from liberal to neoconservative that would turn *Commentary* from a sympathetic resource to an enemy camp. The publication of *Portnoy's Complaint* in 1969, blasted in *Commentary* as elsewhere, changed Roth from a somewhat controversial writer to a storm center and a target. "But the deepest and the unkindest cut of all . . . ," as Joseph Epstein would put it,[1] came in Irving Howe's *Commentary* article, "Philip Roth Reconsidered" in December 1972. Howe gave the intellectual establishment a rationale for joining the chorus of moralists denigrating Roth's achievement. Joseph Epstein asserted in his own *Commentary* attack on Roth in 1984 that Howe's "essay . . . left Philip Roth in the spiritual equivalent of intensive care for . . . more than a decade. . . ."[2]

Howe's revaluation hurt deeply. Not because he thought less than he had previously stated of *Goodbye, Columbus*: so did Roth. Not because he accused Roth of abandoning the serious style of *Letting Go* and *When She Was Good* to achieve popularity: he might just have been expressing his well-known preference for traditional novels that address social issues directly. Not even, though now he was getting close, because he declared *Portnoy's Complaint* to be a cheap string of nightclub shtick that could not pass the test of *re*readability: other reviewers had said that too. What apparently hurt Roth more than all these denigrations of his work was an attack on the man himself, alleging flaws not just of sensibility but of character, intended not to explain, but to explain away, Roth's whole achievement as a writer. Even if Howe sincerely believed that Roth's was a failed art, how he presented that belief must have been to Roth despicable, worthy only of the character Roth would eventually call Milton Appel.

Howe speaks of a ". . . free-floating contempt and animus, which begins to appear in Roth's early stories and grows more noticeable in his later work. Unfocused hostility [he continues] often derives from unexamined depression . . . , which I take to be the ground-note of Roth's sensibility. . . ." He characterizes Roth as "an exceedingly joyless writer, even when being very funny" and his novels as showing "vindictive bleakness." "What," Howe asks,

> does he really have against these unhappy creatures of his? Why does he keep pecking away at them? I think the answer might furnish a key to Roth's work. . . . It is as if, in nagging at his characters, Roth were venting some deep and unmanageable frustration with our common fate.

The translation of this for the lay reader is that Roth has some problem that keeps him essentially an angry adolescent, unable to accept the disappointments of common life or the responsibility for getting on with it. "Unexamined depression" "vented" on the public through "nagging at his characters" adds up to no conscious or serious art, to no ideas deeper in origin than "vindictive" reflexes. With this diagnosis, buoyed by detailed literary analysis, Howe validates attacks of the religious establishment and distributes one-time dispensations to readers guilty of having admired Roth's work, especially *Portnoy*: You laughed; that's all right; it was funny. But joyless, not able to partake of the cosmic laughter reverberating through great comic and satiric writers. Believe me, you would not laugh again! In the guise of saving readers pain, Howe warns them off a course few readers undertake anyway: "The cruelest thing anyone can do with *Portnoy's Complaint* is to read it twice."

Roth did not rush into print to answer Howe. That was not his way. Whether he sat down and composed an answer he never sent, one cannot know, though that was nearer to his way. He had done just that back in the summer of 1969, when Diana Trilling had, in a *Harper's* review, deduced motives and personal qualities of the author of *Portnoy's Complaint* from her reading of the novel rather than confining her comments to the book itself. In that letter he corrects Mrs. Trilling's assumptions about "Mr. Roth": the "Mr. Roth" she posits from reading one book has little resemblance to the author of Roth's four books. To the charge that "Mr. Roth" is a "grimly deterministic" "child of an indiscriminate mass culture" who is in his novel "fortifying a position," he answers that perhaps Mrs. Trilling is fortifying a Freudian position (she speaks at length about "latent content"). And in describing "Mr. Roth's" book as a "farce with a thesis" that tries to make a "pedagogic point," perhaps she is pushing her own classroom analysis at the expense of a receptive reading. Her review limits "Mr. Roth's" talent to reliance on "broad strokes" and an air of "showiness." Roth points out that those were precisely the "airs" no one found, that could not be found, in his earlier novels and are therefore not revelations of the being she calls "Mr. Roth" so much as they are the intentional method of this book, necessary to carry a meaning that goes beyond Freudian or pedagogic analysis. Roth ends the letter he did not send:

> You state at one conclusive point in your review, "Perhaps the unconscious . . . is . . . more hidden from us than the author of *Portnoy's Complaint* realizes." May I suggest that perhaps "Mr. Roth's" view of life is more hidden from certain readers in his wide audience than they imagine, more imbedded in parody, burlesque, slapstick, ridicule, insult, invective, lampoon, wisecrack, in nonsense, in levity, in *play*—in, that is, the methods and devices of Comedy, than their own view of life may enable them to realize. (*RMAO* 30–31)

By the time Roth published this unsent letter six years later in *Reading Myself and Others*, he could group it with other published interviews and inquiries into the composition not only of *Portnoy's Complaint* but also of the other novels and burlesques that had followed it. Among the essays in *Reading Myself and Others* is one in which he does answer not only Howe but, from Roth's standpoint, all critics and reviewers who, like Howe, lack the imagination to conceive the mental and emotional transformation a novelist undergoes in creating a fiction. In "Imagining Jews" he speaks of them as minds wed to categories who either bring their preconceptions to their reviewing or move along on changing tides of fashionable thought. He mentions Marie Syrkin and her limiting sense of Jewishness, her Hitler-Goebbels-Streicher criterion for judging Portnoy. He cites Christopher Lehmann-Haupt for demanding, with the fashions, first visceral, confessional realism ("'I want the novelist to bare his soul, to stop playing games, to cease sublimating'") and later postmodernist "disguise, artifice, fantasy, montage, and complicated irony." Lehmann-Haupt, he says, demands the former ". . . without the slightest understanding that for a writer . . . as for an actor . . . , creating the illusion of intimacy and spontaneity is not just a matter of letting your hair down and being yourself but of inventing a whole new idea of what 'being yourself' sounds and looks like. . . ." And, Roth goes on, when the fashion of the day turns in favor of "artifice," the same reviewer speculates on whether an author he had formerly praised for realism perhaps was not up to the requirements of disguise and fantasy, ". . . no longer had the strength to transmute life into art . . . to turn experience into fiction. . . ." Roth shrugs this off:

> Well, mindlessness marches on. Still, by keeping track of the "thoughts" of a Lehmann-Haupt, one can over the years see just which hand-me-down, uncomprehended literary dogma is at work, in a given cultural moment, making fiction accessible and "important" to insensate readers like himself.

It might not have been prudent for Roth to antagonize the chief daily reviewer of *The New York Times*, who over the years would be in a position to affect his commercial fortunes in the nation's largest book market and whose well-known habit concerning important books was to be the first reviewer into the fray; but the remark is typical of Roth's outspokenness, of his readiness to challenge power. It was a well-grounded trait, characteristic also of the Herman Roth readers would meet in *Patrimony*. In "Imagining Jews" Roth also takes on the *Commentary* establishment. In his view, Marie Syrkin's letter, which was

> . . . published in *Commentary* in March 1973 . . . constituted her improvement on two separate attacks that had appeared several months earlier in *Commentary*, one by Irving Howe directed at my work (most specifically *Goodbye, Columbus* and *Portnoy's Complaint*), and the other by the magazine's editor, Norman Podhoretz, directed at what is assumed by him to be my cultural position and reputation. (*Commentary* associate editor Peter Shaw had already attacked *Portnoy's Complaint* for "fanaticism in the hatred of things Jewish" in the review he wrote when the novel first appeared and which somehow turned up in *Commentary* too.) (*RMAO* 243)

Shaw's attack, "Portnoy and His Creator," had Roth "asserting that it actually is better to highlight Jewish traits that might be regarded as ugly than to hide or gloss over them." By calling Syrkin's letter an "improvement" on these earlier pieces—that is, more strident, but in the same vein—Roth characterizes *Commentary* as a purveyor of a set point of view, not to be taken seriously as a forum for criticism. Set positions stifle response—allow only reaction—to Jewish or literary movements of mind.

In this case, the reviewers had missed what Roth sees as the distinguishing feature of *Portnoy's Complaint*, its having moved into new literary ground by bridging a heretofore tacitly accepted dichotomy in Jewish American literature. The real objection, he insists, was to its having flouted this accepted dichotomy: no other novel had allowed so free-wheeling a character as Portnoy to be identifiably a Jew.

Roth contrasts this seeming paradox with characterization in such representative Jewish works as Bellow's *The Victim* and Malamud's *The Assistant*. Both of those books divide their essential conflict between two characters, one marked by excess of conscience and the other by excess of physical and libidinous aggression, and both assign the moral agency to a Jew and the libido to a Gentile. And that practice of keeping these traits separate—so that either the libidinous character is a Gentile or, if he is a Jew, his Jewishness is in no way an issue—characterizes the novels not only of these authors but of most Jewish authors. For the first time, Roth says, he had placed both the "libidinous slob" and the "disapproving moralist" in one character, Alexander Portnoy. Not surprising that established critics balked at the suggestion, clung to the stereotypes, even though everything they could say in reprobation of Portnoy had been said within the novel by Alex himself.

While Roth in "Imagining Jews" is not making predictions, the response to Portnoy he describes would become fairly widespread and would constitute a well of resentment against its author available ever after to be tapped on cue. The release of libido in a character who was openly and challengingly a Jew, and the ranting tones emanating from one who could not accept in himself what he had been brought up to condemn, would permanently offend certain segments of society. Their defense against these possibilities would be to associate the character with angry self-hatred in his author. The blasts of *Commentary* helped greatly to make the tag stick. It also made the endeavor of close and independent reading less probable. In future fictions Roth would be seen as doing "it" again, not so much writing novels as venting his own anger on his readers through thinly veiled disguises.

But Roth's capacity to scorn what he has considered mindlessness has also been something of a protection. It is not deafness: he has heard very well the criticism, and it has made him appreciate the dangers of the ironic mode. But it also made him know quite early that the commercial success of *Portnoy's Complaint* was unlikely to be repeated and that not his audience—problematic and hard to define—but his own instincts and most deeply felt concerns must determine his subject matter and its treatment. In the two decades since "Imagining Jews" was written, he has both pleased and displeased his readership, but not because he has bent to popular will. At his best, he has delivered the reader into some absurd predicament, surprisingly odd yet familiar, and told a good story: at his worst, being too sparing of his talent, he has sometimes let the *schlemiel* slide into arrogance, the bewildered man of letters into stage directing to make their author's point. Such breach of contract—drying up the springs of sympathy for the protagonist—though rare in Roth, would fuel the contempt of the contemptuous. Others would take disappointment in stride and gamble on their own capacity for surprise: the next production might be totally different from the last. As long as Roth's artistic instincts prevailed, rather than some straining after commercial success, his fate would be in his own hands.

Epstein's characterization of Roth as being in the "spiritual equivalent of intensive care" for over a decade was presumptuous. Not only had Howe not had the last word on *Portnoy's Complaint*, but two decades after Howe's review Harold Bloom could pronounce that *"Portnoy's Complaint* remains wonderfully funny, and is anything but a period piece."³ And in the decade following Howe's review, not only did Roth publish *My Life as a Man*, *The Professor of Desire*, "Looking at Kafka," *The Ghost Writer*, *Zuckerman Unbound*, and *The Anatomy Lesson*, as well as collect his previously written criticism in *Reading Myself and Others* and representative samplings of his fiction in *The Philip Roth Reader*, but he was also busy helping to publish other writers. He was traveling back and forth to Europe, mostly to England and Czechoslovakia, living abroad up to six months of the year, and bringing out the Penguin series "Writers from the Other Europe," designed to make accessible in inexpensive editions translations of the works of Milan Kundera, Bruno Schulz, Jerzy Andrzejewski, Bohumil Hrabal, Tadeusz Borowski, and Danilo Kis. Indeed, Cynthia Ozick dedicated her 1987 *The Messiah of Stockholm* to Philip Roth in appreciation of his having made Bruno Schulz accessible to her in English. Eventually, he would also midwife into an English-language edition Jiri Weil's *Life With a Star*. In 1976 he began sharing his life with actress Claire Bloom, who fifteen years later would become his second wife. And he filled part of his divided time teaching at various universities in America, presenting students with topic-centered readings from several cultures. For some six years after Epstein's "decade," years that would constitute most of the Reagan administration, Roth lived primarily in Europe, not in intensive care, but in intense involvement with the aftereffects of the Holocaust and with the condition of the writer behind the iron curtain. It is a period very much reflected in "The Prague Orgy," *The Counterlife*, and *Deception*. Shortly thereafter, not spiritual but medical intensive care would again become for a while a factor of his career.

Commentary's turn to the right contrasted with Roth's commitment to the values of the left: not so much any political philosophy or admiration of socialism as his suspicion of moneyed establishments and Republicans, his gut certainty of anti-Semitism in the great corporations and of Arabists in the State Department. How could he not, then, feel hostile to *Commentary*, which had accused Roth of aligning himself, in his new financial success, with the "New Class"? This was Podhoretz's term for certain Democrats seen as wealthy knee-jerk liberals who, in the name of democratizing the party, but distrusting the common man, had turned it over to radical forces. Roth thought of himself as a writer sympathetic to the ordinary man, the enemy of privilege. But the very issue of *Commentary* that carried Howe's revaluation also carried another piece on Roth, in which Podhoretz accused him of owing his "centrality" in American fiction to just this snobbish alignment. Podhoretz declares that Roth feels toward Americans of every stripe, a disgust he endlessly explores.

> For [the] overriding purpose [of Roth's stories] is not to question the standard ideas and attitudes which his readers, as members of the educated class, can with complete confidence be expected to entertain about Americans of every other kind; their purpose is, rather, to reinforce those ideas and attitudes, to offer as it were documentary evidence for the complacent thesis that the country is inhabited exclusively by vulgarians, materialists, boors, and bores. Except, that is, for "us": the author and his readers who join together in celebration of their vast superiority to everyone else around them. . . .[4]

For Podhoretz, then, Roth is a member of this self-styled "conscience constituency"—indeed, its laureate—who see themselves above and scornful of the masses. He connects Roth to the new Democratic politics under George McGovern, Joseph Calafano, and Lawrence O'Brien and to the new misguided accent on quotas (*Commentary*'s view of affirmative action), topics also dealt with in this number of *Commentary*. Roth, as the "Laureate of the New Class," is like these politicians capable of supreme ruthlessness

> in . . . pursuit of power . . . status and wealth . . . while excoriating or making fun of the needs and wishes of others and putting them always in the most unfavorable light . . . exempting his protagonists—and, by sympathetic extension, himself and his readers—from the ridicule to which, most often through . . . malicious caricature, everyone else is relentlessly subjected in his work. . . . Philip Roth owes his centrality to the fact that . . . he embodies the ethos [of that group.] The New Class, in short, now constitutes a mass audience in its own right and Roth is the New-Class writer par excellence. No wonder he is such a success.

Commentary was right on one point: the new politics did divide the Democratic party and weaken it for at least two decades by ignoring essential parts of the mainstream. But Podhoretz's association of Roth with an elitism allegedly responsible for that weakening was nothing more than partisanship—grouping together as enemies the various forces that he felt threatening the newly won influence of Jews and the class he thought they could now enter. And Podhoretz may also have identified a source of Jewish resentment toward Roth when, amidst his charge that Roth hates Americans in general, he says, "Since the Americans Roth writes about are more often than not Jewish, some of his critics have charged him with a special animus towards Jews." As a satirist of American life—not the same as a hater of America—Roth may have seemed to target, inordinately, the Jews. But what Roth really opposed was their comfort in associating with groups that either scorned them outright or wooed them to eviscerate them into WASPishness.

Over the years Roth would satirize the Republican presidents and vice presidents—almost, one sometimes felt, for the cleanliness he derived from dissociation. In these pieces he often used the tone of voice as most telling of the particular president's convictions, usually assumptions so deeply held that the speaker himself was oblivious of what he was revealing in his style.

Roth's early piece on Eisenhower at prayer, "Positive Thinking on Pennsylvania Avenue,"[5] is a satire on the Norman Vincent Peale–*Power of Positive Thinking* optimism that Roth associated with WASPS in the fifties. In a way it anticipates the styling of Neil Klugman's prayer at St. Patrick's Cathedral, composed not long after. Just as Roth would have Neil pray to a god of acquisitiveness, he has Eisenhower pray at bedtime (loosely taking off from an account by Mamie Eisenhower conveyed indirectly to Peale), to a god as adjutant, a man-servant of a field commander:

> Lord, I want to thank You for helping me today. You really stuck by me. I know, Lord, that I muffed a few and I'm sorry about that. But both the ones we did all right and the ones we muffed I am turning them all over to You. You take over from here. Good night, Lord, I'm going to sleep.

In a tone as salt-of-the earth as Truman's, but a confidence possible only for one long used to command, Eisenhower is made to show why he could never have accepted a Democratic candidacy but could be comfortable only as a Republican. In the club whose membership was held together by the power of Peale's kind of thinking, Ike and God—a God who knows his station—have rightful places. No place for breast-beating Jews in such cool establishment reverence, where Ike relates to his adjutant on terms that Ike himself has set. "Positive Thinking on Pennsylvania Avenue," which places Ike amidst what

Roth would later call the "native corn," is a mild satire prompted by the very reflex against *goyische* ease that, thirteen years later, would make Milton Lippman rant. In an ease he cannot share, Roth sees establishment complacency he cannot trust.

This 1957 publication occasioned one of Roth's earliest tastes of public reprobation. He was twenty-four, and his satire got two letters of response, one calling it "the most distasteful article I have ever read in *The New Republic*," the other "a fatuous piece of boorishness, and in wretched taste."[6] Ike's prayers were private stuff, one of these writers insisted, and Roth had no business spying and then making them public. Roth replied that it was Norman Vincent Peale who had made them public "by the tens of thousands through the mails" and that Roth agreed, it was "not only bad taste but a blasphemy." With half-concealed bemusement he follows this up in a tone befitting the real (not the correspondent's misplaced) outrage: "to my mind it would be 'cynical and smug' to refrain from picking up the whip of ridicule and driving the exploiters, blasphemers, and money-lenders from the temple."[7] Peale's gossipy, Godly newsletter had been, essentially, a fund-raiser.

Ike was but the first of the Republican presidents Roth would feel constrained to examine. His contempt for Nixon's doublespeak would, of course, surface abundantly in the satire of *Our Gang*, but some twenty months after that work was published, the Watergate hearings now in progress, Roth published a Nixon-like speech called "The President Addresses the Nation."[8] In masterful doublespeak, Nixon refuses to accede to the will of Congress and step down because to do so would be a violation of his oath of office and the trust of the American people who reelected him, and a betrayal of all those wonderful presidents from Washington to Lincoln to Eisenhower who would never have ditched out on their duty, got out of the kitchen, as Harry Truman would say, just because things got too hot. The combination of reverence for the trappings and disdain for the meaning of the Constitution that Nixon embodied emerges from all the "let me make myself perfectly clears" that had become Nixon's giveaway.

That piece on Nixon was a follow-up to others. One, a satire on the war policy that had felled Johnson and that had been amplified by Nixon, had appeared four years earlier and had been based on first-hand knowledge. In 1970 Roth had visited Cambodia, where he saw a peasant population living by the millions in stilt-leg huts shimmering precariously above lakes, eking out livings by fishing in the waters beneath them or toiling in the rice paddies inundated by the monsoon rains. His "Cambodia: A Modest Proposal"[9]—kinder than Swift's— reproved Nixon's anticipated policy of bombing Cambodia's peasantry. Nixon was already floating the idea that with Communists advancing in Cambodia, bombing was necessary to "save" the Cambodian people. Roth asks,

From what? Watching the solitary fisherman push by in their sampans, I could not imagine what there was that could be taken away from them, other than their toil and their arduous lives. Their freedom? They are the slaves of the sun and the monsoon, and always have been. Who in his right mind would plunge this country of peasants into yet another battle for "minds and hearts"? Who in his right mind would ever drop anything on these people other than food, medicine, and clothing? (*RMAO* 187)

Roth's "proposal" to do just that, to drop necessities and, absurdly, *appliances* on this nonelectrified society would accomplish more than the expected bombings and be sound Republican economic policy: ". . . a thousand pairs of boots dropped daily for a week is still cheaper than a single one-thousand-pound bomb. So not only will we be shodding these barefoot Indochinese but there will be an enormous dollar-saving—and thereby certainly the last laugh will be ours." Roth assumes a Swiftian innocence in estimating the risk of hitting and killing some Cambodian child with a "needed" air conditioner; but, he concludes, in a tone anticipating the Tricky Dixon of *Our Gang*, "Let me say . . . I too am

> opposed to the crushing and killing of an innocent Asian child under an American air conditioner. I would go even further and say that I am categorically opposed to the crushing of any child anywhere under an air conditioner, *even a Communist child*. I like to think that I am a humane man. Nonetheless, we must be steadfast in our high national purpose, which has not to do with saving some child somewhere from a falling air conditioner but rather with saving *all* the people of Indochina from a foe whose viciousness and inhumanity exceed the imagination of the American public. And chances are that, with something as heavy as an air conditioner, the child would never know what hit him anyway. (*RMAO* 189–90)

Suffice it to say that *Commentary* and many right-turning American Jews backed the bombing of Cambodia. However, in Roth's writing, even in the fiction, Nixon would remain a symptom of national illness. In *The Anatomy Lesson*, Nixon's writhings during Watergate become an analog to Zuckerman's physical pain in the neck—and nearly its only relief.

During the Reagan years, when Norman Podhoretz and Midge Decter were cheerleading for Reagan at *Commentary* (and perhaps influencing policy through a son-in-law at the State Department), Roth's comments on American policies were indirect at best. His geopolitical interests, irritated by a rising tide of anti-Semitism in Britain, began to move toward growing divisions among Jews in Israel and among thinking people in general over questions of West Bank settlements, as would be recorded in *The Counterlife* (1987) and *Operation Shylock* (1993). But his concern with an American philistinism that could easily and smugly be cemented into policy—foreign and domestic— was as keen as ever. The danger to America and the English-speaking world, as Roth saw it, was not from Eastern totalitarianism, but from Ronald Reagan.

> It wasn't Big Brother who'd be watching us from the screen, but we who'd be watching a terrifyingly powerful world leader with the soul of an amiable, soap opera grandmother, the values of a civic-minded Beverly Hills Cadillac dealer, and the historical background and intellectual equipment of a high school senior in a June Allyson musical.[10]

As the election of 1988 loomed, Roth, back in America, began again to comment on the Republican assumption of America into its exclusionary apple-pie embrace. Not much news about America besides the 1986 World Series championship by the Mets had held his heart from abroad. In an *Esquire* cameo interview subtitled "The Eternal Optimist," he contrasts the little guy, represented by the Mets fan, to the masses that had forfeited their minds for the octopus embrace of the Gipper.

> That year with the Mets was very, very crazy. Men got nutty who aren't ordinarily obsessed with this stuff. That's because the excitement wasn't just about the Mets or baseball. I think that for some of us there may have been something else working on the emotions. At the height of his power and fame, Reagan had become the embodiment of Americanness. I'm an optimistic American, and I don't believe things are destroyed for good by any presidency, but Reagan had tried to co-opt everything called American and had pretty well contaminated the country with his kitsch. So many likable and respectable American things had been pickled in his soppiness, so many things had been taken away from us. But he couldn't take this away.[11]

The "us" was all the outsiders who couldn't get in, and shouldn't be inveigled to try, of whom the Jews had always been prime representatives.

What the *Commentary* mentality seemed to suggest, however, was that Jews could get in, had gotten in, and would continue to get in to office, administrative posts, and presidencies of formerly exclusive Ivy League universities and multinational corporations. They would get in partly because of their unholy alliance with WASP America. This at-homeness, which Roth had also sought and had insisted was the natural next step of acculturation thirty-eight years before in his first trip away to Bucknell, now seemed to him something that could be accomplished only by a sellout of one's immigrant-rooted integrity. Comfort in the establishment was itself suspect, for it required Jews to surrender their traditional function of irritating the complacent, of resisting conformity. The danger was an America resembling Woodenton, where Jews could be invited to come in, be WASP-like, and help keep the next upstarts out. That the Republican right could welcome conservative Jews (and *Commentary* continued to print its share of conservative position papers along with traditional religious stories) to a table set primarily by friends of Jerry Falwell and Pat Robertson made such acceptance clearly a trap for a secular Jew like Roth, whose religion consisted of a more inclusive social agenda, a love of rising inflections, and a distrust of establishments.

The 1988 summer conventions and fall campaign seemed to confirm the latent power of WASPish Republicans over ethnic Democrats. Roth tried to expose that power through humor: a swipe at Dan Quayle for joining the National Guard to avoid the draft during the Vietnam war. It was not so much the choice of service that he attacked, as Quayle's use of family and social position to get correctly placed in the National Guard when others just went to recruiting offices and took their chances. Roth creates a satiric "fable" of a supposed personal experience: his own attempt to join the Guard directly, only to be abused by a recruiting officer for not having used his parents like all good American boys. In this yarn even Roth's own parents become insulted by his abnormal refusal to let them intervene—despite his feeble protests that he is old enough to join the Guard on his own—with the result that his father would not speak to him again for years. He concludes,

> The irony is that, young and raw as I was, I then went off and committed a *totally* abnormal act. I was so angry at the National Guard sergeant, at my mother, at my father—and at America too—that I did the least patriotic thing I could think of. I joined the Army.[12]

Roth could take this high ground because he *had* joined the army after earning his M.A. at Chicago, though he had intended, like Quayle, to further his education. Roth had pursued a Ph.D. for a while after his discharge. Now Quayle was justifying his own hesitation to serve in the military on grounds that he had desired to go on to law school. The contrast between the proletarian G.I. doing what everyone else does and the highly connected National Guard officer who had pulled strings was consistent with Roth's general criticism of the Republican establishment. He would later remain silent on the issue of Bill Clinton's service record. But Clinton, from a proletarian family, would represent a liberal, multiethnic approach to inclusive government.

Roth's use of this fictional self bearing his own name was by this time very much in keeping with his view of the biographical: a fictive self that would irritate the touchy was a tool for peeling masks from readers as well as from the powers that be. And the technique of placing another person in his shoes and tasking him with mixed values was by now a regular Roth ploy to enhance predicament. It would emerge increasingly as the way of his later fiction.

The Bush-Dukakis campaign allowed Roth to elaborate his ethnic thesis. Before the national howl about Willie Horton or the retrospective media analyses, Roth instinctively felt that the issue was old-line establishment versus postimmigrant ethnic intrusion. Amidst a babble of misstated historical facts, Bush anachronistically accused Dukakis of offending the founding fathers by not rallying behind *their* pledge of allegiance (the pledge was not written until 1892). Bush's accusation—of the "stopped beating your wife?" variety—had begun, "What is it about the Pledge of Allegiance that upsets him so much?" And Roth found in Bush's tone and in that question,

> more distressing questions about [Bush] himself. Why is he going around the country leading audiences in the Pledge of Allegiance as though he were the leader of an American priesthood empowered to renaturalize citizens who happen already to be American? Why is he turning the Pledge of Allegiance into a loyalty oath? Why, exactly, at the outset of his campaign, has he seized on the shallowest, most demagogic theme available?[13]

The answer for Roth is not just that Bush's seizing on the shallowest theme, as on the shallowest running mate, owes to intellectual comfort; not a seizing, that is, just "because shallowness stirs him most deeply and fosters his confidence." Rather,

> as permissibly as he can, like a gentleman—yet in a code whose meaning cannot but filter through to those awaiting the message—he is drawing attention to the aura of foreignness emanating from Dukakis's name and appearance. . . . Bush's question, "What is it about the Pledge of Allegiance that upsets him so much?" . . . manages to insinuate that there is something that remains unnaturalized in a man called Dukakis, an ineradicable alienness that prevents him from standing in the same easy, automatic, unchallengeable, seemingly hereditary relationship to America and the Founding Fathers as a George Herbert Walker Bush or a J. Danforth Quayle.

Even in Bush's calling attention to those of his own grandchildren that he referred to as "the little brown ones," a political gesture to confirm his inclusiveness, Bush was showing his discomfort with "physical signs of ethnic or racial difference." And Greek Dukakis, married to Jewish Kitty, was easy to disqualify before a populace being sold Andy Hardy's white-picket-fence America. If Bush was innocent of such tactics by virtue of being just ignorantly insensitive, then Roth would prefer someone downright unprincipled and cynical. In this and other pieces Roth displayed what to him was the strongest aspect of his Jewish legacy: an outsider's assertion of equality with— and distance from—insiders. He could defend that legacy best by challenging a WASP gentility that denigrates demonstrative ethnics.

One possible defense against such WASP attacks was to trump it—myth against myth—by playing the ethnic card. "Ethnic Pop" is Roth's name for the strategy of embodying the immigrant side of the American Dream—father with accent, candy store, sixteen-hour work days, son climbing out through meritorious accomplishment. Mario Cuomo had shown its possibilities in his 1984 keynote speech at the Democratic National Convention. But not even Ethnic Pop could work for Dukakis, whose father was a Harvard-trained physician. In a piece of ironic sociology, "Ethnic Pop and Native Corn,"[14] Roth described the bind Dukakis was in and the stance Bush-Quayle would take to exploit it. Since Greeks had never become fearful enough to Americans "to have inspired an epithet with the pejorative clang of 'wop' or 'mick' or 'kike' or 'spick,'" Dukakis had no "hostile stereotype . . . to oppose." And Dukakis, upper-middle class, Harvard educated, could never be sold as an ethnic exotic, a Zorba the Greek.

> You can sell Ed Koch as Ariel Sharon and Milton Berle all in one, you
> can sell Jesse Jackson as Martin Luther King and Reggie Jackson all in
> one, but you can't sell Dukakis as related in any conceivable way to
> Anthony Quinn.

Taking advantage of this weakness, Bush-Quayle would play to "Native Corn": become the "benign incarnation" of "the lah-di-dah Boss and his pampered Son." It was all a matter of style, demonstrated ultimately by voice: "Native Corn families have spoken unaccented English for more than a mere 50 or 60 years—they have spoken it forever." Roth analyzes the strategic warfare.

> Bush's early obstacle had been to convince connoisseurs of Native
> Corn that he is as potent and authoritarian as he is prosperous and pure
> bred. His mistake was to try so very hard to make regular guys think he
> wanted nothing more than to be a regular guy like them when actually his

Native Corn mission as both Boss and Dad was to inspire in those less powerful the desire to be like him . . . [with] a talent for imposing his will—as is befitting a man of his inheritance—and a subterranean taste for cruelty.

In contrast to the Ethnic Pop son, the Native Corn son accepts the benefits dropped in his lap by the power-wielding father, who "crushes without a qualm what must be crushed." Roth knows how aptly Bush and Quayle can cash in on caste.

Talk about the American Dream! Here is the most seductive, the most magical, the cushiest and dreamiest American dream of them all—winning the capitalist jackpot, the whole damn thing just dropping into your lap out of nowhere. Only for Senator Quayle it isn't a dream—to him this looks like reality. No wonder that of all the performers in the '88 election, he alone plays his role to perfection.

Whatever Dan Quayle's scripted role may have been, and whatever his intellectual breadth or limitation, his outlook on the status and rights of the citizenry was of that conservative stripe Roth distrusted. That Quayle took on as his theoretician William Kristol, Jew, but nursling of the *Commentary* establishment, would have been perfectly consistent with Roth's sense of anathema.

When Roth turned directly to an examination of George Bush, what offended him most was Bush's opportunism amidst his feigned benevolence, a trait that would contribute to his discomfiture four years later. The opportunism was given away by two functions of voice: pronunciation and pronouncement. Roth caught them both. Half a year into Bush's presidency, Roth caricatured what Dana Carvey on "Saturday Night Live" would make Bush's most telling sound, the clipped and elided word endings of the Connecticut Yankee playing John Wayne; and he burlesqued Bush's betrayal of his former pro-choice position in a classically absurd argument lifted right out of Roth's almost two-decades-old *Our Gang*. "Pro-Life Pop"[15] is Bush turned on by the lure of the airwaves to a zealotry worthy of Lippman, but pandering to the Right with a logic echoing Tricky Dixon.

In this burlesque, we meet a Bush who has offered the country a multi-pronged constitutional amendment that would (1) combat abortion (and the spilling of seed or eggs anywhere), (2) fight illiteracy by creating a technically literate but intellectually benighted laboring class, and (3) promote "family values," that is, the prevention of out-of-wedlock births (and wasteful contraception) by mass marriages among ignorant pubescents. The great value of this plan would be its effects: voluntarism and perpetual free enterprise. As the population exploded with kids half of whom would be trained to teach the other half to read (sweet are the uses of illiteracy if it produces perpetual industry) the underclasses would be too busy to rise and too ignorant to challenge "life," whose only value was itself. In this burlesque, part of Bush's proposed constitutional amendment would outlaw not only abortion, but also masturbation and menstruation.

The fatherly Bush voice begins this suggestion with "I think we're on a wavelength here that Americans can be prouda." By the conclusion his faintly veiled ruthlessness sums up the whole Bush value system. Asked by a reporter how he envisions "the states dealing with masturbation and menstruation," Bush, in Roth's script, replies:

> Well, what my sense is, is this: get back to family values. As those boys and girls out there approach puberty, get back to those family values and nip this thing in the bud. Let's take all this stuff out of the realm it's been in and let's get our kids and our grandkids married and havin kids and grandkids of their own to go out sailin with and tossin the ball around with and this amendment won't *need* enforcin. Good clean fun, just like it says in the Bill a Rights. Everybody over twelve married, and big, big families like our own, God bless em, and millions and millions and millions of kids and grandkids, and half of em illiterate, and the other half volunteerin to teach em to read. . . . Call the person sittin in this office a dreamer, but that's the kind of America I can envision for centuries to come.

Roth's implication is clear. The Republican right will advance any seeming value that serves to keep entrenched power and inherited wealth safe from the challenge of the masses.

These excursions out of serious fiction and into broad satire and burlesque permitted Roth to exercise the easy side of writing about the absurd. They kept his liberal passport valid, reassured him of his political integrity, permitted him to exercise a side of his patrimony that he recognized as at once peremptory and pure. He was being Herman Roth's son. At the same time, he maintained another sense of himself as a writer of fiction. This was hardly one-sided. And the satire it engendered was hardly the classic Swiftian view of a social or political wrong that could be righted by humane act or policy. It was a satire, begun in *Portnoy*, stretched to manic limits in "On the Air," and chastened to greater or lesser successes in the fiction of the eighties and nineties, a satire in which the self or the group in which the self rested is assaulted for its easy victimization and defended for its characteristic survival mechanisms. The Jewish issues would be explored by characters publicly insisting on some new idea of themselves while privately asking "Is it me?"

Increasingly, Roth's fascination was with predicaments. "What if?" could be played out imaginatively by placing himself in the predicament of someone who thought or felt entirely differently than Roth was accustomed to thinking or feeling. To the extent that fate is character, how would a personality play out its fate in altered circumstances? How, for example, would Franz Kafka have played out his attempts to be close to women if consumption and death had not claimed him and if he had escaped the Holocaust fate of his three sisters?

"'I Always Wanted You to Admire My Fasting'; or, Looking at Kafka" (1973) is a remarkable work, both for its own moving effect and for its stylistic progress toward the mode of Roth's most controversial pieces of the nineties. Roth was composing it at the very time Howe was composing his condemning revaluation. It begins as a personal essay, a homage to Kafka, and only later moves into the form of a short story, a fantasy upon the implications of that essay. Thematically, the two parts are of a piece: Roth muses on bachelorhood as an aspect of Kafka's entrapment, the son hedged in by a paternal barrier. Kafka, overwhelmed by his father, felt closed off from any domain his father occupied; and in Kafka's view, marriage was such a domain. In the essay part, Roth gazes upon the image of Kafka in the famous photograph, taken when he was forty (Roth's age as he writes), speculates on several Kafka stories of entrapment and on the release from that feeling Kafka must have experienced in his last year with Dora Dymant, a release prompted by her faith in him and by the imminence of death. Kafka did not marry Dora: her father, influenced by the Gerer Rebbe, refused to let her marry a dying man twice her age. And Kafka accepted that—another father's will not to be challenged. But he had in the year with Dora studied Hebrew and written the unfinished story "The Burrow" and had left Roth grounds for speculation. "What if?" Roth asks, not irreverently: What if Kafka had not succumbed to consumption, leaving his manuscripts in Max Brod's rescuing possession, but rather, allowing his novels to perish and himself to survive after studying Hebrew, had taken his pension from the Prague insurance company and come to America just as the war against the Jews was starting? What if he had come to Newark and become a Hebrew school teacher in an after-school setting like Rabbi Binder's? What if in 1942 he had become *Dr.* Kafka, Philip Roth's—and his kibitzing friends'—Hebrew teacher?

This fantasy is not manic, in the mode of "On the Air." It is wistful and profound, linking European Jewish history, Kafka's eminence in twentieth-century German literature, the Holocaust, the relative blessing of the Diaspora, the fragile synapse connecting repressed man and supreme artist, and Roth's own patrimony. The prose of the essay part is masterful: descriptive, evocative of Kafka's almost other-worldly essence, allusive of all the threads the fantasy will braid. The literary analysis, with its tie to Kafka's personal psychology, is equally superb. The story part, introducing the urchins of Weequahic to high-light the predicament of one whose writer's genius cannot shine in mere life, never becomes vicious. Even though it is little Philip who names him *Dr. Kafka* and even though Philip's friends erupt with glee at privately calling him "Franz Kishka," these nine-year-old pranksters sense in the sadness of the man something that deters practical jokes. Philip, the most studious, experiences guilt that "awakens redemptive fantasies of heroism," noting that he has them "often about 'The Jews of Europe.'" Kafka is still a bachelor for reasons the reader understands from the essay, and little Philip and friends discover that he lives in a rented room.

Mostly, the story is a celebration of Roth's own family's mutual support. Philip mentions Dr. Kafka's lonely station, and Mr. Roth sets to matchmaking with Mrs. Roth's spinster sister. Dr. Kafka accepts an invitation to dinner, and Mr. Roth shows him the book of the family circle, with its officers and formal gatherings; Philip recalls his stamp collection (which would emerge as a sore point in *The Facts*) and his apprenticeship to his older brother in fathoming adults, as the two speculate from their bedroom on the progress of diplomacy in the dining room. There Kafka meets Aunt Rhoda and is apparently taken with her and her interest in Chekhov (she is playing in an amateur production of "The Three Sisters"). They date, and an engagement is in the wind.

When all seems to be going swimmingly, Kafka suddenly disengages himself. He is, after all, Kafka. His own patrimony, looming from the past, has blocked access to marriage: that is still his father's domain. The family con-soles Aunt Rhoda and declares Kafka "*meshugeh*." Reality, where character determines fate, has asserted its claim: a Kafka spared from early death would have merely existed and faded, and literature would have been the poorer. The story is almost the obverse of a well-known movie: it is not "a wonderful life" to continue living if that living is mere continuance, while one's death might, by a quirk of fate, have enriched the world. Eventually, this Dr. Kafka dies at age seventy in the Deborah Heart and Lung Center in Browns Mills, New Jersey. The death notice lists him as having been a Hebrew teacher. Like the hunger artist in the story that gives Roth his title, he is cleared out of his confined space and life proceeds.

There is almost a religious fatalism about this "what if?" By contrast it makes the real Kafka's death seem redemptive, for through the agency of Max Brod it allowed the novels to survive Kafka's expressed wish to have them destroyed. The contrast with "normal" life sanctifies Franz Kafka's bewildered struggle. Roth's story pays tribute to the triumph of art and to the arch-victim Jew, with "ears shaped and angled on his head like angel wings" and "an intense, creaturely gaze of startled composure," who produced the finest

German writing in the century of the Holocaust. "Looking at Kafka" has now become available to general readers in a new Schocken Books collection of short stories.[16] Even in a *Commentary* review, twenty years after its writing, the story would be acknowledged to be "richly imagined" and "Roth's love of Kafka, his sense of him as someone uncannily familiar, [to be] very much grounded in the (secular) Jewishness they share."[17]

Fifteen years after writing this story, Roth had a letter to the editor of *The New York Times*.[18] Kafka's handwritten manuscript of *The Trial* had gone at auction to a German buyer for $1.98 million, and the dealer who executed the purchase had said, "This is perhaps the most important work in 20th century German literature, and Germany had to have it." Roth's letter was about the irony that would not have been lost on Kafka. Roth writes,

> Kafka wrote in German, of course, but he was not a German in any way. He was, to the core, a German-speaking citizen of Prague and a son of Prague Jews. In the final, ailing years of his life, when he was, in fact, teaching himself Hebrew, he even occasionally wondered if he ought not to emigrate to mandate Palestine.
>
> If he had not died in 1924, at the age of 41, and had lived on into the 1940's, he would have been murdered at Auschwitz as a Jew. His three sisters, Valerie, Elli, and Ottla, were incinerated there by the Nazis, and there is no reason to think that the author of the most important work in 20th-century German literature would have been spared by the German nation. . . .
>
> If any country had to have the manuscript of "The Trial," it seems to me that a decent regard for historical fact might have placed Germany somewhat farther down the list than England, where the Bodleian has safeguarded Kafka's papers since the 1940's, or Israel, where "The Trial" manuscript found refuge with Brod in 1939 and where it would not have seemed anomalous in the archives of the Hebrew National Library.
>
> It does not strike me as a cause for jubilation that neither of these two institutions was able to raise the money to prevent yet another lurid Kafkaesque irony from being perpetrated on 20th-century Western culture.

Both "Looking at Kafka" and Roth's treatment of holy Jewish themes like the Holocaust and the sanctity of Jewish letters belie the view that Norman Podhoretz posits of Roth as a supercilious member of the "New Class" and the cliché that *Commentary* let pass current for two decades of Roth as a lightweight self-denigrating Jew. Roth characters might hate aspects of themselves, indicating the predicament of a culture that sends conflicting messages, but that is another matter. And when Podhoretz's son John wrote an apprecia-tion of Roth's accomplishment in 1981, he didn't get it published in *Commentary*.

John Podhoretz's piece, "Philip Roth, The Great American Novelist,"[19] subtitled "What do the Jews want?" was published in the conservative *The American Spectator* in 1981 as a revaluation of Roth's standing after the pub-lication of the first two Zuckerman novels. It is clearly a rejoinder to Howe and the *Commentary* thesis of his father. After quoting a passage from *Professor of Desire* showing Jewish solidarity among middle-class kibitzers, he says, "One can see the love with which Roth has written this passage," clearly a rebuff of John's father's position. He says that for all Roth's vulgarity, "behind the bril-liant comedy lies a serious concern with important matters—and when dealing with important matters, he is never vulgar." This and his averring that Roth "was roundly accused of sensationalism at the time of *Portnoy's Complaint*, but it was a false and cheap accusation" seem to be pointed answers to Howe. Indeed, John Podhoretz considers the "Whacking Off" section of that novel "a marvel, one of the most unsettling and brilliant passages in modern literature," for masturbation as treated by Roth, unlike Masters and Johnson, is "a matter of utmost seriousness . . . even as he describes it hilariously he analyzes it gravely."

As to John Podhoretz's chief question about Roth, "Why is he picking on the Jews?" it is not just that they are part of America and he hates America. Rather, it is that

> They are Jews. And what they feel—and what Roth feels, and what I feel—is inextricably linked to that one defining fact.
> . . . despite the harshness, the nakedness, with which he examines the most uniquely beleaguered people who have ever lived, he recognizes the one thing that makes the Jews of the present day still Jews . . . the facts of our ancestry, our family, our membership in a race and in a reli-gion. . . . *I am a Jew*, the characters in Roth's books cry out, *but why?* There is no *why*. The Jews are not a cause, not an issue: They are a peo-ple. The question, thus, is not, Is it good for the Jews? or, as the sancti-monious Judge Wapter puts it in *The Ghost Writer*, "Can you honestly say that there is anything in your short story that would not warm the heart of a Julius Streicher or a Joseph Goebbels?" The real question is, Are You Telling the Truth? Roth does tell the truth.

Inasmuch as the sanctimonious Judge Wapter had taken this line from Marie Syrkin, who had reiterated her position in her letter to *Commentary*, this, too, constitutes a rebuff of that magazine's crusade. And the younger Podhoretz is moved to conclude that "there is no denying Roth his position as one of the foremost of American Jewish writers, and very likely as the foremost American novelist of his generation."

Although *Commentary*'s own staff writers continued to regard Roth with a certain disdain, the magazine after the mid-eighties did publish some pieces that were favorable to Roth, usually pieces by scholars safely regarded as Jewish luminaries. As shall be seen, Robert Alter's review of *The Counterlife* and Hillel Halkin's analysis of Roth's career, focused on the publication of *Operation Shylock*, would tend to restore Roth somewhat among the *Commentary* readership.[20] Indeed, Halkin's estimate of Howe's 1972 revaluation was that it had failed to understand Roth's artistry, however luckily it may have stumbled on the centrality of *Portnoy's Complaint* to Roth's output.

As to Roth's own answer to Irving Howe and *Commentary*, it would come—and be largely misread—ten years after Howe's essay appeared, at the end of Joseph Epstein's "decade in intensive care." It would come in fiction, not as Roth's righteous revenge, but as the absurd obsession of a character who had fully absorbed its message and had taken it, far more than it warranted, to heart.

Chapter 9

ZUCKERMAN BOUND

"The time will come when we are people again, and not just Jews." These words are not Portnoy's. They lack his rancor ("Jew, Jew Jew, I happen also to be a human being!") and are too sanguine in their use of "again." Alex knew of no recent equality for Jews that could justify "again." Many European Jews in the 1930s and 1940s, accepting the myth that they were "people . . . , and not just Jews," had been martyred for their fiction. That martyrdom might bond their successors through worship of their sainthood and even rekindle in a new generation hope of being people. A writer like Nathan Zuckerman, reviled almost from the outset for assuming that right, might redeem himself by embracing, nay by marrying, a sainted martyr who had written those words. If only he could imagine her back to life! *Anne Frank, thou shouldst be living at this hour, Nathan hath need of thee!*

With *The Ghost Writer* (1979) Roth began taking on in fiction the thousand Jewish shocks his writer's flesh had become heir to. For much of a decade Nathan Zuckerman, as Roth's alter ego, would be the arch-assimilated-Jew-writer, whose every word or move exposed him and his people to judgments severest critics had leveled at his author. The Zuckerman fictions are *The Ghost Writer*, *Zuckerman Unbound* (1981), *The Anatomy Lesson* (1983), "The Prague Orgy," now incorporated with the first three into one paperback volume as *Zuckerman Bound* (1985), and *The Counterlife* (1987). As each appeared, it seemed at first a self-contained work, hardly an install-ment in an unfolding saga. Each apparently had something to say about the interaction of a writer's life and his art; then, with the advancing sequence, something perhaps obsessive about Roth's own life and art. By *Zuckerman Unbound* and *The Anatomy Lesson*, the second and third in the series, many reviewers, tired of what they saw as Roth's score settlings, began issuing gra-tuitous advisories that Zuckermania was now exhausted. But some critics had learned not to be so sure, that advisories of Nathan's demise might be prema-ture, that something might still be cooking larger than Roth's rejoinders to them.

Whether *Zuckerman Bound* holds up as a single work only a new reader can tell. Almost no critic read it that way originally or undertook to read the whole thing as if *de novo* when it was published. Most used the occasion, rather, to review the only new part, "The Prague Orgy." The tones of the four component works are different, the quality uneven: the lesser middle two works are narrated in the third person, the first and last by Zuckerman himself. But these, *The Ghost Writer* and "The Prague Orgy," contrast sharply in tone: the one detached, musing, timeless; the other manic, resigned, pinned to its era. Taken together, the four parts explore a question concerning both art and Jewry: whether either can survive without opposition. As freedom betrays family, and intermarriage betrays tribe, so art—especially writing—betrays a culture by opening it to new stories and sharing it with strangers; and the critic, like the rabbi or the parent, is a necessary opponent who calls the artist to account for his betrayals. Zuckerman thinks he can betray benignly and escape behind the walls of his art. Roth uses Zuckerman to tell the world it must let the artist do so, but he brings the world into the books to tell Zuckerman that ain't the game.

The subtopics in *Zuckerman Bound* differ, but as a whole the work sati-rizes an absurdity of the Western intellectual. Whether one is moved to sym-pathy for or anger at Zuckerman—Roth calls him not just an alter ego, but one living life at "a higher valence"—he is a character being wrung out for his focus on himself. Zuckerman is serious about everything, about art, about her-itage, about freedom, about being important. Looking back at him in 1988, Roth could say,

> His comic predicament results from the repeated attempts to escape his comic predicament. Comedy is what Zuckerman is bound by—what's laughable in *Zuckerman Bound* is his insatiable desire to be a serious man taken seriously by all other serious men like his father and his brother and Milton Appel.[1]

That is not the whole of these works; each presents an aspect of Roth's developing view of the artist's predicament. Yet to lose the sense of the absurd operating throughout the series is to lose an important perspective.

The Ghost Writer is about apprenticeship and the madness of art; it is also about substituting fathers, betraying one by adopting another. *Zuckerman Unbound* is about the irony of success, becoming prisoner of a resentful public; it is also about casting off fathers and all they stand for. *The Anatomy Lesson* is about the imprisonment of self-absorption, of inscribing the guilt in the flesh; it is also about hurting fathers and needing their blessing. "The Prague Orgy" is about the impotence of art in totalitarian society; it is also about the misuse of fathers, the ease of betraying them in the name of art.

These works are also tied by a common temporal perspective. Although written and published at two-year intervals between 1979 and 1985 and set at wider intervals spanning twenty years, they are each narrated from some point in 1976–77. Zuckerman begins *The Ghost Writer*, "It was the last daylight hour of a December afternoon more than twenty years ago—I was twenty three. . . ." A little back-reading from the epigraph used to introduce *Zuckerman Unbound* fixes that afternoon as December 9, 1956, and makes *The Ghost Writer*'s supposed composition date some time after December 1976. "The Prague Orgy," a series of Zuckerman's notebook entries, is dated about a year earlier than that supposed time of composition, between January 11 and February 6, 1976. Although Zuckerman's authorship of all these works predates by over a decade Roth's writing of the first of them, the life Zuckerman is writing of, set in 1956, 1969, 1973, and 1976, parallels that of his author: Roth in 1956 was publishing his first controversial stories, in 1969 *Portnoy*, in 1973 *The Breast* (like *The Anatomy Lesson* about entrapment in the flesh), and in 1976 was making one of those *shivah* calls to the once vibrantly Jewish Prague, which, the following year, would inform *The Professor of Desire*.

Since the middle two works are not written in the first person, one might facilely conclude that they come directly from Roth without the intermediate authorial presence of Zuckerman; but shortly before the end of *The Anatomy Lesson*, Zuckerman, in a hospital with his mouth wired shut, writes on a clean notebook page: "WHEN HE IS SICK EVERY MAN NEEDS A MOTHER." That is also—almost verbatim—the first line, 267 pages earlier, of the novel in which he is writing this sentence. Is *The Anatomy Lesson*, then, Zuckerman's third-person account of what has happened to him, begun in the hospital where the novel finally leaves him? Critics who pronounced the exhausted Zuckerman at that point finished as a writer, who were surprised by his return in "The Prague Orgy" and later in *The Counterlife*, might have read more carefully.

In *The Anatomy Lesson* Zuckerman is once more facing the problem of self as subject for fiction—the great accusation against Roth. Enough! He would become a doctor and get involved with "the lowest of genres—life itself," plunge up to the elbows in the gore and blood of other people's stories. As a writer he was trapped in his own stories, his own story. Critics had said if he *was* a writer he could write about things beyond himself. Ah, but "if Zuckerman wrote about what he didn't know, who then would write about what he did know" (544)? The artist, like the Jew, had a Hillelian dilemma. "If you get out of yourself you can't be a writer because the personal ingredient is what gets you going, and if you hang on to the personal ingredient any longer you'll disappear right up your asshole." In a sense, that is what the older Zuckerman writing the first words of this novel about him is doing at the end of *The Anatomy Lesson.*

But even the young Zuckerman who comes to visit Lonoff at the beginning of *The Ghost Writer* has already begun a reverse alimentary passage of sorts. His narrator is himself, already successful and somewhat controversial by the time he composes this ingenu in 1976. Moreover, Lonoff is dead—having died in 1961—and Roth, the author-twice-removed of all of them, is living in a Berkshire farmhouse half of every year. Many critics were quick to identify Lonoff as Malamud—the Malamud of *Dubin's Lives*—whose life of isolated writing took place in the country. Or Salinger. Or a fusion of the two with a seasoning of Chekhov. But Lonoff is also Roth; or, more precisely, half of Roth is Lonoff. And in *The Ghost Writer*, young Roth visiting older Roth, to some extent disappearing up his own persona, is being ghost written by a counter-self. Or is it the other way around? Impatient readers might conclude that Roth is merely playing literary games, that they should just shrug him off as self-indulgently clever. But while the interwoven chronology binds the books, it never dominates them. The reader is hardly aware of it. And if these personae are manifestations of self, none of them is being explored in a vacuum. For the most part these works are good stories, engaging to a reader who may not know their various interconnections. What keeps all the Zuckerman books bound, with their different obsessions with fathers, is the tug of Jewish origins, the father principle in its larger sense, and Jewish authenticity as measured by the bond to fathers.

The simple plots of the novels are occasions to probe two heightened states of existence: the artist and the Jew, both of whom must live with the "unreckoned consequences" of their chosenness. In 1956, twenty-three-year-old Nathan, needing some patting of his writer's ego, visits Emanuel Isidore Lonoff, the dean of Jews who have "got away." Nathan is smarting from an objection by his father to his having written an "Epstein"-like story, an objection seconded by an inquisitorial letter from Judge Leopold Wapter, a leading Newark Jew, about the Julius Streicher–like effects of publishing such a story (Marie Syrkin and Gershom Scholem with a vengeance). Wapter's concluding advice is that Nathan reorient himself to his tribe by seeing the Broadway production of "The Diary of Anne Frank." Nathan, who bristles at Wapter's words, must wince at his father's: their appeal to common sense, less strident than the Judge's indictment for treason, threatens with the simple truth that "People don't read art—they read about *people*." Gentiles will judge Jews by Nathan's depiction of family in-fighting among money-grubbing "kikes." Young Zuckerman's first intimation of the madness of art is of some of the nonartistic uses it can be put to.

Lonoff's farmhouse seems the ideal haven from Doc Zuckerman's and Judge Wapter's strictures. As a Jewish writer, Lonoff has it both ways: he writes about archetypal Jews with immigrant accents while married to a gentile Brahmin, and he eschews company and life in general to immerse himself in turning sentences. Lonoff has invited Nathan because he admires the authenticity of the young writer's "voice." In an overnight encounter with the older writer, amidst talk of other writers, some glimpses of Lonoff's other protégé, Amy Bellette, and a fantasy identifying her with the sainted Anne Frank, Nathan discovers the challenge of a literary life: how to divulge it into fiction and have it too.

A young woman of indeterminate European origins, but faintly resembling and of an age with Anne Frank, Amy Bellette is also having a father experience with Lonoff. She is putting his scattered papers in order for the Harvard library, at night trying to seduce "Dad-da" into running off with her to Italy (but momentarily settling for his imitations of Jimmy Durante), and deluding herself that if she succeeded she could be anything more to the old writer than a substitute martyr for the present Mrs. Lonoff. That forlorn wife, ironically named Hope, says she has gotten more fondling "by strangers on the rush-hour subway during two months in 1935 than . . . up here in the last twenty years!"

In the morning, when Nathan leaves, and Amy Bellette (who is not Anne Frank) leaves, and Lonoff's wife Hope leaves to reach perhaps the bottom of the hill, and Lonoff leaves to bring her back, Nathan is aware that the literary life is no escape from the problems of being a Jew, however fitting it may be as a means to rehearse them. Awareness, of course, is not yet realization, which comes from living. This has been a ritual, a literary bar mitzvah. Lonoff, assuming Nathan will write of this encounter, and "curious to see how we all come out," gravely shakes Nathan's hand "as though having concluded my rites of confirmation" (180). But he has not freed Nathan from the constraints of his Newark upbringing or led him into a world of art as licence. In Lonoff's own writing, unsettled Jewish characters are saved from the consequences of their desires by "the ruling triumvirate of Sanity, Responsibility, and Self-Respect." Lonoff, it seems, is closer to Doc Zuckerman than Nathan has realized. The trading of fathers is not so easily accomplished. Nathan has begun to see that one of the problems of being a Jew—and of being a writer—is trying to live into adulthood without betraying one's father

Anne Frank is a metaphor for that problem. The most widely read writer on the Holocaust had, like Nathan, written about her own personal life and family conflicts, including, with adolescent awakening, a defiant declaration of personal independence, and had expressed assimilationist sentiments; yet she had an authenticity Nathan could never aspire to. The irony is that Anne's authenticity as a writer had required her death; the poignancy of her work rested not so much in her words from the attic as in that sequent event—and its representative historic effect. Were she to have miraculously survived the Holocaust and just come in 1956 to a realization of who she was, she would have to suppress the fact and find some new *achterhuis* to hide out in, for the exposure would compromise her book and betray her father, now riding the lecture circuit as her sole survivor (and owner of her copyright). Nathan fantasizes just such a situation—for his own purposes: he dreams that Amy Bellette is the still-living Anne Frank, whom he will marry and by so doing redeem himself, the wayward son become the Jew of Jews.

Roth's outrageous use of the device, offensive in its very discernment of Anne Frank's anomaly, cuts right to the heart of his own controversy. He did not beard his protagonists or confine them in exotic modes, but put them forth—as Anne would have—as moderns claiming equality in a pluralistic world. Of course, Nathan at twenty-three and Roth writing about him at forty-six were well beyond Anne's naive hopes at thirteen. Roth knew the price of pluralism—not least from *lantzlite*—and he distributed many of the indictments he had come to know in his earliest battles with the Jewish establishment among the characters of the novel. Lonoff's daily mail contains both gratuitous plot suggestions (just as Roth early on had been told what a Jewish writer ought to write) and curses from anti-Semites for assuming he could write also of Gentiles. Anne Frank, we are reminded (in an incisive passage of criticism), gained her wide readership precisely because she was assimilated, not exotic, because she resembled her readers sufficiently to touch them with her hopes of escape into the normalcy of their lives.

The Anne Frank device helps Nathan out of his own imaginative *achterhuis*. Lonoff has made himself and all around him martyrs to art, and Nathan has come as a willing acolyte to the man who acknowledges no other life. As Hope Lonoff says, "*Not* living is what he makes his beautiful fiction *out* of!" In his presence Nathan recalls "Babel's description of the Jewish writer as a man with autumn in his heart and spectacles on his nose." Nathan conjures up Anne Frank, another hero of the imagination, but he knows that her nonliving was not of her own will. She made literature out of *forced* imprisonment, wanting all the time to feel the blood flowing in her veins. Nathan may someday have "autumn in his heart and spectacles on his nose," but now he still feels the "blood in his penis" (49). By morning light he has come to see that hiding, even to write, is but half a life. During the night at Lonoff's he had hid from his father's accusation by placing his writer's imagination at the service of his cringing emotional need. He had conjured Anne Frank to throw her at his father, had reduced her martyrdom by cleverly seeing it as the quintessential martyrdom to art. But he had also exhausted that defense by playing it through to its unreal end, and he had been able to look on at Lonoff's domestic drama with something of a writer's detachment. Now he must get on with his life, write the offending stories, trust the tales to set him free, take the hits. It is 1956, and Nathan's introduction to the madness of art coincides with the adaptation of Anne Frank's story as a Broadway play, a spur and a sop to popular conscience.

Had Roth been so bold as to touch the sanctified Anne Frank in 1956, even to use her in a character's dream, his earliest reception would have been far stormier than in fact it was. Even in 1979 the allusion was a problem: for some critics not even Zuckerman's expressed admiration for Anne as a person and as a writer could erase Roth's fingerprints from the icon. Nor did it help that Bruno Bettelheim and others had scored Otto Frank's bourgeois failure to remove his family altogether from the Holland of his possessions and property rights.[2] Roth must have expected objections to his use of Anne Frank, even while he trusted in the truth of his perceptions to overcome them. At the end of the story his fumbling would-be hero speculates on what the Wapters (for whom read "the Jewish establishment") would think if they knew of his imaginative lifting of Anne "out of her sacred book [to] make her a character in [his] life." It "would seem to them," he says, " a desecration even more vile" than the story his father had sent them. Moreover, in layering the time between those tragic events and their several written revelations, Roth parallels the inevitably receding effects of the Holocaust. Roth must have known that for daring to use Anne Frank in this way he too would be roundly criticized.

The richness of *The Ghost Writer*, as of the other Zuckerman novels, comes not from its simple plot of a visit, an observation of a domestic drama (one can hardly say "crisis," for Hope will not leave Lonoff after thirty-five years for denying her a life, any more than Lonoff will leave her for denying him a fantasy), and a parting on a clear, snow-whitened morning. The richness comes largely from overtones of other literature, that range of experience people of the book draw on to lace themselves into Western civilization. The predicament of this artist and this Jew is not peculiar to these circumstances. It echoes in Anne Frank's *Diary*, in references to stories of Henry James, in allusions to Kafka and Babel, in intimations of Mailer and Bellow, even in the dedication of the book to Milan Kundera. Roth folds other stories into his story like a baker with a spatula, keeping their flavor and enriching his. Nathan's own objectionable short story is entertainingly summarized in the narration of his conflict with his father. James's "The Middle Years" is paraphrased and extensively quoted with telling effect, one of its key sentences that Lonoff has pinned to his wall serving as a linchpin to connect it with Roth's novel: "We work in the dark—we do what we can—we give what we have. Our doubt is our passion and our passion is our task. The rest is the madness of art."

The *Diary of a Young Girl* allows Zuckerman to make a telling comment on anti-Semitism: the Franks, who in their attic had read Goethe and Dickens, not the Bible, had been in all respects indistinguishable from their gentile neighbors; nothing conspicuously Jewish had made them targets, only the technicality that they *were* Jewish. In effect, Roth was repeating the argument he had made a decade and a half before in "Writing About Jews," that anti-Semitism is in no way the responsibility of the Jews and that behaving so as not to create a "*shonda* for the Goyim,"[3] is a betrayal of one's own being. Even among Babel's Jews there are not only characters with autumn in their hearts but also Odessa gangsters, particularly Benya Krik, the charitable but ruthless Jewish gang boss. These polarities had implications for Mailer and Bellow, whose comfort with gangsters and acts of defiant will also expanded the range of Jewish venturings. Compared to mobsters in Odessa, New York, and Chicago, Nathan's own dishonest relative, swindling another member of the family in his short story, was small potatoes. Moreover, in musing on Babel Nathan could implicate yet another martyr to official anti-Semitism—as Babel almost certainly was—and another martyr to art, for Babel had joined the Red Cavalry mainly to write of it. In the confined plot of *The Ghost Writer* Nathan and Lonoff may be just sitting and talking about writing, but their talk bristles with wide-ranging allusions that bear on the theme of the novel. There are many ghosts writing here, threads in the rich fabric of a literary life. Whether Nathan can keep faith with their promise is a question left unanswered at the end of his visit.

Thirteen years later, successful, rich, and notorious Nathan Zuckerman, author of the *Portnoy*-like *Carnovsky*, is tasting other unreckoned consequences of art. He is hounded by his doppelganger, Alvin Pepler (bearing Alex Portnoy's initials), another Jewish victim who would be a writer; he finds his *Carnovsky*-abused mother threatened; and he sees his father die with a word to Nathan upon his lips that might be a curse for the literary abuse of his innocent Jewish family. For *Zuckerman Unbound* Roth drew on his own life—or more precisely, on the public perception of his own life, with its myths and ready criticism. Of course, Roth had no Pepler; his mother had never been threatened; his father had not died or ever thought of cursing him; his only brother was older, not younger, and—far from being unsympathetic to an artist's imaginative needs—had himself been an artist (now an advertising director), indeed, had designed the book jacket for the original publication of *Goodbye, Columbus*. But Roth knew well the fickle mistress fame, which had, since blessing the author of *Portnoy* with financial independence, invoked some unforeseen clauses of the Faustian contract. Whether he could outwit her by writing about her was another matter. Who, after all, has ready sympathy for a millionaire crying that being a success has some drawbacks?

Roth's strategy was the ironic mode: to accept the myth, confess to the charges. Instead of protesting that he was not Jew-hating, family-abusing, and misogynistic, he would let Zuckerman seem to be all those things and induce readers to experience the novel as if they were getting the goods on Roth. What they would find out is that they were themselves myth-makers, that they invested in their public commodity an indebtedness—for which they held the I.O.U.'s—against which they could draw down their own frustrated dreams. But in undergoing some loneliness at the top (even mockingly *in extremis*), they might just glimpse the hazards of an artist's calling.

This was dangerous strategy for comedy, trying to take the tragic emotions of fear and pity and marinate them in satiric irony: they might separate in the stew. At the end what is unbound is Zuckerman from all his roots: family, neighborhood (Weequahic, of course), the Jewish establishment and its demanding critics, the sources of his inspiration. He has just his fame—a literary Sammy Glick! And that fame, like Jewishness itself, or the calling of the artist, disconnects him from the mass of his kind. The Promethean fire that he has brought down, that has freed man from slavish inhibition and tribal myopia—the hot novel *Carnovsky*—has burned him with its identification: now strangers on the street call *him* Carnovsky. Ironic, yes, when all Zuckerman wants is to be left alone in comfortable obscurity. The danger is that the reader may grant the wish. If Roth, echoing Sammy Glick's brother, tells Zuckerman, "You're alone!" will the reader care?

Zuckerman never achieves his author's omniscient perspective; his predicament might be more intense, but not even an ironic turn of mind can get him to see the absurdity of his own seriousness. In this novel, making him fairly naive and yet mildly vicious, like the Roth of myth, leaves him vulnerable to criticism, relatively unsympathetic. And the ploy of irony requires that Roth surround him with characters even less sympathetic, more irritating, than himself. The only developed character besides Zuckerman is Alvin Pepler, unforgettable but obsessed and wearing. The plot is a gauntlet. Zuckerman runs it and emerges having paid some dues but unchastened. There are some ingenious devices along the way, but they touch Nathan without transforming him; they leave him feeling vindicated without vindicating him.

The central fact in *Zuckerman Unbound* is that other novel, the carnal *Carnovsky*, intended by Nathan as a liberating act. Everybody and every episode plays off that offstage event. Zuckerman's novel trails the clouds of *Portnoy's Complaint*: its theme, its reputation. Everybody except Zuckerman's agent and Alvin Pepler sees it as autobiographical and uses it as a point of reference to construct fictions about Zuckerman. It is not just that they have "mistaken impersonation for confession and [are] calling out to a character in a book"; but, taking the fiction for truth, they now go about rewriting Nathan's true life as their fictions. The whole world has become a natter of novelists, collaborating to write the story of the man whose cover picture on *Life* has made him theirs and has ended his privacy forever. The Con Ed meter reader evaluates his sex life. Someone at Bloomingdale's notifies the world Carnovsky is trying out mattresses. Strangers on the street shout, "Hey, careful, *Carnovsky*, they arrest people for that!" Even people who have not read the novel respond to his being pointed out as the man who just made a million bucks by writing it. Since he has not kept the covenant, the sound of a driven leaf will make him afraid, and he will flee when none pursueth. On a New York sidewalk, a year after the Robert Kennedy and Martin Luther King assassinations, someone catches him up from behind, grabs his quaking arm, and struggling for breath, says "Don't"—it turns out to be a little WASP lady with "rimless spectacles"—

> "don't let all that money change you, whoever you may be. Money never made anybody happy. Only He can do that." And from her Luger-sized purse she remove[s] a picture postcard of Jesus and presse[s] it into his hand. (189)

Perhaps Jesus is pictured as Portnoy would have described him, "flowing up to heaven in a pink nightgown."

Zuckerman is everywhere discomfited. His mother is identified as the Sophie Portnoy–like model for Carnovsky's mother, and though he takes out an unlisted number through a phone service, he still gets calls threatening to kidnap his mother. Nathan gets letters, via his publisher, addressed namelessly "To the Enemy of the Jews." At loose ends, he tries to reunite with his third wife, a lawyer dedicated to the antiwar movement whom he once called "an affectless, goody-good Pollyanna WASP." Her saintly disposition so set his teeth on edge that he left her after finishing *Carnovsky*. He realizes she will not have him back, for she has found a soul mate in the movement, a soon to be defrocked priest who is sharing her village apartment. In his mind's ear Nathan hears her saying, "You were perfectly right to go. Having written a book like that, you had to go. That's what writing it was all about."

Nathan's novel has left him bereft; he has no one. His coaching of his mother on how to answer the press does not avail. Guilty over his stroke-reduced father, he remembers that the old man had spent years getting people to appreciate what he considered the *right* art—art that might make Jews accept-able to Gentiles. Doc Zuckerman had once declared that "Tzena, Tzena," the Israeli folk song, might "win more hearts to the Jewish cause than anything before in the history of the world"; later it was "Fiddler on the Roof." He can now accuse *Carnovsky* of single–handedly undoing the good effects of that "art." The older Zuckerman had himself become something of a writer before his illness, sending off hundreds of letters to Johnson and Humphrey opposing the Viet Nam war, compiling a folder "nearly as fat as *War and Peace*." But while Nathan's father and Nathan's third wife, soul mates in the cause, were typing missives to improve the world—Nathan had corrupted it further for profit. At his father's funeral Nathan wishes he were away from the family setting, back writing *Carnovsky*. For him, the liberating effect of that novel had been the act of writing it—an effect disastrously undone by its success.

Alvin Pepler, of the ironic initials (whose crusade against the quiz shows had been Portnoy's cause when Alex was a young prosecutor and who is fic-tionalized better than the merely distorted Herbert Stemple of Robert Redford's *Quiz Show*) needs to believe that Nathan stole *Carnovsky* from his life. He, too, had lived a Newark Jewish boyhood and is something of an onanist. In his warped view, everybody successful has stolen from him—more evidence of the madness of art. The quiz-show people had stolen his real talent and had sub-stituted a right-looking ignoramus who had to be fed the answers because they were interested not in Truth, but in Art. "Art," they had told him, "is *con-trolled*, art is *managed*, art is *always rigged*" (218). Now, having (as he might have said) "accidentally on purpose" encountered Zuckerman in a delicatessen, he wants Zuckerman, who he insists has turned his life into Art, to help him write the book that will turn it into Truth. But Pepler is not above aspiring to art himself. He is trying to get something of his own into production on Broadway, if Zuckerman can only help him polish it a little—a musical based on the "Six-Day War" starring Yul Brynner as Moshe Dayan. To impress Nathan, Pepler invents producers and agents and starlets and might even be the one threaten-ing—for money he thinks he deserves as the true source of Nathan's success—to kidnap Zuckerman's mother. In a wonderful parody of the final "epiphany" scene from Bellow's *Seize the Day*, which Roth had criticized as overdone (*RMAO* 107–8), Zuckerman escapes from Pepler by running into Campbell's funeral home, amidst a maze of gangland mourners, and out the back door.

Even the obvious rewards of success are not so rewarding for Nathan. He cannot travel, dine, dress for the part because he cannot compromise his lower-middle-class sense of himself or his ascetic image of the artist. A date with a legendary Irish movie star promises happiness—two fame-crossed lovers kick-ing their heels at their myths, relaxing in their shared earthiness—until pre-emptive Fame whisks her back to her starring role in Havana: she is the mistress of Fidel Castro. Caesara O'Shea, the raven-haired screen beauty, had gained instant fame on the Dublin stage at age nineteen as the lead in *The Diary of Anne Frank*; that was back when Nathan was publishing his first stories and Amy Bellette was stirring thoughts of another Anne Frank. Now this Anne is life-worn and weary, though still as beautiful as her face on the screen. When Nathan kisses her, it is "staggering to see that face coming up at his . . . like kissing a billboard." They have one beautiful night together, but Caesara can be only a caesura for Nathan. Fidel, who had withstood coups by Kennedy and Johnson and would elude Nixon, could certainly not be toppled in a *bataille d'amour* by Nathan Zuckerman.

Caesara has been reading, and lends to Nathan, a copy of Kierkegaard's *The Crisis in the Life of an Actress*, on the fleetingness of youth and fame. Roth does not develop the Kierkegaard materials beyond the obvious parallels to the life of a writer (Nathan sees himself in "the theater of the ridiculous in which [he] is now a leading character—because of literature") (275). But the Kierkegaard text has a subtle presence, for it underscores the risk involved in the life of the artist. All those nice Newark boys who played it safe in the acceptable professions are free of a danger that Nathan shares with Caesara. The novelist, like the actor—male or female—runs the risk of being ridiculous, or, even worse, of running dry. As the aging actress in Kierkegaard's text finds her beauty fading and her art less sought after, so the novelist—especially the novelist who milks his own biography—runs the risk of faltering reiteration. Telling only what he knows, and knowing for sure only what he has worked through, he may find himself after a time with nothing more to interest the reader. But there is a more poignant application of *The Crisis in the Life of an Actress* to Nathan's newest Anne Frank (the original, he remembers, had pinned pictures of movie stars to the walls of the *achterhuis*). Were it not for her commitment to Fidel, as peremptory as the Nuremberg laws, she might have comforted Nathan now, as a fantasied Amy Bellette might have done thirteen years earlier. Caesara's dark eyes and hair—more Jewish than Irish—and her assertion that she, like Nathan, is "intensity-afflicted," blend in Nathan's mind with Kierkegaard's description of the aging actress to form an object of his longing: someone once innocent, now knowing, who might share his worlds and his responses. His defeat by Fidel adds to his sense that *Carnovsky* has gained him only unrelenting loss.

Nathan's response to all this, the final movement of the book, is tonally at odds with the first parts. The minor mystery of Alvin Pepler, including whether his was the phone voice threatening to kidnap Nathan's mother, is dropped as the publicly beset Nathan becomes the family-beset son and brother, struggling to divest himself of guilt. The irony changes as the loss of Nathan's father and the unbinding of Nathan from all that has plagued and nourished him provoke an almost spiteful gratitude for an isolating and sullen independence. Nathan feels himself almost a tragic hero. Ironically echoing King Lear's five "Never"s—denying that Cordelia was a burden—Nathan declares his whole Jewish Newark past, his burdened role of child to Doc Zuckerman, as "Over" and (going Lear one better) "Over. Over. Over. Over. Over."

In the first half of the book Nathan was very much Doc Zuckerman's son, protest as he might against the association. He was plagued by obligation, his father's most automatic trigger. His father (in *The Ghost Writer*) had operated out of mistaken gratitude to Judge Wapter—who had not even remembered him—for a referral he assumed had gotten Nathan into college; and here it is learned that when Nathan's brother Henry was a college senior, their father had tried to hold him to an "obligation" to continue working summers for some friends who had, three years back, given Henry a summer job—even though Henry now had a career goal totally at odds with such employment. Any satisfaction in independent achievement the sons might have known had been elbowed away by obligation that was no more than Doc Zuckerman's insecurity. Throughout most of this novel Nathan, too, feels beset by Zuckerman obligation: not to be a big-shot, a turncoat against the good Jewish boy from Weequahic. The legacy of his past is expressed by Nathan's embarrassment with success. But he knows that his success is also a mark of his courage. And when, at the end, his brother joins in the chorus of condemnation, Nathan sees how easily resentment comes to one who has failed in courage.

Here is another echo of the Kierkegaard work. Henry Zuckerman, Nathan's younger dentist brother, had wanted to become an actor. It was a summer stock opportunity that had brought Henry into conflict with Doc Zuckerman's "obligation" to continue his obtained summer employments. But Henry's defiance was short-lived. Soon afterward, he came home with the sensible fiancé, pinned and ringed, made the sensible middle-class compromise, pursued the sensible career in dentistry. He had the kids, the home in the suburbs, from his standpoint the responsibility. But he also had mistresses, an occasional need for brother Nathan's apartment, difficulties tolerating his cliché of a wife, and, with all this, jealousy of his older brother for Nathan's myth (certainly not for his hours of typing chancy drafts of fiction). Henry had not risked, as Nathan had risked, failure in art by pursuing the career as an actor. He had not wanted it enough to do that. Now all he can do is berate his brother, using as his whip their father's last word to Nathan. Was that word "faster" or "vaster" or "better," or was it, as Nathan first thought, "Bastard"? Henry insists it was "Bastard!" He turns on Nathan:

> "You *are* a bastard. A heartless conscienceless bastard. What does loyalty mean to you? What does self-denial mean, *restraint*—anything at all? To

you everything is disposable! Everything is *ex*posable! Jewish morality, Jewish endurance, Jewish wisdom, Jewish families—everything is grist for your fun-machine. Even your shiksas go down the drain when they don't tickle your fancy anymore. Love, marriage, children, what the hell do you care? To you it's all fun and games. *But that isn't the way it is to the rest of us.* And the worst is how we protect you from knowing what you really are! And what you've done! You killed him, Nathan. Nobody will tell you—they're too frightened of you to say it. They think you're too famous to criticize—that you're far beyond the reach now of ordinary human beings. But you killed him, Nathan. With that book. *Of course* he said 'Bastard.' He'd seen it! He'd seen what you had done to him and Mother in that book!" (397)

On returning from the funeral in Florida, Nathan takes a detour from Newark airport through the Weequahic neighborhood, past his first Leslie Street apartment and the Catholic orphanage opposite, which had served as the setting for Nathan's early story "Orphans" (and Roth's undergraduate "The Fence"); past his later Leslie Street home, where, asked by a young black man, "Who you supposed to be?" Nathan answers "No one"; past the Chancellor Avenue Talmud Torah that is now an African Methodist Episcopal Church; past the boarded up houses and stores, the detritus of a third-world neighborhood. All this he does in an armed limousine driven by the chauffeur who had escorted him home some days before from Caesara O'Shea's hotel. Inspecting the chauffeur's gun, Nathan muses, "What is art?" This neighborhood gives no answer; it is as yet an unwritten world. His Weequahic, like his father, is gone. His—and Portnoy's—dream that the softball game would survive in perpetuity exists only in *Carnovsky*. Here it is "Over"—to the sixth power. Zuckerman is unbound from his roots. But his assertion of freedom has the ring of over-assertion, of protesting too much: the reader who takes Nathan at his word might also be freed—from sympathy. Still, the ironic tone, which isolates Nathan and leaves him canned in an armed limousine, suggests something premature in such a tossing off.

The extent of Nathan's reduction is made clear in *The Anatomy Lesson*, set four years later. Roth had used physical ailment before in his writing and would again, usually as a metaphor for entrapment or isolation, the graphic symptomology based often on his own experience. Roth's army discharge had been medical, for a strained back, and his short story "Novotny's Pain" is about the emotional persecution of an innocent soldier for just such an inexplicable ailment. Roth's appendicitis and near death from peritonitis are put into *Zuckerman Unbound*, where Nathan suffers the identical illness; and they would be part of Roth's inheritance from his father in *Patrimony*. Entrapment in female flesh is the great metaphor of *The Breast*, and entrapment in a drug-induced emotional state following surgery would be a launching mechanism into *Operation Shylock* (1993). Crippling arthritis would end the puppeteer's career in *Sabbath's Theater* (1995). In *The Anatomy Lesson* Nathan's ailment is not "a disease that anybody could take seriously. Only the pain—in his neck, arms, and shoulders, pain that made it difficult to walk for more than a few city blocks or even to stand very long in one place." It is a vague pain, branching through his torso "like a menorah held bottom side up," but a reductive pain that has kept him from writing anything since *Carnovsky*, a pain for which there may be no medical cure.

Nathan's early treatment is an orthopedic collar and mothering. But his own mother, his last link to Newark, is dead. The collar is like the machine in Kafka's penal colony: when he wears it, unable to "concentrate on anything other than himself," it testifies to his crime of self-absorption. The mothering also takes place largely on his flesh. Four women now minister to him as he lies on his back on a padded juvenile playmat, his head supported by *Roget's Thesaurus*, a bar mitzvah gift inscribed, "From Dad—You have my every confidence." The man who would be free of parents is reduced to infantile dependence, his only satisfaction the parallel suffering of two proclaimed enemies. One is Richard Nixon, "the only other American he saw daily who seemed to be in as much trouble as he was," squirming on TV in the throes of Watergate. Nathan, supine, watches him indirectly through prism glasses. The other enemy will be Milton Appel.

Having declared himself unbound from his Jewish past, Nathan must now devise his own bindings; a quintessential modern, he is a paradigm for the problem of freedom. But none of his four women attendants—each satisfying her own need—is a substitute for his mother. As he has come to learn over three unsuccessful marriages, if you use a liaison to get out of your own past you take on the baggage of someone else's; wives cannot be just mothers, and he is not ready to take on any part of what they collectively represent: the plight of modern woman. His mother dying of a brain tumor three years before had selflessly served others to the last. Deprived of speech and asked by doctors to write her name on a pad—as Nathan would later do—she writes instead "Holocaust," representing a generation never to be replaced.

Nathan's pain is also an analogue to his—and Roth's—writing about Jews: like *Carnovsky*—or Hamlet's madness—it becomes the focus of an internal question in the novel. Everyone in contact with Nathan has a diagnosis and a cure for his ailment. "They just kept coming, these diagnoses. Everybody had a slant. The illness with a thousand meanings. They read the pain as his fifth book" (488). Mostly they see it as sublimated guilt for having written *Carnovsky*, for having been the enemy of his people. Nathan considers this, rehearsing all the possibilities as David Kepesh had done in *The Breast*. He agrees and disagrees with each. But he refuses—as Novotny had forthrightly refused when offered the chance—to give up the idea that physical pain can be real and inexplicable. All the diagnoses are temptations to give in to the tormentors, to break down like the confessor in the police station, and by accepting the received version, be relieved of the condemnation along with his integrity.

But Zuckerman's physical pain, inseparable from his sense of literary pariah, is not like Kepesh's metamorphosis, something he might accept and be the better for (though ironically he interprets it as a signal to change his life, "to *undo* the stranglehold" of writing). Roth has him suffer the pain unremittingly throughout the novel. It becomes a component of his selfhood, like writing, like Jewishness, like obsession with the question of self. "Every thought and feeling ensnared by the selfness of pain" (577). Zuckerman takes every possible kind of painkiller from dope to voltage to sexual treatment, sees every possible kind of doctor, and then, desperate and partly drug-deluded, decides to become a doctor and cure himself (not so much by the science as by the relief from an impossible occupation). His decision to chuck literature and become an obstetrician is announced at the end of a passage exposing the kind of doubts every writer may go through, that Roth surely has gone through (though succumbing to them is another thing):

> "What if twenty years of writing has just been so much helplessness before a compulsion—submission to a lowly, inconsequential compulsion that I've dignified with all my principles, a compulsion probably not all that different from what made my mother clean the house for five hours every day. Where am I then? I'm going to medical school." (508)

But this anodyne too is doomed to fail, for all its sweet irony of fulfilling the clichéd Jewish parent's dream, and for all its clever contrast to writing:

> "Who quarrels with an obstetrician? Even the obstetrician who delivered Bugsy Siegel goes to bed at night with a clear conscience. He catches what comes out and everybody loves him. When the baby appears they don't start shouting, 'You call that a baby? That's no baby!' No, whatever he hands them they take it home. They're grateful for his just having been there . . . imagine what seeing that does to the spirit, *that* every morning as opposed to grinding out another two dubious pages. Conception? Gestation? Gruesome laborious labor? The mother's business. You just wash your hands and hold out the net. Twenty years up here in the literary spheres is enough—now for the fun of the flowing

gutter. The bilge, the ooze, the gooey drip. The stuff. No words, just stuff. Everything the word's in place of. The lowest of genres—life itself!" (509)

The fantasy of going to medical school is like the fantasy of marrying Anne Frank, a palliative for a conscience under siege. The young, hopeful Zuckerman had put his fantasy aside and placed his faith in writing. Now a burnt-out Zuckerman, to whom writing is not a calling but a plague, plunges absurdly into the unreality of his conceit. But the anodyne of medical school must fail because it cannot cure graphomania. Written on Nathan's flesh is the profession of writer, as irreversible as his circumcision. The closest he gets to medical school is as a patient in the Chicago teaching hospital where he has hoped to study, done in by alcohol and Percodan, still compelled to take notes on the miseries around him, to get stories going, even as he denies that he need ever do that again.

Nathan's major dialogues are with himself and his surrogate selves. Even when he is manically driven to outrageous behavior, a common-sense voice in his head presents, in italics, alternatives he will not follow. His dialogues with his four Florence Nightingales and later with a passenger on the plane to Chicago and with the lady chauffeur he employs there only obliquely explore issues; mainly they provide emotional release for pent-up physical and spiritual pain. His conversations, void of affection, touch on the new worlds a deghettoized Jewish writer must live in after parents, after sexual liberation, after the Holocaust, and during the cold war. Any affection that surfaces is for old Jews, cameos who come alive in the text. One, who cures pain with a special pillow, is from the Newark of his father's generation, providing this novel's opportunity for casting back to that vanished world. But the four women enter from colder worlds. Critics would fault Roth, as in *Portnoy*, for making the women caricatures, for not developing them and pursuing the possibilities of the lives they would offer him—still suggesting the novel he should write. But this novel is an internal dialogue in which all the other characters are aspects of Nathan himself.

Including Milton Appel. Especially Milton Appel: the outward description and circumstances are the face and hands of Irving Howe, but the criticism is another self-doubting voice of Nathan Zuckerman, and, in bemused irony, of Philip Roth. Of Philip *Milton* Roth. Nathan tells us in English and in French: M. Appel "Rhymes with 'lapel'"(597). "Je m'appelle Appel" (579). Roth rarely plays conscious hide and seek in his fiction,[4] but he lets Nathan, in a drug-induced manic state, drop that line to acknowledge (and let the knowing reader acknowledge) that Appel is also Roth. Even the most hurtful criticism of one's work—and Roth's animus against Howe had been real enough—is worth taking to heart, since what a writer of the self engages in most is doubt.

The Milton Appel motif is clever but wearing. Nathan's other great irritant, Appel complements the physical pain. And Roth introduces him into the plot to function in a role in Nathan's life that had earlier been Doc Zuckerman's: as would-be savior of the Jewish people. Appel has invited Nathan, indirectly through the mediation of another writer, to compose a piece for the Op-Ed page of the *Times* defending Israel against charges that it was the aggressor in the recent Yom Kippur War. Jewish solidarity should overcome literary differences and hostilities. But Appel has invited him indirectly because he knows Nathan resents the damning review of *Carnovsky*—with its equally damning revaluation of Nathan's earlier work—that Appel has published in *Inquiry* (for which read *Commentary*). Ivan Felt, the mutual friend, instigates the mischief by showing Nathan the confidential letter in which Appel has made the request. Nathan regards the letter as hypocritical: it would use him to get to a part of the reading public that Appel himself scorns. In arrogating to himself a right to tell Nathan his Jewish duty—echoes of Judge Wapter!—Appel sets Nathan's teeth on edge.

The theme of fathers and sons abounds. Felt, a younger novelist, considers Zuckerman his literary father in fictive anger but a hopelessly repressed child in real life, suffering mostly from caged wrath. Zuckerman reads still another father connection into Appel's literary attacks on him. He considers them expiations for Appel's slightings in postwar memoirs of his own Yiddish-speaking, wagon-driving father. Nathan thinks Appel more ashamed than loving of his Jewish background, capable of publishing a book like *World of Our Fathers* to exploit sentiments that Nathan genuinely holds but that for Appel are just so much research.[5] His damning critique of *Carnovsky* reflects Appel's own failings of sensibility as a Jewish son: it sees obvious insults to parents but is blind to any counterbalancing love. Nathan insists that while he has always honored Doc Zuckerman, Appel has merely used his immigrant father, has betrayed not only the man but the vanished world he represents. Repressing a similar guilt, Nathan lashes out at Appel for hypocrisy, among other things for publishing wherever he can gain advantage. "In *Inquiry*, run by the kind of people he used to attack before he began attacking people like me!"

> "The comedy is that the real visceral haters of the bourgeois Jews, with the *real* contempt for their everyday lives, are these complex intellectual giants. They *loathe* them, and don't particularly care for the smell of the Jewish proletariat either. All of them full of sympathy suddenly for the ghetto world of their traditional fathers now that the traditional fathers are filed for safekeeping in Beth Moses Memorial Park. When they were alive they wanted to strangle the immigrant bastards to death because

they dared to think they could actually be of consequence without ever having read Proust past *Swann's Way*. And the ghetto—what the ghetto saw of these guys was their heels: out, out, screaming for air, to write about great Jews like Ralph Waldo Emerson and William Dean Howells." (504–5)

Nathan exclaims that he does not want to hurt the Jews, but he does not feel qualified to write about Israel: "I'm an authority on Newark. Not even on Newark. On the Weequahic section of Newark. If the truth be known, not even on the whole of the Weequahic section. I don't even go below Bergen Street." But neither is Appel qualified to write about Zuckerman because, as Nathan puts it to him, "You lay hold of my comedy with your ten-ton gravity and turn it into a travesty!" To Nathan, Appel is a "sententious bastard" who has never in his "life taken a mental position that isn't a moral judgment" (573).

Nathan spews his venom against Appel into a tape recorder as notes for a planned telephone conversation, rejoices in news that Appel is ill, eventually calls him under the influence of chemical stimulants only to be verbally defeated by Appel's superior rationalism and civility, and gets revenge by manicly degrading Appel to the airline passenger and the female chauffeur in Chicago, both Gentiles. For them he stages a fiction about Appel and stars in the drama himself. He presents himself as Milton Appel, pornographer (of the Larry Flint variety), the publisher of a *Hustler*-like magazine, *Lickety Split*, and proprietor of a sex club, Milton's Millennia. He further identifies, as his now-jailed club manager, *Inquiry*'s editor-in-chief, a Norman Podhoretz–like character, Mortimer Horowitz. Nathan is out to get the whole *Inquiry* establishment. Some of his effects, especially his discomfiture of the polite but scandalized airline passenger, are hilarious. Eventually, his pronouncement of the *Lickety Split* philosophy—grubbily Jewish, he says, and persecuted for being so, but more honest than the air-brushed Hugh Heffner variety—so antagonizes the chauffeur that when he goes over the edge in a drug-induced threat of violence, she applies her jackboots to his jaw, shutting down that offending organ, Zuckerman's mouth.

The theme of hurting fathers and of needing their blessing emerges most strongly toward the close of the novel. Self-deceived into thinking he can get into medical school at his alma mater, the University of Chicago, Nathan contacts his undergraduate roommate, Bobby Freytag, now an anesthesiologist on the medical school faculty. Freytag, who tries rationally to dissuade Nathan, is also somewhat at loose ends. Divorced from a sickly wife, he has in his care his recently widowed father and his profligate adopted son, Gregory. Childhood mumps had left Bobby unable biologically to father a child. Bobby's father, who has followed Nathan's career, remembers Zuckerman warmly as "Zuck," the folk humorist of undergraduate legend. In the old man Nathan sees his own father, both the endearment and the censure.

Old Mr. Freytag is still distraught over the recent death of his wife, a woman of Nathan's mother's selfless disposition and approximate age. Such mothers appear in Roth's novels from *My Life as a Man* on, best represented, perhaps, by the dying mother in *The Professor of Desire* who loads Kepesh's refrigerator with her home cooking before going into the hospital to die. Old Mr. Freytag is mourning what Nathan Zuckerman's dying mother had termed a "Holocaust," the loss not only of his wife, but of all his peers. He tries, himself, to bind the generations by acting as substitute for Gregory's mother, preparing meals and fretting over the adoptive grandson's absences from home and mis-use of money. For his trouble he gets only Gregory's curses. Situated between them, Bobby Freytag feels like the complete failure, as both parent and son. In the Roth cannon, he is another fellow student who remained in Chicago, per-haps indicating what the Herzes' adoptive fate might have been had their story been played out beyond the end of *Letting Go*.

Now in Chicago himself, Nathan hears from Bobby the problems of fatherhood and feels responsible in his own childlessness for killing off a branch of the Zuckerman line. Drug-primed into fits of sentimentality and anger, he volunteers to take old Mr. Freytag to visit his wife's fresh grave. But in his hired limousine he continues abusing his gentile chauffeur with his sleazy pretense of being the pornographer, the fictive Appel. As they arrive at the Freytag's house, she telling him off for his warped values, he interrupts, "Be out in ten minutes. Just going in to get laid." But old Mr. Freytag mistakes the arriving car for a funeral limo. The sight of the old man's bewildered face rekindles in Nathan the conflict with his parents' generation.

> Even in his stupor, Zuckerman understood. Who is dead, where is the body? What savage catastrophe, the old man was asking, had overtaken which of his beloved, irreplaceable kin? They belong to another history, these old Jewish people, a history that is not ours, that we do not want for ourselves, that would be horrible for us, and yet, because of that history, they cannot leave you unaffected when their faces show such fear. (655)

Thoughts close to those he has ascribed to Appel are still unresolved in Nathan. The old man, torn between going and waiting for his two-day absent grandson, embarks in Nathan's hearselike limo just as it begins to snow. Their drive through graffiti-defaced neighborhoods moves the old man to comment on the difference between the hard-working Jews that are gone and the reviled ethnics that have replaced them. In a scene reminiscent of Roth's early "The Day It Snowed," they reach the cemetery and walk through family plots, the old man narrating the foibles of the buried Jews and lamenting his son's fate. Were it not for the damaging effect of childhood illness, he says, Bobby might have had the pick of wives and a good child with *our* rather than *their* genes. His temper growing as he blames Gregory for his eugenic disappointment, old Freytag shouts, ". . . I'll break his neck for what he's done to this family! I'll kill that little bastard! I *will*!" The unbalanced Nathan can take no more of Jewish sanctimony. Roth's narrative moves quickly.

> Zuckerman, with what strength remained in his feeble arms, pounced upon the old man's neck. *He* would kill—and never again suppose himself better than his crime: an end to denial; of the heaviest judgment guilty as charged. "Your sacred genes! What do you see inside your head? Genes with JEW sewed on them? Is that all you see in that lunatic mind, the unstained natural virtue of Jews?"

Maybe Henry had been right: maybe he had killed his father. Nagging doubt would be put to rest by this murder of the surrogate father Freytag. Nathan continues, "We are the dead! These bones in boxes are the Jewish living! These are the people running the show!" Old Freytag escapes his grasp and heads for the gate shouting for help. Zuckerman slips and, sitting in snow amidst the lettered gravestones, shouts their names in a mocking decalogue: " 'Honor thy Finklestein! Do not commit Kaufman! Make no idols in the form of Levine! Thou shalt not take in vain the name of Katz!'" Then sliding on his knees toward Freytag, his clothes filled with freezing slush, and crying, "Freytag! Forbidder! Now I murder *you*!" he is stopped by Ricky, the gentile chauffeur, always pictured with one blonde Teutonic braid hanging down her uniformed back. Or rather, what stops him are Ricky's jackboots, well placed, reminiscent of the most efficient enemies of the Jews. "'This'—Zuckerman laugh[s], spewing flakes of burning ice—'this is your protection, Poppa Freytag? This great respecter of the Jews?' . . . 'Out of my way, you innocent bitch!' But [the episode concludes] against Ricky's boots got nowhere." With the broken jaw Ricky has paid Nathan back as much for the tasteless "Appel" shtick as for his present aggression.

Her act both defeats and liberates Nathan. Appel and old Freytag are sentimentalizers of the old Jewish world from which he would be unbound and for which unbinding he needs to be punished. In provoking Ricky to do to him as the feigned Appel what Nathan wishes he could do to the real Appel, Nathan has brought punishment down at once upon his enemy and his guilty self. Ricky, as his surrogate, has prevented him from committing battery and has given him, in place of a vague, untreatable pain, a treatable battered face. It is in the hospital at the end that Nathan plays out his doctor fantasy and perhaps gets back to the task of writing that has been burned into his flesh.

Earlier in *The Anatomy Lesson* Zuckerman suffers some of the same abuse for his mother's death that he had suffered in the previous novel for his father's. His brother, Henry, grabs the filial spotlight with an overblown funeral oration; his sister-in-law, Carol, avoids him out of fear of being turned—if she so much as expresses a thought—into a character in his fiction; someone leaves in a mailbox for him words spoken by the Satanic spirit in Blatty's *The Exorcist*, "May your mother suck cocks in hell—and you soon join her! You deserve it. One of your many foes." All this because of *Carnovsky*.

The passing of innocence with his mother's generation had already been symbolized by Nathan's four modern women. Only one of them is Jewish; the other three are a latter-day Pumpkin and Pilgrim and—perhaps the most poignant of all—a representative of iron-curtain despair. To the extent that *The Anatomy Lesson* is a self-satirizing defense of *Portnoy's Complaint* (alias *Carnovsky*), the four stereotypical women may also be an ironic way of rubbing in the method of that book. Young Alex was the sexual seeker; infantile Nathan is the sexually sought. Women come to him as he lies helpless in his Upper East Side brownstone.

> On his back he felt like their whore, paying in sex for someone to bring him the milk and the paper. They told him their troubles and took off their clothes and lowered their orifices for Zuckerman to fill . . . the more conspicuous his helplessness, the more forthright their desire. Then they ran. Washed up, downed a coffee, kneeled to kiss him goodbye, and ran off to disappear in real lives. Leaving Zuckerman on his back for whoever rang the bell next. (417–18)

Unthreatened—even released—by his helplessness, each woman represents a different aspect of joyless modern feminism.

Gloria, the one Jew and wife of Nathan's devoted accountant, is liberated to the extent of feeling that she deserves the rewards of the sexual revolution. A good wife and mother, she is not drawn to Nathan against her better judgment like some Anna Karenina; Nathan is not even her only extramarital affair. But she is a sobering statement about the world that has passed, as she plays at whorishness, naked and equipped from the sex shop, seeking the adventure that has gone out of her marriage. The second woman, Jenny, is an artist, marginally independent, a Pumpkin without Daddy or a real income, who lives upstate in a rural setting convincing herself she is not lonely, until disarmed by a moment of *chic* in an outfit from Bergdorf's Nathan has staked her to. She would marry Nathan if he allowed himself to get close enough. His response is that she is a potential repeat of his three previous mistakes.

Diana Rutherford (one remembers what the actress of that surname had meant to Portnoy) is "a student at Finch, the rich girls' college around the corner where the Nixons had sent Tricia." This jaded "twenty-year-old girl from an ultraprivileged Christian-Connecticut background" has known men since being abused by a chauffeur at age ten and comes to the author of *Carnovsky*, whom she has recognized on the street, "as if Temple Drake had hitched up from Memphis to talk about Popeye with Nathaniel Hawthorne." For this latter-day Pilgrim there are ". . . no more parents. Parents are over." She has skipped right out of her generation into Nathan's. Since he cannot physically sit at a typewriter, she agrees to serve as his part-time secretary, but balks at writing a tell-off letter he wants to send to Appel. She will not abet a sick obsession. Instead, she preaches forgiveness. Abused by the chauffeur—representing the class structure of her WASP world—she still clings to the superiority of her Christian teaching, contrasting it to Nathan's unforgiving Old Testament vengeance. "That stonelike book. Eye for eye and teeth for teeth and never forgive anybody." Yet her refusal of complicity in writing the letter is what drives Nathan to admit that part of the reason he hates Appel's guts is that Appel may be right. "What if my writing's as bad as he says? . . . He's one of the few around who make any sense at all. Let's face it, even the worst criticism contains some truth. They always see something you're trying to hide" (507). Half his age but twice as worldly, Diana unlocks a fear that has intensified Nathan's pain.

But Roth contrasts this fear, which can elicit at least infantile hope in a fantasy of medical school, with total despair. The fourth woman is Jaga, a defector from Poland. Nathan meets her at a hair-restoring clinic, where she works as a scalp massage technician. He has gone there partly out of vanity, partly out of need to succeed in *some* kind of therapy (though this is as futile as the treatments for his branching pain), and partly because the hair loss threatens him with the spectre of his father's generation. Jaga's frail cynicism, anticipating "The Prague Orgy," is beyond anything in Nathan's experience. He can but abuse it by observation; even his sympathy is for the story he can extract, as Jaga well knows. But Roth uses it beautifully to suggest closures in the East that eclipse Nathan's relative loss of freedom in the West. As a sufferer, Jaga is transcendent, her face and body at once tired and young. She wants to escape into Nathan, into wine, into fantasies of ethical purity, while needing to be held close and not lied to or patronized with false cheer or the facade of American optimism. She has done it all: suffered from politics; mothered a child, now thirteen, who once thought her meatballs the best in the world; taken a husband and a wild lover—lovers—from whom she was rescued by a boy brave enough to want to remove her from abuse. She lives with that boy, now an unmanned adult, in a Bronx neighborhood void even of

as much redeeming architecture as might be found in the smallest towns of
Poland, lives with him not out of love but out of gratitude, dressed in a shoddy
coat "once stylish elsewhere." She fingers Nathan's books, chooses some to
borrow, but never removes them from his brownstone, rather piling them up on
a desk corner she calls her "spot." She often leaves Nathan's apartment drunk.
In America she appears a victim and is victimized, once even raped by a
Polish limousine chauffeur who finds her staggering away from Nathan's
house and abuses her for a fare she cannot pay. The rape means to her not what
it would to an American, still capable of outrage. Hers is limited to the irony of
having escaped from Warsaw only to be raped by a Pole. She has more of a
story, but it is hinted at and made believable from its effects on her without
having to be told.

The fifteen pages of Jaga's exchanges with Nathan are Roth's strongest
prose in *The Anatomy Lesson*, a terse depiction of betrayal expected and therefore received.

> "I will let you do anything you want to me, but I will not fall in
> love."
> "Fine."
> "Only good, only fine? No, in my case it is excellent. Because I am
> the best woman in the world for falling in love with the wrong man. I
> have the record in the Communist countries. Either they are married, or
> they are murderers, or they are like you, men finished with love. Gentle,
> sympathetic, kind with money and wine, but interested in you mainly
> as a subject. Warm ice. I know writers." (538)

Zuckerman's curiosity evokes her despair. "And again she offered to assume
any position for penetration that would please and excite him. 'Come however you like and don't wait for me. That is better for a writer than more questions.' . . . She wanted to collapse and be rescued, and she wanted to be heroic
and prevail, and she seemed to hate him most for reminding her, merely by taking it all in, that she could manage neither." What sustains Jaga is permanent
exile from optimism. She has a darkness to go back to if not a home. And she
knows Nathan will not love her. "'All I'm saying is, after you get tired of fucking me, I'll understand—but, please,' she said, just as his body, playing yet
another trick, erupted without so much as a warning, 'please, don't just drop me
as a friend.'"

Nathan's questioning and listening anticipate the detached Philip in
Roth's *Deception*, the writer as tabula rasa. As Nathan speculates on his own
failure of sympathy, an accusation his author knew well, his thoughts ironically
echo his brother Henry.

Monstrous that all the world's suffering is good to me inasmuch as it's grist to my mill—that all I can do, when confronted with anyone's story, is to wish to turn it into *material*, but if that's the way one is possessed, that is the way one is possessed. There's a demonic side to this business that the Nobel Prize committee doesn't talk much about. It would be nice, particularly in the presence of the needy, to have pure disinterested motives like everybody else, but, alas, that isn't the job. The only patient being treated by the writer is himself. (540)

Nathan by now has lived James's stricture: "Our doubt is our passion and our passion is our task." For writers, physicians who heal themselves on paper, doubt is symptomology, the neural ache that prods creation. In Nathan's view, the novelist who loses his doubt loses his soul and becomes a polemicist.

But cherishing his own doubt is one thing; requiring it of the nonartist is another. Milton Appel, old Mr.Freytag, brother Henry take set positions, but they are not novelists. Nathan hates them for being unbound by his restraints, for inhabiting a real world that exists for reasons beyond its effects on their creative sensibilities. Altruism is wide open to them, and Roth leaves the reader to grasp or miss the irony of Nathan's wishing "to have pure disinterested motives like everyone else."

Many readers will find it easier to hate Nathan (and Roth) for confusing—or at least associating—such seemingly disconnected, sometimes sacred, ideas as the Holocaust, the passing of post-immigrant Jewish America, the iron curtain, the sexual revolution, and the public reaction to *Carnovsky*. To Nathan they are symptoms of a world unhinged, promising only exile and death. Readers, too, after the death of optimism in the sixties, may feel rootless and exiled. But to feel sympathy for Nathan, they require some connection with him, some mutual concern. Many will find the muttering Nathan distant from them, isolated in his big bucks, paranoid fixation, and solipsistic scorn of their world.

The Anatomy Lesson has a problem, then, with its protagonist: his obsessions make him an antagonist. Though suffering physically, he is writhing more in hatred than in pain. And the hatred Nathan would enlist his audience in, not for a villain or a sociopath, is but a writer's animus toward a critic—for differences of judgment or taste. Few lay readers could be expected to join the jihad. The reader is bombarded by catalogues of pharmacology, effects of multiple-drug combinations, obsessive clinical details, even in mordantly humorous inventions like *Lickety Split*. And although these are ironically combined at the expense of Zuckerman, his agony is unseasoned with even the capacity for humility. He is sententious even as he inveighs against the "sententious bastard" Appel. The corpus of the novel is largely exposed nerve, not sheathed

in discovery of character or seductions of plot. Nathan is neither young and idealistic as he was in *The Ghost Writer*, nor nobly defeated by an external world.
It was, after all, Nathan who wrote *Carnovsky*.

Part of the problem is Roth's treatment of the absurd. The wish to be
released from the chosenness of being a writer, as if writing were as innate as race
or sexuality, has about it something slightly ridiculous. Not false, but slightly
ridiculous: for some such need *is* innate. Having to tell one's story, Roth had long
since come to see, is a basic human trait, whether or not one is driven to do so in
books. But Nathan, decrying the agony of writing, trivializes what most readers
will see as the larger agonies of life, not to mention the reader's own integrity in
having committed to the very enterprise Nathan condemns.

That commitment may be overtaxed here because Roth's invention seems
to bear so little fruit in verisimilitude or ideas. The metaphor of inscribing the
compulsion in the flesh works partly, but does not account for Nathan's other,
purely physical, pain. Roth needs that pain to justify the taking of Percodan and
a dozen other drugs, and he needs the drugs to justify the manic rushes that
inspire *Lickety Split* and the abuse of Poppa Freytag. But one cannot escape the
feeling that the physical pain is more of a device than an idea. Besides the
absurdity of a writer's trying to abandon his calling, Zuckerman stands for
very little. He wants Jews to be able to get on with modern living, to accept
having outgrown immigrant accents and apparent victimizations; but Nathan,
who elsewhere could eschew myth while upholding some moral imperative,
here is defined only by such negations. His energies are marshaled to redress
abuse with abuse. The reader sees him as his own worst enemy but is given little reason to want to be his friend. Not of a man who acts out infantile fantasies.

Yet Roth uses Nathan to represent an absurdity he takes very seriously, a
man whose only authenticity is as a writer, and whose writer's authenticity
exists in direct proportion to strong tribal feelings he intellectually rejects. If
Nathan were the target of traditional satire, to be reduced and risen above, the
effect would be a sly satisfaction. Roth is trying for something different here,
something harder. He invests Nathan with a gnawing suspicion, which readers
would associate with himself:

> . . . he had half begun to believe that if it hadn't been for his father's fraz-
> zled nerves and rigid principles and narrow understanding he'd never
> have been a writer at all. A first-generation American father possessed by
> the Jewish demons, a second-generation American son possessed by
> their exorcism: that was his whole story. (446)

And maybe half of Roth's story. Perhaps that is why Nathan in this state is
mocked but not despised. Throughout *The Anatomy Lesson*, Roth holds Nathan

close and the reader somewhat at bay. But the novelist who distrusts the reader sins against his art. Roth would commit that sin again in *Operation Shylock*, with even heavier consequences than here in *The Anatomy Lesson*.

Roth's tone changes immediately in the "Epilogue" to *Zuckerman Bound*, when Nathan, free of pain, goes to Prague and enters a world entirely like that from which Jaga had defected. "The Prague Orgy" is no less manic than *The Anatomy Lesson*, but here it is the society that is frazzled and reactive. The protagonist, a babe in the woods, is humbled. Whatever his own story is, and will always be, Nathan can at least tell it (and tell it and tell it). But in the seventies and eighties there were still stories in Eastern Europe that could not be told, that might be lost forever, despite Roth's achievement in getting some of them published in the "Writers from the Other Europe" series. The tragedy of that loss, and the despair of societies where life survives at the price of sealed lips, makes Nathan's battle with critics and doctrinaire Jews seem trivial—and ironically a right worth hollering and screaming for. "The Prague Orgy," published in the first year of the Gorbachev regime but set in 1976, sums up the mind-numbing legacy of communism.

The plot is very simple. Sisovsky, an exiled Czech writer, half-Jewish on his father's side, accompanied by his actress-mistress, visits Nathan to persuade him to go to Prague to rescue a Yiddish-language manuscript of some two hundred stories written by his father, a man who had been shot by the Nazis two months before Sisovsky's birth in 1941. The manuscript is in the possession of Sisovsky's estranged wife, herself a prominent (but now disgraced) Czech writer of biographic vignettes that capture the Czech soul. The wife occupies a garret atop Sisovsky's former palazzo but, out of hatred for him, will not let the stories out to be published. Nathan, as a hero of sex and Jewish literature, can seduce the wife and get the stories.

Nathan goes to Prague and at an orgy meets the wife—now degenerated into a total voluptuary—who begs Nathan to marry her and take her to the West. Back at her palazzo Nathan tries to get her to accept the idea of a green-card marriage with someone else. He would arrange it in exchange for the manuscript, which she despairingly shows him but which he cannot decipher (he cannot read Yiddish). She is scornful of Nathan's alleged dedication to art, since he would not make the ultimate sacrifice to it by marrying her himself. Nonetheless, she lets Nathan take the manuscript. But in Prague all rooms, from the orgy apartment to Nathan's hotel room to the palazzo, are bugged by the secret police, who arrest Nathan as he returns to his hotel, confiscate the manuscript, threaten him with multiple prison terms for espionage, escort him to the airport, and put him on a plane back to the West. The great Jewish writer on a mission of cultural rescue is disposed of like a firefly that has strayed through the screen door.

But the plot is only the framework for a tale none of whose particulars are necessarily what they seem (to poor Nathan) to be. Sisovsky, the exiled Czech writer, may be motivated by a desire to rescue worthy literature and establish his Holocaust-victim father's reputation, or he may wish to exploit that father by publishing the stories under his own name and live on the certain wealth they will bring. His actress mistress, once the goddess of the Prague stage, is not Jewish but is increasingly being reviled as such, a tribute to her most memorable debut back in 1956 as Anne Frank. The motif, of course, is deliberate: Anne Frank can be used by everyone, everywhere in *Zuckerman Bound*. As Yevtushenko can inhabit Anne's memory in "Babi Yar," so the whole Eastern world can wield her to prove conscience even as they enclose people in an *achterhuis* of meaningless routine and physical adaptation. Now Eva Kalinova, the actress, is paying for having—at age nineteen—used Anne to launch a career in a society indifferent to her tragedy. Eva, an iron-curtain version of Ceasara O'Shea, would find no romance in flying back behind that curtain, as Ceasara did to Fidel, for there she would be jailed for her defection, but neither has she any longer a stage career outside the land of her native Czech tongue. The artist's need to be nurtured by his own culture—Roth's and Nathan's theme in the American quilt—operates everywhere. The awareness doubles the reader back to *The Ghost Writer*, to Nathan's early need for Amy Bellette, and the "unforeseen consequences of art."

> I am remembering the actress Eva Kalinova and how they have used Anne Frank as a whip to drive her from the stage, how the ghost of the Jewish saint has returned to haunt her as a demon. Anne Frank as a curse and a stigma! No, there's nothing that can't be done to a book, no cause in which even the most innocent of all books cannot be enlisted, not only by *them*, but by you and me. Had Eva Kalinova been born in New Jersey she too would have wished that Anne Frank had never died as she did; but coming, like Anne Frank, from the wrong continent at the wrong time, she could only wish that the Jewish girl and her little diary had never even existed. (759)

The "too" suggests Nathan, born in New Jersey, who had had need of Anne alive. But an actress cannot, any more than a writer, control the unforeseen consequences.

In Czechoslovakia in 1976 writers are assigned manual labor, and everything requiring brains is done by drunks and crooks—they get along better with the Russians. Nathan, who has spent two books protesting his treatment as a writer, wryly muses on what would happen were America to fall under such a regime:

> I imagine Styron washing glasses in a Penn Station barroom, Susan
> Sontag wrapping buns at a Broadway bakery, Gore Vidal bicycling
> salamis to school lunchrooms in Queens—I look at the filthy floor and
> see myself sweeping it. (759)[6]

In Czechoslovakia, where expression is stifled but the need to tell stories persists, fictions are more acceptable than facts. The chief occupation of half the ordinary people is spying on the other half. No one who seems trustworthy can be trusted. Sisovsky, the exiled writer, may be lying. He says his father's shooting death had been the result of an exchange between two drunken Gestapo officers. One had protected his father to keep him as a chess partner; the other had protected a Jewish dentist to work on his teeth. When in the quarrel (so his story went) one Gestapo officer shot the other's dentist, that gallant retaliated by shooting Sisovsky's father. Both officers were officially reprimanded for their drunkenness.

Nathan has carried the story in his mind from America to Prague, but Olga, Sisovsky's wife, mentions it as a myth her despised exile uses to gain sympathy. Olga, the writer "with the best legs in Prague," is more despairing even than Jaga, more in need of any sensation that can confirm that she exists; and yet, at the end Nathan is not sure that she was not the one who called the secret police to arrest him with the manuscript. And on the way to the airport, Novak, the arresting officer, regales Nathan with the story of *his* father's life, that of a true Czech patriot—a conformist loyal to every contrasting political administration since early in the century, because self-abnegating conformity is the way of Eastern survival. But, Nathan says at the end,

> I also have to wonder whether Novak's narrative is any less an invention
> than Sisovsky's. The true Czech patriot to whom the land owes its sur-
> vival may well be another character out of mock-autobiography, yet
> another fabricated father manufactured to serve the purposes of a story-
> telling son. As if the core of existence isn't fantastic enough, still more
> fabulation to embellish the edges. (783)

Nathan cannot flee from his theme.

In Prague, where everything is done obliquely, people consciously live their fictions. No apparent motive is real. Pederasts use women to entice boys. Writers get themselves locked in sanitaria to be able to continue writing. Ennui, desperation, degradation are all ways of standing fast against an oppressive conformity that has the license to despise these defenses. Here there is beautiful architecture unknown in Jaga's south Bronx, and no drugs.

No drugs, but plenty of whiskey. You can fuck, you can masturbate, you can look at dirty pictures, you can look at yourself in the mirror, you can do nothing. All the best people are there. Also the worst. We are all comrades now. Come to the orgy, Zuckerman—you will see the final stage of the revolution. (723)

But the orgy he visits in Prague is thick with a depressing opacity Nathan could not conjure in his airy phantasm of "Milton's Millenia."

And this is the world that his grandparents, by leaving Europe, had spared Nathan from knowing, just as they had spared him from dying in the Holocaust. Like Portnoy before him, Nathan flies back to America on a plane, not cured of his particular resentment, but having seen from a personal fiasco in a contrasting society that the America that abuses him also nurtures him and gives him vent. The passport inspector at the Prague airport—after perusing Nathan's biographic details "to determine, you see, if I am fiction or fact"—has the last word. "Ah yes, . . . Zuckerman the Zionist agent. An honor to have entertained you here, sir. Now back to the little world around the corner."

Zuckerman, of course, is fiction; and the inspector's final words are an echo out of radio land, out of "Mr. First Nighter." From the standpoint of the East, Zuckerman lives in a make-believe world. But has not Roth been saying so too? Roth has entertained the idea of Zuckerman (in his little theater around the corner) as the doubly burdened sensibility, the artist-Jew, testifier to a process of emergence from forebears and old stories that cannot be discarded. The Jew who would not write to the *Times* to defend Israel is "the Zionist agent."

As a conclusion to the "Epilogue," and thus to the trilogy, this is a subtle summing up. Zuckerman is again driven in a chauffeured car and politely dispatched. The trilogy has been punctuated by ubiquitous chauffeurs—efficient, polite, on hand to protect a privileged class (and ready to abuse any infiltrators from their own class)—as it has been punctuated by the various manifestations of Anne Frank: both motifs mocking pretensions to freedom with displays of control. And throughout these novels, fathers, sought or shunned, underscore the patrimonial continuum that the Jew must work out. Nathan can redeem himself, he thinks, for having rejected his own father's world by embarking on the quest for Sisovsky's father's manuscript. In his own mind he fails. But Doc Zuckerman might have chuckled (or beamed) at Nathan's being called a Zionist agent. Not to be at ease in Zion or in his own flesh is Zuckerman's destiny. The subtlety of the ending stands in sharp contrast to a too-sanguine declaration of independence that Nathan delivers in *The Anatomy Lesson* when describing his undergraduate stance back in Chicago:

. . . to be raised as a post-immigrant Jew in America was to be given a ticket out of the ghetto into a wholly unconstrained world of thought. Without an old-country link and a strangling church like the Italians, or the Irish, or the Poles, without generations of American forebears to bind you to American life, or blind you by your loyalty to its deformities, you could read whatever you wanted and write however and whatever you pleased. Alienated? Just another way to say "Set free!" A Jew set free even from Jews—yet only by steadily maintaining self-consciousness as a Jew. That was the thrilling paradoxical kicker. (480)

Roth here credits the undergraduate Zuckerman with considerable early aware-ness. He himself had come upon the "kicker" somewhere between Bucknell and the end of studies at Chicago, and most of his subsequent fiction testified to the growing insight. But it is doubtful that he knew he could attain freedom "only by maintaining self-consciousness as a Jew" anywhere near that early. Roth would still be peeling the onion of that insight for another decade. Meanwhile, the critics could take the word "Epilogue" at face value and declare the Zuckerman adventures over and done with. They were wrong.

Chapter 10

ZUCKERROTH

Jews are to history what Eskimos are to snow.
—Nathan Zuckerman, 1978

While immersed in the act of writing, every novelist practices impersonation, becomes a character who can summon other spirits into his written world. In almost a decade of inhabiting Nathan Zuckerman, Roth had turned the practice of impersonation inside out. Nathan was not only a writer, he was *the* writer whose public history was closest to Roth's own. Wallach and Tarnopol might have been closer to Roth's private history, but their readership in the sixties and seventies had not been invited to leap to biographic conclusions. However, in contriving Nathan, Roth had taken distorted public perceptions of himself and had distorted them further, to intensify the predicaments of his character and the issues those predicaments embodied.

Often, Roth would complicate those predicaments by pouring fantasy on fantasy, letting one outrageous complication for Nathan undercut another. In *The Anatomy Lesson*, for example, giving Nathan the escapist fantasy of being a pornographer subverts his other escapist scheme of becoming a doctor. As Roth would later muse, Zuckerman lets "each of his escape-dreams of self-transformation subvert the meaning and mock the intention of the other."[1] Zuckerman's absurd savoring of his victimization as a writer finds its correlative in these mutually canceling fantasies. A man taking himself that seriously loses perspective and the ability to choose real freedom.

Yet in the unwritten world Jewish self-transformation was taking place in ways Nathan could but fumble to assess. In Israel, grandchildren of men whose beards had been pulled in the streets of Europe were signing treaties and shouldering Uzis; in America, grandchildren of Jewish peddlers were senators and CEOs. Even Zuckerman would come to believe that Jews could now define themselves—as men and as Jews—while just getting on with life. Roth's books of the late eighties and nineties are assertions of a Jewish self not so much arguing over as shrugging off the fine print of the covenant. Now confirmed Jews reach across national borders and into the past for the wider ties and conflicts that their self-acceptance contracts them to.

This Jewish self-acceptance of the later Roth hero intersects a wider historical development. For the first time in Western Jewish history a Jew of Roth's adult generation could choose to be a Jew. Before, he could try to choose not to be, but that was almost as ridiculous as a black's choosing not to be black. Now, however, in the public arena a Senator Goldwater or Cohen, or a Defense Secretary Schlesinger could be Christian and not viewed behind his back, like Mendelssohn, Marx, or Disraeli, as a turncoat Jew. Jews could actually sigh with relief that the erratic Bobby Fischer was no longer one of them. And precisely because a Jew or child of a Jew could choose not to be a Jew, Jews in general could now choose to be Jews. Choice rather than compulsion meant freer Jews able to define their Jewishness. Secularists or atheists identifying themselves as Jews could criticize their people without fear—or need—of being labeled outsiders. Jewish consciousness required neither traditional observance nor open rebellion.

From "The Prague Orgy" (1985) and *The Counterlife* (1987) through *Operation Shylock* (1993) Roth's Jews enter into, rather than flinch from, involvement with identifiably Jewish pursuits. From "the Zionist agent" Nathan's failed rescue of a Jewish manuscript (a motif Cynthia Ozick would also use in *The Messiah of Stockholm*) to *Counterlife* Nathan's attempts to parse the moral issues of West Bank settlements and genteel British anti-Semitism to Roth's reconsideration of his own whole struggle for personal freedom and the claims of his heritage in *The Facts* to his embracing of his father's life and struggle in *Patrimony* to his character "Philip Roth"'s involvement with the Mossad in *Operation Shylock*, Jewish issues are central to Roth's work. And at the same time, the chosenness of story telling, the endless reconsideration of self and attempts to answer "Is it me?" link the personal and the tribal histories. In most of these works a Jew seeks to identify his moral center so he can confirm his interaction with the world as a Jewishly transforming act. Going beyond the last rope is no longer pushing beyond parental or tribal restraints but carrying the rope out farther, expanding its demarcation to include new depths.

Working close to real history, Roth could construct seemingly real biography. But his "Philip Roth" is as much a character inhabited for the transforming purposes of fiction as was Nathan Zuckerman. The ultimate stage trick, it derives from the art of the ventriloquist, about whom Roth had said in 1984, that while he

> speaks so that his voice appears to proceed from someone at a distance from himself, . . . if he weren't in your line of vision you'd get no pleasure from his art at all. His art consists of being present *and* absent; he's most himself by simultaneously being someone else, neither of whom he "is" once the curtain is down.[2]

In creating a character with his own name, Roth had decided to play a variation of the ventriloquist's game. If not Edgar Bergen, then Jack Benny. For what impressed Roth about Benny was how he could for decades play that stingy, mean character *in his own name*. Considering Benny's ploy, Roth had said, "It excited his comic imagination to do this. He probably wasn't all that funny as just another nice fellow writing checks to the UJA and taking his friends out to dinner." And in a similar way it excited Roth's imagination to create Nathan Zuckerman as a thinly disguised, and "Philip Roth" as an open, representation of the myth his readership had created about him.

It was a myth of a more public man than Roth had ever become. In truth, as far back as *Portnoy*, when readers had him jet setting with Barbra Streisand, Roth had hidden for three months at Yaddo, because the recognition "was too big" for him to "begin to deal with."[3] And later, in his comings and goings to London, Prague, and Jerusalem, he had kept a low profile, absorbing current ideas in cafés and at dinner tables. He would stir them into drama only through endless hours of trying out predicaments on his typewriter, of inhabiting a character and staying open to the possibilities that the page gave back: a nugget here, a complication there, or a beginning that may have been composed as a conclusion months and hundreds of pages before.

Roth's habits of writing had become pretty well set before this period. Whether living in his 1790 farm house in Connecticut or in Claire Bloom's Chelsea home in London, he did his writing in a separated studio, either the converted cottage at the edge of his farm property or a rented room at a place like the Royal Automobile Club in Pall Mall. Each had a desk, an identical IBM golf ball typewriter, some books and pictures, lamps and chairs. A day's work consisted of both reading and writing, often without yet having outlined a specific tale, working sometimes on what would become parts of separate works. In England, he engaged in limited society, read newspapers, conducted correspondence, and thus gauged the forces affecting his life. It was there that his own leftward-leaning politics was brought up short by attacks against Israel—attacks from a smug British-left establishment that smacked to him of anti-Semitism.

While living largely abroad for six years, Roth had become somewhat disentwined from problems of American-Jewish identity. The discovery he made on resuming life primarily in America in the latter eighties was at once heartening and disconcerting. On the one hand, Jews were accepted almost everywhere as just people or as models of achievement, and no longer as exotics; and many fewer, even among Jews, now regarded Israel as a sacred cow to be loved uncritically. Moreover, in the cities he could breathe among unrestrained ethnics expressing joy or telling one and all off—there was some salt left in the earth. But on the other hand, the achievement of American establishment culture was now material and superficial beyond expectation. In high culture *chic*, everyone knew the references, but no one cared to know much of the substance. Intellectual and cocktail party conversation was not about books but about movies; the dues were two hours in a multiplex. News sources specialized in one-paragraph or fifteen-second capsules. Everyone could mouth the current ideas without much thinking. Books were collections, lists, how-tos, fantasy slicks. People read to escape from or confirm who they were, few to challenge or reconsider. Meanwhile, suspicious of being easily understood, Roth had been grappling to create a literature of misunderstanding, of irony whose response is never so much agreement as irritation. His maverick reputation might be a useful device for irritating a public to think. As it turned out, those new reading habits would combine with a new emphasis in the academy on ethnicities "of color" to ease Jewish writers off the required reading lists; and in addressing an older constituency, Roth would be sidetracked from his role of irritant onto a more sympathetic path by physical crises, his father's and his own.

Yet personal illness was far from his mind when, in writing *The Counterlife*, Roth used cardiac trouble and the aftereffects of a beta blocker to set Zuckerman's sexual predicament. That Roth himself would need a multiple bypass within three years of giving Nathan Zuckerman the fatal choice to undergo that procedure was sheer ironic chance. Nathan's (and in turn brother Henry's) illness, rather, would be a device for constructing a moral bind with absurd overtones, a challenge to unexamined, normative living. Illness could be the one threat to personal freedom unasserted by a group or culture. From Epstein in the 1950s, through to Novotny, Portnoy, Kepesh, and Zuckerman, insisters on personal sovereignty had received mocking ailments of the groin, the back, the flesh, the neck, or—now—the heart. They could defy the body politic but not the body somatic. Illness as a metaphor was the perfect answer to arrogations of will. Roth himself exercised regularly, was lean and fit, needed no trouble; but he had Nathan at the mercy of his imagination.

Illness prompts *The Counterlife*'s explorations of self-doubt, multiplied—beyond anything in *Zuckerman Bound*—by the novel's shiftings of fictive ground. The story being read is soon seen as a story within a story and then as a story within a story within a story. Its center is the question of Nathan's physical survival as a family man whole enough both to procreate and to influence his child's conflicted posterity. It is about the passing on of Nathan's kind of Jewishness. At several levels the Nathan and Henry of these pages try to fathom themselves and their Jewishness. And the tone is less strident than in the middle *Zuckerman Bound* novels, where Nathan's predicament is but the product of his vocation. Here a maturing, musing Nathan is seen *in* his vocation, through his writing, plumbing his own character and at the same time inducing readers to discover theirs.

Fiction writers lie their way to truth. Nathan's imaginings embody the truths he is seeking about himself; he projects his own story onto the lives of those closest to him, those invested with elements of himself. Nathan's credo is that all people—not only novelists—become themselves by constructing and then settling into the right fictions. No one simply *is*. Every mind creates fictions: creates the selves it shows to others, creates the others it responds to, the places of familiarity, allegiance, comfort. All of us, Nathan believes in his heart of hearts, are different people *to* different people because we are different people *with* different people. The healthy ones create the people, places, and values with which they can most be themselves, including, if they happen to be Jews, their Jewishness. *Their* Jewishness, which is not necessarily the same as anyone else's. *The Counterlife* presents the necessity and the absurdity of being oneself in a world of allegiances.

The five sections of Roth's novel, named for places in Nathan's head, are drafts of Zuckerman's writing: "Basel," "Judea," "Aloft," "Gloucestershire," and "Christendom." The reader, engrossed in these scraps, often does not know whether he is in Roth's or Nathan's fiction and only slowly sorts out the fictions within the fiction. "Basel" takes place in New Jersey, "Gloucestershire" in New York, and "Christendom" in England. The only thing Swiss in "Basel" is a woman we do not actually meet, a former mistress of Nathan's dentist-brother, Henry. In Nathan's fictional account, she is Henry's missed opportunity to escape from middle-class Jewish family life, a woman who would escape her own bourgeois Swiss life by wearing black lace camisoles to bed and pretending whorishly to take money. She is based on an early affair Henry had confided to Nathan. Neither the real Henry nor Nathan's fictive Henry ever goes to Basel. But Nathan's manuscript account of Henry's affair has Henry suffer cardiac arrest and beta-blocker impotence over not going. Basel also carries overtones of Judea; it is the place where Herzl summoned the first

World Zionist Congress. The real Henry never goes to Judea either, but Nathan creates his imagined *aliyah* to a right-wing orthodox settlement, so that Nathan can try fictively to rescue him (and in the bargain get to consider The State of Israel as a state of mind in the Jewish and non-Jewish worlds). "Aloft" lets Nathan inhabit the mind and persona of a hijack victim, "Christendom" that of an expatriate American stunned by fashionable English anti-Semitism. The stories of Henry's death in New Jersey and alternate life in Israel, and of Nathan's possible death in New York and alternate life in London, range over a menu of Jewish living. All these scraps of writing are Nathan's "useful fictions" to explore his later life as a man and as a Jew. In the novel, Nathan Zuckerman is composing fiction about a character with his own name and circumstances, as Philip Roth would later do in *Deception* and *Operation Shylock*.

Nathan's most immediate pressing conflict, although the reader does not know it is *Nathan's* conflict until the fourth section, is sexual impotence. Physical impotence, not the psychological impotence of a Portnoy or the mere writer's block of Tarnopol. Nathan's is the very condition the reader has been led to associate, in the fictive tryout, with Henry: a side effect of that beta blocker, the only drug that can spare him life-threatening cardiac surgery. But Nathan cannot tolerate his impotence because he loves a woman he wishes to marry and father a child by (and because it reduces "the aggressiveness of sex"). The woman fears the operation too much to want him to go through with it, is willing to continue a sexless affair with Nathan. But she is an English woman, mother of a young child and wife of a diplomat. To continue seeing Nathan, her neighbor in their New York apartment building, she would have to stay married, for her child's sake, to an abusive husband who—Nathan's real horror—still uses her sexually. And her husband's shifting venues would make her locale not Zuckerman's New York, where any free-thinking Jew could comfortably rebel against his people, but Christian London, where in constantly facing down anti-Semitism a relocated Nathan would have to become the ultra-Jew. The problem that Roth gives Nathan Zuckerman, which Nathan tries out fictively on Henry Zuckerman and on the woman Nathan would marry and on the reader of his and Roth's novel, is, again, "Is it me?"

In distorting others to discover himself, Zuckerman risks the accusation of betrayal, a pain Roth has known. And as he sees his own Jewishness evoking reactions—scorn from the Zionist zealot, resentment from the bourgeois brother, soft-soap anti-Semitism from the liberal Gentile, shouted insult from the open bigot, even his own dilemma after intermarriage about his child's heritage—Zuckerman must reckon the Jew in himself. But since Zuckerman thinks truth resides in story, he would first arrest us in his fictions, then peel them away like a plastic surgeon's bandages to reveal the new face they have helped to create.

Roth changes voices and tones to maneuver the reader into Zuckerman's shoes and those of the other characters, letting the reader re-create himself through encounters with many possible selves. Roth lies so well on his way to truth that, even warned, the reader succumbs to his—or to Nathan's—fictions. Like a sleuth tripping on hasty conclusions, the reader cannot but form new ones; and each shift of perception flushes out a new insight to the frail business of being a modern Jew.

Between the lines—perhaps of a second reading—one may find not so much a storytelling strategy, a la *Rashomon*, as a display of a novel's natural growth, of its shaping itself from a number of materials composed under the impetus of their own urgency, and a confirmation that what the novelist does most alone in his workroom is doubt. Early in the Henry story, Nathan is faced with the task of possibly speaking at Henry's funeral. He goes to his notes, years of random writing, thoughts that had been dressed in episodes, scraps that had urged themselves into being in the loneliness of the writer's studio. From these he culls a story that he cannot use for a funeral. The words do not praise Henry; they doubt the surface of Henry's life, imposing Nathan's values and assumptions about that life. Nathan gives over the task and declines to speak. But in Nathan's attempt the reader sees his writer's mind at work. Doubt makes Nathan turn and turn his subject, bring in as many conflicting perspectives as there are questions to test certainties, and expand—endlessly expand—that subject until it becomes not Henry's or Nathan's life but the human fiction-making capacity itself. Nathan is demonstrating Roth's mode of working as a novelist: composing fictions that may become useful as he gets closer to a sense of his next novel.

Even a first reader, sifting the false leads and mirrored identities, comes to realize that only once in the book, well into the fourth of five sections, is the narrator possibly not Zuckerman. But by then a reader has become too chary of conclusions to say that it is Roth. One is content to just stay open, to let any conclusions be drawn not *away* from the book but back into it, to deepen its mystery and enrich its life. And what the narrative voice that may not be Zuckerman's establishes during its short reign in the fourth section is that Zuckerman may now be dead, but being a writer he still lives in the fiction he has left us to read. And reread. For in that light one must newly consider not only the upcoming fifth-and-final chapter (by Zuckerman) but also Zuckerman's first three sections. Now ideas about fiction subtly take on over-tones as ideas about Jewishness, which like good fiction, is seen less as a tangible set of particularities than as a rich and creative state of mind.

Without defining "Jew," Roth raises more Jewish questions in *The Counterlife* than in any of his previous works: whether Israel will survive through intransigence or compromise—or survive at all; whether a secular

Diaspora Jew needs its survival, or even needs Jewishness; whether that is not but an ancient guilt, like *koshrut*, keeping him from mixing completely with his species; why he cannot mix with the gentile world without feeling *tref*; why he cannot shed the feeling that whatever craziness his Jewish heritage burdens him with, it is more commonsensical than the mythology of Christianity that surrounds him; whether *aliyah* is not just a fiction that troubled Jews use to evade their real problems; whether the self-made international man is not but another myth, or rationality but another fiction; whether zealotry is not but heritage impassioned; and, finally, why the mission to advance Jewish history is felt in the bones of even the most secular Jew.

The Counterlife does not answer these questions, but it raises them vividly as only fiction can, in guises that make the reader entertain them even as they entertain him in transcendent musings. Roth makes the unbelievable believable through a conflict of inseparable character, situation, and ideas. And the ideas come more frequently and more naturally than in any of his previous fiction, enhancing the famous "voice" in a way that multiplies the rewards of characterization and dialogue. The effect is even more pronounced by comparison with precisely contemporary works. In 1987 Bellow produced *More Die of Heartbreak* and Ozick *The Messiah of Stockholm* (dedicated to Philip Roth), both deemed lesser novels (in the year that Roth carried off the critical awards) because in neither did sympathy for or nuanced behavior of characters fully enrich the thematic premise. It is Bellow's and Ozick's way to provide philosophic debate in alternations of narrative and expository passages. In *The Counterlife* Roth engages the intellect every bit as fully as they, yet in a way more legitimately fictive, fusing narrative and philosophy so that where the characterization or the plotting or the dialogue is most inventive, the philosophical speculation is most inextricably intertwined. The greater the contention of thought, the more intense is the feeling transfused through it. *The Counterlife* satisfies the intellect by moving readers not as philosophy but as story. It is finally Roth's generosity to the reader of fiction that makes it a fine novel.

Nathan Zuckerman's problem of "Is it me?" is complicated by his living in a world whose temporary experiment with universal brotherhood has run its course, where everyone is back to being comfortable with his own kind and expressing that comfort as principled isolationism. Zuckerman, still dedicated to universalism, is isolated. Yet, because he is willing to die trying to be himself, he emerges whole, victorious and vindicated.

The counterlife in the title is more than the written world, more than every man's fictive power to create himself, his close ones, his enemies, his needed deaths, countries, salvations. It is also work, patriotism, or devotion to one's roots, any imaged and reified alternative to one's seeming life. In the land of the Gentiles it is being a Jew; in the land of the Jews it is being a Gentile. It is life created and intensified by a consciousness sustained through contrast, needing the conflict without which everything won begins to lose its definition and therefore its meaning. It is life only with the risk of death, and meaning-in-death only while the very circumstances hold the promise of intensified life. Roth examines every allegiance that defines a man to himself: allegiance to parents, siblings, tribe, adopted culture, beloved—and finds them all culturally contrived yet essential, constricting the self but rooting it in the world.

The nexus of Roth's story is the conflict between the brothers Zuckerman. Henry is a family man, bourgeois; Nathan, like his biblical namesake, a troubling voice. The locus of both their callings is the mouth. And a "calling" Henry thinks his dentistry is, though for three novels, since he gave up a youthful chance at being an actor, he has represented the overserious, narrowly focused "professional" deeply in need of respectability.

The conflict of these brothers opens the story out in all its other dimensions: Nathan now wants love and family on *his* terms (a gentile wife and a Jewish son), but in Henry's view he is the undeserving prodigal who has refused to pay the price of tribal confinement. Perhaps that is why Nathan imagines Henry trying to break out of the family mold. In "Basel" he makes Henry a desperate philanderer (Nathan throws him into the teeth of his calling by having him violate his hygienist's mouth with merciless oral sex), but a philanderer requiring, to preserve his affair, the surgery that kills him. Resurrecting him for "Judea," Nathan then sends him off into radical Zionism and posits himself as Henry's failed rescuer. Nathan must then face doctrinaire accusations. First the latter-day Lippman, a Kahane-like settlement leader, counts him, like the "goodies and niceys in Tel Aviv," among the spineless sellers out to the at-least-admirably dedicated Arab enemies (two positions for the narrative price of one). Then a young fanatic, first seen as a novitiate Hasid but also a reader of modern novels and a rabid Zuckerman fan, thinks Nathan has made the perfect escape from Jewishness:

> ". . . I want a shiksa just like the shiksa that married dear old Z. Teddibly British. Do like you do—The Yiddische disappearing act with the arch-goy, the white priestess. . . . You really got the inside track on how not to be a Jew. You shed it all. You're about as Jewish as the *National Geographic*." (*C* 169)

The envious fan is the schizoid Jimmy Ben-Joseph, author of "The Five Books of Jimmy," one-time baseball enthusiast who can imagine a great DiMaggio-like leaping catch against the Wailing Wall.[4] Having met his idol Zuckerman,

Ben-Joseph (his real name is Lustig, of the West Orange Lustigs) is now on the plane back from Israel, plotting a hijacking and dragging Nathan, through flattery, into seeming complicity. Moments later, Nathan, spread-eagled by two El Al security guards who have wrested a hand grenade from the psychotic Jimmy, is shown what it feels like to be a total outsider. The guards, humorless, as the situation warrants, and unwilling to believe that this seeming companion of the hijacker is what he calls himself, a creator of fiction, demand that he show some proof of kinship with Israel, a demand hardly satisfied by Nathan's using the enemy's term to declare that his brother lives in a "West Bank" settlement. The rectal inspection that completes the indignity dispels Nathan's last personal fiction that Israel is a haven for uncertain Jews.

But these fictive contentions with Henry and their ideational offshoots are parts of Roth's now-you-see-it, now-you-don't stage illusions, strategies of tone, playful and tender at the same time. It is a practice begun before the first word of the novel, where, playing off his own clichéd image, he has dedicated the novel—lovingly, but also ironically—"To my father at eighty-five." And from Roth's dedication—separating him from Nathan—the reader plunges into Nathan's first section, a draft piece in which he tries killing off the brother who once accused him of patricide. Nathan's estimate of Henry as "not quite coarse enough to bow to his desires, and yet not quite fine enough to transcend them" describes a Henry who has always played it safe while—nicely confusing autobiography and the autobiographical impulse in fiction—exonerating himself in resentment of Nathan. Later it is Henry who self-protectively destroys a considerable portion of the dead Nathan's fiction before anyone else in the novel—anyone, that is, except the reader—can peruse it.

Thus destroyed, and dead to all eyes except the reader's, is the account of the mad trip to Israel and back. But not destroyed by Henry is Nathan's final story, the one left for the eyes of the British woman Nathan loved—she for whom Nathan underwent the fatal surgery. "Christendom" is a story written in New York from hints she had given him about her life in England but, from her point of view, another distortion, another imagining of Nathan. In this story Jimmy Ben-Joseph's wild words are put to proof. Returning from Judea, not to New York but to London, Nathan posits himself now married to the British upstairs neighbor. But as the Jew trying to live a counterlife in Christendom, Nathan faces the threat to yet another marriage. Nathan depicts the major difficulty that intermarriage demands: mutual acceptance of the other's way. In the culture of Nathan's beloved British wife, it is fashionable to regard Jews as somewhat odd. But Nathan's Jewish paranoia, and his sense of self, render him unable to slough off fashionable anti-Semitism. So in this story, which ends the novel, the British wife, having "had it," wants out. In a letter Nathan imagines she could write him, she says that Nathan, the writer of other people's existence, has created her to comfort himself, has made her no more than a character in one of his novels. She wants not just out of the marriage, but out of the novel—even names the page early in *The Counterlife* on which doubt is first cast on their possibilities for a successful life together. Nathan, in reply, tells her why she can't have out—because the fiction is all. Since we are all one another's creations, there is no out. There is only perpetual and incomplete learning to stay in.

Roth wrings out his protagonist in an inquisition into the need for art or Jewishness. And Nathan's answer, disappearing back into his fiction, is Roth's testament of faith in his lifelong enterprise. *The Counterlife* sets out both despair at the existential condition of a person of the book (by implication, of any Jew or any artist) and the spark of hope that refuses to be extinguished. In the last chapter, Zuckerman's eloquent declaration of faith in fiction and Jewish resilience is sublime writing from an author not usually associated with sublimity.

As a bridge from *Zuckerman Bound* to the work of the nineties, combining ironic commentary on zealotry with faith in fiction, *The Counterlife* moves further into the cosmic Jewish predicament than Roth's previous fiction had seemed to do. At the beginning of the novel, while others still universally view Nathan as the libidinous author of *Carnovsky*, Nathan's own sympathies show him in a kinder light. The internal writer of his own namesake's experience, he reveals a warm regard for his parents' generation and a desire to continue their patrimony. He posits in Henry's father-in-law yet another shoe store owner, this time a man from Albany who can't stay in business because his Christian customers won't tolerate his catering to the new black residents of the neighborhood. Yet this old man lacks Papa Freytag's bitterness, rather taking his troubles out on his own body and warding them off with nitroglycerine pills. Conflicted Jews in this novel pay the somatic price, while those of fixed purpose retain their vigor. Nathan's Uncle Shimmy, wealthy and "arguably the family's stupidest relative," built in the solid Neanderthal mold of Mr. Patimkin and holding between his teeth a chunk ripped "out of life's raw rump," is one example. Yet to Nathan he is an essential part of the immigrants' success in America:

> . . . pain and suffering did not deter [men like Shimmy] for half an hour from their intention of living. Their lack of all nuance or doubt, of an ordinary mortal's sense of futility or despair, made it tempting sometimes to consider them inhuman, and yet they were men about whom it was impossible to say that they were anything *other* than human: they were what human really is. While [Nathan's] own father aspired relentlessly to embody the best in mankind, these Shimmys were simply the backbone of the human race. (*C* 38)

Shimmy's views are uncomplicated. For Israel's foreign policy, his solution is "Bomb 'em, bomb the Arab bastards till they cry uncle. They want to pull our beards again? We'll die instead." Nathan's Aunt Essie has her nephew's instinct for ironic reflection and perhaps a better ability to balance myth and skepticism. She, too, is solidly for Israel, but she sees it as capable of self-criticism and adjustment—she gives to the U.J.A., she says, because in Tel Aviv they tell better anti-Semitic jokes than in Miami—and, in this early part of the novel where Henry is dead, Essie sees through the widowed Carol's fiction that Henry had risked his operation to preserve their marriage. Nathan completes the picture of his parents' generation with old Grossman, the melancholy relative who had survived the death camps and whose pessimistic view of everything is excused by the family as the price they must all pay for the Holocaust, while behind these still-living characters lurks the ghost of Nathan's father, who had held them all together as family archivist and sheepdog. Doc Zuckerman as remembered seems more and more like the anticipation of the Herman Roth that would come forth in *Patrimony*.

The public and private Nathan are thus in conflict in the novel, as Nathan increasingly feels love for his heritage replacing resentment. But his own myth is still useful to him. When Nathan declines to speak at his brother's funeral, he can depend on his vague excuse going unchallenged. Carol fears him too much as the feeder off and betrayer of family secrets to trust him far with a task of sentiment. Yet trying vainly to compose Henry's death has set Nathan to revaluating his own childhood, his views of family, his responses to Jews. We see him hankering after some home for his Jewish heart. And at the end, trying to be at home in gentile England amidst his wife's family (called Freshfield), he is bursting to defend Jews against latent English anti-Semitism. His renewed respect for America is associated with being himself: it is a place where he is not in diaspora.

To Nathan diaspora is not geography, not the same as *the* Diaspora (that is, everywhere outside of Israel). He can be in diaspora in Israel. He is most in diaspora when he feels least at home, least himself. By contrast, his Zion is any place where Jews feel collectively secure enough to be themselves, where they are not forced to distort their beings by exaggerating some part of themselves to defend against terror of body or spirit. And he hopes he is reaching the point in his own life where that Zion can be carried with him, where he can be himself regardless of geography. *The Counterlife* does not answer geographically the question of where Jews belong. But it does challenge all general answers. Jews had been celebrating for years their ability to feel so at home in Israel—with its Jewish cop and its Jewish laborer and its Jewish bully—that anti-Semitism there had seemed to vanish from consciousness; but one does not escape Roth's ironic reminder that the country is surrounded and infiltrated by sworn enemies to its Jewish aspirations and that the extreme positions Jews are driven to in order to defend it create their own distortions of the Jewish self. Nathan's Israeli journalist friend Shuki says that in Israel Jews are living "the kind of imperiled Jewish existence we came here to replace." It is an existence "excitable, ghettoized, jittery." Ironically, as the American Jew needed to think less and less about how to defend his Jewishness, the Israeli Jew needed to think more and more about how to defend his life. The reminiscence at Lippman's settlement about the brothers' boyhood radio days makes the idealized Weequahic still the perfect Zion of Nathan's experience. But that serves for one Jew, reified by one life experience, and "On the Air" had already shown it to be a flawed experience. Neutral (irritatingly, to some) about the true Zion, *The Counterlife* was nearly a year into publication when the first stones of the *intifada* were being thrown. They would be hurtling through the novel in which Nathan's successor, "Philip Roth," returns to Israel.

Still, Israel is the setting for some of *The Counterlife*'s most contentious conflicts, presenting a fairly large cross-section of opinion on the Jewish question circa 1978. But it is not Roth's purpose to make this a novel about how or whether Israel should survive. His leftist Israeli journalist and his right-wing Gush Emunim zealot both argue eloquently for their causes and rebut vehemently the other's position. But both are creators of fictions in which they hope to live, each trying to enforce his scenario into existence. Roth may be closer to the journalist, Shuki, than to Lippman, but he is not Shuki. These antagonists share that aspect of their creator shared by all the other characters in the novel: a need to create vital fictions. Nathan's British wife is an amateur writer, Jimmy is a would-be literary prophet, Carol writes the obituary delivered over Henry, Henry by destroying and preserving Nathan's writings becomes Nathan's editor and executor: they all try to compose fictions in which they can live unthreatened. Roth makes their ideas reflective of their characters, makes believable their resolutions of identity; he does not use them to promulgate some polemic of his own with planted demurrals for seeming effect (the prolepsis of Marie Syrkin's old accusation). Of course, once he allows a character to speak passionately for a political position, he risks making enemies among advocates of the counter-position. That is Roth's history. What is true of the plot is also true of the polemics within the plot. Rather than advancing, the plot comes (as one reviewer put it) "to a number of screeching halts, . . . each new beginning . . . a refutation of what has gone before, [but] the individual scenes inspire absolute belief."[5] So do the disquisitions on Jewishness by the main characters. Each forces Nathan to ponder its thesis and ask, "Is it me?"

Jewishness tags everyone in the novel. In "Judea," Henry, having survived his bypass operation and gone off on a snorkeling vacation to Eilat, happens into Mea She'arim, the ultraorthodox neighborhood of Jerusalem. Here, feeling his comparative lack of Jewish identity, he resolves to undergo a spiritual bypass to match the physical. Having failed earlier to chuck the New Jersey bourgeois Jewish life and go to Basel with his *shiksa*, he now chucks it to go to Judea as a supermilitant Zionist. Away from Carol, the kids, and America into another life, he will make bypass a solution. *Aliyah* will give him a new identity as Hanoch, a pistol-toting follower of the humorless Lippman. He will find a self in something larger than himself, complete with religious discipline. Indeed, the novel's various shiftings of fictive grounds are explorations of bypasslike cures for impotence—attempts to change one's life through extrication from pressing predicaments—real bypasses in this novel being the surgery that kills. And Judea, for all the political accuracy and realism of its descriptions, is not just a place in the Middle East, it is also an item on the menu of personal Jewish choices. It is the primeval tribal state. Nathan, impotent and having tried out stories on Henry, also seeks his Judea. As a writer, he has his namesake fly to London to settle into bourgeois family life among the Freshfields. "Christendom" is his Judea; his escape is a mirror-reversal of Henry's. Ironically, he is trying to follow the old injunction of Rilke's poem: "You must change your life!" To do so, he realizes, is for him as for the Zionist, to create "a counterlife that is one's own anti-myth." But for Nathan the thing larger than himself will turn out to be not his new country but his renewed dedication to the truth of fiction—including his own ability to script a personal Jewishness.

Nathan's wife in this fifth section sees his trip to rescue Henry as having been a journey into "the Jewish heart of darkness." To Nathan, trading literary allusions, it was a brief stay aboard a Pequod headed for destruction, with Lippman as Ahab. Their conversation takes place along the Thames, a somewhat foggy Thames that might suggest also the beginning of another Conrad voyage of destruction in "Youth," aboard the ship *Judea*, whose motto is "Do or Die!" This marriage is do or die for Nathan, but like young Marlowe he has always considered himself just an observer in the Jewish voyage of older people, seeing a mere quaintness in their ancient rituals. The day before, on Dizengoff Street in the real Judea, a Nathan defensively casual about his Jewishness, had told Shuki that circumcision, like all biblical commandments, "was probably irrelevant to my 'I'." But now as he converses with a wife pregnant with what he can only consider to be a son, and already forewarned by a sister-in-law that the Freshfields will expect baptism, Nathan imagines the coming conflict over circumcision. He grows adamant that his son will bear the tribal mark, which, he now declares, is no more brutal than life, is indeed a good first exposure to its reality. As a novelist, Nathan can insist that he has no "I," that he is like a method actor or like that sensibility Keats calls the poetic character: having no personality of his own, no self. Indeed, he insists that the very idea of a self is a bad joke that people allow their circumstances or their families to impose on them. Nathan protests too much:

> What I have instead [of a self] is a variety of impersonations I can do, and not only of myself—a troupe of players that I have internalized, a permanent company of actors I can call upon when a self is required, an ever-evolving stock of pieces and parts that forms my repertoire. (*C* 321)

But if Nathan has no self, he has a history, and a psychological identity within that history, which is Jewish; and so he insists that whatever his son's Jewishness will be, it should begin with the sign of the covenant in his flesh. "Circumcision confirms that there is an us, and an us that isn't solely me and him."

Ironic, that the shape of the unborn child's possible penis will finally focus the whole identity theme—but consistent with the imagery of the book. For the penis as symbol exists throughout—the other great symbol in the novel besides the mouth. The novel, which ends with Nathan's musing on his erection, had begun with Henry's predicament over restoring his. The penis remains in focus through surgical attempts to resurrect it. Symbolically, as a pistol, it sits in Lippman's holster to intimidate his Arab opposites. In "Christendom," it marks boundaries: for Nathan, foreskinned is forearmed; circumcision becomes the palpable focus of Jewish tribal history. Ironic, too, that this most Portnoyish association should cinch a hero who fully transcends Portnoy.

The main difference between the protagonists of that early and this later novel is that Nathan, unlike Alex, is a writer; and the writer in Nathan can command the doubts that wracked Portnoy (in contrast to the Alex-like flailings of Henry). Trusting doubt, Nathan can also trust his feelings to prevail over settled doctrine. He can even face his wife's despair over what she considers his Jewish paranoia, face it not by giving up his protective instincts or embracing baptism but by insisting their difference can be lived with and worked through. Whereas a young Portnoy lets the Pumpkin go for not wanting to convert to Judaism, a mature Nathan—in a more secure time—insists that his child of a Christian wife can be a circumcised Jew and that the couple can struggle to stay together. It is not a polemical point of Roth: he is not advocating intermarriage—or decrying it. Indeed, for Nathan, it is a struggle against very strong feelings, for, in truth, the religious trappings of Christianity repel him:

> It never fails. I am never more of a Jew than when I am in a church when the organ begins. I may be estranged at the Wailing Wall but without being a stranger—I stand outside but not shut out, and even the most ludicrous or hopeless encounter serves to gauge, rather than to sever,

my affiliation with people I couldn't be less like. But between me and church devotion there is an unbridgeable world of feeling, a natural and thoroughgoing incompatibility—I have the emotions of a spy in the adversary's camp and feel I'm overseeing the very rites that embody the ideology that's been responsible for the persecution and mistreatment of Jews. (*C* 256)

His wife's comfort with church service and baptism he will never share; it is another side of a very difficult issue, evidence that all relationships are struggles over identity. That awareness forces Nathan to ask, and his wife to ask, why people marry.

Maria and I were not anthropologists in Somaliland, nor were we orphans in a storm: she came from somewhere and so did I, and those differences we talked so much about could begin to have a corrosive effect once the charm began wearing thin. We couldn't just be "us" and say the hell with "them" any more than we could say to hell with the twentieth century when it intruded upon our idyll. (*C* 308)

What Nathan will fight for at the end is the worth of a life beyond the idyll. What Kepesh could not face without loss of desire, Nathan now sees as desirable. He invites his wife to grasp it with him, symbolically in a shared erection. All the Christian mistresses and wives in this novel are named Maria—Nathan's projections onto the Zuckerman brothers of their fascination with female Christian archetypes. An issue of Diaspora life, they are the price of resisting a self-diminishing comfort in religious exclusion. It can be argued that Roth is presenting a false conflict, that Nathan really has no choice since the child of a Christian wife cannot be considered a Jew under Jewish law. But that, too, is an issue of Diaspora, facilely dismissed only by Jews who can dismiss grandsons and cousins and aunts.

Jewishness and fiction, seen as open states of higher truth, are Nathan's hope, worth reaching for. Ironically, even as they call in question notions of the authentic self and the authentic Jew—who is always slightly wounded, slightly alienated—their confluence as the novel's final testament produces for the reader a rush of optimism. But after the experience of the novel there seeps in a counter-irony: Nathan himself may not have survived its composition. That final section of the novel is being read by his New York Maria after a failed bypass surgery has probably killed him. *The Counterlife* is quintessential Philip Roth, and as such, not his last word on where Jews belong.

Critical reception of *The Counterlife* divided over the issue of universality. Some readers, liberated by doubt, felt themselves soaring in its openness;

others saw old Roth being poured into new tricks. These polarities were nicely set for the largest potential market by the daily and Sunday *New York Times* reviews. Christopher Lehmann-Haupt, seizing the first available Monday before publication, saw Roth cleverly reiterating his same old theme that characters are not their authors. But to Lehmann-Haupt the shifts of plot, by subverting verisimilitude, undermined credibility and therefore fictive power.

> By the time we have finished "The Counterlife," we have begun to wonder if Mr. Roth has anything to write about except his fear of being misjudged as an artist. . . . We respect the tricky epistemology. And go hungering for something more substantial.[6]

On the following Sunday, William H. Gass declared that "Philip Roth's magnificent new novel, a remarkable change of direction itself," constituted "a fulfillment of tendencies, a succesful integration of themes, and the final working through of obsessions that have previously troubled if not marred his work." Gass adds, "I hope it felt, as Mr. Roth wrote it, like a triumph, because that is how it reads to me." Gass specifically denies that Roth is settling scores (he sees him as having done that in the Milton Appel episode of *The Anatomy Lesson* and elsewhere); he finds that Roth has achieved, rather, a style "no longer . . . at war with itself. . . . Its combativeness is no longer pointed at the reader, the critic, the family or some other ancient adversary."[7] Most of the reviews leaned toward agreement with Gass. Perhaps by this time the most influential Jewish scholar-critic was Robert Alter, whose works on biblical narrative and poetry had enhanced his already considerable prestige. Alter did what is almost never done: he reviewed the same book in two different periodicals; he could do so by making his second entry part of a longer essay, a critique of new works by two influential authors. His first review appeared in the February 2 *New Republic*; his second, as a comparison of Roth's book with Cynthia Ozick's *The Messiah of Stockholm*, in the July *Commentary*. The combination of Alter and Ozick was a shoehorn that could slide even Roth into the graces of the *Commentary* readership. Both of Alter's essays on Roth's novel were highly favorable, the *Commentary* one even contrasting Roth's hit to Ozick's near miss.

Alter saw how Roth, in focusing "suggestively on the ambiguous transactions between fiction and life," had hit upon Israel as the Jews' fictional resolution for tensions best left open, especially as every faction's view of Israel was a different story.

> *The Counterlife* . . . uses the fictional medium to wrestle with the intractable question of Jewish identity (hence the appositeness of the

theme of self-making.) And this involves an imaginative confrontation within the fictional frame of clashing Jewish ideologies . . . [which makes this] . . . one of the best American examples . . . of the Jewish fiction of ideas.[8]

And its considerations of Israel, Alter suggests, are timely, since Israel had itself become an idea within Judaism, one that needed to be considered without the devotional reduction of an *Exodus*. To Alter, "Philip Roth's ability to imagine Israel in depth as an inexorable component of the Jewish struggle for identity is what gives his latest book the unusual resonance it possesses." Alter praises the novel's accuracy in describing and interpreting the various ideological positions it reflects. In the end, he declares,

> it is hard to say what is concluded ideologically because ideas and outlooks remain, as they should, in restless circulation. But the Zuckerman of the final section does resolve to resist all visions of a harmonious accommodation with reality—all 'pastoral' prospects, as he calls them, whether in assimilation or in Zionist normalization of Jewish existence. This resistance is itself a minimal Jewish credo.[9]

The Counterlife won the National Book Critics Circle Award for fiction. When it also won the distinctly Jewish *Present Tense/* Joel H. Cavior Literary Award, Roth, in thanking the board, was moved to remind them that his career had been made "in response to" well-placed Jews who had contradicted his "sense of the contradictions of Jewish life." He concluded, "I mean only to warn of possible consequences if your unprecedented tribute becomes universal throughout the Jewish world. You could well be initiating the destruction of a career."[10] That would prove the least of his fears and one entirely within his control.

The most obvious change in Roth's books following *The Counterlife* is the departure of Nathan Zuckerman: in the next four books, until the arrival of Mickey Sabbath in *Sabbath's Theater* (1995), the primary voice would be posited as Roth's own. But, depending on what that "own" might mean, the change might be merely one of masks. For in these books, the ventriloquist, speaking no longer through the dummy, but directly, takes on many of the dummy's mannerisms and assumptions, reducing the distinction implied by a different voice. Indeed, the demands on the reader become greater, for what Roth leaves behind in shedding Nathan are some of Nathan's endearing foibles. "Philip Roth" is harder. In order to digest him, the reader not only is expected to believe—at some level—that the character speaking, narrating, or being spoken about is *the* Philip Roth but also is expected to know, at least minimally,

Roth's life and most recent works—certainly, the Zuckerman books.

The first three of these post-*Counterlife* works, *The Facts*, *Deception*, and *Patrimony*, are all autobiographical fiction or autobiography using devices of fiction. They present respectively a past, present, and future blurred by doubt: was it me? is it me? will it be me?—quite Jewish questions. The biblical YHWH defined himself to Moses only as the puzzle of being—"I am that I am"—and named his people Israel: "the man who struggles with God." To struggle with "I am" is—for the creature made in the image of "I am"—a life-long enterprise. If all Roth's stories come back to Ozzie Freedman's question, "Is it me?" this obsessed Jew's questioning of his identity may indeed be a Jewish quest; and fiction, the medium of that quest, his counter-devotion to ritual worship. Just as in medieval literature courtly love could become a religion contending with Christianity, so for Roth fiction as the way to truth may almost be a religion contending with Judaism. If so, the struggle is essential to its doctrine, and the incorporation of the rival is essential to its life.

But if the whole point of Roth's quest for identity were only personal, that dedication to fiction would be merely solipsistic. A new division between Roth's defenders and his detractors would be over whether the character "Philip Roth" is to be taken as the author (or only the author) or as a representative figure whose personal doubts are representative doubts. And the answer to the question is inseparable from the quality of the writing, for it is in its ability to engage the reader that universality in fiction or biography attests itself. If it holds and moves us, it is about us too; if not, it is not.

To compose fictions from small narratives independently spawned is to "work in the dark." That might not have been the sense James intended in the words from "The Middle Years" that E. I. Lonoff posted on his bulletin board. But the continuation of that quotation might contain the essence of Roth's religious calling: "Our doubt is our passion and our passion is our task." As for the leap of faith the religious make to trust in some transcendent *other*, "The rest is the madness of art." Working in the dark for Roth, the fiction writer, meant writing small pieces that could be woven together or rewritten as the sense of a larger fiction formed in his mind. Bits might be left out or left over, perhaps to be used another time. What these pieces did on their own was to assert their life. They talked back to their author. No sooner composed than doubted, they were put through grillings and transformations, grapplings with their authenticity that were no mere prolepsis. In *The Facts*, the letters to and from Zuckerman that form the frame; in *Deception*, the dialogue debates that punctuate brief encounters; in *Patrimony*, the questions to and comparisons with Herman Roth by a Philip needing to identify the true patrimony before losing his status as child: these are the products of dialogue between the writer and himself over the question of his being. To engage a general reader, they would have to be put in

a context of recognizable conflict, of an outward danger to a vulnerable protagonist. Roth's problem in inhabiting his myth himself, without the slight but
protective *schlemiehldom* of Nathan, is that the irritating character contrived in
his own name might have little empathic vulnerability.

In some respects these first three outright autobiographic books are
responses to Roth's immediate circumstances, treadings of water between the
meatier *Counterlife* and *Operation Shylock*. And many reviewers would treat
them, like the three immediate successors to *Portnoy's Complaint*, as solipsisms
to be suffered before Roth could again confront the cosmic irritations of modern Jewish life. While all three address, however deceptively, Roth's personal
life, they do imply much more; and one may read them for ideas and for understanding of Roth as a complex representative Jew. But it would take prior
interest in Roth to read either *The Facts* or *Deception* with anything like total
understanding.

As products of Roth's personal life, these works were born of a stormy
time. Twice again in this period—as when he had been floored by peritonitis
for three months in 1967—Roth would be brought by illness to the verge of
death. Speak of life imitating literature (and to speak of it is to invite skepticism from those long predisposed to distrust Roth), his life at this point might
seem like an ironic commentary on his own 1960s indictment of fiction as
inadequate to plumb the horrors of reality. Shortly after the publication of
The Counterlife, in the spring of 1987, a failed knee surgery—the simple kind
that is done in offices every day—left him in sleep-reducing pain for which
one drug and then another and finally a combination of drugs was prescribed
that pushed him psychologically beyond anything that Nathan Zuckerman
had known in *The Anatomy Lesson*. He became so depressed that he contemplated suicide without ever realizing or being medically advised that this condition was possibly drug-induced. Roth's psychic energy was wholly diverted.
Philosophic contemplation of how to be gave over to fighting the pull of not to
be. Under that impetus Roth began writing *The Facts* for the most primitive of
human reasons, to find himself by reasserting to himself who he had been in
the earliest unwritten reality of his life. Indeed, it worked so well that before he
was finished with the book he could compose that frame dialogue with
Zuckerman—testimony to his recovery into self-questioning skepticism. Then,
two years later, while helping his tumor-reduced father resolve his own question of life or death, Roth suffered a heart attack that would have killed him
had a doctor not been present in its earliest stage; his life was spared by multiple bypass surgery. Throughout these episodes, Claire Bloom was at hand to
keep his life somewhat on keel, and in 1990 he married her. All these events
would become part of the background for *Operation Shylock*, which bases its
action on a transformed Roth myth.

Roth never stopped writing. The jottings for *Patrimony*, not yet an actualized book, would be begun during his father's last sinking year, and the materials of *Deception* were near at hand even as *The Counterlife* was being finished. These tentative excursions reflected Roth's long-standing practice. They could be shaped into books, and they might even incorporate wider issues sensed through personal involvement in a politicized world. For years the cold war had induced Roth to ponder on paper the literary differences between East and West. Outright censorship in the East had made sex a substitute for politics and talk of sex a substitute for literature. And in its demanding way, the opportunity of freedom in the West had all too often turned strident self-definition into alienation. Now the cold war was coming to an end. What of all those Jagas and Olgas and Professor Soskas (retired by the government at age thirty-nine in *The Professor of Desire*), of the Czechoslovakia from which Roth had been banned in 1975 and the Holocaust-emptied Poland whose exiles from communism he had come to know over the years? Their rootlessness in the West had become more poignant during his own brief diaspora in England. Roth's personal life had been full of associations that suggested themes for writing if he could distance them enough to transform them into universal predicaments. And his being Jewish had provided him with another slant on their plight and on their attitude toward him. He would find, almost despite himself, that when he directly addressed his own life, it was his Jewish identity that magnetized concerns about his past, his most recent associations, and his patrimonial continuum.

Perhaps the effect of these changes was to give Roth a new attitude toward, or relationship to, his role as writer. The one-time *enfant terrible* was less *terrible*, even to Jewish readers, than when Jews had felt threatened in America; and the ascent of film and television, the trivializing of culture, meant a limited readership for introspective American ironists. But beyond America, overall Jewish fate was still being spun amidst what Roth had once characterized in himself as "fanatical security, fanatical insecurity." In England and among Europeans, being Jewish was still problematic.

Writers who mine their own lives for material are often played out by their mid-fifties. Either they are revisiting their youth for diminished ore or are reasserting mid-life convictions now *passé* to their readers. But Roth knew things about turnings from cold war and sexual war, about ossified ideals clung to in eddying streams. He also knew some ironies about reputation not grasped by Zuckerman's rasher sensibility; he had the perspective of that older man whose blood is not quite tame but whose need is not quite urgent. In an autobiographic mode he might still play out these less frenetic themes and on his own wrists might take the pulse of late twentieth-century Jewishness. As a Jewish writer traveling in Europe and Israel, he had cultivated friendships with

Holocaust survivors from Primo Levi to Aharon Appelfeld. He had attended the trial of John Demjanjuk, had defended the Israelis among the Brits, watched the rising factionalism, seen, despite the safety of secularism, how aloofness might diminish one's own sense of Jewishness. Indeed, more and more he was engaging the question of his own Jewishness not to give the world prescriptions but to answer for himself a nagging irrational question: what role does allegiance play in identity? His experience could be subject for ironic engagement without pietism.

In *The Facts* Roth had sought for his early identity out of dire personal need and then had challenged it out of respect for art. He had published it against Zuckerman's advice and had at once given his readership sentimental grounds to accept him as himself and ironic grounds for doubting anyone so self-exonerating. It was biography and it was fiction. What had been had not necessarily been the way he had so very badly needed it to be. But for the first time Roth had offered the public a man called Roth. The younger man who had been full of Jewish prejudices and spites had been he. His loving mother—no Sophie Portnoy—had yet been moved to revulsion at accepting his first wife's laundry in her washer, that taint on underwear of goyish female excretions representing for at least one critic the uptight prejudice that was Roth's whole problem.[11] The charge of misogynist was thus confirmed for some, of chauvinist for others, but for all who might be interested there was a book about Roth (not about his writings) by Roth. It was a step toward achieving a different kind of authenticity than before, a different use of facts: not only transformation by imaginative assault, but also domestication by seeming self-acceptance.

Roth's next three books were commissioned as a package under contract by Simon & Schuster, powerful and determined to create commercial success. The first book was *Deception* (1990). And its first deception was the cover: a partial glimpse of two naked bodies lying horizontally, the man's arm caressing the woman's waist, air brushed into a lace sheet merging with a white background. The sexy cover, intended by the new publisher to exploit Roth's vaguely rakish reputation among general readers, was not dishonest, just deceptive. The second deception was the blurb on the book jacket flap, which begins by calling this "Philip Roth's most provocative novel about the erotic life since *Portnoy's Complaint*." "About" is not "of," but the reader is invited to associate *Deception* with *Portnoy*—rather than with the thirteen books in between—as another sex bomb. After purchase, the reader might enter the world of the deception. Conversation in the book is largely postcoital, reflective rather than arousing. When it is precoital, it is playful rather than stimulating. Or the conversation is negotiative, the friendly talk of persons who have had an affair, who are resuming it after an absence (the text spans five years), but who are careful to begin with civilized updatings. Some of it is phone conversation, not all with lovers. Mostly it is Philip in his London writer's studio inducing talk from women, making probing observations that keep the burden on them. Their talk is familial, social, vaguely political. Sometimes it reveals what for him is evidence of anti-Semitism inherent in their being Christian, for them merely assessments of the status of Jews in England. Iron curtain lovers still embody the question of freedom. Love is sometimes sympathy and mutual taking without undue hurting, need seen from a jaded perspective. Sometimes it is just expression of sympathy intended to induce further talk. As Jaga, Carol, Henry, and Maria had complained of Nathan, these people, including even Philip's wife, accuse Philip of engaging them not for themselves but for their stories.

Deception continues two themes pursued in The Counterlife: the intermingling of fiction and real life (the theme also built into the sandwich structure of The Facts) and the contrast between British and American Jewry. It also carries forth an experiment in style that Roth had conducted sparingly before, as far back as Our Gang and more recently in the fourth section of The Counterlife. Toward the end of that section, the ghost of Nathan, who has died in surgery, returns to converse with the British neighbor for whom Nathan underwent the operation, she who had inspired the fifth section's Maria Freshfield Zuckerman and is the interior reader of that book. Whether Nathan here exists only in her head or is staging some supernatural visitation is immaterial. The exchange is pure dialogue, without narrative or attribution to guide the reader. In Deception Roth goes further, stripping the whole work to almost pure dialogue. And some of that dialogue—about the composing of The Counterlife—is held now with two "real" British women on whom "Philip" had supposedly based Nathan's inspiring neighbor. Its veiled allusions to that novel and those women can be fully comprehended only by readers of the earlier work, just one of many such demands. At one point Philip's principal lover plays at being the biographer of Philip's fictional characters: the now-dead Zuckerman and the long-dead Lonoff.

Thus Deception requires more of its reader's attention and thought than any other of Roth's novels, yet it repays the reader with only slight, though stunning, dividends. It is fiction about fiction—deceptive in using a form that gives the illusion of nonfiction—but without compelling conflict: it presents no suspenseful danger to its hero that might create what Roth elsewhere calls "predicament." It forfeits mimesis for technique, experience for teasing curiosity about the source of the experience. Part of its deception is its invitation to keep interchanging "Philip" and Roth. But without "predicament" it is—by Roth's own lights—ungenerous, giving the reader no personal conflict to share. The lovers' evaluating the genre of biography by reference to Roth's own past work is but one example of Roth as author hiding and seeking among his past and present characters. Here the woman required to imagine herself a biographer engaged to do Zuckerman falls into the game by saying she hopes to keep it a simple task with a fast payoff, not—like the (imagined) chore of having done Lonoff's biography—needlessly difficult and unremunerative. Although the speaker is twice removed from these strictly fictive events, she imagines being a male biographer put off by the task as if he were doing real persons. She (he) is peeved by Lonoff's having buried so much in his turned sentences and by the still-living Hope Lonoff's having offered so little help. In a few swift turns, we are out of the studio room and into a whole fictive history being created by allusion. At another point, all of the novel we have so far read is identified as the contents of a notebook found by Philip's wife, who sees it as evidence of the adultery it is—or may be, since he defends it as not life but imagined life. She asks that he at least rename his character Nathan—give all this over to identification with Zuckerman and spare her at least the embarrassment of being considered betrayed. (Interestingly enough, at the time of the writing, Roth and Bloom were not yet married, nor is the reader anywhere invited to identify the wife.) He ignores her request and continues his imagined manuscript (that is, this book) and later comments on it as a real manuscript in a final conversation with his problematic British lover. Indeed, at this point, the very end of the novel, it seems as if most of what we have previously read has been the writer's notebook for *The Counterlife*, predating that work; and this later conversation, following publication of *The Counterlife*, is being held with one of the original British women on whom Roth had based Maria.

Deception, as Hermione Lee has pointed out, is not betrayal; this is not Pinter's play. "Betrayal is an act, deception is a craft. Betrayal is a crime, deception is a practice. Betrayal is exposure, deception is concealment. This book isn't nearly so much about adultery as it is about writing."[12] To the one mistress, fiction, Philip is absolutely faithful. Those in the novel who want him to tone down his writing or conceal its more revelatory moments are asking for betrayal of his art and therefore of his own being. He will provide deception because it is not personal; it may even be kind, protecting identities, precluding pain. But he will not provide betrayal. When he goes as far as to admit that there is a kind of betrayal in having made up "little conversations" with fictional lovers while sitting in the very bedroom where his wife may at that moment have been sleeping, his wife, in frustration, exclaims that these creations of his must be real women. He denies that and refuses to revise them, insisting in turn that for him to yield to the censorship of taste or humiliation or avoidance or doubt about the security of his marriage—a natural part of which institution, he claims, is strains against the marriage—would be to betray his art. As professional imaginer and scribe of his own imaginings, he cannot be censored. Not by his wife, and not by the lovers themselves, who feel betrayed in having become grist for his fiction mill. Philip tells them he has had no contract with them not to use their stories, that in effect his known past at the time of their entering the relationship is a sort of contract of expectation that he *would* use their stories. He cannot promise to love and be silent, only, as a gentleman, to conceal the identities. But to both wife and mistresses, his defense is that the more apparently fact-based his narratives, the greater the achievement in having made them up. The more compromising they seem, the more fully imagined they must have been. Objectionableness is almost, therefore, a test of his art.

Like the characters, who are sometimes directly challenged to do so, the reader has to pay close attention. And even so, one may miss the shifts of character or of speaker within the dialogues. Sometimes the reader will not know until well into a section that the dialogue is with a character other than the one he had thought. Misreading and retracing are actually part of the reader's expected task in this book. The fourteen dialogues with the internal author that constitute the novel move back and forth between the main love affair with the married British woman and seven other conversations with various people and Philip's wife. All but one are women.

The one man is the irate émigré husband of a Czech girl who has sought Philip's friendship in compensation for a disintegrating marriage that has left both partners stranded. At loose ends in the West, she has had an affair with a black man, which itself cannot hold. Her husband, Ivan, even as he despairs of the East's subjugating paranoia, needs to blame Philip as a representative of the West's cash nexus and mongrelizing permissiveness.

> ". . . she has too much love for that black guy. He's unable to take that, especially if there's no money forthcoming. He's too primitive. He doesn't understand it. He'll leave her. She will return to Prague because she will have nowhere else to go. But this is the Soviet Union she will be dealing with, not a washed up old emigre like me—never again will she be able to go to America. Authorities will always be worried that she is a spy. All because of his long black prick! He did not fuck her the way you fucked her, for her stories. He fucked her for fucking. You are more interested in listening than in fucking, and Olina is not that interesting to listen to. She is even less interesting to listen to than to fuck."
>
> [Philip protests that there has been no sexual relationship, but Ivan proceeds.]
>
> "Other men listen patiently as part of the seduction leading up to the fuck. That is why men usually talk to women—to get them in bed. Other men let them begin their story, then when they believe they have been sufficiently attentive, they gently press the moving mouth down

on the erection. . . . It is not emotionally conventional to ask so many questions. Do all Americans do this? . . . With the nigger it's his prick and with the Jew it's his questions." (*D* 92–93)

Ivan's iron-curtain mentality is unicultural. He can see no merit in ethnic diversity. He is a reason that the end of the iron curtain will be the beginning of Balkanization in Europe. His literary imagination is similarly limited. Wanting to blame Philip for his wife's disintegration, he calls Philip's use of her stories in his fiction a weakness in his art; but since it was Philip's fiction that convinced Ivan to view him as no more than a seducing ear, Ivan's concern really testifies to the strength of that art. Philip refuses to accept blame for the husband's sense of his wife's betrayal. Juxtaposed to his own wife's accusation of him, Ivan's illusion that he has had this encounter strikes Philip as another testimony to his art. One is almost led to accept the defense, to forget that this is a hand from a stacked deck, Philip or Roth commanding the play of these characters.

Yet, one may be grateful for this last glimpse of iron-curtain psychology before the end of that era, just one of three provided in this novel. Still another concerns a second Czech woman who has left her English husband. The gap between the two cultures has left her stranded like Liza Doolittle:

"I hate Czechoslovakia because it has very set rules. You can't breathe. I don't particularly like England because it has another set of rules. Of little houses and little vegetable gardens, and all their life is to get something like that. . . . [Her British husband] . . . wasn't like the majority of people here, who are typically English and don't know much about the outside world. He knew what I was like and we could talk about a lot of things. It was wonderful. I felt totally different, I enjoyed being here. That's why I was so hurt [by his leaving], because I'm back being a— well, now again, I have my distance. Because I was educated I more belong to the class that I don't have the money to be in. I have much more in common with these people than with the people I belong to because of money. I'm misplaced. Totally." (*D* 63–64)

Another iron-curtain émigré, a Polish-woman translator, had never known Jews in her Jew-depleted native land. She first met them in Long Island, when her husband pointed out a group getting on the train. Her image of Jews is for her very strange: men not in sidelocks but in business suits going off to make money. Part of her attraction to Philip is his intense preoccupation with Jews and her need to be acquitted of what he cannot but suspect: that anti-Semitism is in the bones of his gentile fellows-in-exile, their last supercilious balm for their own political discomfiture. But it is part of the psychology of these Eastern European women to accept exile as a condition preferable to tyranny. They get out of loveless marriages. The British mistress stays in. More than anything, though, these exiles mirror Philip's own unease in England.

Another relationship is conducted on the phone with a girl in America. She is an ex-student of Philip's with whom he had an affair when he lived on Eighty-first Street. She is a product of a Jewish social-climber of a mother and a WASP of a father, a good ex-student who had insight into literature but a penchant for the dangerous life of the sex industry and drugs. She has had shock therapy. Still another in America is a British woman, who had been his neighbor on Eighty-first Street. It is unclear whether she or the one he is seeing now is *the* neighbor who first inspired Maria Freshfield. She may have suggested Maria in New York; the other, Maria in England. Now she has cancer and takes chemotherapy and has lost her hair and wears babushkas. She phones and he phones her out of an old sense of friendship, mostly to tell her she will not die. He hints to her that he will soon move back to New York and promises to call her on his arrival.

The main relationship, the one with the current British woman, is presented in many tones, as a long-standing, often uncertain affair should be. Philip feels no commitment beyond great friendship, but finds sexual expression of that feeling right. Why he is betraying his wife is a question he will not let his paramour entertain, though she presses to know. (He knows hers is really a question about his feeling for her.) And all the reader can have of a principled answer is that it is, among other forbidden appetites, one that he finds it natural to sate, more natural than exclusivity. He says, "I followed temptation where it led me. I do that now that I'm older." When he announces his impending fifty-first birthday, she asks why he's upset. His answer: "Because life will be over soon, that's why. I'll be dead." Among their games, which they use to create rules for and understandings of their relationship, are composing a questionnaire, pretending to subjugation (though never exercised abusively), and "reality shift," a game of exchanging places and speaking from the other's or from an imagined perspective (that Roth had reportedly played with Claire Bloom). Success in this last is sexually stimulating: cleverness begets adoration. At one point the woman pretends to be his accuser in an Eastern-style court (the tone reminiscent of Milan Kundera) on the charge of being a sexual harasser and seducer. The episode is a deflating satire on a theme Roth would take up more seriously in *Sabbath's Theater*, the new feminist power inherent in accusations of sexual harassment:

> "First you patronize us with a lecture on literature; now are we to have a lecture on *love*? From *you*? Be careful, sir, how far you go with

your insulting ironies. The court may feel obliged to have patience with such behavior but, I must warn you, the vast, indignant television audience that watches these trials is not bound by the legal niceties that obtain here. You were an adulterer were you not?"

"Still am."

"With the wives of friends?"

"Sometimes. More often with the wives of strangers, like you."

"And with whom was the treachery more perversely enjoyable? Whom did you delight most in sadistically betraying, friends whose wives you ruthlessly seduced or strangers whose wives you ruthlessly seduced?"

"Oh, you *are* a wonderful girl! You *are* clever! You *are* beautiful!"

"Your Honor, I must ask the court to instruct this *man* that I am not a 'girl'!"

"Come over here, prosecutor, would you please—"

"Your Honor, I *beg* you, the defendant is *blatantly*—"

"I want to ask your expert opinion about this— this—"

"Help, help, he's exploiting me, he's defaming me, he's attempting with this gross display of phallic—"

"You delicious, brilliant, lovely—"

"He's maligning me, Your Honor—in a court of law!"

"No, no, this is fucking, sweetheart—I'm fucking you in a court of law."

"Your Honor, the television—this is pornography!"(*D* 116–17)

Such intermittent flashes of fun convince the reader that the relationship is wholesome, even if imagined. The questioning is also stimulating, not so much of sex as of a sense of open possibilities. The adultery allows both of them to question the meaning of their choices in ways marriage does not—since in marriage the choice is beyond questioning. She can pursue the ethnic difference and declare that maybe his motive is anthropological, that he is ". . . the Albert Schweitzer of cross-cultural fucking." His answer, laughing: "Well not *so* saintly. The Malinowski will do." Beyond the strategies and banter are real concerns for her marriage and for her achieving personal independence—either in or out of that marriage—traced over a period of time and change, ending finally in a last phone call from Philip, now relocated in America, where he is at home among the ethnics he had missed.

With Philip's wife the novel is less concerned. She is a given, and in his limited dialogue with her he seems to test (testily) his own freedom by demanding that she not confuse his art with his life. The dialogue takes place at home, where she has been upset by reading his notebook, and he is sufficiently tender to acknowledge her pain and to want to relieve her of it. He insists that some of the intimacy she has read of reflects his premarital affairs, but he also insists that he is faithful except in his imagination, to which he must give full rein.

> "To compromise some 'character' doesn't get me where I want to be. What heats things up is compromising me. It kind of makes the indictment juicier, besmirching myself. As is proved, if you still doubt me, by this fucking argument."(D 184)

That is also a test for her—he can be hard with her—for he expects her to know him and accept his seeming dualities as part of one artistic personality. To this theme of artistic independence all the Czech and Polish material is counterpoint; they coalesce when Philip, refusing to change the protagonist's name from his own to Nathan—maintaining, that is, a distinction between his novel in progress, *The Counterlife*, and this notebook in progress, which will become *Deception*—says,

> "Jesus Christ, *is* this Eastern fucking Europe? I will not be put in that position! That is *too* absurd! I won't have it! You cannot stop me from writing what I write for a simple and pathological reason—because I cannot stop myself! I write what I write the way I write it, and if and when it should ever happen, I will publish what I publish however I want to publish and I'm not going to start worrying at this late date what people misunderstand or get wrong!" (D 191)

That reference echoes others to Eastern Europe. He tells his mistress about his fascination with and visits to Czechoslovakia, which began in a casual 1971 driving trip and ended in his being harassed in 1975 and denied further visas. One of the Czech women reminds him of his having invited her to an Orgy, reminiscent of "The Prague Orgy." We cannot know which of these are Roth's own experiences and which were merely his earlier inventions for the fictions they elicit. But they continue to raise the question about biography as itself possible deception. At one point he alludes to a confrontation in a Chelsea street while walking with Israeli writer Aharon Appelfeld and his son Itzak. Philip is insulted by an Englishman dressed enough like him to be his doppelganger, differing only in Philip's having been bearded (Roth sported a beard on one return from Israel). The Englishman has mumbled something indefinite, at which Philip has taken offense, assuming it to be an anti-Semitic attack on the Jew for dressing like the Englishman. This, like the remark of a woman in a restaurant in *The Counterlife*, may contain a good admixture of reportorial paranoia.

Neither Philip nor then Nathan provides sufficient evidence to back his interpretation of the event. Roth leaves the reader to sift that for himself. But by working in the Appelfeld episode, he connects the work to the *New York Times* piece that Roth had actually written and thus the character Philip to himself. So, too, of another personal allusion. At one point Philip tells that during one of his stays in Connecticut, his father had called from New Jersey to complain of an impending marriage between his grandson, identified as the son of Philip's brother Sandy, and a Puerto Rican young woman. Philip says he had driven down and told his father off with a sincere argument (that turns out to be a piece of blatant sophistry).

"I said, 'Your father, at the turn of the century, had three choices. One, he could have stayed in Jewish Galicia with Grandma. And had he stayed, what would have happened? To him, to her, to you, me, Sandy, mother— to all of us? Okay, that's number one: ashes, all of us. Number two. He could have gone to Palestine. You and Sandy would have fought the Arabs in 1948 and even if one or the other of you didn't actually get killed, somebody would have lost a finger, an arm, a foot, for sure. In 1967, I would have fought in the Six Day War, and at the least have caught a little shrapnel. Let's say in the head, losing the sight in one eye. In Lebanon your two grandchildren would have fought and, well, to be conservative, let's assume only one of them got killed. That's Palestine. The third choice he had was to come to America. Which he did. And the worst thing that can happen in America? Your grandson marries a Puerto Rican. You live in Poland and take the consequences of being a Polish Jew, or you live in Israel and take the consequences of being an Israeli Jew, or you live in America and take the consequences of being an American Jew. Tell me which you prefer. Tell me, Herm.' 'Okay,' he said, 'you're right—you win! I'll shut up!' I was delighted. I had him out-foxed and wouldn't let him go either, not quite yet. 'And now you know what I'm going to do?' I said. 'I'm going out to Brooklyn to talk to the girl's mother. I'm sure she's down crying on her knees too, giving her rosary beads a real workout. I'm going out to Brooklyn to tell her the same goddam thing I told you. "You want to live in Puerto Rico, your daughter marries a nice Puerto Rican boy all right, but you all have to live in Puerto Rico. You want to live in Brooklyn, the worst that happens is your daughter marries a Jew, but you get to live in Brooklyn. Take your choice."' Well, this starts my father right up again. 'What kind of comparison is that? What do you mean, "the worst that can happen"? The woman ought to be tickled to death who her daughter's marrying.' 'Sure,' I said, 'she is—tickled to death just about as much as you are.'"(*D* 81–83)

"Herm," as faithful readers would have known by then, was the name of Philip Roth's father, Herman Roth. And the son, or a character expected to be taken 98 percent for the son, is turning the tables with a piece of well-known psychology: it is perhaps best known in a Jewish joke, the one about the boy who tells his parents he's coming home with his new mate, a black man, so that when he revises the story to tell them that it is not so and he has merely failed a course, they will take the failure as a reprieve. Whether the episode with "Herm" is a true story or not should be beside the point (it may elicit Gabe's trip to Brooklyn to see Paul's parents in *Letting Go*). The reader of a Roth novel should not particularly care about Roth family affairs. But the reader of this novel, as of the two books that follow, is being drawn into a different contract, a contract of misreading Roth's life and of misunderstanding, requiring another processing of its information—one of interruption of the narrative, of reintroducing the suspended disbelief and unraveling the deception. Counterlife, unlike life, did not necessarily happen but might have.

Here the anecdote, though it anticipates the relationship that will be pursued in Roth's next book, *Patrimony*, has no plot purpose other than to introduce an American contrast to Jewish life in Britain, Roth's view of comparative diasporas. It reaffirms his view that the American Jewish experience, taken all in all, is a historical blessing, intermarriage notwithstanding. Total democracy and Jewish exclusivity are incompatible. A society both pluralistic and tolerant of Jewish life cannot guarantee safety from intermarriage. But such a society does strengthen what to Roth are the worthier Jewish values: openness, fairness, crediting of another's person, not just his background.

Roth's stance is the same as it was twenty years before in "On the Air," where he had Lippman pathetically listing the Jews "we got" to excel in the categories of entertainment. But denying exclusivity as a value is as far as he will go in exploring the American Jewish question in this work. Herm's initial reflex may suggest that there is more at risk in arguments about intermarriage than the value of openness; indeed, Roth says nothing about what will keep Jews together—aside from danger. And those hypothetical (and highly questionable) losses of life or limb in Poland or Israel that he lays on the old man would have been sustained on behalf of Jewish solidarity, not, like intermarriage, on behalf of dilution. Philip will not admit that Jewishness is not just democracy, as in another part of his being, Roth knows. But the closest affirmation Philip gives to Jewishness itself in *Deception* is to a sentiment: his love for brashness and the camaraderie of ethnic bonding. At the end of the novel, Philip, having returned to America, walks the streets and sees something he had terribly missed in England. On the transatlantic phone, his recent British mistress asks,

"What's that?"

"Jews."

"We've got some of them in England, you know."

"Jews with force, I'm talking about. Jews with appetite. Jews without shame. Complaining Jews who get under your skin. Brash Jews who eat with their elbows on the table. Unaccommodating Jews, full of anger, insult, argument, impudence. New York's the real obstreperous Zion, whether Ariel Sharon knows it or not."

"So England *was* too Christian for you."

"Tel Aviv's too Christian compared to this place. After London even Ed Koch looks good." (*D* 204)

And he goes on to explain who Ed Koch is and to admire his style.

In that phone call, which takes place sometime after the publication of *The Counterlife*, the mistress threatens the final deception of this novel—to write a book about Philip, exposing their affair, to be called *Kiss and Tell*. He advises her to go right ahead, more fiction is the way to go. One never knows whether she is to be taken as real and threatening or contrived and threatening, that is, Philip's last imagining of this book, but she is unhappy about some of the uses he made of her in giving her to Nathan in *The Counterlife*. It is assumed here that she is the model for the British episodes of the Maria Freshfield character. As the conversation grows from flirtation, to confession, to nervous irritation, it seems increasingly authentic. Roth thus delivers the reader firmly back into doubt.

But never into danger: this novel in the form of a novelist's notebook is always under Philip's control. Nor into striving. He yearns for nothing more than self-knowledge, themes for writing, and return to a milieu closer to that of his childhood. All the mistresses, the wife, the answers to his questions and questionnaire have been subject to his selective editing, and what he delivers of them is only as much as will justify his self-justification. His author may use the autobiographical element (achieved by denarrating the novel into notebook entries) to vindicate the ordinariness of a writer's life; but for this drab achievement, he risks foregoing the drama needed to give it urgency. The personal conundrums of *The Counterlife* were enriched by the pressure of the subtext, with its threats of death or discontinuity—to Nathan, his counterself, and the Jewish people as embodied in the State of Israel. But some of these same conundrums, without the elasticity of striving or any empathic danger, can be shrugged aside like a crossword puzzle. As an experiment in an art form, *Deception* should be credited for taking risks; Roth is not resting on any laurels. But paradoxically, this is a novel in which the protagonist, as distinguished from the artist, takes almost no risks; and Roth goes to such great pains to tease the reader out of distinguishing the protagonist from the artist, that Philip's safety becomes the reader's disincentive to care very much.

And that, too, was the apparent response of the public. *Deception* was interesting to a limited few, but not exciting. It may even be more interesting the second time through. But word of mouth never advanced the message of the cover. The optimistic first printing of 100,000 copies[13] was never justified in sales. Simon & Schuster may have gotten review copies into some friendly hands, but it could not elicit raves. Fay Weldon in a generally positive Sunday *New York Times* review would describe it as "swift, elegant, disturbing." But in the daily pages, where Christopher Lehmann-Haupt urged Roth to "stop analyzing his imagination and start exercising it," the characterization of the book as just a return to tired themes probably cut closer to the public perception.

Roth's second book for Simon & Schuster, *Patrimony* (1991), would do better. It would succeed (moderately) among Jewish audiences, would provide a good set piece for reading on the lecture circuit, and would win another National Book Critics' Circle Award, this time in the genre of biography. *Patrimony*, subtitled *A True Story*, chronicles a death, pays homage to a life, and connects two generations of storytellers. It acknowledges a gift beyond genes and reciprocates a lifetime of fathering by honoring the parent's terminal dependency as the natural obverse of the son's infant dependency. Roth's earliest work had focused upon the parents' obligation to let go of the child; this book would work through the harder problem of the child's letting go of the parent.

For Herman Roth, child of the immigrant generation saved from the Holocaust and imbued with a duty to transmit the spared heritage, the patrimony was inextricably Jewish; but Philip's father knew it was a Jewishness that had already slipped from the definings of his own father's generation, that America had shaved it and dressed it in pastels and white loafers, and the aged Herman was not sure just what he had preserved to be passed on. *Patrimony* attests that it was not so much religious content as the process of transmission itself. He had given Philip memory untinged with sentimentality, a love of hard work, and a reflex of hard questioning. He had also given a tribal allegiance very much subject to that reflex.

In *The New York Times* of Friday, October 27, 1989, the following obituary appeared:

Herman Roth

Herman Roth, a retired district manager for the Metropolitan Life Insurance Company and the father of Philip Roth, the novelist, died of a brain tumor on Wednesday at St. Elizabeth Hospital in Elizabeth, N.J. He was 88 years old and lived in Elizabeth.

Mr. Roth worked for the insurance company from 1932 until he retired in 1964. He was born in Newark.

Also surviving are another son, Sanford, of Chicago, and two grandchildren.

By that Wednesday on which the father concluded his dying, much of the son's account of it had already been committed to typed sheets. Herman Roth would not be a new subject. He had been presented to the reading public in *The Facts* as the hard-working eighth-grade graduate who had overcome prejudice in rising to district manager at Metropolitan Life. He had been the stern voice from whom Philip had had to flee to Bucknell, who had early feared for Philip's morals (*Facts* 75) and later fiercely defended his son against accusations of family betrayal in his literature. He would not now be in a position to defend Philip against such an accusation as it affected his own physical deterioration and dying; but the son, who had long grappled with the charge of using other people for his stories, was prepared for any reraising of it here. If he was violating his father's being in telling a story the old man probably would have preferred left untold, the old man was also beyond hurting. The son needed to memorialize him, and the writer—accepting the "unseemliness of [his] profession"—needed to explore the question, What is the true patrimony?

Roth embodies the question in three vivid symbols, none of which answers it. Like the three manifestations of nature that Elijah witnesses on Sinai, they but limn the elusive spirit he seeks. The *tefillin* (prayer phylacteries), which Herman Roth leaves in a locker at the Y because he knows that neither son will use them, is not the patrimony; the shaving mug that Philip finally settles for after regretfully turning down insurance money suggests, but is not, the patrimony; and the most powerful image, as hard for the reader to erase from memory as for Philip to erase from the surfaces of his bathroom after Herman "beshat" himself—the shit the son had to take literally and figuratively from the father—teases up, but is not, the patrimony. Roth himself dwells on this last; but no symbol will suffice here any more than the wind, the earthquake, or the fire would suffice to encompass the still small voice that Elijah finally heard. The patrimony, which can be told but not displayed, is a sharing of values, temperament, and place. The telling is this book. The place? Among the Jews and in America.

The *tefillin* and the shaving mug had been passed down from Sender Roth, the Yiddish-speaking grandfather who had studied to be a rabbi but who, like the pious immigrants in *The Rise of David Levinsky*, had learned that America required him to earn money and so had spent his life in a hat factory. His son Herman, though not a ritual praying man, knew that *tefillin* were not to be thrown out or destroyed; and so his transmittal to whoever would rescue them from a locker in a Jewish Y was his way of securing for them a Jewish, if anonymous, posterity. The mug, inscribed in faded gold Gothic lettering with Sender's first initial and surname and date of 1912—evidence that Sender had aspired to be more than the chain-smoking hat blocker with too small a head that his grandson remembered—could be transmitted to Philip but not to a fourth generation. The shit, too, would end with Philip, nothing of whose own body, no seed, would live in any posterity. There would be no grandson for Herman on Philip's side. The immortal part of Herman that Philip could pass on would be this book.

In *Patrimony*, since Roth generally restrains his novelist's imagination to tell *A True Story*, some unusually dramatic passages may seem dubious. Scenes like one with a father-hating cab driver who mistakes Roth for a complicitous soul mate and even the vivid scene of Herman Roth's "beshitting" Philip's Connecticut bathroom, reminiscent of Maureen's calling card in *My Life as a Man*, have a certain fictive convenience. But Roth employs well his storyteller's sense of structure and sequencing of events—including the suspenseful drama of his own heart attack—to keep the book moving. Enough is convincingly reconstructed dialogue to provide the tensions and immediacy of a good story, and much will touch a reader's own life sufficiently so that he will not need to have known Roth's. As a result, the book is more accessible than *Deception*.

One may read *Patrimony* as a description of social intrusion, of the way the medical bureaucracy tries to script its final set chapter to what should be an individual life. In that respect the book is very much on the Rothian theme of who or what shall have jurisdiction over one's life—in this case over the leaving of it. Herman, his face partially paralyzed, must consider surgery to remove the cause, a probably benign brain tumor; but while the procedure might prevent further deterioration, it will not restore already curtailed functioning. The father and son together determine against having the old man undergo two fourteen-hour operations on his eighty-six-year-old brain, from which it would take him months to achieve a dubious recovery. They settle instead for minor cataract surgery and its gift of somewhat better eyesight for the two years remaining. But beyond the question of medical jurisdiction, the book is more richly read as a clue to the personality of its author and to what that personality tells about the conflicts between Jewishness and individualism and between individualism and alienation.

Herman Roth outlived Bess Roth by eight years, the last two in the throes of this final illness. After his wife's death, he began immediately to dispose of her personal things, not out of absence of feeling but out of an almost compulsive pragmatism. She was gone; she couldn't use them; certainly, he couldn't. The same sense limited his period of mourning and his abstinence from relationships with other women. A minimalist in amenities of living, he had kept a cleared desk in his business life. Long a decision maker at Metropolitan Life, he was still that man who had whipped off his sweaty clothes at Bradley Beach and had made directly for the water. The close of every transaction for Herman signaled a turn to some next transaction.

But Herman Roth had retired from business at the age of sixty-three, and, fidgety and needing something to administer, had become impatient with and bullying of his wife, to the point that she once contemplated (but only contemplated) leaving him. He would transfer these habits of domestic interference to his life with the widow he took up with later. And he would be open to other involvements; retirees are easily ambushed by organized activity. Herman, not a regular synagogue-goer most of his life, began attending *shul* and the Y for classes or card playing or lectures or musicals and followed a similar regimen during winters in Florida. Inevitably, the Jewish setting heightened awareness of Jewish concerns and of organized Jewish life. The natural skepticism of the secular man was now in conflict with the habits of a congregant. Fierce independence had once fit him to lead a regional office or a family circle; he would bristle as a mere functionary, quietly submerged in group activity. Opinionated, given to quick and emotional reactions, he was not an easy congregant. Yet, that pragmatic need to get on with things and to choose for himself would mark the heroism of his final decision.

On the lecture circuit for almost two years following publication of *Patrimony*, Roth gave dramatic readings of one of its chapters, one whose juxtaposition of father and son would gratify Jewish audiences. Even in March 1993, a month into the publication of *Operation Shylock*, when public appearances might have been used to advance the sales of that chancy new work, he still chose to read this *Patrimony* excerpt to a sold-out audience at New York's 92nd Street Y. Its poignancy, heightened by his coached and practiced reading, would engage that audience from the opening pronouncement of its title: "Will I Be a Zombie?"

Herman Roth's central question about the operation broods over this recounting of a week spent assimilating the diagnosis. It is a narrative of phone conversations, a walk and drive through old neighborhoods, a consultation with a surgeon, and the return afterward to Herman's apartment. It includes a role reversal surprising even to Philip. Herman, depressed, doesn't want to go out for the walk; Philip speaks four words: "Do what I say!" and Herman obeys. Into these activities are poured the effluence of memory. Sites evoke events, relationships, names of neighbors, relatives; they fix Herman in his past and set Philip, like a jewel, into the ring of memory. We learn of the extensive family circle—150 members at its height—with its own newsletter and dues structure, serving that traditional *tzedakah* function of rescuing

European family members and tiding over those in dire straits. Herman, a former president, is the last survivor among nine siblings. Memory is linked to place and events, but not, for Herman, to possessions. We see him divesting himself of everything impractical, passing glassware and knickknacks to Philip, as if to lighten the final task of divestiture after death. Everything worth saving is in his brain, threatened with displacement by the growing tumor. Among its precious stores is postimmigrant history, called up by landmarks in the neighborhood and questions from the son. Early in the century Sender's shaving mug, in a row with other men's mugs, had sat on a barber-shop shelf, to be taken down for what seemed his one relaxing moment, the sabbath shave, and had moved with the man to other addresses and other barber shops—all in that widening ghetto. Herman could divide that history into the eras of his youth and his young manhood, separated roughly by World War I. During the thirties and forties insurance agents would make weekly rounds to housewives' doors to collect the three or four cents that constituted premiums on their husbands' or fathers' lives. Bizarrely, decades after the death of some insured, especially among the black community, relatives would continue to pay the weekly ritual without understanding that they had had to declare the deaths that could end their debits and pay them their benefits.

That insurance business had left Herman with a practical hold on life's transactions, more useful for making his present decision than a college education. He appreciates the actuarial unlikelihood of his long surviving an operation. To the surgeon—the first of a few he will consult—he comes prepared with a list of questions, more incisive than his son could have mustered, about his final chances and their price in pain and reduced quality of life. At his apartment later, he impatiently attempts to regain control of everything, including the preparing of canned soup, which he wrests—despite objections—not yet heated from the stove. He hardly feels its cold as it dribbles from the downspout that has become the corner of his mouth and tints his shirt before his tear-restrained son.

Into "Will I Be a Zombie?" Roth inserts flashbacks, family history, examples of Herman's peremptory nature and inflexible morality. His hatred of Reagan (always pronounced Ray-gun), not shared with all his cocongregants,[14] his break and reconciliation with a brother, his moralistic interferences in the lives of his children, all are offshoots of assumed responsibility. Once, as president of his elementary school class—in a building still standing on the route of their drive to the surgeon—he appointed as class treasurer another Jewish boy who turned out dishonest; in job after job on into manhood Herman kept rescuing the fellow from consequences of his dishonesty. The once extensive Jewish neighborhood, spanning parts of Newark and Elizabeth, from which emerges a roster of names and memories, is seen as that fountain world of

Roth's imagination; and the man formed by it, the peremptory, relentless, and tactless Herman Roth, appears more and more as Philip's natural progenitor. The core message of this chapter, echoed throughout the book, is one about memory. Roth often completes the details of his father's recollections, fusing their sensibilities. For his father, like himself, "To be alive . . . is to be made of memory—to him if a man's not made of memory, he's made of nothing." For his public readings of "Will I Be a Zombie?" Roth shaped a self-contained narrative by omitting and rearranging details of the printed book, but what his audiences in effect heard was a voice saying, I loved that old man—honest, emotional, peremptory, tactless—very much like me.

In a review of *Patrimony*, Neal Kozodoy, editor of *Commentary*,[15] faults Roth for his disaffiliated, and therefore flawed, Jewishness; but he does so by a circuitous comparison. Some unnamed celebrated Jewish intellectual had once applied to Kozodoy for nursing-home connections to help his own declining father, and then, after availing himself of the assistance, continued to berate middle-class Jewish life as a betrayal of some proletarian ideal. The reference is greatly reminiscent of Zuckerman's charge against Milton Appel. But Roth's treatment of his own father in no way resembles that warehousing; the only justifiable point of comparison is the two sons' lack of involvement in organized Jewry's formal "modes of perpetuation." Roth's informal perpetuation, the review implies, is not Jewish.

Roth and his father shared a great deal, from the continued habit of swimming for exercise to their history of burst appendixes and near deaths from peritonitis, to their politics, personal dispositions, and preoccupations with family relationships, neighborhood lore, and Jews. Philip had put it well in his presentation of Herman in *The Facts*: "Narrative is the form that his knowledge takes, and his repertoire has never been large: family, family, family, Newark, Newark, Newark, Jew, Jew, Jew. Somewhat like mine."[16] But the filial sharing was also warm and lively, from transatlantic phone calling to check on the doings of the Mets to visits in New Jersey or Connecticut to this last two-year vigil. For them, Jewishness was their own continuity of experiences that had begun in Jewish settings. If Philip had his own pool in Connecticut, while Herman still swam at the Y—still enjoying the comradeship of sweat and failing flesh once found in the men's bathhouses of their youth—that was partly because as an artist and a cosmopolite, Philip had drifted farther from his immigrant center. The neighborhood of Roth's adult affiliations was not geographic but intellectual and artistic. Disaffiliation is a complex charge; many people remain affiliated out of xenophobia, while distance and comparison may let others achieve insights into their own religion that some of the totally affiliated never achieve. Certainly Jewishness is ubiquitous in Roth's work. One does not ask about the synagogue attendance of Bellow or Appelfeld—or the editorial board of *Commentary*. It is doubtful that a tax-exempt dues contribution to a Jewish organization would have redeemed Roth for Kozodoy. Roth's sponsored readings, his participation in panels, his interviews and articles probably put him into such contexts more often than many of his affiliated Jewish readers. But Kozodoy's essay is less a review of this book than of its author's career; any redemption would have required, long ago, Roth's dropping the irony, not tasking his people so. And yet there is little irony in *Patrimony*. Memory is pure, details abundant, the filling in of a history. Even tedious details are summed up in appreciation of the American Diaspora, shared by father and son.

> All the privation and rebuilding and regeneration, all those *people*, all that *dying*, all their *work*—how could anyone fail to be moved and even, ultimately, to be as awestruck as he was by how, in America, our Roths had persevered and endured? (*Pat* 191)

Kozodoy is not moved; he pursues his indictment and includes Herman— for having been "spiritually stymied" and Jewishly "befuddled," as indicated by the way he disposed of his unused *tefillin*. He finds Herman unworthy of being the subject of such a book as this and his son, now "filially devoted" to cleaning up his father's shit, "futilely protecting it [and their apostasy] with art."

Kozodoy dismisses Roth and his book because he sees it, like the utterances of his own Appel-like intellectual friend, as Roth's way of unloading some well-deserved guilt. As proof he cites this passage in which Roth muses over his having to clean up after his father's incontinence:

> So *that* was the patrimony. And not because cleaning it up was symbolic of something else but because it wasn't, because it was nothing less or more than the lived reality that it was.
>
> There was my patrimony: not the money, not the tefillin, not the shaving mug, but the shit. (*Pat* 176)

Kozodoy grasps only the surface of Roth's enigmatic utterance, failing to see that words are always symbols of something else. He sees the literal reality of "shit"—smell, slime—to Kozodoy the natural emanation of Roth's "cloacal vision of what constitutes 'lived reality,'" but not its metaphoric use, as in to "take shit" from someone. Roth is using both senses as "lived reality."

Sons escape from the shit of their fathers, try out the shit of the world, and ultimately, if they are lucky like Roth, return to see the shit they were escaping as an essential part of themselves. Herman enabled Philip to surpass him educationally and culturally—to seek more respectable fathers in books—while

Philip guiltily saw Herman mired in shit he had escaped. A central conflict of Jewish postimmigrant literature is about resisting the pull to return to the family's mold—betraying its expectation by having one's own. Roth's treatment of the conflict is largely through characters who resist the return by spewing shit of their own. But while Kozodoy and others never could credit their diarrhea of the mouth as anything but meanness of spirit, Roth was presenting something more complex: defiance of the parental virtues as character. If his protagonists were verbally incontinent, it was because the world given them was so continent, demanded so much holding in. The fiction writer impersonates the unvirtuous other and exercises through his uncompliant counterself a self-seeing criticism of the life the compliant take for virtue. But always at a price: the protagonist's assertion of self leaves him outside the familial or tribal embrace. Yet since the conflict implicit in his effusions includes the patrimonial point of view, he is never outside their range. *Patrimony* is about what was there all the time the younger generation were fighting their war of sovereignty. And what holds it and binds the generations is memory. Roth's parental antagonist had been not only his double but his muse and as the representative Jew for Roth, almost his deity. "He wasn't just my father; he was *the* father, with everything there is to hate in a father and everything there is to love." Perhaps the final appeal of this book would be in that love, outstripping intimations of hate, and without ironic undercutting as Zuckerman would have expressed it. Roth as memoirist could recapture part of an audience unavailable to the author of *Deception*, an audience more easily moved by a true story and by sympathetic protagonists.

In the two years of their final closeness, Roth observes his father so as not to lose the memory of him. Herman meets humiliation of the flesh with a certain resilience and candor but meets remissions from functional loss sometimes by grasping at straws. At one point he takes the doctor's uncertainty about the time remaining to him to its logical infinite end: first, why not ten years rather than two, and ultimately, "Why should a man die?" What had once infuriated the son in his "stubborn prick" of a father now inspires admiration. He views him naked in the tub, seemingly helpless—Roth venturing close to the sin of Ham—and observes that the old man's penis is thicker than his, perhaps gave greater sexual pleasure. Here gentle irony is permitted in the service of love. In admiration, reversing the sin of Ham, Roth uses *Portnoy*'s primary symbol to undo any lingering association with Alex's resentments of Jack. And Herman goes Philip one better. He says of his final dependence on his son that Philip has been like a mother to him. Not like a father; Herman will not give over his sovereignty. Politically, the mother is but second in the family; Herman ever holds first place.

There are other flashes of grim humor, scenes of geriatric dignity amidst declining power: a still older friend in Florida whom a frail Herman has to induce to take walks; attendance at a recital in a senior center where people whose inclinations are to chat or sew or nosh or relieve their bladders force their attention to the music as homage to culture; Herman's bringing to dinner a Holocaust survivor, now a furrier, who has written a personal account of the Holocaust that perhaps, through Philip's connections, *they* can get published.

The survivor's account turns out to be a piece of pornography (Herman has not read it), and the furrier is not above offering a bribe—an ermine and sable coat for Claire—to get it published. Including this slight piece amidst serious talk of Holocaust literature, of Philip's connections and responses to Aharon Appelfeld, Primo Levi, and the Demjanjuk trial may seem to desecrate that sacred history. It does not, it complements it: even the Holocaust, especially in those who learned to survive by barter, had its unlikely characters and therefore its touchable reality. Roth, like Appelfeld, would resist giving it a sacredness so untouchable as to be iconographic. There is a perverse humor in the affinity between son and father, the one a renowned author, editor of European Holocaust literature, widely read interviewer of survivors; the other, a card-table crony of one hustler with a number on his arm.

That affinity had connected Roth to his patrimony, had supplied him with raw material as yet undiminished by fictive refraction or interpretation. The father had always been so straightforward, and therefore so definite in his values, that he had been untouched by the sophisticated questionings of the son. But Philip had gone beyond the eighth grade; and later, as he tells it, "I had the impassioned, if crazy, conviction that I was somehow inhabited by him and quickening his intellect right along with mine," that Herman was "the intellectual homunculus for whose development I felt as responsible as I did for my own"— a response not unlike that of Alex Portnoy. From at least college on, Philip had thrashed about to replace those values with the authority of other—mostly literary—fathers. Ironically, his reading and that of his peers had widened

> the poignant abyss between our fathers and us . . . that they themselves
> broke their backs to give us. Encouraging us to be so smart and such
> *yeshiva buchers*, they little knew how they were equipping us to leave
> them isolated and uncomprehending in the face of all our forceful babble.
> (*Pat* 159)

Now Roth's quest out has brought him back to his source, and so what he values, what he piles on, is specific events—places, people, the father's recounted, uninterpreted memories, lived realities—all Roth's rescored Newark material heard pure again from the mouth of the original muse.

In a Jewish funeral a closed casket keeps the body from view. Yet after Herman Roth's funeral, Philip had a dream: his father came back and screamed at him for dressing him in a shroud and not a presentable suit. Philip sees the shroud as this book, unseemly from the father's point of view. Philip does not speak of the book as his own child, of all his books as his own and only children. He does not accuse them of what they have exacted from him. Rather, he harks back to their connection with Herman.

> The dream was telling me that, if not in my books or in my life, at least in my dreams I would live perennially as his little son, with the conscience of a little son, just as he would remain alive there not only as my father but as *the* father, sitting in judgment on whatever I do. (*Pat* 237–38)

There follows a coda to that statement. It is the admonition, the covenant, the patrimony Roth derives from a century of Jewish-American history. He inscribes it into the millennia-old history of the people of the book as the last, one-line paragraph of *Patrimony*:

"You must not forget anything."

Chapter 11

Operation Shylock

When Roth signed his three-book contract with Simon & Schuster in 1990, he reportedly had one novel ready for completion (*Deception*), a book about his father in progress (*Patrimony*), and sketches begun for a novel on an undisclosed subject. Completing the contract in a timely manner should not have been a problem. His notebooks hinted at material he had barely touched in recently published manuscripts: *Patrimony* mentions his having attended the John Demjanjuk trials; *The Facts* cites his near breakdown from medications following knee surgery. Both *Patrimony* and *Deception* allude to Roth's relationship with Aharon Appelfeld and *The New York Times* interview on that Israeli writer's fiction. What had largely energized *The Counterlife* and *Deception* was the question of where geographically Jews belong. A recurrent feature of all Roth's writing had been the appearance of the doppelganger. From these clues it might have been possible to guess where Roth would be heading in his new novel. In the brilliance of hindsight one might also dwell on that statement by Philip in *Deception*, "To compromise some 'character' doesn't get me where I want to be. What heats things up is compromising me."

Roth's challenge would be to link personal and tribal obsessions, to expose as inherently absurd the presumtion that this successful writer or the

Jewish State or the Jewish people were secure. Israel was a sovereign state, yet much of the world still questioned the legitimacy of Jewish existence, however defined. To add to the absurdity, Israel, as a moral exemplar, was tasked with being particularly virtuous if it were to continue. Aharon Appelfeld had said, in Roth's 1988 interview, that "Today we have redemption, tomorrow darkness. Writers are also immersed in this tangle. The occupied territories, for example, are not only a political issue but also a literary matter."[1] What Roth now had in mind was a novel merging personal and public themes to examine a critical moment in Jewish history. He was not going to propose a solution to the Middle East conflict; solving problems had never seemed to him the fiction writer's job. But showing the absurdity of fly-by-night solutions, the power of group hatred to overwhelm personal feeling, the impossibility of maintaining neutrality about Jews or about Israel, and even—though irrational—fear for the survival of a Jewry concentrated within the bulls-eye of Israel itself, all this could occupy a novelist committed to peril.

For Roth, the problem would be how to inhabit—to "compromise"—his character without forcing the materials. He had come to a point where he considered his once-cherished privacy less useful than the mythic persona he had recently cultivated. By using autobiographic characters to explore the artist's conflict between real and imagined life, he had placed himself in a position to play the public figure in a novel that might require one. And the essential absurdity to be explored in *Operation Shylock* would require a victim for a crackpot's scheme of Jewish salvation: someone suspended in reputation between Jewish hero and self-hating Jewish enemy, who could be embraced for the wrong reasons by anti-Zionists and employed at the same time by Israeli intelligence. Here would be a tale of the reluctant Zionist spy who came in from the Diaspora cold. What better lead character to play that *schlemiel* than Philip Roth himself?

Such a project would require delicate irony toward the protagonist and a balanced examination of the geopolitical picture. Israel as an idea and as an imperiled polity was potentially explosive. It could not be a mere background for a psychological examination of stolen identities. Israel was not a symbol like Kafka's bureaucratic office maze or his castle, or a state so secure that it could be satirized without threat to the daily lives of its inhabitants and to much of Roth's readership. Anything too zany could repel. *Operation Shylock* would be subtitled *A Confession*, a term perhaps as deceptive as "Deception." The title might mean that Roth was confessing to betrayal or to fictionalizing betrayal; however, this blurring of fiction and fact, not merely personal but historical, was dangerous as literary enterprise: fantasizing history could seem like trivializing history. From the outset—whether or not he fully appreciated it—Roth was skating on very thin ice.

Operation Shylock meets the ironic challenge brilliantly for almost one hundred pages of a book that, unfortunately, runs almost to four hundred pages. Roth's problem artistically was one that he had encountered—but never solved—in *The Great American Novel*: accommodating such a wealth of material, having so much to include, that the sheer weight might overwhelm the spirit of the book. In *Operation Shylock*, the material had to be distributed evenly if the ice was not to crack; but unfortunately, at key points Roth stops moving and lets his polemical or philosophic load sink through a splintering surface. Redistributing this material for a more even effect probably would have required months or even years of disciplined rewriting. But it was also material fraught with expiration dates. The Demjanjuk trial was winding down, the Israeli Labor government's peace initiatives were under way, the 1988 *intifada* events he wished to narrate were already three to four years past—to push their projected 1993 publication back to 1995 or 1996 might sap their vitality altogether. And Roth had to complete the contract for which he had, uncharacteristically, taken an advance from Simon & Schuster.

Not least of the problems was how writing the book would affect Roth himself: how much wearing the mask of his mythic self in a character haunted by his double and namesake would, by blurring the line between fiction and fact, indeed compromise him. When review copies were being sent out in January and February 1993, Simon & Schuster kept changing the designated review categories from fiction to nonfiction and back again to fiction, and reports from within the walls of the publisher had a frenzied Roth haunting the precincts with changes and expressions of anxiety. One periodical, *Library Journal*, reviewed the book in the category of fiction but appended the following disclaimer to its review: "[Roth reported in *The New York Times*, March 9, 1993, that all events depicted in this book are in fact true but that the Mossad insisted that he bill it as fiction.—Ed.]"

That is also the position of the "Philip Roth" within the novel concerning the undisclosed spying mission whose code name is the book's title. He even goes so far as to say that he has written a full account of the mission in a chapter he has had to delete under pressure from the Mossad. "Philip Roth" the interior narrator of the novel must be allowed his fictive license. But what of Philip Roth the author? Following his 398-page, allegedly incomplete narrative, author Roth posts this disclaimer:

Note to the Reader

This book is a work of fiction. The formal conversational exchange with Aharon Appelfeld quoted in chapters 3 and 4 first appeared in *The New York Times* on March 11, 1988; the verbatim minutes of the January 27,

1988, morning session of the trial of John Demjanjuk in Jerusalem District Court provided the courtroom exchanges quoted in chapter 9. Otherwise the names, characters, places, and incidents either are products of the author's imagination or are used fictitiously. Any resemblance to actual events or locales or persons, living or dead, is entirely coincidental. This confession is false.

With the last sentence, the disclaimer is possibly disclaimed. Because the title of the whole work includes the words, "A Confession," this last sentence can be read as saying either that the whole confessional work is false or that the confessional "Note to the Reader" is false (and, therefore, the work true). As in all his later books except, perhaps, *Patrimony*, Roth continues to insist on the ambiguity of his truth.

As publication approached, author Roth obliged with promotional interviews and side bars. He both told truth and played games—consistent, from his point of view, with the higher understanding that fiction was itself an indirect apprehension of truth. He acknowledged, on the one hand, a diminishing readership both for himself—his old adversaries having mellowed or died off—and for serious literature, and, on the other hand, newly rising ethnic interests that left Jews no longer the central testers of the American dream. But he also responded to straight interview questions about his book with fictive answers. Perhaps as the apostle of ambiguity, in whose gospel all report is point of view, he expected not to be taken straight but to be allowed the *game* of deception— different from *outright* deception. In any case, one piece of gamesmanship reveals the contradiction on which Roth would eventually be impaled. It shared a front page of *The New York Times Book Review* with D. M. Thomas's review of the novel and was titled, with delicious Rothian ambiguity, "A Bit of Jewish Mischief."[2]

First assuring the reader that he is "as hopelessly addicted" to "predictable, plausible reality . . . as any other human being," Roth repeats, with one deviant detail, the controversial assertion of his novel:

> A man of my age, bearing an uncanny resemblance to me and calling himself Philip Roth, turned up in Jerusalem shortly before I did and set about proselytizing for "Diasporism," a political program he'd devised advocating that the Jews of Israel return to their European countries of origin in order to avert "a second Holocaust," this one at the hands of the Arabs.

The one discrepancy is that while the novel sets all this in 1988, Roth here asserts that it happened in 1989.

Roth then spends the better part of the next five paragraphs analyzing the difference between mischief in life and in art. He knows the difference well, he says, because his doppelganger's "imposturing" created "a crisis [Roth] was living rather than writing." Roth characterizes the "imposture" as

> a form of self-denunciation that I could not sanction, a satirizing of me so bizarre and unrealistic as to exceed by far the boundaries of amusing mischief I may myself have playfully perpetrated on my own existence in fiction.

The tone is seductively sincere. Of course, if this imposture had never happened—and no reputable commentator believes it ever did (in either 1988 *or* 1989)—then any distinction between a crisis Roth was living and the many he had written (and was at this very juncture again writing) is at once absurd and wonderful. It places the author with the reader indignantly against the event, *as if* they have been mutually offended. Here, as in the novel, Roth is elevating a possible improbable into a probable impossible—that is, an emotionally satisfying, a *pleasurable* fictive truth. Other assertions of the alleged imposture outside the novel would be less pleasurable; in what seemed like a campaign, Roth iterated to interviewers that "something" had happened—triggered by this imposture—that had led him into espionage in Athens to uncover Jews contributing to the PLO.

In this *Times* piece, the primary mischief is Roth's guileful celebration of mischief itself and its connection to this supposed event. "Mischief," Roth says, "in life as in art, . . . can be a relief from all the prescriptions." In that light, he considers his own career, his special place as mischief-maker among the Jews. His intention had always been to provide some comic relief from the trying Jewish "predicament," relief that Jews have always given themselves through humor and self-satire, "even in the most superdignified Jewish circles." But what he has always viewed as relief, others have mistaken for betrayal, affecting his credibility. The danger Jews felt from Roth's having exercised among them what Poe called "the Imp of the Perverse," their seeing him as having committed "not amusing mischief but serious mischief, not responsible mischief but irresponsible mischief . . . [which] . . . trivially misrepresent[ed] things that all Jews are haunted by, including themselves as Jews" has made it impossible for some people to accept now his assertion that he encountered his double in Jerusalem. Well, he says, with Falstaffian generosity, he can forgive them! *Now*, having, like them, been abused by

> the double who turned up in Jerusalem in 1989 to demythologize Israel and pathologize me—that criminal impersonator who usurped my biog-

raphy as well as my name while all but calling himself the Messiah—I now understand a little more subjectively something of the disorienting extremes of distress with which my books are said to bedevil these readers.

Roth disclaims any special authorial knowledge of where the other Roth came from or what his real motivations were and, as indignant as his readers, charges the imposter with being "deformed, deranged, craven, possessed, an alien wreck in a state of foaming madness—someone, in short, who isn't really human at all." (A nice ambiguity, that: one antonym of "really human" might be "an imagined character.") While it is not lost on Roth that these are the very charges that his audience has long leveled at him, he nevertheless pardons his readership and begs their pardon in return: "Those whom I've offended should be happy to hear that I now have more than a faint idea of why they have wanted to kill me and of what, rightly or wrongly, they have been through."

Wonderful!—*except*. Except that in other interviews at this time he was acknowledging that those furiously offended readers had all but drifted away or lost their fury, that any likely readership for serious novels was somewhere around four thousand to eight thousand people and any readership more sizable would be totally indifferent to the persona "Philip Roth" he was positing for this novel. He was writing a work requiring his own importance for a readership fast turning to Michael Crichton and Robert Ludlum. In the novel he might have to tell readers how wonderful some people once thought him, but that would be a dangerous ploy. Readers like to decide those things for themselves. If Roth seemed to be blowing his own horn, readers might be less offended by the "craven" imposter or less accepting of the duality called for in the novel. The imposter requires a famous, respected Jew to pin his scheme on; the Mossad requires a baffled *schlemiel* to ensnare in its trap—no easy combination. Novelists can concoct fictitious heroes, but offering oneself as Mr. Wonderful might seem hubristic beyond toleration to the new readership Roth admitted had taken over. And though high praise of Philip Roth is offered primarily by deranged characters in this novel, one might wonder about the gall of an author who composes these encomia even for such mouths.

Ideas in *Operation Shylock* revolve around its locales, its people, and the topics of its obsessive discussions: the Holocaust, the creation of Israel, Israeli justice, "Ivan the Terrible," gentile anti-Semitism, rights of Palestinians, the Jew in history, and, of course, the Jewish writer. All are paradoxes: they are what they seem and they are also the direct opposites of what they seem. The Holocaust, which to the Israelis is indisputable proof that a Jewish state must exist, is to the Palestinians a renewable Israeli rationalization for continuing to deny them their homeland. That argument resonates amidst benign descriptions of Israelis trying to coexist and to retain their souls as occupiers. Israeli justice, showcased for its fairness in the Demjanjuk trial, is accused by the Palestinians—and occasionally by Amnesty International—of railroading young *intifada* sympathizers into star chamber courts and illegal detentions. The charges are made not without cynicism. Palestinian radicals play them off against countercharges by state prosecutors as part of a game—more benign than either lets on—implicit to the political stalemate. Demjanjuk, whose trial hit new snags with the disclosure of Soviet counter-evidence just as Roth was completing the novel, is himself a great duality: he is both the murderer "Ivan the Terrible" and a gracious grandfather whose son is at his side convinced— and trying to convince the world—it is all mistaken identity. Gentile anti-Semitism, the scourge of modern Jewish history, is posited by Roth's double as a disease, treatable by a program like Alcoholics Anonymous, making victimizers as sympathetic as victims. In his mad scheme, recovered anti-Semites will turn into righteous Gentiles. Former Polish children who mocked the boxcars with pantomimes of throat-slitting will joyously welcome their redispossessors back into their villages. The absurdity of the idea notwithstanding, the notion of disease takes a certain root in the brain of the most righteous reviler of anti-Semites and struggles like Jonah's vine for some ascendancy there. Roth is using absurdities to test the traditional Jewish defenses. Even the title tests through its associations. Shakespeare's *Shylock* (as John Gross was pointing out)[3] had fixed the Jew in the gentile mind. From his first words, "Three-thousand ducats," he had seemed to come among them to collect interest on Judas Iscariot's thirty pieces of silver. That Roth's double is raising money to return Jews into the bosom of Europe's Gentiles is one twist on "Shylock." That Philip Roth could become a paid agent for betraying Jewish contributors to the PLO is still another twist. All this underscores the paradoxical conditions of Israel and Jewry in *Operation Shylock*.

The action of the novel encompasses three days in Jerusalem plus a prologue and epilogue that take place in America. During those three days, in which "Roth" is there primarily to interview Aharon Appelfeld, he also attends the Demjanjuk trial; meets his doppelganger twice; has two close encounters with the doppelganger's mistress; is taken by a Palestinian friend to a trial on the West Bank; runs into an Israeli patrol's ambush; is told of a conspiracy to harm Demjanjuk's son, which he tries haplessly and needlessly to foil; takes the doppelganger's place at the King David hotel; is sought after for lectures by a class of Israeli schoolchildren; is given a copy of a supposed diary by Leon Klinghoffer, the martyr of the *Achille Lauro*, with a request that he write the introduction; encounters a Ukrainian Catholic priest from his old Manhattan neighborhood; is kidnapped and held dubious prisoner in a Jerusalem schoolroom; is presented with the opportunity to spy for the Israelis; and refuses (but subsequently agrees) to undertake the mission. All the actions in Jerusalem may or may not have been induced by the Mossad to set "Roth" up for the final proposition. The epilogue is about publishing the book in progress and determining how much to reveal or suppress. But throughout, the frenzied action is at odds with the retarded pace of the dissertations that punctuate it.

This summary cannot convey the experience of the novel, which varies between bumbling curiosity and polemic assault. The plot of passive political seduction and bewildered escape is little more than a line to hang ideas on. But since the book is a game with the reader, in which even the preface and the afternote are parts of the plot, its essential energy comes from incongruity, from "predicament" intended to keep the reader off balance. Each predicament reflects some aspect of the cosmic Jewish predicament, yet what animates the story are devices of comedy: absurd schemes, misperceived motivations, and frenzied responses. Such comic rhythm is hard to sustain; it must maintain its inconsistencies consistently. But some of Roth's characters deliver essays, which, like an Alan Jones song in a Marx Brothers movie, interrupt the comic rhythm. These set pieces must be got through, but they cannot be absorbed into the whirl. And midway through the book they begin to pile up and retard the pace to a near halt. Tone, a writer's handshake with a reader—whether firm or loose, curt or broad—is an unwavering contract. In letting the comic tone escape him, Roth violates the contract.

But in those opening hundred or so pages (about two-fifths of the first major movement of the novel), what Roth attempts is fascinating. (And in a second reading, where Le Carré-like suspense no longer matters, some of the ambiguities and subtleties of discourse seem even richer.) Beginning in the world of personal memoir, Roth sets his namesake character as a man overwrought by those suicidal effects of Halcion that he had known following his own knee surgery, and this is made even more real by his inveighing against the Upjohn company for placing the volatile tranquilizer on the market. From the perplexing haze of that real postsurgical nightmare, Roth slips into another, this time fictive, perplexity. Imperceptibly, author becomes interior narrator. And narrator Roth has heard about that double in Jerusalem, attending the Demjanjuk trial, propounding Diasporism, already said to have gained for Philip Roth the approval of Lech Walesa. The sources of this information seem credible enough to further fog the already blurred line between fact and fiction. Aharon Appelfeld, whom Roth (both author and narrator) is actually to interview shortly in Jerusalem, and a supposed cousin who lives there have both informed him of press stories about "him" in Israel. Still unsettled after the Halcion nightmare, the Roth character makes a series of decisions against his own interests that slowly pulls him into the aura of his double's perverse logic. His initial response to the imposture is outrage, and his wife, Claire Bloom (though in actuality they were not yet married in 1988), advises him to have a lawyer nip it in the bud. Hers is one of those sensible pieces of advice that Roth heroes get, agree with in principle, and violate even as they think they are still entertaining the possibility.

Instead, Roth makes an overseas call to the King David hotel, where the imposter is allegedly staying, and asks to speak to Philip Roth. When the double gets on, Roth, fascinated, impulsively takes the guise of a French journalist—one Pierre Roget—and, with that accent, lures the imposter to confirm that he is the author of *Portnoy et sonne complexe*. In one unthinking stroke, Roth has reversed roles. Now *he* is an imposter interviewing a celebrity, a celebrity who has convinced journalists, statesmen, and half of Israel of his authenticity. Pierre Roget, with the same initials as Philip Roth, was the compiler of the thesaurus, the master of verbal substitutions. Roth, with only a written life to speak of, is hooked by his writer's fascination for the alternative possibility. Slowly he begins to move into the guise of Diasporist himself.

If all this "Roth"ing is confusing, we might well avail ourselves of the scheme used in the novel to distinguish two of these characters. The internal narrator labels his imposturing double, "Moishe Pipik" (or as one speaking Yiddish with a Litvak accent might say, "Moishe Pupik"). Literally "Moses Bellybutton," the name is well understood by people of a Yiddish-speaking background to mean a child's imaginary alter ego or the child himself when he is intruding into adult business. It was a name with which grandparents or uncles would fondly dispatch *nudnik* children. Irritant that this third Philip Roth is to the second (narrator) Roth, the putdown dispatches him nicely—for a while. As to the "real" Philip Roths, let us call the writer we have been talking about for the last few hundred pages Roth and the interior narrator of *Operation Shylock*, Philip. Philip, then, carries the burden of the myth Roth has been building for several books, and Pipik is an irritant to Philip and a lookalike to both. It is Roth's noble gamble in this book to entice the reader into thinking all that happens to Philip has happened to him. And for a while, the reader indulges Roth in his attempt, though after the first quarter of the book with growing resistance.

Pipik has been attending the Demjanjuk trial and giving interviews to promote Diasporism. Philip, ignoring Claire's advice and lying to her to cover his misdemeanor, goes to Jerusalem for his scheduled interview with Appelfeld, attends the trial himself (that Roth had attended) where he is seen by Pipik, and has the interview with Appelfeld that Roth had had. He even spells out the interview questions that Roth had published in *The New York Times*, so that the questions and answers concerning a Holocaust survivor living in Israel and assimilating Holocaust-affected life into his stories become intertwined with the questions being raised in Roth's present narrative. Philip and Pipik encounter each other in a hotel lobby, where both have found refuge from the rain after one of the Demjanjuk sessions, and Pipik immediately fawns over Philip and admits that he has been allowing people to identify him with Philip Roth so he can do his great good for the Jewish people. Philip is outraged both on his own behalf and on that of the Jews, but as he studies the man, he finds his outrage infinitesimally undercut by the striking similarity of appearance, down to the odd wayward threads betraying a missing button on Pipik's identical jacket. Pipik is, if anything, better looking, not marred by the sunken chin that Roth shared with Sender Roth and that Philip acknowledges to be a flaw in his own profile.

Pipik has persuaded Philip to have lunch with him, although Philip is late for his scheduled luncheon interview with Appelfeld. As they wait in the empty dining room, there is something in Pipik's manner that transfixes Philip, like the wedding guest before the Ancient Mariner, so that he cannot help but hear. At first, Pipik's logic is quite simple. He cannot praise Philip enough as the novelist who has fully understood the Diaspora contribution to Judaism. And the Philip Roth reputation is a kind of currency, he says, with value that must be wisely spent. Of course, not every man is a man of action; it has been enough for Philip to have been a man of words. But Pipik, who asserts that his real name *is* Philip Roth, sees himself as being the Roth capable of action who can use to best Jewish advantage the reputation of Roth, man of letters. He sees Israel as having been but a stage in Jewish survival and insists that now the Jewish people must no longer have all its eggs in one basket so accessible to its Arab enemies. Peace will be possible between Arabs and Israeli Sephardim once the Ashkenazi Jews have returned to their European places of origin. And, of course, Christian Europe will welcome them back—he has Lech Walesa's word. He shows a passport with a picture Philip believes to be one taken of himself a few years earlier, but it is marked with stamped destinations to countries Philip has never visited. Pipik defends the resemblance, and the name, by citing Jung on "synchronicity," the law of averages, and his own Holocaust theory to show that it is not so unlikely for an earlier strain in a greatly reduced blood line to have produced them both.

Even the Pollard case is a point in Pipik's arsenal. Indeed, as one later discovers, the Israelis's hanging Pollard out to dry may have been the trigger that set Pipik against the Jewish state. Israel presents a duality of loyalties in which well-meaning Jews—including these two Roths, if they had the chance— might be tempted to become spies, so as to save Jewish lives. Remove the possibility of double loyalty, Pipik asserts, and you also remove a weapon from the arsenal of the anti-Semite. Of course, this last well-known argument is absurd: it can be heard among anti-Semites anywhere. No one who knows Roth's history can believe he accepts it; as troubler of the scene, he is mischief maker enough just to present it. Pipik is shaken by Philip's rejection, shows some marks of weariness, and confesses to being a terminally ill cancer patient on a desperate timetable of his own. This remark sufficiently disarms Philip so that he hands back the passport, instead of confiscating it and forcing the legal showdown that might have ended his ordeal. Lunch is never served: the hotel restaurant is on a later schedule. Philip runs off to his other luncheon meeting with Appelfeld.

After the Appelfeld interview (the first of two whose transcripts will be intruded into the story), Philip is sitting in the garden of his own East-Jerusalem hotel when a "voluptuously healthy-looking creaturely female" of about thirty-five places a note in his hand. It (and she) is from Pipik, a second conciliatory plea for acceptance. He cites Roth's reclusive habits and pleads to be allowed to "EXIST" to spend "the renown you hoard." Asking to be judged "not by words but by the woman who bears this letter," he calls himself "THE YOU THAT IS NOT WORDS" and signs himself, "Philip Roth." Her name, prophetically, is Jinx.

Wanda Jane "Jinx" Possesski, nurse and lover of Pipik, is a "recovering anti-Semite" whose speech, when she gets around to relating the details of her life, shows how easily recovery can give way to relapse. At one point, she says, she hated the young Jewish doctor who could not save one of her cancer patients from death. But in her account of how that failure rekindled her father-transmitted hatred of Jews, she rises to such vituperative use of "Jew" that the speech might have come from the mouth of a Louis Farrakhan lieutenant. Roth's irony here is magnificent, for he never lets Philip—who is attracted to Jinx—acknowledge the discrepancy between her present philosophy and her slip into the vitriolic. However, when he gives her no quarter on the matter of Pipik's fraudulent impersonation, she exits, throwing at him another document: "THE TEN TENETS OF ANTI-SEMITES ANONYMOUS." It seems that when she fell in love with Pipik, she confessed to him her hatred of Jews, from which Pipik deduced that it was an illness curable only by active participation in the cure of another anti-Semite, on the model of A.A.; and so he founded the complementary movement to Diasporism, the education movement that would prepare all recalcitrant Gentiles for the return of European Jewry—Anti-Semites Anonymous.

Some time after Jinx leaves, Philip begins to edit those "TEN TENETS." He can see immediately the weakness in their language and how put into more logical order they could guide a novitiate in firm steps from hatred to tolerance. Pipik's first few tenets echo Roth's old argument in "Writing About Jews" that anti-Semitism is not the fault of Jews but of haters prone to scapegoating prejudices. Philip is slowly buying into the program. When he next meets Appelfeld, he weaves a whole scenario about how the imposter could be sincere—even in identity—and how perhaps the cancer-wracked Pipik had been moved by Jinx's love to keep himself alive through espousing this noble cause that she inspired him to propound. Imagining their collaboration, Philip flies into a passion of his own and, as he improves upon their "Tenets" for A-S.A., acts like Colonel Nicholson (the Alec Guiness character) in *The Bridge Over the River Kwai*: almost embracing the enemy's plan in his enthusiasm for outdoing it. When he brings himself up short in laughter at this absurd impulse, Appelfeld asks, "What's so hilarious? His mischief or yours? That he pretends to be you or that you now pretend to be him?" Asked to define "mischief," Appelfeld continues, "To a mischief-maker like you? Mischief is how some Jews get involved in living." Philip knows there is something phony about Pipik, that "he emanates the aura of something absolutely spurious, almost the way Nixon did." Appelfeld responds, "A vacuum, a vacuum into which is drawn your own gift for deceit." And Appelfeld concludes, in an oracular sadness mixed with bemusement, "You are going to rewrite him."

The opening exposition of the novel is juicily cinched at this point. Philip and Appelfeld are approached by an elderly crippled Jew who apparently takes Philip for Pipik, that is, for the famous novelist Philip Roth, known to be proselytizing for Diasporism. He declares himself to be a Holocaust survivor who, after the camps, succeeded in the jewelry business in New York, saved his money to come to Israel, and is now unhappy, wanting only to return to his native Poland. He tells Appelfeld to get his family out of Israel, that "Philip Roth is right!" Before the next Holocaust, in which the Arabs will be God's instrument, as was Hitler, Appelfeld should leave! The old man's religious conviction comes down to this declaration:

> A Jew knows God and how, from the very first day He created man, He has been irritated with him from morning till night. That is what it means that the Jews were chosen. [Theirs is] a God Who does not ever stop, *not once*, to think and reason and use His head with His loving children. To appeal to a crazy, *violent* father, that is what it is to be a Jew.(*OS* 110)

With that, pulling an envelope out of his pocket, and identifying himself as Mr. Smilesburger, he hands Philip a check for a million dollars as a contribution to Diasporism. Philip does not open the envelope and discover the sum until well after Smilesburger has disappeared from the café and into the Jerusalem street. From here on, Philip's responses are all part of a test: as he holds onto, eventually to lose, the check, allows others to tag him with Pipik's ideas, and gets inveigled into a trip to a West Bank court, he is being set up for his mysterious mission. Of course, the reader does not know that Smilesburger is an operative for Mossad, though the name—right out of John Le Carré—might have suggested it. This Smiley's first name is not *George*; the "George" will be reserved for the next character dragged into the now dubious and increasingly contrived plot.

One irritating contrivance is the polemical or philosophical set piece. Early in the novel, when the rain-soaked Pipik meets Philip in a hotel and praises in detail the whole Roth ouevre, the reader does not yet feel choked by the encomium, though it may make him gag a little. But the interviews with Appelfeld are another matter. The transcript of Roth's *Times* interview, profound as it is for the interested reader of literary criticism and apposite as it may be to the themes of the novel, is a detour from the predicament being shared with the reader. It may serve to reassert Philip's connection to Roth, but it is not the stuff of fiction. That will be the problem with other set pieces as well. Whereas in *The Counterlife* declamations had animated the conflict, here they tend to suspend it. But it is not dramatic suspension, not a Homeric simile or recollection, or a *Moby Dick* whaling dissertation. Those interrupt the plot to engage the reader in an alternative action, a substitute conflict that then is brought to bear on the main plot conflict. They are robust narrative devices that also clarify matters for the reader. But where narrative gives way to dissertation in *Operation Shylock*, one feels that the character delivering the dissertation has been brought into the novel specifically to do so, not speech clarifying essential character but character contrived for the speech. Such, despite strains of gusto, is the case of George Ziad.

Philip is on a Jerusalem market street heading for a meeting with his Israeli cousin when he hears his name called; the middle-aged Palestinian bearing down on him sings out that he is Philip's old university friend "Zee." Ziad, who back in Chicago in the fifties had been the urbane Arab counterpart of the urbane Jewish graduate student, is much the worse for wear. Here in Jerusalem he is presented as the ghostly opposite of the American Zionist, the Arab who has returned from diaspora against all personal advantage because he is haunted by his patrimony—the Palestinian cause. Roth's model for Zee is not necessarily any one real person, but the reader might easily consider what Edward Said might have deteriorated into had he been moved by a personal demon to give up all and return to his homeland. Such an association may explain why the once-scrupulous fact checkers and editors at *The New Yorker* failed to correct the spelling of Ziad's name in John Updike's review, where it was consistently "Zaid."⁴ Ziad, too, raves about Philip's writing and career. Now a paunchy, smoke-dissipated professor in Israel, he teaches *Portnoy's Complaint* to his Arab students "to convince them that there are Jews in the world that are not in any way like these Jews we have here." His lengthy dissertation on how the American Diaspora had opened Jews to their best potential while Israel has shrunk them into narrow bigots is concluded with praise for Philip's clear-eyed promulgation of Diasporism. Having mistaken Pipik's pronouncements for Philip's, he now adds his admiration for his friend's courage. Philip, he is sure, must have breasted personal danger—threats from the Zionist government—but Zee is not surprised: this bravery is but an extension of Rothian career-long iconoclasm. Ziad ends by insisting that Philip accompany him to a kangaroo court on the West Bank to see how the Israelis treat Palestinians trying to exercise *their* freedom of expression.

Ziad's words of praise for Roth's writing, added to Pipik's, and later to those of several others all the way down to a late rave from Smilesburger, are often tonally in conflict with their ironic function. The reader is always aware of Roth, like the mother of a young vaudevillean, pushing Philip to take his bows. If it is hard to find Minnie Marx, Rose Hovac, or Mother Berle endearing, it is at times insufferable to hear Roth ventriloquize self-praise through a trunkfull of dummies, especially when each of these encomia interrupts the action. And since the theme of their praise is often how right Roth was all along, the running polemic is at odds with the need for perplexity in the character.

Philip is greatly perplexed following his trip to the West Bank settlement. He has seen the court session—less indicting of the Israelis than Ziad and his militant friends have tried to make it—and has met other Arab zealots, who seem to accept less readily Ziad's characterization of him as a Diasporist. To prove his loyalty, and assure his safety, Philip allows himself to float freely in the guise of the Diasporist, allows Ziad's mistake not only to go unchecked but to set the agenda for extensions of Pipik's fantasy. Invoking their old Chicago camaraderie, he rises to flights of rhetoric about the advantages of the American Diaspora (a position that Roth has often taken) and soars to manic praise of Irving Berlin as the savior who, with two lyrics, equaled the genius of Moses. As Moses got the Ten Commandments to give the Jews a sacred morality, "Easter Parade" and "White Christmas" desanctified Christianity and so reduced its power to hurt the Jews. "*He turns their religion into schlock. But nicely! Nicely! So nicely the goyim don't even know what hit 'em.*" Ziad is comforted to see in these flights his old Philip of *Portnoy* days.

Philip even shows Smilesburger's check as proof of his allegiance to Pipik's cause. But with these pronounced sympathies, he finds himself caught in a conflict between Ziad and his wife. She, too, is dissipated by the whole Palestinian experience, but, unlike her husband, she wants to go back to America, to take their impressionable son away from this militancy and single-minded self-torture. She sees no high moral purpose in their martyrdom to George's notion that his father's plot of ground is sacred, not when they had wonderful apartments and a lively cultural life in the States.

What soon perplexes Philip even more is simpler than all that. On his return trip after dark, his Arab driver gets lost, or stops to relieve himself, or is driving him into an ambush, or violating a curfew, or some other suspected but unknown horror that the West Bank visit has enabled Philip to imagine. Alone, and seemingly abandoned here on the road, he feels the danger implicit to Israeli society. Suddenly, he is surrounded and threatened by Israeli soldiers, but just as suddenly he is rescued when one of their officers turns out to be a young Roth fan. He has just that day been reading one of Philip's books and identifies himself as a man in conflict with his own father, losing his soul to the duties of occupier but understanding his father's dedication to the country. He, too, wishes to go to America; but for now he can just drive Philip back to Jerusalem. In contrast, Philip, who can pack up and leave in a moment, is drawn lingeringly into experiencing the Diasporist's conflict.

Into the ensuing episode Roth pours all the bite, the wit, the reversals, the off-balance speculation on appearance and reality—indeed, the myriad of criticism of his own career—that he can muster. At times it is brain-tingling. But it is never convincing, and for one reason. Whatever germ Diasporism might have in an idea or a philosophical position, as a program of political action it is nothing that anyone sane can take seriously, not even to mock it. The term, as Robert Alter[5] points out, has real roots in a book by R. B. Kitaj, a British painter and "friend of Roth's," called *The Diasporist Manifesto*. But the program, even though presented and embraced in this novel only by madmen or plotters, is everywhere an impediment to total suspension of disbelief. Not Smilesburger as old Holocaust victim (before we learn he is a Mossad agent) nor even Ziad as cause-blind zealot, not to mention a range of journalists and dignitaries, can be expected to respond to a notion so preposterous. So when, in this next episode Philip returns to his hotel to find Pipik—who as his look-alike has gotten his key—searching his room for Smilesburger's check (which Philip has apparently lost on the road), the exchange between them—potentially wonderful on the subject of the doppelganger or the duality of human nature—becomes hollow because of their silly belaborings of Diasporism. Nor is it quite enough for a reader involved in the surrounding realities of the *intifada*, the Demjanjuk trial, the Israeli tightening security, to be told that Philip himself doubts the reality of the Diasporism-related events. His wondering whether this could not all be but a dream, another side-effect of Halcion, does not suffice to bridge the gap in verisimilitude. Still, as the reader is plunged forward toward a conclusion of the first movement of the novel (well better than halfway through), certain rich fictive speculations—on Jews and Gentiles, on Israel and its difficulties, and on Roth and his old susceptibility to dependent gentile women—still exercise an engaging power, made possible by the off-balance insecurity of Philip.

In Philip's room, Pipik searches, pleads, and, exhausting himself, falls asleep on Philip's bed. Philip answers the phone and recognizes the voice of

Jinx, who thinks she is talking to a furtively searching Pipik; in whispers, he works her up into autoerotic stimulation a la Nicholson Baker's *Vox*. Pipik, awakening but shriveled sufficiently to reveal his cancerous state, displays knowledge of Philip's entire life, Newark childhood and all, in an attempt to get the check. Philip goes as far as to admit that there may be "a mad plausibility" about Diasporism and the "Eurocentricity of the Judaism that gave birth to Zionism" and from that concession induces Pipik to reveal his true identity: he says that he has been for much of his life a private investigator. But, Pipik insists, he has always been mistaken for Philip, even by John Kennedy in the old days when he was detailed as a Presidential bodyguard. Philip does not know, and the reader does not know, whether this is not all just a life lifted from television soap opera and detective shows, but through it all Pipik's detective impersonations and fiction spinnings mirror the vocation of the novelist confronting him. Idea is reinforced by appearance: Philip notices that their hair is even parted, mirror-image fashion, on the opposite side. The episode ends in Philip's declaring the "comedy" over. Continually raised to a peak of hysteria himself, he struggles for his own sanity by regarding all this only as some divinely scripted piece of absurdity. His own literary education can provide him with classifications into which to fit and thereby control the experience. And the class of comedy he considers them to have been engaging in is Aristophanic old comedy, the kind that in the ancient Dionysian festival was characterized by highjinx of exaggerated phalluses and multiple goosings. Pronouncing the million-dollar check irrevocably lost, he claims victory and an end to hostilities.

> "A million bucks blowing away across the desert sands, probably halfway down to Mecca by now. And with that million you could have convened that first Diasporist Congress in Basel. You could have shipped the first lucky Jews back to Poland. You could have established a chapter of A-S.A. right in Vatican City. Meetings in the basement of St. Peter's Church. Full house every night. 'My name is Eugenio Pacelli. I'm a recovering anti-Semite.' Pipik, who sent you to me in my hour of need? Who made me this wonderful gift? Know what Heine liked to say? There is a God, and his name is Aristophanes. *You* prove it. It's Aristophanes they should be worshipping over at the Wailing Wall—if he were the God of Israel I'd be in shul three times a day!" (*OS* 204)

Philip's hysteria is answered by Pipik's lunge at him, directly across the bed, pelvis first, led by a very Aristophanic erection cranked up on a penile implant. "There's reality," he shouts. "Like a rock." And in the ensuing fight, Philip breaks Pipik's dropped glasses, throws him out of the room, takes a phone message from an anonymous Holocaust victim cursing God for having been absent between 1939 and 1945, and answers a knock on the door from a hovering figure whom he has taken throughout the episode to be the hotel detective but who, it seems, is merely a pervert offering oral sex. Throughout the episode, an admixture of adolescent adventure and heady danger has been stretching the plot line to near tremor, its reality dubious even as it is being spun. Yet, it might have kept the reader off balance and engaged were it not for the one implausibility that in this case cannot be written around—not in the serious geopolitical circumstances of this novel. However well Pipik may serve for psycho-literary exploration of the counter-self, he has been placed here in Philip's room and life by a different convergence of events. On the primary level, he is there because he has been honored by Lech Walesa, interviewed by the Israeli press, sought after for political alliances by the PLO, and contributed to by disaffected Jews worldwide. But this is hardly acceptable as a premise for serious fiction and not farcical enough for Aristophanic comedy. The modern Jew, unlike the ancient Athenian, is too insecure to licence a send-up of his most sacred institutions.

Philip now determines to quit Israel the following day. Pipik's hope and energy having flown with his check, the doppelganger seems less of a threat—although the vision of him going around Jerusalem with his implanted erection unretracted, telling everyone he is Philip Roth, is still disconcerting. Philip will spend the night preparing questions for his final interview with Appelfeld, the original legitimate purpose of his trip to Israel, and will depart after delivering the questions in the morning. But his hotel, in the Arab quarter, is not safe. He has seen from his windows, moving through the night, like shadows, kaffiyeh-masked Arabs gathering stones from a nearby construction site for who-knows-what demonstration and Israeli soldiers loading onto buses for patrol in the West Bank. In the same hotel are Demjanjuk's son and his American and Israeli law team plotting strategy for the father's defense, and Philip has been speculating on the safety of that young man in Jerusalem amidst so many embittered Holocaust survivors. This speculation is always somewhat admiring of Israeli civility, the safety of young Demjanjuk contrasted to the likely danger to a similarly placed Jew in some terrorist-dominated society. But, then, the novel would be published a year before the 1994 Hebron massacre.

Philip bars his hotel door by moving a dresser in front of it, both to keep danger out and to keep himself in, despite many possible temptations. The act illustrates the tenuousness of his resolve. But after some time there is a knock on the door, and, in whispers, Jinx Possesski identifies herself. When Philip refuses to admit her, she slips a yellow cloth star under the door, the kind Holocaust victims had to sew on their clothes, and says it is a gift from Lech Walesa. She avers that she has left Pipik and means Philip no harm. She is not looking for the million-dollar check, but she must tell Philip of the danger the loss has created. On the condition that she will reveal Pipik's true identity, a condition Philip offers against his better judgment—and in full realization of her attractions—he admits her. Pipik, she blurts out, in desperation, has contacted Meir Kahane, and together they are planning to kidnap Demjanjuk's son, intending to amputate increasingly vital parts of the youth and send them to his father until the old man confesses to being "Ivan the Terrible" of Treblinka. To the Polish-fathered Wanda Jane, this turn has realized the greatest fears of her childhood indoctrination, the Jews performing the blood-libel ritual of redemption on a Christian child. All her Anti-Semite Anonymous training is perilously threatened because of Pipik's reduced state. In the subsequent hours of the night, Jinx tells her life story, a model of the hard life of the *shiksa* that had dominated Roth's novels of the sixties and seventies. It is a narrative of how Wanda Jane, the innocent child, easily abused and easily misled by father, priests, and born-again ministers preaching a Christianity of personal unworth, became Jinx, the sexy, worldly woman turned nurse, beyond their abuse and saved by her "Philip." She has also been his savior: for her he underwent the stone penile implant, which must be manually ratcheted up, restorer of his tenuous manhood.

Philip, listening to her life story, hears in it echoes of Roth's life with Maggie. Toward the end of her narrative, as she talks about men's ogling her breasts (her "cross," Philip calls them "carried before instead of aft") and as she offers to read his fortune in his palm, the attraction increases and he does "the stupidest thing I'd yet done in Jerusalem and perhaps in my entire life. I got up from the chair by the window and stepped across to the bed and took hold of the hand that she was extending" (*OS* 237). He knows, like many a Roth hero before this, what he should not do. He tells himself, "Stop. Breathe. Think. She believes you are in possession of Smilesburger's million and is simply changing sides. Anything could be happening and you'd be the last to know." Then Philip concludes this part of his confession, "I should have fled. Instead I implanted myself and then I fled. I penetrated her and I ran. Both. Talk about the commonplace at its most ridiculous" (*OS* 238).

Up to this point, the novel has been a mixture of fantasy and adventure, some of it silly. The fantasy, except for some philosophic tomes, takes the reader fictively along as participant in the episode in progress. Now, suddenly, Roth, disregarding the reader's primacy in the ordinary fictive contract, interrupts the suspended disbelief—not, as in *The Counterlife*, to replace one fictional situation with another, but to declare, seemingly as narrator, that this has been only an experiment in fiction. He backs away from the story line and contemplates what he has been telling—he summarizes, analyzes, and evaluates the very story in which the reader has so far been imaginatively transported despite some rough edges. His new chapter, called, "The Uncontrollability of

Real Things," begins: "Here is the Pipik plot so far." And with that announce-ment he launches into a five-page bare-bones summary of all we have so-far read, concluding it, like "On the Air," with a series of questions that a "soap" would answer for anyone who might "Tune in next time!" But this is not radio. The plot summary gives over instead to a literary evaluation of what has just been recounted.

> This is the plot up to the moment when the writer leaves the woman still dolefully enmeshed in it, and, suitcase in hand, tiptoeing so as not to disturb her postcoital rest, he himself slips out of the plot on the grounds of its general implausibility, a total lack of gravity, reliance at too many key points on unlikely coincidence, an absence of inner coher-ence, and not even the most tenuous evidence of anything resembling a serious meaning or purpose. (*OS* 245)

Roth (or is it Philip?) then proceeds to blast the whole Pipik idea as based on an undeveloped character (interestingly, Updike will consider Pipik better devel-oped than Philip) "*trying* to be real without any idea of how to go about it":

> His being as an antagonist, his being *altogether*, is wholly dependent on the writer, from whom he parasitically pirates what meager selfhood he is able to make even faintly credible. (*OS* 245)

But what underlies this evaluation is the observation that geopolitical intriguers, like con men or detectives or just you and I, always script themselves (well or poorly); and that their plots—important as they may be to the course of his-tory—are not unlike a novelist's plots. The same word applies to both. In this respect, no "reality" is to be completely trusted, no motive, however righteous, completely pure. Roth's fictive purpose emerges from his analysis: to suggest in the very unlikelihood of these seeming events a confusion of mind in Philip, a weakened sense of reality amidst which he can be inveigled into the climac-tic espionage that will be the subject of the ultimately deleted chapter on the spying mission.

But this first such change of narrative mode is so abrupt that the reader cannot enter it as part of the fiction. Until Philip steps in (six pages into the chapter) to identify the inserted summary as his own thoughts, the reader won-ders why the novel has stopped sounding like a novel and started reading like publisher's notes on a book proposal. Still later, in Pipik's room, Philip listens to tapes made for Anti-Semites Anonymous, tapes that compress into one long diatribe the illogical rantings of a quintessential anti-Semite. This seven-page monologue, poured forth in a voice perfect for a gentile locker room or bar anywhere in the Western world, is certainly provocative on its own, but it, too, interrupts the pace of the novel. Roth's intent in this rant is to expand Philip's predicament, to universalize it as the cosmic predicament of the Jew. But in place of narrative interweaving, there is mere insertion. The material is thematically rich but fictively unassimilable. What Roth is now practicing is not so much the art of the novel as a juxtaposition of voices, a presentation of various views of the Jew held by real groups of people at the end of the twentieth century, voiced at extreme pitch. But the reader had been somewhere in the middle of a story, and a narrator-host may not with impunity become indifferent to his reader-guest. Trying to expound the predicament of the Jews, Roth loses the predicament of his main Jew.

Although such tomes tend to sink the narrative line, shorter asides can sometimes jump start the action. In a one-paragraph essay, Roth produces a remarkable analogy between the eternal conflict of fathers and sons—Freudian and, oh, so Rothian—and the conflict of the three major religions competing in Israel. Judaism, after all, is the father of Christianity and Islam. Philip has noticed *The Jerusalem Post*'s practice of triple-dating its first page, on this occasion 1988, 5748, and 1408, and he takes off on the implications of the discrepancy: "a matter not of decades or even a few little centuries but of four thousand three hundred and forty years."

> The father is succeeded by the rivalrous, triumphant firstborn—rejected, suppressed, persecuted, expelled, shunned, terrorized by the firstborn and reviled as the enemy—and then, having barely escaped extinction for the crime of being the father, resuscitates himself, revives and rises up to struggle bloodily over property rights with the second-born, who is raging with envy and the grievances of usurpation, neglect, and ravaged pride. 1988. 5748. 1408. The tragic story's all in the numbers, the successor monotheists' implacable feud with the ancient progenitor whose crime it is, whose *sin* it is, to have endured the most unspeakable devastation and still, somehow, to be *in the way*.
> The Jews are in the way. (*OS* 266)

Much of the thesis of the book is contained in that last line. It is what much of the world continues to think and what a reader might be moved to test on his own pulse. Wouldn't the Middle East problem be solved if the Jews would just go away? Or the Farrakhan problem? Or the Crown Heights problem? Or the separate education problem? Or the denial of the Holocaust or the banning of *Schindler's List* in a host of Moslem countries? Or the recurrent doubts about Christ's divinity? Couldn't the Jews just get off the stage and let the drama of history go on?

"The Jews are in the way" takes on all these overtones, but for the Diaspora Jew that Roth represents, it has additional irony. For the Diaspora Jew, Israel itself often seems to be in the way. And that annoying realization about this new fountainhead of his legitimacy compromises his independence. America is only a safe place for Jews as long as they have an alternative homeland, like all the other immigrant groups whose assimilation is desirable as long as they need not disappear into the mix. That had never been conceded in a Roth novel before, but it is implicitly conceded throughout this one.

That little essay ending in "The Jews are in the way," sets up a new episode begun in the very next line—a series of speeches by Israeli schoolchildren who stop Philip at the King David elevator. This episode elaborates the mistaken identity theme: the children had written to him, but Pipik had gotten their letters. Roth evidently wants them to be puzzled about why someone would try to resettle their families in Europe, and he makes them politely undertake that very Western schoolchild exercise, literary criticism. But at this point they are keeping Philip from pursuing urgent business, another plot interruption. Roth, using them to suggest still another Zionist *raison d'être*, wants them to sound like second-language English speakers trying to be precise; but as they continue to query a frustrated Philip on present implications of "Eli, the Fanatic" and "Defender of the Faith," they succeed mostly in irritating the reader with a robot tone and considerable fawning: "We were impressed by the beautiful style of literature you write, but still not all of the problems were solved in our mind." Of course, in both those early stories set in America, the Jews are in the way, even of themselves, as they cannot possibly be in Israel. The theme of *Operation Shylock* is being advanced, the story line retarded.

A reader may even be impressed here by Roth's knowledge of Hebrew expressions like *hozer b'tshuva*, just as throughout the book one may sense that his proclaimed ignorance of Judaic learning is set amidst not unimpressive displays of Jewish history and doctrine. But such set pieces fail to satisfy an artistic purpose. Take Smilesburger's extended diatribe on the teachings of the Chofetz Chaim, the popular name for the Polish Rabbi Israel Ha-Cohen, a sage who died at ninety-three the year Roth was born. His message is about speaking ill, the laws of *loshan hora*. Replete with folkloric examples of the many ways one may unintentionally sin in speaking ill—even of oneself—this six-page passage might have been written for a collection of wisdom literature. It repeats and repeats its Talmudic terms, all the while Philip is sitting as a virtual prisoner about whom the reader is still sufficiently curious to want to get on to what may happen next. Every one of these set pieces has a bearing on Roth's theme, which is complex and even profound, yet mostly they stop the story in ways that leave the first-time reader so stranded that he is unable to appreciate them.

What they are punctuating is the last movement of the Jerusalem narrative—begun after Philip tiptoes out of his West Bank hotel. Having started for the airport to leave Israel, he is brought up short by a realization. Indeed, it is a realization that suggests much about Roth's reaction to the British in his previous few books. Philip remembers a political cartoon he had seen in the British papers in which the Israelis were pictured like the typical big-nosed kikes of Nazi propaganda, standing shruggingly and disavowingly over a pile of dead Arab bodies. He realizes he must try to save Demjanjuk's son from Kahane. "When he starts slicing off the boy's toes and mailing them one at a time to Demjanjuk's cell, the *Guardian* will have a field day." So he has himself driven instead to the King David hotel "to face down this bastard [Pipik] once and for all" only to find that Pipik has checked out and Jinx has checked out, gone possibly to Romania, and that there is no evidence of any contact between them and Kahane. He takes Pipik's room—claiming to be his twin brother—searches it and finds the A-S.A. tapes (linking the Jews to every evil from the JFK assassination to fixing the SAT scores to faking the Holocaust) and in checking out the next morning is accosted first by the schoolchildren and then by two men, one who assumes he is a loyal Zionist and another who assumes he is an anti-Zionist. The first is Mr. Supposnik, a bibliophile who wants him to read and compose an introduction for the Klinghoffer manuscript (we later learn that he and the diary are products of Mossad). He holds Philip in another set piece, a dissertation on the role of Shylock in Jewish history, and touts the diarist Klinghoffer (another K. in Roth's Kafka-dominated imagination) as a second Anne Frank (referencing for the Roth reader Zuckerman's multiple uses of Anne, and thus for Philip, a known obsession).

The second man waiting for him is George Ziad, who wants him to meet higher-ups in the PLO so that through them he can get to Jews who wish to donate cash to the Diasporist-compatible Palestinian cause, to be arranged through a connection in Athens. Philip stuffs the supposed diaries in his pocket and rushes off with Ziad to the Demjanjuk trial to see if Pipik might be there and to check on young Demjanjuk. The scene is filled out by a long cross-examination of a death-camp survivor, which pretty much fixes Demjanjuk's culpability despite superficial conflicts of testimony. But young Demjanjuk is well and safe. Outside the courthouse the Ukrainian priest is attempting to distribute leaflets he asserts can help prevent a sure anti-Semitic reaction if Demjanjuk is convicted. Roth brings in the question of Chielmnicki, as he has Philip remember Ukrainian festivals in the East Village of the early sixties (the setting of *My Life as a Man*) and people costumed as that Cossack hero—who is to Jews the reviled butcher of 1648. After a Jewish giant of a man scatters the priest's leaflets—eliciting a comparison to the Golem of Prague—Philip feels himself being lifted from the ground and, amidst the swirl of the crowd, whisked into a car, whence he is driven to an abandoned schoolroom around the corner from the market at which he had first met Ziad. The last part of the Jerusalem materials takes place in the schoolroom.

Philip's two Mossad kidnappers are men he has seen before, one in the market where he had spoken to Ziad, the other the supposed pervert at the hotel. Left in the schoolroom, whose open window and unlocked door invite possible escape, he is transfixed like a Kafka character by some sense of a superior will keeping him from leaving. Instead, he reads the Klinghoffer diaries, skeptical of their authenticity; and thus, while he waits uneasily for whatever fate has in store, he speculates on the victim of the *Achille Lauro*, another Jew who was in the way. On the blackboard are words written in Hebrew that Philip avers he cannot understand or even read, having lost his early Hebrew-school training. Complete with vowels (not likely for an Israeli school room), it is a quotation from Genesis 32:24, "So Jacob was left alone, and a man wrestled with him until daybreak." The rest of the novel is a wrestling match over the loyalties and conscience of a Jew.

Eventually Smilesburger comes in and compliments Philip on his silence and his decision to remain, assuring him that from the moment he entered the schoolroom no compulsion has been exercised to keep him. Indeed, his staged Mossad abduction in front of witnesses has almost certainly guaranteed his acceptance as Diasporist and ally of the people he would be recruited to deal with. The omniscient spymaster, Smilesburger hints that he has been using Philip's reaction to Pipik and his accidental meeting with Ziad to load the espionage deck, but he denies that either of these two is, as Philip has come to suspect, parties to the Mossad plot. Smilesburger takes the line that E. I. Lonoff had taken at the end of *The Ghost Writer*: "I cannot believe . . . that this has been an ordeal that will scar you forever. You may even be grateful someday for whatever my contribution may have been to the book that emerges" (*OS* 348).

Philip is rightfully offended at his detention, but he resists his own impulse to leave long enough to ask a question: "These Jews who may or may not be contributing money to the PLO, why haven't they a perfect right to do with their money whatever they wish without interference from the likes of you?" It is a defiant question, Philip asserting on the one hand his independence from this official Jew and on the other his support of acts of conscience. But it is also a self-deceiving question, for it invites a response that will bypass the defiance and coax him into an act of tribal loyalty. The answer Smilesburger offers is consonant with Philip's principled view of himself: such Jews, he says, have a perfect right, nay a moral duty, to follow their consciences and contribute to the PLO if they think that is right. Indeed, the Jews owe the Palestinians reparations, have done them great harm. Like his earlier pronouncement about the injustice of God to His people, he accepts that there is injustice in the politics of the region. "Irrespective of terrorism or terrorists or the political stupidity of Yasir Arafat, the fact is this: as a people the Palestinians are totally innocent and as a people the Jews are totally guilty." His line has overtones of that taken by Mordecai Lippman in *The Counterlife*: survival is a matter of power, not of ultimate principles. Smilesburger continues, "I am a ruthless man working in a ruthless job for a ruthless country and I am ruthless knowingly and voluntarily." Indeed, his most astounding statement, what he would say to a war crimes tribune if it came to that, sounds as if it were being spoken by Iago at the end of *Othello*: "'I did what I did to you because I did what I did to you.' And if that is not the truth, it's as close as I know how to come to it. 'I do what I do because I do what I do.'" It is also the deepest truth of this book, disturbing but inescapable. People are born to the sides they are born to, and betraying those sides, even for causes as righteous as their own highest moral teachings, leaves them without identity. Scoffingly, Smilesburger calls Philip the blessed American Jew—"blissfully unblamable," "truly liberated," "not accountable," "*comfortable*," "*happy*," "condemned to nothing, least of all to [Israel's] historical struggle." As if dispensing with his prisoner, he concludes, "Go. Choose. Take. Have." Philip answers from conscience by refusing to partake of his plot. But when we have turned the page we see that it is some time later and he has partaken. Like all his weak acts against his better judgment, where instinct and disposition have won out, his act on behalf of the Jewish state is beyond his reason. It is of his being.

There is no return to the Pipik plot, except as an imagined speculation in the epilogue. As in Roth's earlier use of harassment by a doppelganger—that of Alvin Pepler in *Zuckerman Unbound*—this one, having served its purpose, is dropped. True, Philip does continue to imagine himself being set up by Pipik all the way into the schoolroom episode, until he fully understands that the real *deus ex machina* is Smilesburger; and, true, it is Pipik's initiatives in the first half that have left him vulnerable to PLO exploitation in the second half, convenient for the Mossad counter-espionage. But the first half of the novel, though fictively more engaging, is only a set-up for the concentrated ideas served at, but not to, the reader in the second part.

In the epilogue, titled "Words Generally Only Spoil Things," Philip is back in America some three years later, ready to publish this story, as Smilesburger had predicted. Still unable to account for his participation in the espionage, he is about to meet with Smilesburger, who has retired from the service to some grandfatherly cultivation of a little plot in the Negev and some catch-up reading that includes the works of Roth. Smilesburger has asked to read the manuscript before it is published and is flying into New York to meet with him. As Philip thinks about Pipik and Jinx, he imagines a letter that she could have written him, a device that had worked well in *The Counterlife*. The imagined letter is so cleverly absorbed into the reader's conciousness that one is likely to recall its contents as the true conclusion of the Pipik-Jinx story; but their story needs no true conclusion in a novel in which they were only a supposition to begin with. It is an amusing tale in which after coming to New Jersey, they move to, and ultimately settle in, the Berkshires not far from Roth, where Pipik dies. What finally kills him is the first news of the Iraq war, with its threats of missile destruction to Israel. He dies thinking that his worst Diasporist fears have been realized. But Jinx, "[f]or two days, wearing her nightgown and watching CNN, . . . remain[s] beside the body in the bed" comforting it with news of Patriot missiles and Israeli survival and—using Pipik's penile implant—engaging in necrophilic sex with her beloved. And Philip, still compromising Roth, imagines the possibilities of a visit from so near a neighbor.

Philip invites Smilesburger to meet him in his favorite Jewish foodstore-restaurant on the Upper West Side of Manhattan. Less posh and more earthy than the Upper East Side, there he can wave across the room to Ted Solotaroff and his son, a sign of Roth's return to the fold of *menschlichkite*. Smilesburger, insisting that he no longer has authority over anything and is speaking only for himself, strongly advises Philip to suppress the one chapter that narrates the espionage mission. Philip, back to protesting his independence and artistic integrity, mocks any suggestion that he is in Rushdie-like danger if he exposes what he has done; but Smilesburger gently yet firmly presses upon him the likelihood that such an exposure would compromise other lives and would not be allowed to go unanswered in some fashion suitable as a lesson to future spies. Smilesburger, though retired, says he feels responsible for Philip, wishes not to leave him exposed as Jonathan Pollard's handler had done. He praises all Roth's works, from *The Great American Novel*, least understandable to a foreigner like him, to the more autobiographical novels for their implicit concern for the Jews. When Philip suspects that the old spy was indeed sent here on another mission, Smilesburger assures him, in lovely double entendre, that

> "I come quite on my own, at substantial personal expense actually, to ask you, for your own good, here at the end of this book, to do nothing more than you have been doing as a writer all your life. A little imagination, please—it won't kill you. To the contrary." (*OS* 387)

When Philip still balks at removing the last chapter of a work that was a product of his only true allegiance, his art, Smilesburger responds in a speech that readers may speculate contains much of Roth's answer to himself.

> "Why do you persist in maintaining that you undertook this operation as a writer only, when in your heart you know as well as I now do,

having only recently enjoyed all your books, that you undertook and carried it out as a loyal Jew? Why are you so determined to deny the Jewish patriotism, you in whom I realize, from your writings, the Jew is lodged like nothing else except, perhaps, for the male libido? Why camouflage your Jewish motives like this, when you are in fact no less ideologically committed than your fellow patriot Jonathan Pollard was? I, like you, prefer never to do the obvious thing if I can help it, but continuing to pretend that you went to Athens only for the sake of your calling—is this really less compromising to your independence than admitting that you did it because you happen to be Jewish to the core? Being as Jewish as you are is your most secret vice. Any reader of your work knows that. As a Jew you went to Athens and as a Jew you will suppress this chapter." (*OS* 388)

A moment later he continues by asking what Roth would be without the Jews, without their driving him crazy—no writer at all. Mere gratitude, Smilesburger says, demands that Philip sacrifice something—one-eleventh of this book—for them. He also informs him that George Ziad is dead. In questionable circumstances, as all such deaths are, he was killed before his son's eyes either by Palestinians pretending to be Israelis or Israelis pretending to be Palestinians—or some other permutation of those possibilities. Such carefully maintained mysteries govern the lives of those interdependent populations. Ziad's son and wife have returned to Boston, and Philip speculates on the burden his friend's death will be to the lad—another son never to be free of the father's quest. Finally, Smilesburger advises Philip to call his book a piece of fiction. It is not very believable, and those parts that come close to revealing state secrets—once the Athens chapter is removed—will be less anxiety producing if they are seen as fiction. The two agree that in the comedy of life, as in Roth's art, it is the "pervasive uncertainty" that keeps things going. And just before the ending, Philip concludes—for himself and for his author—

> Yes, Smileburger is my kind of Jew, he is what "Jew" *is* to me, the best of it to me. Worldly negativity. Seductive verbosity. Intellectual venery. The hatred. The lying. The distrust. The this-worldliness. The truthfulness. The intelligence. The malice. The comedy. The endurance. The acting. The injury. The impairment. (*OS* 394)

It is not praise contrived to make the rabbis love Roth.

Finally, Smilesburger insists on giving Philip money—to defray his expenses involved in the mission. Philip refuses—and probably winds up taking it. Was Smilesburger really on his own? He says he was given the money and will be in difficulties himself if he does not deliver it. Philip, protesting that taking the money would make him no better than Pollard and scornfully repeating the password used throughout his Athens mission, "Three thousand ducats!" tries to pawn off the suitcase of money on some sleeping homeless people. Smilesburger warns him to take it, lest the Mossad play "hardball" and ruin his reputation.

> "Lead them not into temptation, because their creativity knows no bounds when the job is to assassinate the character even of a *tzaddik* like you . . . Philip, pick up the attache case, take it home, and put the money in your mattress. Nobody will ever know."
> "And in return?"
> "Let your conscience be your guide." (*OS* 398)

And so, cleverly omitted is the adventure that also never happened. We may be 99 and 44/100 percent sure, as the radio ads used to say, that it never happened. The other 56/100 is the province of the fictive imagination, another "what if?" in the series of speculations on the conflicting pulls of Zionism and Diaspora life, of Israel's role among nations, of the place of the Jew in the contemporary world that is *Operation Shylock*.

Had Roth chosen to publish the book as fiction, without all the silly pretense about its being a confession of a real event, he would probably have had a better time with the publication. So lasting, even after all these years, was Roth's reputation for being the bad boy, that the play-acting for the interviewers may have turned away readers. The difficulties of the Pipik premise would turn away many more. Reviewers treated the novel with more or less respect, few with profound respect. The conflict of form and theme made it difficult for many to read. John Updike's *New Yorker* review is a good example. It commends Roth "for facing the fact that a fiction writer's life is his basic instrument of perception" and for his achievement in "the post-Proust, postmodern, post-objective world of American fiction" where

> Roth stands out as a working theorist of fictional reality, a marvelously precocious and accomplished realist who has tested the limits of realism . . . has feverishly paced its boundaries and played games with its pretensions [so that] the act of writing has become his fiction's central dramatic action.

But Updike does not offer even this limited praise until late in the review, until after turning off less dedicated readers with quite another assessment. "Somewhere," he says, after the sleeping-with-Jinx episode, "the novel stops pretending to coherence and becomes a dumping ground, it seems, for every-thing in Roth's copious file on Jewishness. . . ." Updike finally recommends the novel for "anyone who cares about (1) Israel and its repercussion; (2) the devel-opment of the postmodern novel; (3) Philip Roth." In the absence of a final con-junction, one cannot say for sure whether Updike requires just one of those con-ditions or all three. It was not an encouraging review.

Nor was the first prepublication exposure of Roth's text a help to sales. Such a device is often used to stir interest within book-buying circles, but this time a beginning excerpt was placed in the still relatively new English-lan-guage weekly *Forward*, a periodical with a very limited circulation even among Jews. The novel never made its way onto even the tail end of the best-sellers lists despite being named an alternate selection of the Book-of-the-Month Club. Simon & Schuster, which began with full-page ads in the book review sections, did not push hard beyond the first month. Indeed, in the year in which they had blockbusters of questionable merit from Rush Limbaugh and Howard Stern, their efforts seemed directed elsewhere. Even as the Christmas gift season approached and Simon & Schuster presented full-page spreads showing book jackets of dozens of its best offerings of 1993, it left *Operation Shylock* out of the picture. It did, however, submit the novel for the competitive PEN/Faulkner Award for Fiction, which amidst great surprise, *Operation Shylock* won over 288 other entries in April 1994 (providing Roth a prize of $15,000).

The effects of this checkered reception are hard to assess, especially as regards Roth's relationship to the Jews. He was reported to be distressed, even depressed, by the end of 1993. In January 1994, nationally syndicated gossip columnist Liz Smith reported a breakup with Claire Bloom in which Roth allegedly asked her to move out. Smith explained, "Roth is said to have been quite depressed of late over the failure of his book 'Operation Shylock,' which received some poor reviews. He felt that this was his seminal statement, and that it was much misunderstood." Whatever the motive, the break was real; and Roth's next novel would be fairly hard on the institution of marriage. Claire, who had been married twice before the long relationship with Philip, was reported to have said that "Marriage gets vulgar after the second time." Perhaps the statement is best taken as a commentary on other people's interest. At any rate, Roth was, of course, busy on *Sabbath's Theater*. Whatever the effect on his personal life, he was not without his occupation.

The curse of writers, that they need their best time to themselves, appears intensified for Roth. Despite the guises, his writing is so deeply concentrated in engagement of himself, in finding in the act of writing a representation of engagement with life, that he is always at personal risk of becoming an E. I. Lonoff—or perhaps worse, a hunger-artist who needs his fasting to find his center. And that concentration on self affects his Jewishness. A Jew without a minyan, he has had, as Hillel Halkin put it, ". . . a sheer, almost abstract passion for being Jewish . . . almost as a pure, attributeless Jew-*an-sich*."[6] Nathan Zuckerman at the end of *The Counterlife* contemplated some such pure state, a Jew "without Jews, without Judaism, without Zionism, without Jewishness, without a temple or an army or even a pistol, a Jew clearly without a home, just the object itself, like a glass or an apple" (*OS* 324). The evidence of *Patrimony* and *Operation Shylock* suggests a change. Confronting his Jewishness, Roth seems to have added "without forgetting, without failing to acknowledge kinship, without—however illogical to the man of pure reason—neglecting allegiance." A year after the meager-saled publication one could find some stirrings of recognition for *Operation Shylock* among Jews, some of whom, like Cynthia Ozick, see it marking Roth's return to the fold. Halkin's almost celebratory analysis of Roth's oeuvre applied to *Operation Shylock* was published in *Commentary*. Perhaps even establishment Jews were beginning to grant his nonestablishment Jewishness its own authenticity.

Operation Shylock* was released in a paperback edition in March 1994, joining new editions of *Goodbye, Columbus*, *Portnoy's Complaint*, and *My Life as a Man*. That same March, Brandeis University announced an award to Roth of a prize for fiction, so the PEN/Faulkner Award in April capped a season of recognition perhaps reversing the time of despair. Whether the reading public would be able to absorb the ironies of a self offered up as both representation and sacrifice and whether Roth could find enough distance and predicament to transform that self into the readers' surrogate as well as his own would remain a question—and perhaps a test—for both. His next production would shake them even more.

Chapter 12

MASTER BAITER: SABBATH'S THEATER

Maybe, as Liz Smith reported, Roth had considered *Operation Shylock* his "seminal statement," but he apparently had another seminal statement still to make. Not so much about Jews as about semen; and not so much about semen as about the energy it suggests. Just what Portnoy would have wished for: *Sabbath's Theater* (1995) puts the id back in Yid with a Dionysian vengeance.

Roth returns ironically to the domestic questionings of his youth to view America through the eyes of one of its certified discontents. Mickey Sabbath is dangerous. More than that, the facts of the case prove him despicable: he seduces women, corrupts youth, betrays wives, encourages women to betray husbands (even when the husbands are his rescuers), steals money, tempts alcoholics to drink, even urinates on a grave. But for Roth, the facts are never the story. It is what the imagination does with the facts that counts. And the imagination, Keats tells us, "has as much delight in conceiving an Iago as an Imogen." There is delight in Mickey Sabbath, for reader as well as writer: despite the facts, he is deeply human. Good bait for the trap Roth can set in the groves of complacency!

Sabbath, aging, defeated, underclass Jew—physically grotesque and angry—curses those who have achieved power without talent by playing the system. But while he rails at their cant, he suspects his own. His consciously outrageous acts are partly stylings for himself, covers for his obsessed need to test assumptions, including the necessity of his own life. These stylings are just one of the meanings of "Theater" in the title.

To Sabbath most of life is a stage; people script themselves into roles of dubious significance. "That unaccountable exaggeration, significance: in Sabbath's experience invariably the prelude to missing the point" (*ST* 378). Sometimes the scripting is just "the need of [one's] spiritual being for a clarifying narrative with which to face day after day . . ." (*ST* 38). But often the needs and the roles are more sinister: self-scripting guardians of morality who resent erotic love script Sabbath at age sixty-four into a permanent sabbatical. Mickey submits to the verdict, prepares for his death, but won't shut his mouth.

Sabbath's Theater challenges the notion that at sixty-four the heyday in the blood must be tame and baits the would-be moralist with possible bests yet to be. It explores forbidden pleasures of the erotic life, a life almost everyone lives in fantasy but condemns when it threatens to lurch into reality. Despite absurdist comedy decades after *Portnoy*, and seeming obscenity, Roth delivers some passages that approach the erotic in a novel of often lyric virtuosity. This is a love story. Sabbath has known, outside marriage, a love whose depth, devotion, and selflessness the reader may well envy, though some may be disturbed by his reiterated assurance that such a love within marriage is all but impossible. Sabbath follows his impulses, trusting them, more than formal covenants, to lead him to some spiritual height. His predilection may suggest that Jewish paradox of Sabbatianism earlier posited for Alex Portnoy, the teaching that holiness may emerge from immersion in sin; but Sabbath pursues sexual liaisons not to break the grip of eroticism, but rather to challenge its sinfulness. This is also in part a tragic story, haunted, like *King Lear*, by a sense of loss. The death, early in the novel, of the woman Sabbath loves leaves him bereft, ill, and feeling his age. *Lear*-like, too, may be its place in Roth's cannon: his most moving work, its richest passages are inseparable from its text.

Sabbath's Theater does not explicitly address the state of the Jews, though that state is implicit in Roth's examination of this unlikely Jew. No geopolitics as in *Operation Shylock*, no mini-essays on the Holocaust, the State of Israel, the future of Jewish life in America. All of these topics appear in the most natural way as affecting the protagonist's sense of himself; they are absorbed into the story, which is very much Mickey Sabbath's self-exploration and his declared anger at what he has missed or will miss. He acknowledges himself to be self-centered, but the real center of his being is a felt loss of what family might have given him had it not been wrenched away in his earliest life. At his most bereft he talks to the ghost of his mother.

Roth scrambles the usual autobiographical elements in this novel. Morris "Mickey" Sabbath is older, shorter, poorer, less well educated than Roth's standard protagonist. He is still from New Jersey, but from the wrong side of the tracks—or of the summer vacation grounds. While Roth, like Alex Portnoy and Nathan Zuckerman, comes from the Weequahic section of Newark and vacationed with family at Bradley Beach, Mickey Sabbath is *from* Bradley Beach—year-round—the poor kid who grew up amidst Italians and Irish (who have made Morris into Mickey) envying the Newark Jews who joined him for the summer on LaReine Avenue. Sabbath was born four years earlier than his author into a family of peddlers: from trucks his father sold butter and eggs, his uncle, vegetables, purchased from nearby farms. But the World War II death of Mickey's idolized older brother desolates his parents and triggers his own interminable rage. Mickey never goes to college but becomes a merchant seaman right out of high school and gets his education partly, like Conrad, from books read at sea, but mostly—further breaking the Jewish stereotype—in the whorehouses of the world's great ports.

Mickey Sabbath is doubly an outsider, a Jew and an artist, and highly unorthodox in both, for his art outrages public morality. He is scarred with Roth's theme, even if he bears no physical resemblance. Short, bearded, barrel-chested, strong in hands and arms from scraping barnacles off ships, Sabbath returns to New York—after stints in the service and in Rome studying puppetry under the GI Bill—returns in his mid twenties, without that high respect for teachers and institutions that marked his fictive predecessors, to become a street theater performer. He carries his own small stage in front of him, and from behind the curtain, using fingers as puppets or in puppets, engages people in spontaneous dialogue, luring them in close for verbal exchanges while he attempts, if they are women, to fondle or unbutton them. That is his art, and absurdly but profoundly it raises the question of the license art may demand. If, either in his early-1950's street theater or in the later theaters of his life, Mickey can fascinate women into sexual partnership, is that illegitimate use of art? It is one question with which Roth baits the reader. Sabbath's answer, somewhat like his author's, is to go as far as he can and then, heeding Rilke, change his life.

A street theater fondling episode, back in 1953, ends with Sabbath's being arrested by a Jewish cop on 116th Street and Broadway, just outside the Columbia University gates, over the protests of a Columbia co-ed, who, far from feeling victimized by his act of fondling her, tries to defend Sabbath's artistic freedom. That episode, a central metaphor for Sabbath's life, is told in flashback as is the succession of events that form his earlier history. Found guilty and forced to abandon the street, he is championed by two young producers who set him up in an East Village duplex theater. Upstairs, his Indecent

Theater of Manhattan features sexually stimulating puppetry; downstairs, his Bowery Basement Players, a repertory for the classics, lets Sabbath develop his natural talents for directing young actors. From this theater the beautiful young actress he has married and has been directing as Cordelia disappears one night when he is off having an affair with the puppet maker who will later become his second wife.

His first wife's disappearance, like his brother's death in a felled warplane, haunts him and drives him out of New York to northern New England, where he becomes a professor of puppetry in a consortium program of colleges, and his new wife becomes an art teacher in the local high school. As the novel opens in 1994, she is a recovering alcoholic and he has been disemployed—given permanent sabbatical—both because crippling arthritis of the hands has ended his puppetry and because he has been scandalously taped having telephone sex with an undergraduate of twenty. That affair has not at all affected the deeper one he is having with his beloved mistress. She, too, has long since given over sex in her marriage, but while remaining a virtuosa of the practice with many men, loves only Sabbath. It is her death that sends him into a quest for the meaning of his voluptuary life amidst the sham moralizings of all who play life safe.

Roth's own art fuses with Sabbath's. Like his protagonist, Roth entices the reader to participate in the outrageous and to suspend moral judgment, his seamless prose, like Sabbath's finger patter, blending memory and present action in surges of sorrow or joy. But Roth's art cannot be summarized without reducing imagination to fact—absent suspension of disbelief, to despicable fact. Take the single most outrageous fact, Sabbath's urinating on his beloved's grave. This comes at the end of the novel, after a flashback to a moving episode of total sexual abandon where, in the middle of a cleansing brook, the couple had engaged in mutual urination as part of their sex play. In that earlier scene the improbable had been made not only possible but aesthetically urgent, even to seem—beyond the imaginings of D. H. Lawrence—pristine and healthy, the ultimate knowing of one person by another. As fact these episodes may be censurable, but into such reading Roth embeds his trap of moral outrage. Anyone sanctimonious enough to take the bait becomes game for Sabbath's derision.

Sabbath's Theater is also tragi-comedy, full of surprises which become less unlikely as one intuits its dual tone. The comedy arises largely from Sabbath's quest, on a return to New York and New Jersey, to comprehend before his death the earlier life he had led and to exorcise its ghosts. But throughout the book fun arises also from parodies of or just salutes to earlier literature, much of it Roth's own. Without specific mention of source, there is, here and there, an episode paralleling or a name returning from the literary past. Motifs from his own art include a struggle in the snow of a cemetery as in

The Anatomy Lesson, a challenge to a spouse to "Throw me out . . ." as in *The Ghost Writer*, wives who transfer hatred of fathers to hatred of husbands as in *When She Was Good* and *My Life as a Man*, and reference to the tenets of Alcoholics Anonymous as to those of Anti-Semites Anonymous in *Operation Shylock*, a book from which Roth also lifts the buxom blonde nurse in the cancer ward where Sabbath's beloved is dying, a nurse he cunningly names Jinx. Amidst explanations of the affair with the student that has lost him his professorship, as in David Mamet's *Oleana*, there is a footnote giving the whole telephone-sex dialogue, as in Nicholson Baker's *Vox*. This lengthy footnote, sufficiently erotic to have its own prurient interest, forces the reader to choose whether to continue in the narrative and then come back to the footnote or, more likely, to complete the footnote—which involves turning many pages— and then return to the narrative. Part of the double take is the realization that the choice affects the narrative because the footnote mitigates the innocence of the student. It supports Sabbath's view that she is being used by a feminist academic establishment to justify its outrage with him. The twenty-year-old student is already living with another young man, and the footnote lets Sabbath raise the question of who is best qualified to initiate twenty-year-old women into the mysteries of sex.

Part of Sabbath's rage is against tendencies in movements like feminism or Alcoholics Anonymous to demand adherence to their own scripts. Personal sovereignty, always an issue with Roth, is too easily sacrificed to such orthodoxies. For Sabbath these have replaced fascism and communism as the ideologies allegedly helping "good" people fight "oppressors." Once it was Aryans damning racial inferiors, then workers damning the rich, now women damning men. Declares Sabbath, "The holder of the ideology is pure and good and clean and the other is wicked. But do you know who is wicked? Whoever imagines himself to be pure is wicked! (*ST* 274)" In the new technocracy all values are measurable; accountability, like credentialism, is reduction to numbers and categories. An alcoholic's recovery is evaluated by the calendar, a twenty-year old's virtue is defined by her being a student, and Sabbath's accusers must be just, for as professors they can define his telephone sex talk as harassment. "Harassment?" he protests to the student. "I remember the good old days when *patriotism* was the last refuge of a scoundrel. Harassment? I have been Virgil to your Dante in the sexual underworld! But then how would those professors know who Virgil is? (*ST* 237)" The generative impulse in the world is quickened, Sabbath insists, not by sanctimony, but by treachery and danger, as is proven by the Jewish Bible:

What in all of creation is as nasty and strong as this god who gives life? The God of the Torah embodies the world in all its horror. And in all its truth. You've got to hand it to the Jews. Truly rare and admirable candor. What other people's national myth reveals their God's atrocious conduct *and* their own? (*ST* 278)

The death of one of his two former producers brings Mickey, after thirty years, back to New York for one funeral and then to New Jersey to arrange his own. Bearded, ragged in dirty country clothes (he has driven down directly from a roll on the ground at his mistress's grave), he is taken for a derelict, the paper coffee cup in his hand soon stuffed with money. And Sabbath enjoys the role playing. A hilarious episode in the Central Park West apartment of the surviving former producer provides him with money and the reader with faint echoes of *Six Degrees of Separation* as this latter-day Rip Van Winkle tasks and tests his "successful" urban Jewish contemporaries. His drive down to Bradley Beach to find his family burial plot and arrange for his own spot there is poignant as the whole family life he fled at seventeen comes back in upon him. His finding, and leaving, his one-hundred-year-old Uncle "Fish" Fischel, an episode reified by Roth's unerring rendition of senile speech, helps Sabbath, and the reader, fill the lacunae of his adolescence: his mother's reaction to his brother's death and the strong family ties severed by that death. And while Fish's memory summarizes a century of Jewish-American history, his fate, after surviving his children, his peers, and the removal of his kin from the changing neighborhood, testifies to the frailty of dignity to fend off the aloneness of extreme old age. Mickey's problem of finding an appropriate way to die (the second half of the novel is called "TO BE OR NOT TO BE") so he can be at one with his dead mistress becomes an absurdity in itself, and the reader who has gotten to know Mickey Sabbath well by this time should be able to guess, with a growing sense of satisfaction, how he will resolve that piece of theater.

Sabbath's Theater is filled with passages so beautifully composed, so able to fuse idea with apt emotion, that one emerges aware of having been in the hands of a master writer. An account of Sabbath's experience of his beloved's descent into cancer death is a haunting dirge punctuated by the phrase "Got used to. . . ." With each physical reduction the refrain tolls the lovers' sense of impending loss, but also of acceptance and spiritual elevation. Constant refrains from *King Lear*, weaving Lear's life with Sabbath's actual and theatrical lives move the reader to sense the limits on freedom imposed by age. However, other refrains in the novel are intended to trouble some readers. Four-letter words are commonplace but not, as used, unseemly; "fuck," the most common verb for sexual activity, suggesting not anger but candor and even love. Still others will be most disturbed by a refrain not of language but of incident: the repeated suggestion that marriage restrains spontaneity, repressing not just variety but risk, whereas living fully is living at the brink of danger. The refrain signals that this angry Jew, deprived of family early on, is no marriage haven for emotionally needy *shiksas*. But Mickey Sabbath is not a misogynist. If he constantly hurts weak women, it is in a continual search for strong ones. In only one is he not disappointed, and her death is the hardest blow of his adult life. All others he takes in as theater.

In Mickey Sabbath, Roth baits establishment America, whose rock is the marriage contract. The triumph of *Sabbath's Theater* is that Mickey has so much humanity, and beneath the anger, so much vulnerability, that every baiting act, hurtful to others, is potentially even more hurtful to himself. Others in the novel find solace in marriage. As we get to know and accept Mickey Sabbath, we do not want solace for him. At least during the reading—one of the graces of fiction—he is that outcast part of ourselves that holds out for more. The Dionysian reel, as in Euripides' *The Bacchae*, is more of a danger to those who, like young Pentheus, condemn it than to the rest who, including the old, make a place for it. What place, one is left wondering, does that ancient Greek religious warning have in modern American life?

Chapter 13

IRONY BOARD

Over the years, reviewers and critics have had a strange response to Philip Roth, one unparalleled in their responses to other writers. It can be found in the titles of their essays, in the drawings that accompany them, in the extent to which these writers have laid aside moderation and taken positions—almost as if their subject were not a writer but some force let loose among them. Consider the titles: "Son Stroke," "Waking the Dead," "Rothballs," "Schlongmeister," "Deja Jew," "Sermons and Celery Tonic," "The Suburbs of Babylon," "Reading Philip Roth Reading Philip Roth," "The Shiksa Question," "Coriolanus in New Jersey," "Alexander the Great," "Sex Novel of the Absurd," "Tropic of Conversation," "Wild Blue Shocker," "Mrs. Portnoy's Retort; a Mother Strikes Back," "Philip Roth: Days of Whine and Moses," "What Does Philip Roth Want?" "A Sort of Moby Dick," "Philip Roth Between the Peaks (Piques?)," "Waxing Wroth," "Sonny Boy or Lenny Bruce?" "The Fun of Self-Abuse," "What Has Roth Got," "The Gripes of Roth," and a legion of titles using "Complaint."[1] They echo known titles and sayings in an effort to be clever, almost to compete in cleverness with their subject. It is a powerful temptation, to which this writer has succumbed. And the pictures! Roth as Moses with the tablets, Roth as the Sphinx, Roth in Victorian fog as sinister villain, Roth perplexed, Roth defiant, seldom just Roth, never Roth looking relaxed. Perhaps it is the nervous response to an ironist, to one who at almost any juncture may be inserting his scalpel into a most sensitive part of the critic's own epidermis.

These reactions are also a tribute. The scalpel has touched a nerve the critic can no longer pretend is not there, or if always acknowledged to be there, not as well insulated as the critic might once have thought. The responsive irony is a parrying thrust. But the nerve being touched is not just the critic's nerve. From *Portnoy* on there has been another actor in this ironic interplay. To represent his vulnerable public, Roth has used a character easily identified with himself, more susceptible of hurt than the reader, suffering more from the condition at question than reader or critic is likely to suffer. The Rothlike character is there to absorb the ironist's abuse, to be the public. And by turning the irony on this surrogate, Roth has perversely led the charges against himself. The absurdity of the protagonist's predicament, not immediately recognized as a representative Jewish predicament, opens the character to a degree of contempt, easily turned against the author. There is a tradition for that representative sufferer, a tradition with ancient origins. It is the tradition of Hosea and Jeremiah moderated in this century by Kafka.

It may be overstating things to suggest that Roth's relationship to the Jews has been prophetic, but that is a matter of degree. Twentieth Century America promised Jews—along with its other newly enfranchised populace— freedom to become whatever their individual talents might let them become. Roth, the innocent, began by asserting his characters' independence to pursue those talents. At first these characters saw parents and tribe as inhibiting rather than fortifying them in their quests. When in their thrashings about they were seen as attacking the tribe, they, and their author, were further isolated as enemies of their people. But the people themselves were often diffident in their new surroundings and reluctant to proclaim or claim their rights, and that made them apt subjects of irony as well as sympathy. Roth has especially chronicled lower-middle working class Jews, uncomfortable in WASP America but willing to venture in stages into individual enterprise, management, institutional professions like teaching and government administration, and—most exposed and chancy of all—the arts. They have journeyed from fearfulness as seen in "On the Air," to claim staking in the academy as in *Letting Go* and *The Professor of Desire*, to the thwarted freedom of the writer as in the Tarnopol and Zuckerman novels, to the cosmopolite's testing of international freedom through Diaspora and Zionism as in the novels since *The Counterlife*. Freedom, for Roth's latest hero, even implies the right to choose how and when to die. Among the final epiphanies of *Sabbath's Theater* is one of Mickey Sabbath, a *yarmulke* on his head and an American flag wrapped *talis*-like over his shoulders, making his existential way over a flotsam-strewn beach—the lone

American Jew for whom each minute's experience, disconnected from the next, is vaguely bound by symbols once communal.

Roth has charted journeys of anticipation, exploring problems of which the public was not yet fully aware. The agonizing virtue of the biblical prophets was being able to transform into powerful images some change just afoot. Personalizing it and dramatizing its likely pain was the task of their artistry. While they attacked the tribe, they also personified the tribe; and Roth's journey back into personal identification with his patrimony has added a richness to his struggle to remain his own man.

"Is it me?" "Is it us?" There is no way to pose these questions from the outskirts of the congregation and not be lonely. For Roth, there is no way to pose them from within the center of the congregation and not be co-opted. Jewishness is about allegiance, individualism is about betraying allegiance. There are people whose whole sense of being comes from continual reasserting of allegiance. Roth's characters sense themselves in their resistance to such assertions, a resistance they see as for the good of the congregation itself. But, perhaps to his own amazement, Roth's resistance has brought him around to a paradoxical allegiance of his own. He could confidently assert in mid voyage that his allegiance was to art, and it has never ceased to be, but like the protagonist of *Operation Shylock*, he has been unable to refuse the demands of his Jewishness. As he sees it, these are to doubt it, to challenge it, to make it assert its best instincts in response to the probings of artists like him.

Ironic personal immersion, compromising himself, that turn in Roth's art not anticipated in his startings out, have been this artist's courageous responses to forces he has engaged since confronting the mythic promises of his youth. Roth's earliest stories expose sides of Jewish life; his early novels reveal some of their complexity for the liberally educated, supposedly liberated Jew; his later novels internalize those issues by embodying them in characters suffering for them publicly. That scornful question continually raised by critics and some readers since the early seventies—Who needs all that personal stuff?—is answered by a simple realization: that is how Roth gets at general stuff. His characters are in a sense witnesses. Writing, which for Roth is how he begins wrestling with the problems of his times, becomes a character's engagement and ultimately a people's memory.

Jews are better able to participate in the promise of America in the mid 1990s than they were when Roth started writing in the mid 1950s. To travel through the psyches of Roth's characters—to experience them as they experience themselves—is to journey through those changing stages of Jewish security. Whatever the next stage may be, Philip Roth will probably be wrestling with it in fiction at the edge of Jewish society well before teachers and critics begin labeling and analyzing it at the congregational center.

NOTES

CHAPTER 1

1. In 1971 Ruth R. Wisse called Alexander Portnoy "The most popular protagonist of American fiction since George F. Babbitt." Ruth R. Wisse, *The Schlemiel as Modern Hero*. (Chicago: University of Chicago Press, 1971) 118.

2. *The Ghost Writer* (New York: Farrar, Straus & Giroux, 1979); reprinted in *Zuckerman Bound* (Farrar, Straus & Giroux, 1985); containing *The Ghost Writer*, *Zuckerman Unbound*, *The Anatomy Lesson*, and *Epilogue: The Prague Orgy*; hereafter cited in text as *GW* with page references to *Zuckerman Bound*.

3. *The Counterlife* (New York: Farrar, Straus & Giroux, 1987); hereafter cited in text as *C*.

4. *Deception* (New York: Simon & Schuster, 1990); hereafter cited in text as *D*.

5. *Operation Shylock: A Confession* (New York: Simon & Schuster, 1993); hereafter cited in text as *OS*.

6. *Goodbye, Columbus and Five Short Stories* (Boston: Houghton Mifflin, 1959); hereafter cited in text as *GC*.

7. *Sabbath's Theater* (New York: Houghton Mifflin, 1995); hereafter cited in text as *ST*.

8. As Saul Bellow did in his preface to Allan Bloom's *The Closing of the American Mind*.

9. John Leonard's complaint that "The trouble with reviewing [any Roth novel] a few weeks late is that Roth has already explained it for us. He is ever explaining . . . he can't shut up" (*New York Review of Books* 2 September 1979:) may show the frustration of the reviewer, but it does not suggest that Roth had at that time used extraliterary

occasions to insinuate himself into public consciousness or to make himself rather than his fiction a public topic.

10. Anatole Broyard, "The Voyeur Vu," [Review of *Zuckerman Unbound*] *New York Times* 9 May 1981: 13.

11. *The Facts: A Novelist's Autobiography* (New York: Farrar, Straus & Giroux, 1988); hereafter cited in text as *Facts*.

12. *Patrimony: A True Story* (New York: Simon & Schuster, 1991); hereafter cited in text as *Pat*.

13. Anatole Broyard, "Moving Day: The Books I Left Behind," *New York Times Book Review* 19 November 1989: 39.

14. Ruth R. Wisse, "Philip Roth Then and Now," *Commentary Summer* 1981: 56.

15. As Rabbi Eugene Borowitz referred to them ten years later. "*Portnoy's Complaint*," *Dimensions* Summer 1969: 48.

16. *Portnoy's Complaint* (New York: Random House, 1969); hereafter cited in text as *PC*.

17. Denis Donoghue, "Nice Jewish Boy," *New Republic* 7 June 1975: 23.

18. Bellow's concluding statement in *Seize the Day*. Bellow may have fashioned the sentence after this one by C. H. Grandgent in the introduction to the Vintage edition of *The Divine Comedy*: "The final vision is the consummation of the pure heart's desire." Dante Alighieri, *The Divine Comedy*, trans. Carlyle-Wicksteed (New York: Vintage Books, 1950) xiv.

19. Wisse, "Philip Roth Then and Now," 56.

20. I include "On the Air" [see Chapter 7], which though set just before American entrance into World War II is really a second look at that era from the point of view of one who has outgrown its falsifying nostalgia.

21. Philip Roth, "Recollections from Beyond the Last Rope," *Harper's Magazine* July 1959: 42.

22. "Recollections from Beyond the Last Rope," 44. It was not until *Patrimony* (1990) that he would write acceptingly of a Persian Jew, one of the doctors treating his father, p. 135.

23. Philip Roth, "Writing About Jews, " *Commentary*, December 1963; reprinted in Philip Roth, *Reading Myself and Others* (New York: Farrar, Straus & Giroux, 1975) 158; page references hereafter cited in the text as *RMAO*.

24. Leslie A. Fiedler, "The Image of Newark and the Indignities of Love: Notes on Philip Roth" [a review of *Goodbye, Columbus*], *Midstream* Summer 1959: 96.

25. "Recollections from Beyond the Last Rope."

26. As indicated by the whole tone of "Recollections from Beyond the Last Rope."

27. Saul Bellow, "The Swamp of Prosperity," *Commentary* July 1959: 77.

28. Charles S. Liebman, *The Ambivalent American Jew* (Philadelphia: Jewish Publication Society, 1973) 26.

29. Liebman, 27.

30. Robert Alter, "When He Is Bad," *Commentary* November 1967: 86.

31. John Gross, "Marjorie Morningstar PhD, *New Statesman* 30 November 1962: 784ff.

32. Reprinted in Philip Roth, *Reading Myself and Others* (New York: Farrar, Straus & Giroux, 1975,) 137–48; hereafter cited in text as *RMAO*.

33. Reprinted in Philip Roth, *Reading Myself and Others* (New York: Farrar, Straus & Giroux, 1975) 149–70; hereafter cited in text as *RMAO*.

34. Philip Roth, "Author's Note," *Reading Myself and Others* (New York: Farrar, Straus & Giroux, 1975) xi; hereafter cited as *RMAO*.

35. Wisse, "Philip Roth Then and Now," 57.

36. Hermione Lee, *Philip Roth* (London: Methuen, 1982) 14.

37. *The Breast* (New York: Holt, Rinehart & Winston, 1972; rev. ed., New York: Farrar, Straus & Giroux, 1980); hereafter cited as *TB*, with page numbers referring to the 1980 edition as reprinted in *A Philip Roth Reader* (New York: Farrar, Straus & Giroux, 1980).

38. *The Professor of Desire* (New York: Farrar, Straus & Giroux, 1977); hereafter cited in the text as *POD*.

39. *My Life as a Man* (New York: Farrar, Straus & Giroux, 1974); hereafter cited in text as *MLAM*.

40. Zuckerman's earlier successful publication, *Higher Education*, is similarly to be identified with Roth's *Goodbye, Columbus*.

41. On the Air," *New American Review 10*, July/August 1970.

42. "'I Always Wanted You to Admire My Fasting'; or, Looking at Kafka," *American Review 17*, May 1973; reprinted in Philip Roth, *Reading Myself and Others* (New York: Farrar, Straus & Giroux, 1975) 247–70.

43. In *Zuckerman Bound*; hereafter cited in text as "PO" with page references to *Zuckerman Bound*.

44. *Our Gang* (New York: Random House, 1971).

45. *The Great American Novel* (New York: Holt, Rinehart & Winston, 1973).

46. *Letting Go* (New York: Random House, 1962); hereafter referred to in the text as *LG*.

CHAPTER 2

1. Philip Roth, "The Box of Truths: A Story of a Young Man," *Et Cetera* [The Undergraduate Literary Magazine of Bucknell University] October 1952: 10.

2. Philip Roth, "The Final Delivery of Mr. Thorn," *Et Cetera* May 1954: 22.

3. Philip Roth, "The Fence," *Et Cetera* May 1953: 10–12. In *Zuckerman Unbound* Roth gives the provenance of this story, a fenced-off Catholic orphanage that had been located opposite the house in which he spent his earlier Newark years.

4. Philip M. [sic] Roth, "Philosophy, Or Something Like That," *Et Cetera* May 1952: 5, 16.

5. Philip Roth, "The Day It Snowed," *Chicago Review* Fall 1954: 34–45.

6. Albert Goldman, "Wild Blue Shocker," *Life* 7 February 1969: 62.

7. From Fleg's *Pourquoi je suis juif*, 1927, a credo in the form of a tract, which had been translated into English in 1943 by Victor Gollancz (*Why I Am a Jew?*) and which was frequently used as material for silent meditations.

8. Oscar Janowsky, *The American Jew* (Philadelphia: Jewish Publication Society, 1964) 225.

9. Laurence Perrine. *Literature: Structure, Sound, and Sense.* (New York: Harcourt, Brace, & [World] Javonovich): [numerous editions since 1956; "Defender of the Faith" since 1963].

10. Irving Howe, "Philip Roth Reconsidered," *Commentary* December 1972: 72.

11. I have taken this passage (interrupted by Howe's comment) from page 200 of the Bantam Windstone paperback edition of *Goodbye, Columbus* (July 1981) rather than from pages 276–77 of the original Houghton Mifflin edition because it was that slightly different version that Howe quotes and comments upon. Although Bantam declares that its edition ". . . contains the complete text of the original hardcover edition. NOT ONE WORD HAS BEEN OMITTED," there are telling changes in the text of "Eli, the Fanatic" that show Roth's practice of continually editing up to the minute of final publication.

12. Saul Bellow, "The Swamp of Prosperity," *Commentary* July 1959: 78.

13. *Commentary* July 1959: 77–79.

14. Philip Roth, "Preface" to the thirtieth anniversary edition of *Goodbye, Columbus*, (New York: Houghton Mifflin, 1989) reprinted in *New York Times Book Review* 1 October 1989: 14.

CHAPTER 3

1. A notable exception was Jeffrey Berman's chapter on "Philip Roth's Psychoanalysts" in his *The Talking Cure* (New York: New York University Press, 1985). Berman shows the close link between Roth's actual analysis and two works, the chapter of *Portnoy's Complaint* called "The Jewish Blues" and Tarnopol's conflict with the same psychiatrist over the unwarranted use of Roth's psychoanalytic material in *My Life as a Man*.

2. *When She Was Good* (New York: Random House, 1967).

3. Asher Z. Milbauer and Donald Watson, eds. "An Interview with Philip Roth," *Reading Philip Roth* (New York: St. Martin's Press, 1988) 10.

4. See Philip Roth, "This Butcher, Imagination," *New York Times Book Review* 14 February 1988: 3.

5. Identified by friends who knew Roth at that time and named by Roth in the dedication to *When She Was Good*.

6. See Philip Roth, "In Response to Those Who Have Asked Me: 'How Did You Come to Write that Book Anyway?'" *Reading Myself and Others*, 33–41.

7. "Recollections from Beyond the Last Rope," 47–48. The extra three dots in the text before "Finally, I would watch him . . ." are not ellipsis periods but Roth's own textual indication of pause.

8. "Just a Lively Boy," a conversation with Molly McQuade (1991) reprinted in *Conversations with Philip Roth* ed. George J. Searles (Jackson: University Press of Mississippi, 1992) 283–84.

9. McQuade, 284.

10. Norman Podhoretz, "The Gloom of Philip Roth," *Doings and Undoings* (New York: Farrar, Straus & Co., 1964) 239.

CHAPTER 4

1. Most notably the 1948 *Apartment for Peggy* with Jeanne Crain, William Holden, and Edmund Gwenn, which romanticized the struggle of young married students.

2. See *The Ghost Writer* (in *Zuckerman Bound*) 117.

3. James Atlas, "A Postwar Classic," *New Republic* 2 June 1982: 29.

4. "Marjorie Morningstar PhD,": 784.

5. Nat Hentoff, "The Appearance of Letting Go," *Midstream* December 1962: 104–105.

6. "The Grey Plague," *Time* 15 June 1962: 86. *Time* maintained a policy, later abandoned, of giving no bylines and often of writing not only news, but also features, by "committee." This review has the sound of a single voice, but it is unidentified.

7. *New York Times* 15 June 1962: 25.

8. "Hammer Locks in Wedlock," *Saturday Review of Literature* 16 June 1962: 16.

9. *New Yorker* 22 September 1962: 176.

10. Arthur Mizener, "Bumblers in a World of Their Own," *New York Times Book Review* 17 June 1962: VII:1.

11. Irving Feldman, "A Sentimental Education Circa 1956," *Commentary* September 1962: 275.

12. "The Gloom of Philip Roth," 240–41. (The essay was originally published in 1962.)

13. Feldman, 276.

14. Stanley Cooperman, "Philip Roth: 'Old Jacob's Eye' With a Squint," *Twentieth Century Literature* July 1973: 215–16.

15. Atlas, 28–32.

16. See Robert Alter, "When He Is Bad," *Commentary* November 1967: 86–87 and Jonathan Baumbach, "What Hath Roth Got," *Commonweal* 11 August 1967: 498.

17. Judith Paterson Jones and Guinevera A. Nance, *Philip Roth* (New York: Frederick Ungar, 1981) 53.

18. Albert Goldman, "Wild Blue Shocker," 63.

19. Albert Goldman, "Laughtermakers" *Jewish Wry*, ed. Sarah Blacher Cohen (Bloomington: Indiana University Press, 1987) 84.

CHAPTER 5

1. Albert Goldman, "Wild Blue Shocker," 63.

2. Eugene Borowitz, "Portnoy's Complaint," *Dimensions* Summer 1969:48–50. This is a publication of the Union of American Hebrew Congregations.

3. Donald Margulies, "A Playwright's Search for a Spiritual Father," *New York Times* 21 June 1992: H5.

4. Marie Syrkin, "The Fun of Self-Abuse," *Midstream* April 1969: 64–68.

5. Syrkin once urged upon this writer sympathy for all those who had subordinated their art to the Zionist cause, mentioning specifically Meyer Levin. As a supporter of the Labor Party and the early work of the *Hagganah*, she was not at all proud of the Stern gang.

6. Scholem wrote two pieces, one ("Some Plain Words") in answer to a May 22, 1969, review by Robert Weltsch, and one ("Social Criticism—Not Literary") in counter-reply to objections to his first essay by Dr. Benjamin Kadar and Daniel Gedanke. The essays were translated by Edgar E. Siskin and published as: Gershom Scholem, "*Portnoy's Complaint*," trans. E. E. Siskin CCARJ (Central Conference of American Rabbis) June 1970: 56–58.

7. H. E. Retik, "Postscript to *Portnoy's Complaint*," *Israel Magazine* Summer 1969: 40–42.

8. "Poles Hear Portnoy's Complaint," Associated Press story from Lodz, Poland, 11 February 1988.

9. See Jacob Katz, "Accounting for Anti-Semitism," *Commentary* June 1991: 52–54.

10. Robert S. Wistrich, "Once Again, Anti-Semitism Without Jews," *Commentary* August 1992: 45–49.

11. Judah Stampfer, "Adolescent Marx Brothers," *Jewish Heritage* Summer 1969: 13.

12. Peter Shaw, "Portnoy & His Creator," *Commentary* May 1969: 77.

13. Stampfer, 15.

14. Shaw, 78.

15. Bruno Bettelheim, "Portnoy Psychoanalyzed," *Midstream* June-July 1969.

16. See Retik, 42.

17. Trude Weiss-Rosmarin, "On Jewish Self-Definition," *Reconstructionist* XXV, 2. 6 March 1959: 22–25.

18. Trude Weiss-Rosmarin, "*Portnoy's Complaint*" (editorial), *Jewish Spectator* April 1969: 6.

19. Jewish Spectator Winter 1985/Spring 1986: 46–47. When I asked Weiss-Rosmarin why this dismissive piece was the most important editorial among all the

issues of 1969, she answered, perhaps cryptically with triple underlining of the year, "I thought that this 'dismissive review' was appropriate in *1969*."

20. Sermon delivered March 7, 1969, at Fairmount Temple, Cleveland, Ohio. Reprinted with omissions as Arthur J. Lelyveld, "Old Disease in New Form: Diagnosing 'Portnoy's Complaint,'" *Jewish Digest* Summer 1969: 1–4.

21. In *The Ghost Writer* the question, "Do you believe Shakespeare's Shylock and Dickens's Fagin have been of no use to anti-Semites?" becomes one of Judge Wapter's "Ten Questions for Nathan Zuckerman." (102–3).

22. A shortened form of this review, with the references to and quotations from *Portnoy's Complaint* here used omitted, appeared in *The Jewish Spectator* for Fall 1974.

23. Sanford Pinsker, "Surviving History: Updated notes on the American-Jewish Dream," *Jewish Spectator* Summer 1988: 21.

24. Franklin Zimring, "Portnoy's Real Complaint," *Moment* December 1980: 58–62.

25. Helen Weinberg, "Growing Up Jewish," *Judaism* Spring 1969: 241–45.

CHAPTER 6

1. Sanford Pinsker, "Philip Roth and the Jewish Problem," *Reconstructionist* 2 May 1969: 26.

2. Roth would use Rilke's line again in later fiction to set forth the challenges of manhood and of art. See, e.g., *The Ghost Writer*, p.27.

3. Jeffrey Berman, "Philip Roth's Psychoanalysts," *The Talking Cure* (New York: New York University Press, 1985) 239–69.

4. Roth had used a psychiatrist named Spielvogel as early as 1963, six years before the publication of *Portnoy's Complaint*. See Philip Roth, "The Psychoanalytic Special," *Esquire* November 1963: 106–110, 172–176.

5. See Berman.

6. "The Art of Fiction LXXXIV: Philip Roth," an interview with Hermione Lee, in *Conversations with Philip Roth*, ed. George J. Searles (Jackson: University Press of Mississippi, 1992) 171. Originally printed in *The Paris Review*, 93 (Fall 1984).

7. He is called in the book "Vice-President What's-his-name" with the addition "of Greek descent." *Our Gang*, 17.

CHAPTER 7

1. Philip Roth, "On the Air," *New American Review* 10, August 1970: 7–49.

2. Genesis 12:2,3.

3. *The Counterlife*, 114.

4. *The Counterlife*, 133.

5. Roth has confirmed the borrowing. When I presented him this notion of the two Lippmans sharing an identity, he smiled and congratulated me on discovering his little joke.

CHAPTER 8

1. Joseph Epstein, "What Does Philip Roth Want?" *Commentary* January 1984: 62.

2. Epstein, 62.

3. Harold Bloom, "Operation Roth," *New York Review of Books* 22 April 1993: 45.

4. Norman Podhoretz, "Laureate of the New Class," *Commentary* December 1972: 4,7.

5. Philip Roth, "Positive Thinking on Pennsylvania Avenue," *New Republic* 3 June 1957: 10-11.

6. *New Republic* 24 June 1957: 3, 23.

7. Philip Roth, "Eisenhower and God" (letter) *New Republic* 15 July 1957: 23.

8. Philip Roth, "The President Addresses the Nation," *New York Review of Books* 14 June 1973; also included, somewhat abridged, as a skit in *Watergate Capers*, a satirical review performed in repertory at the Yale Drama School in November and December 1973. Reprinted in *Reading Myself and Others*, 59–64.

9. Philip Roth, "Cambodia: A Modest Proposal," *Look* 6 October 1970. Reprinted in *Reading Myself and Others*, 185–90.

10. Hermione Lee, "The Art of Fiction LXXXIV: Philip Roth," in Searles, 178.

11. "Philip Roth," *Esquire* June 1988: 137.

12. Philip Roth, "Oh, Ma, Let Me Join the National Guard," *New York Times* 24 August 1988: A25 (Op-ed).

13. Philip Roth, "My Problem with George Bush" (editorially subtitled ROTH'S COMPLAINT), *New Republic* 26 September 1988: 12.

14. Philip Roth, "Ethnic Pop and Native Corn," *New York Times* 19 September 1988: A23 (Op-ed).

15. Philip Roth, "Pro-Life Pop," *New York Review of Books* 17 August 1989: 5.

16. *Writing Our Way Home: Contemporary Stories by American Jewish Writers*, ed. Ted Solotaroff and Nessa Rappoport (New York: Schocken Books, 1992) 246–66.

17. Evelyn Toynton, "American Stories," *Commentary* March 1993: 53.

18. Philip Roth, "Kafka Would Have Savored the Irony of Being a German Treasure" (letter), *New York Times* 24 November 1988.

19. John Podhoretz, "Philip Roth, The Great American Novelist," *American Spectator* September 1981: 12–14.

20. Hillel Halkin, "How to Read Philip Roth," *Commentary* February 1994.

CHAPTER 9

1. Milbauer and Watson, 9.

2. Bruno Bettelhim, "The Ignored Lesson of Anne Frank," *Surviving and Other Essays* (New York: Alfred A Knopf, 1952).

3. This was also Alan Dershowitz's reiterated theme in *Chutzpah* a decade after *The Ghost Writer*.

4. Although Roth did admit to playing the game with Lippman in *The Counterlife*; see Chapter 7, note 5 above.

5. Among the books Hermione Lee noted in Roth's London workroom at the Royal Automobile Club during the writing of *The Anatomy Lesson* was Howe's recently published *A Margin of Hope*, in which Howe's treatment of his father is frankly dutiful but not loving, and the embarrassment of bringing young friends home is touched on but not dwelled on. Suggestions like these were seeds for Roth's imagining of Appel, not, as Roth well knew, facts about Howe.

6. The writer as sweeper was the subject of Jewish Czech novelist Ivan Klima's *Love and Garbage*, published after the lifting of censorship in 1990. See Philip Roth, "A Conversation in Prague," *New York Review of Books* 12 April 1990: 14.

CHAPTER 10

1. Hermione Lee, "The Art of Fiction LXXXIV: Philip Roth" in Searles, 166.

2. Searles, 167.

3. Searles, 176.

4. The text never uses the proper term, "Western Wall."

5. Paul Gray, "The Varnished Truths of Philip Roth," *Time* 19 Jan. 1987: 78–79.

6. *New York Times*, 29 December 1986: C19.

7. William H. Gass, "Deciding to Do the Impossible," *New York Times Book Review* 4 January 1987: 1, 24–25.

8. Robert Alter, "Deja Jew: *The Counterlife* by Philip Roth," *New Republic* 2 February 1987: 37.

9. Robert Alter, "Defenders of the Faith," *Commentary* July 1987: 55–56.

10. Reprinted in *Present Tense* July-August 1988: 54.

11. Georgia Brown, "Shiksa Bashing," *7 DAYS* 30 November 1988: 66.

12. Hermione Lee, "Kiss and Tell" [a review of Philip Roth's *Deception*], *New Republic* 30 April 1990: 39–42.

13. Roger Cohen, "Roth's Publishers: The Spurned and the Spender," *New York Times* 9 April 1990: C11.

14. See Philip Roth's letter to the editors of *The New Review of Books* 13 June 1991: 60.

15. Neal Kozodoy, "His Father's Son," *Commentary* May 1991: 52–54.

CHAPTER 11

1. Aharon Appelfeld in Philip Roth, "A Talk With Aharon Appelfeld," *New York Times Book Review* 28 February 1988: 29.

2. Philip Roth, "A Bit of Jewish Mischief," *New York Times Book Review* 7 March 1993: 1,3.

3. John Gross, *Shylock: A Legend and Its Legacy* (New York: Simon & Schuster, 1993).

4. John Updike, "Recruiting Raw Nerves," *New Yorker* 15 March 1993: 109–112.

5. Robert Alter, "The Spritzer" (a review of *Operation Shylock*), *New Republic* 15 April 1993: 32.

6. Halkin, 48.

CHAPTER 13

1. Those not previously mentioned in this book include: "Son Stroke" under a picture of PR in Rhoda Koenig, "Waking the Dead" (a review of *Patrimony*), *New York* 21 Jan. 91 and Peter Prescott, "Sermons and Celery Tonic" (a review of *The Counterlife*), *Newsweek* 12 Jan. 87.

SELECTED BIBLIOGRAPHY

PRIMARY SOURCES

Books

The Anatomy Lesson. New York: Farrar, Straus & Giroux, 1981

The Breast. New York: Holt, Rinehart & Winston, 1972. Rev Ed., New York: Farrar, Straus & Giroux, 1980.

The Counterlife. New York: Farrar, Straus & Giroux, 1987.

Deception. New York: Simon & Schuster, 1990.

The Facts: A Novelist's Autobiography. New York: Farrar, Straus & Giroux, 1988.

The Ghost Writer. New York: Farrar, Straus & Giroux, 1979.

Goodbye, Columbus and Five Stories. Boston: Houghton Mifflin, 1959; 30th Anniversary edition, 1989.

The Great American Novel. New York: Random House, 1973.

Letting Go. New York: Random House, 1962.

My Life as a Man. New York: Farrar, Straus & Giroux, 1974.

Operation Shylock: A Confession. New York: Simon & Schuster, 1993.

Our Gang. New York: Random House, 1971.

Patrimony: A True Story. New York: Simon & Schuster, 1991.

A Philip Roth Reader. New York: Farrar, Straus & Giroux, 1980.

Portnoy's Complaint. New York: Random House, 1969.

The Professor of Desire. New York: Farrar, Straus & Giroux, 1977.

Reading Myself and Others. New York: Farrar, Straus & Giroux, 1975.

Sabbath's Theater. Boston: Houghton Mifflin, 1995.

When She Was Good. New York: Random House, 1967.

Zuckerman Bound. New York: Farrar, Straus & Giroux, 1985. Containing *The Ghost Writer, Zuckerman Unbound, The Anatomy Lesson,* and *Epilogue: The Prague Orgy.*

Zuckerman Unbound. New York: Farrar, Straus & Giroux, 1981.

Stories and Articles

Five stories from *Et Cetera* [The Undergaduate Literary Magazine of Bucknell University]:
> "Armando and the Fraud." October 1953: 21–28, 32.
> "The Box of Truths: A Story of a Young Man." October 1952: 10–12.
> "The Fence." May 1953: 18–23.
> "The Final Delivery of Mr. Thorn." May 1954: 20–28.
> "Philosophy, Or Something Like That." May 1952: 5,16.

"A Bit of Jewish Mischief." *New York Times Book Review,* 7 March 1993: 1,3.

"Cambodia: A Modest Proposal." *Look,* 6 October 1970; reprinted in *Reading Myself and Others,* 185–90.

"The Contest for Aaron Gold." *Epoch 7–8,* Fall 1955: 37–51.

"A Conversation in Prague." *New York Review of Books*: 12 April 1990: 14–22.

"The Day It Snowed." *Chicago Review,* Fall 1954: 34–44.

"Eisenhower and God." Letter. *New Republic,* 15 July 1957: 23.

"The Eternal Optimist." *Esquire* June 1988: 137.

"Ethnic Pop and Native Corn." *New York Times* 19 September 1988: A23.

"Heard Melodies Are Sweeter." *Esquire,* August 1958: 58; reprinted October 1973.

"Herman Roth." Letter. *New York Review of Books* 13 January 1991: 60.

"'I Always Wanted You to Admire My Fasting'; or, Looking at Kafka." *American Review 17,* May 1973; reprinted in *Reading Myself and Others*: 247–70

"Jewishness and the Younger Intellectuals." Forum contribution. *Commentary,* April 1961.

"Kafka Would Have Savored the Irony of Being a German Treasure." Letter. *New York Times* 24 November 1988.

"My Problem with George Bush." *New Republic* 26 September 1988: 12–14.

"Oh, Ma, Let Me Join the National Guard," *New York Times* 24 August 1988: A25.

"On the Air." *New American Review 10*, July/August 1970, 7–49.

"The Psychoanalytic Special." *Esquire*, November 1963: 106–10, 172–76.

"Positive Thinking on Pennsylvania Avenue." *New Republic* 3 June 1957: 10–11.

"The President Adresses the Nation, *New York Review of Books* 14 June 1973; reprinted in *Reading Myself and Others*, 59–64.

"Pro-Life Pop." *New York Review of Books* 17 August 1989: 5.

"Quote/Unquote." Remarks made at the *Present Tense*/Joel H. Cavior Literary Awards; reprinted in *Present Tense*, July-August 1988: 54.

"Recollections from Beyond the Last Rope." *Harper's Magazine*, July 1959: 42–48.

"A Talk With Aharon Appelfeld." *New York Times Book Review* 28 February 1988: 29+.

"This Butcher, Imagination." *New York Times Book Review* 14 February 1988:3.

"Writing about Jews." *Commentary*, December 1963; reprinted in *Reading Myself and Others*: 149–69.

SECONDARY SOURCES

Books and Bibliographies Specifically about Roth

Baumgarten, Murray, and Barbara Gottfried. *Understanding Philip Roth*. Columbia: University of South Carolina Press, 1990.

Bloom, Harold, ed. *Philip Roth* (Modern Critical Views). New York: Chelsea House, 1986.

Halio, Jay. *Philip Roth Revisited*. New York: Twayne Publishers, 1992.

Jones, Judith Paterson, and Guinevera A. Nance. *Philip Roth*. New York: Frederick Ungar, 1981.

Leavey, Ann. "Philip Roth: A Bibliographic Essay (1984–1988)." *Studies in American Jewish Literature* 8 (Fall 1989): 212–18.

Lee, Hermione. *Philip Roth*. London: Methuen, 1982.

McDaniel, John N. *The Fiction of Philip Roth*. Haddonfield, N.J.: Haddonfield House, 1974.

Milbauer, Arthur Z., and Donald Watson, eds. *Reading Philip Roth*. New York: St. Martin's Press, 1988.

Pinsker, Sanford. *The Comedy That "Hoits": An Essay on the Fiction of Philip Roth*. Columbia: University of Missouri Press, 1975.

———, ed. *Critical Essays on Philip Roth*. Boston: G.K. Hall, 1982.

Rodgers, Bernard F., Jr. *Philip Roth*. Boston: Twayne Publishers, 1978.

———. *Philip Roth: A Bibliography*, 2nd ed. Metuchen, N.J.: Scarecrow Press, 1984.

Walden, Daniel, ed. *The Odyssey of a Writer: Rethinking Philip Roth*. Special issue of *Studies in American Jewish Literature* 8 (Fall 1989).

OTHER ARTICLES AND BOOKS CITED

Alter, Robert. "Defenders of the Faith." *Commentary*, July 1987: 55–56.

———. "Deja Jew: *The Counterlife* by Philip Roth." *New Republic* 2 February 1987: 37.

———. "The Spritzer." *New Republic* 15 April 1993: 32.

———. "When He Is Bad." *Commentary*, November 1967.

Atlas, James. "A Postwar Classic." *New Republic* 2 June 1982: 26–32.

Barret, William. "Let Go, Let Live." *Atlantic*. July 1962: 111.

Baumbach, Jonathan. "What Hath Roth Got?" *Commonweal* 11 August 1967: 498.

Bellow, Saul. "The Swamp of Prosperity." *Commentary*, July 1959: 77–79.

Berman, Jeffrey. *The Talking Cure: Literary Representations of Psychoanalysis*. New York: NYU Press, 1985.

Bettelheim, Bruno. "The Ignored Lesson of Anne Frank." *Surviving and Other Essays*. New York: Alfred A. Knopf, 1952.

———. "Portnoy Psychoanalyzed." *Midstream*, June-July 1969.

Bloom, Harold. "Operation Roth." *New York Review of Books* 22 April 1993.

Borowitz, Eugene. "Portnoy's Complaint." *Dimensions*, Summer 1969: 48–50.

Brown, Georgia. "Shiksa Bashing." *7 DAYS* 30 November 1988: 66.

Cohen, Roger. "Roth's Publishers: The Spurned and the Spender." *New York Times* 9 April 1990: C11.

Cohen, Sarah. "Philip Roth's Would-Be Patriarchs and their *Shikses* and Shrews." *Studies in American Jewish Literature 1*, (1975): 16–22.

———, ed. *Jewish Wry*. Bloomington: Indiana University Press, 1987.

Cooper Alan. "Philip Roth Between The Peaks (Piques?)." *The Jewish Frontier* August/September 1984: 20–23, 25.

———. Letter. "What Does Joseph Epstein Want?" *Commentary*, April 1984.

———. "The Jewish Sit-Down Comedy of Philip Roth." In *Jewish Wry*, ed. Sarah Blacher Cohen. Bloomington: Indiana University Press, 1987: 158–77.

Cooperman, Stanley. "Philip Roth: 'Old Jacob's Eye' With a Squint." *Twentieth Century Literature*, July 1973.

Epstein, Joseph. "What Does Philip Roth Want?" *Commentary*, January 1984.

Feldman, Irving. "A Sentimental Education Circa 1956." *Commentary*, September 1962.

Fiedler, Leslie A. "The Image of Newark and the Indignaties of Love: Notes on Philip Roth." *Midstream*, Summer 1959.

Gass, William H. "Deciding to Do the Impossible." *New York Times Book Review* 4 January 1987: 1, 24–25.

Goldman, Albert. "Wild Blue Shocker." *Life* 7 February 1969, 58–64.

Gray, Paul. "The Varnished Truths of Philip Roth." *Time* 19 January 1987: 78–79.

"The Grey Plague." *Time* 15 June 1962: 86.

Gross, John. "Marjorie Morningstar PhD." *New Statesman* 30 November 1962: 784.

———. *Shylock: A Legend and Its Legacy*. New York: Simon & Schuster, 1993.

Halkin, Hillel. "How to Read Philip Roth." *Commentary*, February 1994: 43–48.

Hentoff, Nat. "The Appearance of Letting Go." *Midstream*, December 1962: 103–6.

Hicks, Granville. "Hammer Locks in Wedlock." *Saturday Review of Literature* 16 June 1962: 16.

Howe, Irving. "Philip Roth Reconsidered." *Commentary*, December 1972: 69–77.

———. "The Suburbs of Babylon." *New Republic* 15 June 1959: 17–18.

Janowsky, Oscar. *The American Jew*. Philadelphia: Jewish Publication Society, 1964.

Katz, Jacob. "Accounting for Anti-Semitism." *Commentary*, June 1991: 52–54.

Kazin, Alfred. "The Earthly City of the Jews." In *Bright Book of Life*. London: Secker & Warburg, 1974.

Koenig, Rhoda. "Waking the Dead." *New York* 21 January 1991.

Kozodoy, Neal. "His Father's Son." *Commentary*, May 1991: 52–54.

Landis, Joseph C. "The Sadness of Philip Roth: An Interim Report." *Massachusetts Review*, 3 (Winter 1962): 259–68.

Larner, Jeremy. "Conversion of the Jews." Review of *Goodbye, Coumbus. Partisan Review,* 27 (Fall 1960): 760–68.

Lee, Hermione. "Kiss and Tell." *New Republic* 30 April 1990: 39–42.

———. "The Art of Fiction LXXXIV: Philip Roth."(originally in *Paris Review* 1984) in George J. Searles, ed. *Conversations with Philip Roth*. Jackson: University of Mississippi Press, 1992.

Lehmann-Haupt, Christopher. "The Counterlife." *New York Times* 29 December 1986: C19.

Lelyveld, Arthur J. "Old Disease in New Form: Diagnosing 'Portnoy's Complaint'." *Jewish Digest*, Summer 1969:1–4; a reprint with omissions of a longer sermon delivered at Fairmount Temple, Cleveland, Ohio, 7 March 1969.

Levine, Mordecai H. "Philip Roth and American Judaism." *CLA Journal,* 14 (December 1970): 163–70.

Liebman, Charles S. *The Ambivalent American Jew*. Philadelphia: Jewish Publication Society, 1973.

Margulies, Donald. "A Playwright's Search for a Spiritual Father." *New York Times* 21 June 1992: H5.

Mizener, Arthur. "Bumblers in a World of Their Own." *New York Times Book Review* 17 June 1962: VII: 1, 28–29.

Mudrick, Marvin. "Who Killed Herzog? Or, Three American Novelists." *Denver Quarterly*, 1 (Spring 1966): 61–97.

Pinsker, Sanford. "Philip Roth and the Jewish Problem." *Reconstructionist* 2 May 1969.

———. "Surviving Jewish History: Updated Notes on the American-Jewish Dream." *Jewish Spectator*, Summer 1988.

Podhoretz, John. "Philip Roth, The Great American Novelist." *The American Spectator*, September 1981: 12–14.

Podhoretz, Norman. "The Gloom of Philip Roth." *Doings and Undoings*. New York: Farrar, Straus, & Giroux, 1964.

――――. "Laureate of the New Class." *Commentary*, December 1972: 4,7.

"Poles Hear Portnoy's Complaint." Associated Press story from Lodz, Poland, 11 February 1988.

Prescott, Peter. "Sermons and Celery Tonic." *Newsweek* 12 January 1987.

Retik, H. E. "Postscript to *Portnoy's Complaint*." *Israel Magazine*, Summer 1969: 40–42.

Saks, Robert. "Gershom Scholem's *Sabbati Sevi*." *The Jewish Spectator*, Fall 1974.

Schechner, Mark. "Philip Roth." *Partisan Review*, Fall 1974: 410–27.

Scholem, Gershom. "*Portnoy's Complaint*" trans. E. E. Siskin. *CCARJ* (Central Conference of American Rabbis) June 1970: 56–58.

Searles, George J. ed. *Conversations with Philip Roth*. Jackson: University Press of Mississippi, 1992.

Shaw, Peter. "Portnoy & His Creator." *Commentary*, May 1969: 77.

Sheed, Wilfred. "The Good Word: Howe's Complaint." *New York Times Book Review*, 6 May 1973: 2.

Solotaroff, Theodore. "Philip Roth and the Jewish Moralists." *Chicago Review* 13, no.1 (1959): 87–99.

――――. "The Journey of Philip Roth." *Atlantic Monthly*, April 1969: 64–72.

――――. "The Diasporist." *The Nation*, 7 June 1993: 778–84.

――――, and Nessa Rappoport. *Writing Our Way Home: Contemporary Stories by American Jewish Writers*. New York: Schocken Books, 1992.

Stampfer, Judah. "Adolescent Marx Brothers." *Jewish Heritage*, Summer 1969: 13.

Syrkin, Marie. "The Fun of Self-Abuse." *Midstream*, April 1969: 64–68.

Tanner, Tony. "Fictionalized Recall—or `The Settling of Scores! The Pursuit of Dreams!' (Saul Bellow, Philip Roth, Frank Conroy)." In *City of Words: American Fiction 1950-1970*. New York: Harper & Row, 1971.

Toynton, Evelyn. "American Stories." *Commentary*, March 1993

Updike, John. "Recruiting Raw Nerves." *New Yorker* 15 March 1993: 32.

Weinberg, Helen. "Growing Up Jewish." *Judaism*, Spring 1969: 241–45.

Weiss-Rosmarin, Trude. "On Jewish Self-Definition." *Reconstructionist* XXV, 2. 6 March 1959: 22–25.

——— . *"Portnoy's Complaint"* (editorial). *Jewish Spectator*, April 1969: 6, 31; reprinted *Jewish Spectator*, Winter 1985/Spring 1986: 46–47.

Wisse, Ruth. "Philip Roth Then And Now." *Commentary*, Summer 1981: 56.

——— . *The Schlemiel as Modern Hero*. Chicago: University of Chicago Press, 1971.

Wistrich, Robert S. "Once Again, Anti-Semitism Without Jews." *Commentary*, August 1992: 45–49.

Zimring, Franklin. "Portnoy's Real Complaint." *Moment*, December 1980: 58–62.

A

B